INSIGHT GUIDES
SRI LANKA

☀ INSIGHT GUIDE

SRI LANKA

Editorial

Project Editor
Alexia Georgiou
Series Manager
Rachel Lawrence
Designer
Tom Smyth
Map Production
**Original cartography Berndtson &
Berndtson, updated by
Apa Cartography Department**
Production
**Tynan Dean, Linton Donaldson and
Rebeka Ellam**

Distribution

UK
Dorling Kindersley Ltd
A Penguin Group company
80 Strand, London, WC2R 0RL
customerservice@dk.com

United States
Ingram Publisher Services
1 Ingram Boulevard, PO Box 3006,
La Vergne, TN 37086-1986
customer.service@ingrampublisher
services.com

Australia
Universal Publishers
PO Box 307
St Leonards NSW 1590
sales@universalpublishers.com.au

New Zealand
Brown Knows Publications
11 Artesia Close, Shamrock Park
Auckland, New Zealand 2016
sales@brownknows.co.nz

Worldwide
**Apa Publications GmbH & Co.
Verlag KG (Singapore branch)**
7030 Ang Mo Kio Avenue 5
08-65 Northstar @ AMK
Singapore 569880
apasin@singnet.com.sg

Printing
CTPS-China
© 2012 Apa Publications (UK) Ltd
All Rights Reserved
First Edition 1992
Seventh Edition 2012

CONTACTING THE EDITORS
We would appreciate it if readers
would alert us to errors or out-
dated information by writing to:
**Insight Guide s, PO Box 7910,
London SE1 1WE, England.
insight@apaguide.co.uk**

ABOUT THIS BOOK

The first Insight Guide pioneered the use of creative full-colour photography in travel guides in 1970. Since then, we have expanded our
range to cater for our readers' need not only for reliable information about
their chosen destination but also for a real understanding of the culture
and workings of that destination. Now, when the internet can supply
inexhaustible (but not always reliable) facts, our books marry text and pictures to provide those much more elusive qualities: knowledge and dis-
cernment. To achieve this, they rely heavily on the authority of locally
based writers and photographers.

Insight Guide: *Sri Lanka* is structured to convey an understanding of the
country and its people as well as to guide readers through its attractions:

◆ The **Best of Sri Lanka** section at the front of the guide helps you to
prioritise what you want to do.

◆ The **Features** section, indicated by a pink bar at the top of each
page, covers the natural and cul-
tural history of the country as well as
illuminating essays on the Sri
Lankan economy, daily life, architecture and the arts.

◆ The main **Places** section, indicated by a blue bar, is a complete
guide to all the sights and areas
worth visiting. Places of special
interest are coordinated by number
with the maps.

◆ The **Travel Tips** listings section,
with a yellow bar, provides full information on transport, restaurants,
hotels, activities from culture to shopping to sports, an A–Z of essential
practical information, and a phrase-
book with Sinhala and Tamil expres-
sions. An easy-to-find contents list for
Travel Tips is printed on the back flap,
which also serves as a bookmark.

Stephen, a foreign correspondent who covered the Indian Ocean tsunami for *The Independent* newspaper group, contributed a feature on the disaster as well as updating the South and East Coast text. Tom, a resident of Sri Lanka, completely overhauled the sections on the Cultural Triangle, as well as contributing to the listings. The photo feature on Ayurveda was written by **Claudia Klages**.

Authors who worked on previous incarnations of this guide include the following: **Tania Brassey**, part-Sinhalese, part-Irish, who wrote the earlier chapters on Festivals, Food and Drink, Veddhas, Colombo, Hill Country and the East Coast. **Jeanne Thwaites**, who comes from one of Sri Lanka's oldest Burgher families, contributed the Tamil essay, while **Feizel Mansoor**, himself of Muslim descent, wrote on Muslims. **Dr H. Tamitegama** wrote the sections on the Sinhalese, Tea, Ayurveda and Kandy. Leading biologist and conservationist Dr Ranil Senanyake contributed the old Sanctuary essay. **Ralph Fouldes**, environmental scientist, wrote Wildlife. Polonnaruwa and Anuradhapura were written by **Samantha Elepatha** (of German and Sinhala descent), while Tania's daughter, **Pikka Brassey**, wrote about crafts – now in Shopping – and the South and West Coast chapters. **Dr Vessantha Abeysekera** wrote on Sigiriya. The chapters on Sri Lanka's complex history were initially provided by **Rowlinson Carter**, who also contributed on many other issues.

Many of the excellent photographs are the work of photographer **Sylvaine Poitau**. Thanks go to **Paula Soper** who edited this guide, **Jan McCann** who proofread it and **Penny Phenix** who indexed it.

The contributors

This new edition of Insight Guide Sri Lanka was put together by Insight Guides editor **Alexia Georgiou**, and updated by **Gavin Thomas**, who expanded the Best of Sri Lanka section and provided extra material for the chapters on the East Coast and Jaffna and the North.

The current text draws on previous editions of this guide, more lately a complete reworking on the part of **Gavin Thomas**, **Stephen Khan** and **Tom Parker**. Gavin is a freelance author and editor who has extensive experience of travelling in Sri Lanka. He completely revised or wrote from scratch the chapters on Geography, History, People, Contemporary Society, Religion and Festivals, Food, Art and Architecture, Performing Arts, Shopping, Wildlife, Colombo, the West Coast, Kandy, the Hill Country, Jaffna and the bulk of the Travel Tips.

Map Legend

━━━━━	Province Boundary
─ ─ ─ ─	District Boundary
─ • ─ • ─	National Park/Reserve
─ ─ ─ ─	Ferry Route
✈ ✚	Airport: International/Regional
🚌	Bus Station
➊	Tourist Information
∴	Ancient Site
✝ ✝ ✝	Church
৬	Hindu Temple
🏛	Buddhist Temple
☾	Mosque
∩	Cave
⚊	Statue/Monument
★	Place of Interest
⌐	Beach
🗼	Lighthouse
❈	Viewpoint

The main places of interest in the Places section are coordinated by number with a full-colour map (eg ➊), and a symbol at the top of every right-hand page tells you where to find the map.

Contents

Maps

Travel Tips

THE BEST OF SRI LANKA: TOP ATTRACTIONS

From the Buddhist temples and palaces of Kandy and the ancient ruins, art and architecture of the Cultural Triangle, to the altogether simpler pleasures of a good rice and curry.

△ **Galle Fort.** A perfectly preserved colonial time capsule, the quiet streets of Galle Fort ooze old-world atmosphere, with characterful Dutch-era mansions encircled by a venerable chain of ramparts and bastions, and the crashing waves of the Indian Ocean breaking just beyond. See page 178

▽ **Kandy.** The cultural capital of Sri Lanka has a vibrant traditional arts scene, a superb array of Buddhist temples and palaces, and a beautiful location amidst the island's precipitous central hills. See page 191

△ **Pinnawela Elephant Orphanage.** Touristy but undeniably enjoyable, the Orphanage is home to the world's largest troupe of captive pachyderms, from majestic old tuskers to the cutest of newborns. See page 197

△ **Polonnaruwa.** This is where you'll find Sri Lanka's finest collection of ancient Buddhist art and architecture, from the magnificent rock-carved statues of the Gal Vihara to the exquisitely decorated temples of the Quadrangle. See page 245

△ **Yala National Park.** Sri Lanka's foremost wildlife destination is home to the world's highest concentration of leopards, alongside elephants aplenty, fabulous birdlife and skittish monkeys – plus a wonderful landscape of unspoilt jungle and salty lagoons. See pages 134 and 185

◁ **Sigiriya.** The unforgettable rock-fortress of Sigiriya towers high over the surrounding plains, one of Sri Lanka's most dramatic natural sights, and brimful of historical interest too. See page 255

△ **Whale-watching.** Southern Sri Lanka offers arguably the best place in the world to see both blue and sperm whales together, along with lots of dolphins. See page 133

▽ **World's End.** The hill country at its most dramatic: the sheer cliffs of World's End fall away beneath one's feet for the best part of a kilometre, offering heart-stopping views over the distant plains below. See page 212

▷ **Rice and curry.** For the true flavour of Sri Lanka, tuck into an authentic Sri Lankan rice and curry, a miniature banquet of contrasting ingredients and flavours – with a fair bit of spice thrown in. See page 118

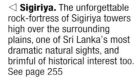

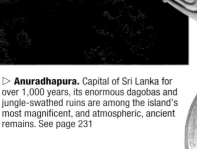

▷ **Anuradhapura.** Capital of Sri Lanka for over 1,000 years, its enormous dagobas and jungle-swathed ruins are among the island's most magnificent, and atmospheric, ancient remains. See page 231

THE BEST OF SRI LANKA: EDITOR'S CHOICE

Sri Lanka's temples, wildlife sanctuaries, scenery and cultural highlights... here, at a glance, are some recommendations to help you plan your journey.

BEST WILDLIFE

Yala National Park
Best known for its remarkable population of leopards, but great for all sorts of other wildlife as well. See page 185.

The Gathering, Minneriya National Park
The world's largest gathering of Asian elephants, who congregate here in their hundreds yearly from June to September. See pages 132 and 253.

Birdwatching in Bundala National Park
The lagoons of Bundala support an amazing array of aquatic birds, including great flocks of pink flamingos. See page 185.

Uda Walawe National Park
Modestly sized and yet one of the best places in Sri Lanka to see elephants in the wild. See page 216.

Sinharaja
A superb stretch of lush and unspoilt tropical rainforest, and home to some of Sri Lanka's rarest birds. See page 215.

BEST BUDDHIST TEMPLES

Temple of the Tooth, Kandy
The most important pilgrimage place in Sri Lanka, and home to the revered Tooth Relic of the Buddha, believed by many Buddhists to be the most precious thing in the world. See page 191.

The four *devales*, Kandy
Untouristy little shrines offering a picture-perfect snapshot of Buddhist art and architecture. See page 193.

Dambulla Cave Temples
Dating from the 1st century BC, these are the most beautiful temples in Sri Lanka, festooned with a marvellous array of sculptures and murals. See page 224.

Mulgirigalla
Wonderfully atmospheric sequence of cave temples carved out of the flanks of a towering hillside in the rural depths of the south. See page 184.

Kelaniya
Vibrant modern temple on the edge of Colombo, an attractive colonial-era building. See page 161.

ABOVE: Dambulla.
LEFT: leopard at Yala National Park.

BEST CULTURAL EXPERIENCES

Esala Perahera, Kandy
Sri Lanka's finest festival: an extraordinary pageant of drummers, dancers and elephants. See page 192.

Kandyan dancing
Spectacularly costumed dancers perform acrobatic choreography to an insistent accompaniment of high-octane drumming. See page 99.

Kataragama
Buddhists, Hindus, Christians and Muslims alike flock to the shrines at Kataragama, the island's most eclectic religious site and home to an extravagant summer festival. See page 184.

A cricket match
Join the crowds at a test or one-day match for an insight into Sri Lanka's other major religion: cricket. See page 306.

Nallur Festival, Jaffna
Sri Lanka's biggest and most spectacular Hindu festival, a pageant of colour, crowds and religious devotion. See page 279.

ABOVE: elephants draped in their finery for the Esala Perahera. **BELOW:** aromatic cardamom seeds.

BEST VIEWS

Horton Plains National Park and World's End
Marvellous landscape of bleak upland plains dotted with beautiful stands of cloudforest and bounded by the stunning cliffs and viewpoint of World's End. See page 211.

Lipton's Seat
Fabulous perch just outside Haputale, and a favourite haunt of great tea magnate Thomas Lipton, after whom it's named. See page 212.

Ella
Idyllic little village with gorgeous hill country scenery and one of the island's best viewpoints through the dramatic Ella Gap. See page 213.

Knuckles Range
Rugged and little-visited uplands east of Kandy – Sri Lanka at its wildest and least developed. See page 199.

Adam's Peak
The summit of Adam's Peak towers over the hill country – and doubles as one of the island's most important pilgrimage sites. See page 209.

ABOVE: Adam's Peak.

BEST FOOD

Sri Lankan seafood
Feast on crab, lobster and succulent prawns. See page 120.

Hoppers
A staple of Sri Lankan street cafés, these delicate little bowl-shaped pancakes are great either on their own, eaten with curry or cooked with an egg broken into the centre. See page 120.

Kottu rotty
Sri Lanka's answer to the stir-fry, with slices of doughy bread (kottu) mixed up with meat or veg and cooked on hotplates by cleaver-wielding chefs – just follow the noise of chopping and banging. See page 119.

Lamprais
A portion of rice, egg and meat baked in a plantain leaf. See page 119.

BEST BEACHES

Unawatuna
Pretty little horseshoe beach backed by one of Sri Lanka's most enjoyable villages. See page 180.

Bentota and Induruwa
One of the finest stretches of beach on the west coast, running south from the magnificent Bentota lagoon and lined with a string of alluring hotels. See page 172.

Arugam Bay
Famous for its surf, this remote beach and village in the far east also has bags of laid-back charm

and a number of interesting sights nearby. See page 270.

Mirissa
One of the south coast's most intimate beaches, with a picture-perfect arc of sand screened by toppling palms – and a great place to go whale-watching too. See page 182.

Uppuveli
Proximity to the former war zone means that this superb swathe of sand remains remarkably sleepy and undeveloped – visit now before it all changes. See page 269.

BEST OF COLONIAL SRI LANKA

Villas in Galle
Stay in one of the superbly restored old Dutch colonial villas in the historic city of Galle. See pages 178 and 291.

Hill Club, Nuwara Eliya
One of the island's finest period pieces, this marvellously time-warped British country club seems scarcely to have changed since the days of the Victorian tea planters who built it. See page 207.

Catholic churches, Negombo

Florid and colourful Catholic churches can be found scattered throughout Negombo and the surrounding district, a lasting reminder of the mass conversions seen here during Portuguese times. See page 166.

Dambatanne Tea Factory, Haputale
Classic British-era tea factory, complete with much of its original Victorian machinery, some of it still in use today. See page 212.

Old Jaffna
Despite the war, the core of old Jaffna remains remarkably peaceful, with shady streets dotted with churches, colleges and colonial villas – and the country's most impressive Dutch fort. See page 278.

ABOVE: Bentota beach.
LEFT: St Mary's Church, Negombo.

BEST AYURVEDA RESORTS, SPAS AND ECO-LODGES

Ayurveda Pavilions, Negombo
Idyllic little hideaway in bustling Negombo, with bijoux private villas and gardens and a wide range of rejuvenating treatments. See page 290.
Amangalla Spa, Galle
One of Sri Lanka's finest spas, set in the memorable Amangalla hotel. See page 291.
Barberyn Reef, Beruwala
Long-established, soothing and refreshingly

unpretentious Ayurveda resort – or head to the sister establishment in Weligama. See page 290.
Kumbuk River, near Kataragama
Award-winning eco-lodge with accommodation in an enormous thatched elephant. See page 308.
The Mud House, Anamaduwa
Traditional Sri Lankan village architecture given a contemporary twist – surrounded by lakes and wildlife. See page 293.

ABOVE: Yapahuwa, stone staircase and gateway.

BEST OFF THE BEATEN TRACK

Yapahuwa
Absorbing remains of one of Sri Lanka's many abandoned capitals, centred on a spectacular ceremonial stone stairway, lined with intricate carvings and statues. See page 223.
Mulgirigalla
Marvellous sequence of elaborately decorated cave temples benefiting from a dramatic hillside setting – high above the coast at Tangalla. See page 184.
Arankele
Atmospheric forest monastery, with ancient remains scattered amidst beautiful tropical jungle. See page 223.

Maligawila
A pair of majestic Buddha statues stand enigmatically in the jungle near the remote village of Maligawila. See page 271.
Batticaloa
Bustling Batti is the east's second city – long isolated during the war years, but now offering a rewarding destination for the few travellers who make it here. See page 269.
Jaffna Peninsula
One of Sri Lanka's most fascinating areas, dotted with Hindu temples, gorgeous beaches, windswept islands and assorted reminders of the now vanquished LTTE. See page 279.

ABOVE: meditating at the Ayurveda Pavilions.

MONEY-SAVING TIPS

Sri Lanka's thriving package-tour industry means that it's often a lot cheaper to pick up a flight-plus-hotel deal, rather than booking each separately.
Most people hire a car and driver to get around, although public transport reaches virtually everywhere you might want to go, at virtually zero cost – not as comfortable or

convenient as a car, but saving plenty of cash and also offering a closer and more memorable view of the island (just remember to pack light, and take a rucksack rather than a suitcase).
There's not much you can do about the inflated admission prices to the major tourist sights, although you can cut costs when visiting national parks by sharing a jeep with others

(ask with the person arranging the tour, or at the park entrance).
Always agree a fare before setting off in a tuktuk, and check with your hotel to find out roughly how much you should be paying – rogue tuktuk drivers, con artists (see page 317), and strangers trying to take you to shops or sell you gems should be avoided like the plague.

REMEMBER MY NAME

Sri Lanka's many different names are a
reflection of its fascinating history.

The island currently going by the name of Sri Lanka
has had a string of other names and identities over
the centuries. Prince Vijaya and his followers called
the island Tambapanni, after the copper-coloured beach
at which they landed on the west coast. In the reign of
the Roman Emperor Claudius, a sea captain working for
Annius Plocamus, a tax collector in the Red Sea, suffered
the misfortune of catching a monsoon that swept his boat
off course and dumped him on the island 15 days later.
For him, and other Roman and Greek callers, Tambapanni
was too much of a mouthful and became Taprobane, a name that survived in Western use for hundreds of years, even cropping
up in Milton's *Paradise Regained* (where it is described as the
"utmost Indian Isle Taprobane") and Cervantes' *Don Quixote*.

Arab traders could have told Annius Plocamus's captain
that if he waited a while a different monsoon would blow
him back to Arabia or, if he liked, East Africa. They relied on
these winds to go back and forth, knew the island well and
called it Serendib, a corruption of the Sanskrit Sinhaladvipa.
This was the name that 18th-century English novelist Horace
Walpole used for his fairy tale, *The Three Princes of Serendib*,
coining the word "serendipity" (Sirinduil is another variant).

Edward Barbosa, a Portuguese captain who visited in 1515, tried to
persuade his countrymen to adopt Tennaserim, which in some ancient
Indian language meant "Land of Delights", but they had already settled
on Ceilão which, thanks to medieval Europeans like Marco Polo, became
Seylan. The Dutch worked out their own derivation to produce Zeilan;
the English compromise was Ceylon.

Through all of this, the Sinhalese had long ago decided it was Lanka,
and it officially changed to Sri Lanka in 1972 (Sri means "holy" or "beautiful"). The words Prajathanthrika Samajavadi Janarajayi (Democratic
Socialist Republic) were tacked on in 1978. It's quite a mouthful, but
your mistakes will doubtless be forgiven: Sri Lankans are used to people
getting their name wrong.

PRECEDING PAGES: temple at Seenigama Island, near Hikkaduwa; in Galle Fort;
Pinnawela Elephant Orphanage. **LEFT:** a Thai Buddha statue at the Seema Malaka,
Colombo. **ABOVE, FROM LEFT:** wall panel, Anuradhapura; Bentota Beach.

LIE OF THE LAND

From tropical beaches and lagoons to arid savannah and craggy mountains, Sri Lanka crams a hugely varied range of landscapes into its modest dimensions.

The outline of Sri Lanka on the map has evoked visions of a teardrop falling from the tip of India, a pearl, a pear, a mango and – in Dutch eyes somewhat insensitive to the misgivings of the Muslims and vegetarian Buddhists who live on it – a Westphalian ham. Lying just a few degrees north of the equator in the balmy waters of the Indian Ocean, the island boasts an incredibly diverse range of landscapes, from the sultry tropical beaches, coconut plantations and lowland jungles of the coast to the cool green hill country, with its mist-shrouded mountains, crashing waterfalls and endless tea plantations.

Sri Lanka is a small country, with a land area of 64,740 sq km (25,000 sq miles) – roughly the size of Ireland – around 430km (270 miles) from top to bottom, and 220km (140 miles) from east to west at its widest point, though the range of contrasting landscapes and cultures packed into such a small space can make it feel much bigger. Most of Sri Lanka is flat and hot, though the uplands of the hill country, occupying the central southern portion of the island, rise to cool, mist-shrouded heights. The island's highest point is Pidurutalagala, near Nuwara Eliya, which reaches 2,524 metres (8,281ft), though its most famous mountain, the sacred Adam's Peak, is a little smaller at 2,243 metres (7,359ft).

Rocks of ages

The rocks that now underlie much of Sri Lanka originally formed part of Gondwanaland, the great southern supercontinent which until about 150 million years ago contained the disparate landmasses which are now Africa, Antarctica,

India and Australia. Geologically, Sri Lanka is part of the Indian continental plate. Indeed, until quite recently India and Sri Lanka were connected by a land bridge, perhaps 100km (60 miles) wide or more, until rising sea levels divided the two around 7,000 years ago. The two countries still remain tenuously connected by Adam's Bridge, a slender chain of islets and sandbanks; temple records in India suggest that parts of the "bridge" remained above water until as recently as the 15th century, offering migrants an easy passage between India and its island neighbour.

The peaks of Sri Lanka's hill country are also intimately linked to the subcontinent, being a continuation of India's Western Ghats. These mountains were formed during the subcontinent's split from the African continental plate,

LEFT: the coast at Galle, southern Sri Lanka.
RIGHT: Adam's Peak in the hill country.

and consist of rock sediments dating back 2 billion years – some of the oldest rocks in the world, and now the source of myriad precious stones, which are washed down out of the hills in rivers and mined in various parts of the island, most famously in the countryside around Ratnapura.

Wet and dry zones

These central hills play a pivotal role in shaping Sri Lanka's weather patterns. Sri Lanka experiences two separate monsoons, which arrive on opposite sides of the island at different times of year. The barrier presented by the central

hills means that rain carried by these monsoons is unable to travel right across the island, but instead affects only the coast on which it arrives. From around May to September the heavy southwest, or Yala, monsoon inundates the southwestern quarter of the island, the so-called wet zone, which receives far more rainfall than the rest of the island. Covering about a third of the island, the wet zone is Sri Lanka at its most lushly tropical, stretching from around Chilaw (north of Negombo) on the west coast to just east of Tangalla on the south coast. Much of the land is covered in a dense canopy of greenery, with many kilometres of coconut and rubber plantations, and clusters of fruit trees and spice bushes in every garden.

The remaining two-thirds of the island's lowlands are known as the dry zone, a predominantly arid region that receives little rainfall except for sporadic deluges during the northeast (Maha) monsoon, which hits the eastern side of the island from roughly October to March. The lowland areas of the dry zone mostly comprise scrub-covered savannah, predominantly flat, although often dotted with dramatic mountainous outcrops, such as that at Sigiriya, or the huge granite formations that dot Yala National Park.

Beaches and hills

Virtually the whole of the island's 1,340km (830 miles) of coast is low-lying, shelving gently into the Indian Ocean. Much of the seaboard is fringed with golden beaches and thick stands of coconut palms, backed in many places by extensive, meandering lagoon systems, while the section of coast from Negombo north up to Puttalam is bisected by an old canal built by the Dutch to transport spices.

Heading inland from the coast into the hills, the land climbs up through a series of different climatic zones, each with its own associated set of flora and fauna. Sinharaja, on the low, southwestern flanks of the hill country, preserves the country's finest tract of undisturbed rainforest, while heading further up into the hills one finds beautiful pockets of cloudforest at places like Horton Plains National Park and Adam's Peak, a misty and mysterious world of stunted grey trees covered in mossy epiphytes. Much of the hill country's original forest cover, however, was cleared in the 19th century to make room for tea plantations, whose small and carefully trimmed bushes, dotted with strategically

---

WINDS OF FORTUNE

The trade winds, on which the monsoons are carried to Sri Lanka, not only keep the island watered, but also helped make it rich. The winds are named for their old commercial connections: in former centuries they provided a reliable shuttle service for traders sailing from Greece, China, Arabia and Rome. These traders came to Sri Lanka primarily for spices and gems. Having landed and concluded their business, they had to wait for the winds to change direction before they could head back home – and by the time they did, many of these visitors had become so attached to the island that they decided to settle for good.

positioned eucalpytus trees (planted to provide shade, and as a source of commercial timber), are now the highlands' most characteristic sight.

Rivers, wetlands and lagoons

The map of Sri Lanka is scored with dozens of rivers, which flow down from the highlands into the sea on both coasts, often forming spectacular waterfalls en route as they tumble out of the hills – the island's highest cascade, at Bambarakanda, is 241 metres (790ft) from top to bottom, almost five times taller than Niagara. The biggest rivers are called *ganga* (a North Indian word, referring to the Ganges, brought

wetlands at Bundala National Park are the most famous, principally for their rich birdlife, but those at Muthurajawela (near Negombo), Bentota, Koggala and Batticaloa are also interesting.

Water tanks

Many of the island's most striking water features, however, are not the work of nature, but of the ancient Sinhalese. Arriving in the arid plains in the north, the Sinhalese faced the problem of storing sufficient water to cultivate rice on a year-round basis. The resultant irrigation works, constructed between *c.*400 BC and the fall of Polonnaruwa in 1215, changed the physical face

to the island by early Sinhalese settlers), while smaller seasonal rivers are called *oya*. Sri Lanka's pre-eminent river by far is the mighty Mahaweli Ganga, which twists and turns for 335km (205 miles) between its source in the highlands near Adam's Peak, through the Kandy area and down to the sea near Trincomalee.

As they approach the coast, many of the rivers spread out into enormous lagoon and wetland systems, often fringed with mangroves and hosting significant populations of aquatic birds, crocodiles and other fauna. The lagoons and

ABOVE, FROM LEFT: Duhinda Falls; Kandy River; fishermen returning with their catch to the shores of Mahakanadarawa Tank, near Anuradhapura.

of Sri Lanka forever, and the map of the country is still studded with over 18,000 of these ancient reservoirs (generally referred to as "tanks"; in Sinhala, *wewa*) (see page 249). Some of these are little more than modest ponds, but many are staggering feats of hydraulic engineering, with circumferences of 8km (5 miles) or more being fairly common. Particularly famous examples include the trio of tanks which surround Anuradhapura; the vast Parakrama Samudra at Polonnaruwa; the tanks in the national parks at Minneriya and Kaudulla; and the Kala Wewa, north of Dambulla near the Aukana Buddha – although the island's largest tank is the little-visited Padawiya Tank in the far north, near Vavuniya, close to the former front line of the civil war.

DECISIVE DATES

Pre- and Early History

c.10,000 BC
Sri Lanka's first Stone Age culture emerges.

543 BC
Death of the Buddha in India and arrival of Sinhalese in Sri Lanka, led by Prince Vijaya.

Early Anuradhapura Period

c.250–210 BC
Reign of Devanampiya Tissa. Indian emperor Asoka sends missions to Lanka and converts population to Buddhism.

161–137 BC
Reign of Dutugemunu. For the first time Sri Lanka is unified under a single Sinhalese monarch.

35–32 BC
Pali scriptures committed to writing.

AD 276–303
Reign of Mahasena; foundation of the Jetavanarama, the largest dagoba in the world.

303–31
Reign of Sirimeghavana; arrival of the Tooth Relic; apogee of first Anuradhapura period.

432–59
Tamil invasion and end of first Anuradhapura period.

Late Anuradhapura Period

459–77
Reign of Dhatusena; end of Tamil domination.

477–95
Reign of Kassapa and construction of Sigiriya.

495–512
Reign of Mogallan I; capital returned to Anuradhapura.

618–84
Internecine struggles; Tamil interventions; finally Pallava domination.

684–718
Reign of Manavamma; alliance with the Pallavas.

835–53
Reign of Sena I. Pandyan conquest.

c.947
Chola expedition; Anuradhapura is plundered; the king flees to Rohana.

993–1017
Capture and sack of Anuradhapura. Chola victory at Polonnaruwa. Collapse of irrigation system and destruction of many religious foundations.

Polonnaruwa Period 1073–1215

1055–1110
Reign of Vijayabahu; kingdom liberated from Cholas.

1073
Capital transferred to Polonnaruwa. Religious foundations and irrigation works.

1153–86
Reign of Parakrama I (the Great). Polonnaruwa becomes undisputed capital, beginning a period of political, religious and material reconstruction.

1187–96
Reign of Nissanka Malla; further grandiose buildings erected.

Period of Ephemeral Capitals 1214–1597

1214
Kalingan Invasion.

1215–36
Tyranny of Magha. Destruction of Polonnaruwa.

1505
Portuguese arrive, establish fort at Colombo, and soon occupy the island's coastal areas.

1550–97
Dom Jão Dharmapala set up as puppet king by the Portuguese.

Kandyan Period 1597–1815

1597
Capital moved to Kandy.

1619
Portuguese capture Jaffna.

1656
Dutch arrive and oust Portuguese after both land and sea battles.

1796
Dutch surrender to the British, who have become interested in Trincomalee's fine harbour.

British Colonial Period 1802–1948

1802
Ceylon becomes a Crown Colony.

1815
The last Sinhalese king, Sri Wickrama Rajasinha, deposed and exiled.

1867
First commercial planting of tea and construction of first railway line, from Colombo to Kandy.

PRECEDING PAGES: an Esala Perahera procession celebrates the arrival of the Buddha's Tooth Relic. ABOVE, FROM LEFT: a view from 1864 of the Thuparama dagoba at Anuradhapura; a Ceylon postage stamp from the reign of King George VI (1936–52); portrait of a Sri Lankan army soldier at Anuradhapura.

1919
Foundation of Ceylon National Congress, first nationalist political party.

1931
Universal franchise granted.

Independence 1948– Present

1948
Independence declared.

1959
Prime minister S.W.R.D. Bandaranaike assassinated by Buddhist monk.

1960
Mrs Bandaranaike becomes world's first female prime minister.

1971
Armed rebellion by Maoist JVP in south leaves thousands dead.

1972
Country changes its name from Ceylon to Sri Lanka.

1983
"Black July" sees thousands of Tamil civilians murdered by Sinhalese mobs in Colombo. Outbreak of civil war between the Sri Lankan Army (SLA) and the LTTE (Liberation Tigers of Tamil Eelam) in the north.

1987
Indian peacekeeping troops sent in.

1987–88
Second JVP insurrection. Thousands more die in the south.

1990
Departure of Indian troops.

1993
President Ranasinghe Premadasa assassinated.

1996
World Cricket Cup victory.

2001
Truce agreed between government and LTTE.

2004
Boxing Day tsunami ravages coastline: 30,000 lives lost and 100,000 left homeless.

2006
Mahinda Rajapakse becomes president. Steady upsurge in violence leads to renewed fighting between SLA and LTTE.

2007
SLA succeeds in driving LTTE out of eastern Sri Lanka.

2009
In May, SLA defeats LTTE forces in the north, reclaiming all rebel-held territory and killing Tiger supremo Vellupillai Prabhakaran.

2010
Rajapakse re-elected president, defeating former army chief Sarath Fonseka.

2011
The final report of the Lessons Learnt and Reconciliation Commission clears government of alleged war crimes; the international community remains unconvinced.

ANCIENT CIVILISATION

Sri Lanka's ancient chronicles stretch back into the
far distant past, where history melts into myth.

Myths about ancient Sri Lanka are plentiful, but actual archaeological evidence
of the island's prehistory is slight. The
first humans to arrive in Sri Lanka were the
Veddhas (see page 63), who walked across from
India not later than around 16,000 BC, or perhaps as early as 125,000 BC. Their impact on
the island was minimal, as they lived mainly by
hunting and gathering, although archaeological evidence of domesticated animals and iron
has been found from around 800 BC. The dis-
covery of so-called Black and Red Ware pottery
in both Sri Lanka and India, as well as shared
types of burial mound, suggests that there was
contact between the two countries long before
the arrival of the Sinhalese, although exactly
what form this took is unknown.

The Sinhalese

Around the 4th century BC, waves of immigrants from north India began to arrive in the
island – the ancestors of the modern Sinhalese.
The Sinhalese traced their lineage to the union
between a lion (*sinha*, hence Sinhalese) and a
princess in Bengal. The story of their ancestry
and how they came to arrive on the island is
described in the curious legend of Prince Vijaya
(see page 64).

At first the Sinhalese were confined to coastal
river valleys, these being the only areas suitable
for the cultivation of their staple crop, rice.
Gradually, however, they developed skills in irrigation and the building of reservoirs (or "tanks",

LEFT: one of the enormous Buddha images that make
up the Gal Vihara at Polonnaruwa, where solid rock
has become a masterpiece. **RIGHT:** the revered mount
of Adam's Peak.

THE MAHAVAMSA

In the 5th century AD, Buddhist monks began
writing the *Mahavamsa* (Great History) on palm-
leaf *(ola)* tablets. Like the Old Testament, this is a
chronicle of ancient kings interwoven with the
theme of a Chosen People guided by the True
Faith. In this case the heroes were the Sinhalese,
and this national story was (and still is) a way of
asserting their inherent claim to the island. It was
written at a time when the Sinhalese capital,
Anuradhapura, was beset by armies from southern India who threatened to imitate the actions of
the Visigoths and Vandals who had, half a world
away, recently sacked Rome.

as they're known in Sri Lanka) which allowed them to convert the arid northern plains to agricultural use. Moving slowly inland, they established the first significant Sinhalese capital at Anuradhapura, in around 380 BC.

The arrival of Buddhism

Sri Lanka's great historical chronicle, the *Mahavamsa (see box)*, indulges in a spot of wishful thinking when it recounts the Buddha's three visits to the island when the only inhabitants were *yaksas* and *nagas*, who flitted through the jungle so elusively that they could have been spirits and demons. Although the Buddha's

The turning point was their appeal to India's emperor Asoka the Great. With the characteristic zeal of a new convert, Asoka dispatched missionaries in all directions, including Egypt, Syria and Greece. The conversion of Lanka, meanwhile, was entrusted to Asoka's own son, Mahinda.

Asoka directed his son to King Tissa of Anuradhapura, who was out hunting deer on a mountain side at Mihintale, not far from his palace, when he was confronted by Mahinda. The missionary prince tested the king with searching questions about mango trees, an interrogation that survives verbatim, but is

appearance struck fear into their hearts, they were not suitable disciples.

The chronicle also asserts that, just as Prince Vijaya and his followers reached Sri Lanka, the Buddha lay down between two sala trees in a remote part of northern India and attained Nirvana. His parting words, according to the *Mahavamsa*, were to pronounce a blessing on Vijaya's enterprise. Prosaic history records that in 543 BC, the traditional date of Prince Vijaya's landing, the Buddha would have been about 20 years old. He died around 60 years later, after eating some off-colour pork prepared by a disciple named Chunda.

For two centuries after the Buddha's death, his teachings met with only moderate success.

more or less unintelligible to anyone not steeped in Buddhist theology. The king's replies were totally satisfactory and, in turn, he was left in no doubt about the validity of the Buddha's beliefs. His conversion was sealed by the new title Devanampiya (Dear to the Gods) and the arrival of Mahinda's sister, a nun, with a collection of holy relics: the Buddha's begging bowl, his collarbone, and a cutting from the sacred Bo tree beneath which the Buddha had achieved enlightenment. The cutting was planted next to the royal palace and orders were given for the building of a temple to house the begging bowl and collarbone.

Some 23 centuries later, the tree still stands – albeit propped up on crutches – one of the oldest documented trees on earth and, for Buddhists, the most sacred. The texts that Mahinda brought over with him were translated into Pali, the language of Buddhist scripture, and Anuradhapura blossomed with grand buildings in honour of the new religion. Lanka was on the verge of a civilisation that would last 1,000 years and be ranked among the wonders of the ancient world.

The Tamils take control

Although a few Tamils had settled in the north of the island, and perhaps also in the east in the 3rd century BC, the main migrations did not occur until the 10th century AD. Today they represent about 18 percent of the population. The Sinhalese descendants of Prince Vijaya appealed to their south Indian neighbours to form their armies, in order to appease their Buddhist abhorrence of killing anything, even cockroaches, which left them vulnerable. If their Tamil mercenaries mutinied, there was nothing the Sinhalese could do about it. In 237 BC, only a few years after Devanampiya Tissa's death, two Tamil captains in the Anuradhapura army staged a coup and ruled Anuradhapura for 22 years before they were murdered. The Tamil general Elara was quick to step into their shoes and his rule lasted 44 years.

Getting about through the jungle was slow and difficult, so Elara carved the land into manageable chunks under quasi-feudal barons who called themselves kings. The perfect impartiality referred to by chroniclers suggests that some of these kings, perhaps the majority, were actually Sinhalese.

The rise of Dutugemunu

This was certainly the case in the south of the island, Ruhuna, where the king was so satisfied with existing arrangements that at table one day he asked his 12-year-old son and heir apparent to swear faithfully that he would never lift a finger against Elara. The prince flung his rice bowl from the table, said he would rather starve to death than make such a pledge, and soon after the meal sent his father some female baubles to show what he thought of his obsequiousness. The prince subsequently took to sleeping in

the foetal position, explaining to his mother that he felt unable to stretch out between a Tamil tyrant and the sea. When the prince had a Buddhist relic set into the shaft of his spear, there could be no doubt that he, Dutugemunu, was the right man to topple Elara.

The preliminaries took 11 years and were a matter of picking off the feudal dependencies and their collaborator kings one by one, Dutugemunu sharing the battle honours with his enormous elephant Kandula. On one occasion, when they stormed the gates of a fortress and were showered with rocks and molten lead, the elephant had to dive into a nearby tank to

cool off. Then, under a protective shield of buffalo skins, they re-entered the fray and demolished the gates like matchsticks.

The war reached a dramatic finale with Dutugemunu and Elara facing one another in single combat on elephants. Dutugemunu won, but he was magnanimous in victory, giving the fallen general an honourable burial and decreeing that anyone passing his tomb, even royalty, should dismount out of respect. It is said that as recently as 1817 – more than 2,000 years after the event – a Kandyan noble on the run from the British climbed out of his hiding place on tottering legs to comply, although these days, curiously, no one seems sure where the Tamil general's last resting place can be found.

ABOVE, FROM LEFT: a 19th-century photograph of Veddhas records a way of life that was unchanged for millennia; a Buddha sculpture from the 6th century.

The golden age of Anuradhapura

Dutugemunu's triumph was celebrated with an orgy of new building works in the capital, including parks, temples and palaces, the greatest being his copper-roofed Brazen Palace – though this wasn't for himself (the chronicles take care to mention) but for the city's monks. He also oversaw further additions to the island's increasingly vast network of irrigation works, comprising hundreds of enormous tanks and thousands of kilometres of channels. Ambitious projects such as these demanded a high degree of centralised authority, which in turn was paid for with taxable agricultural surpluses. It was

as she got bored with a succession of five lovers, including "a gigantic Malabar named Wattuka". Unable to find any more volunteers to share either the throne or, even fleetingly, her bed, she reigned alone for four months before being murdered by her stepson. The chroniclers could take this sort of thing in their stride; it awaited a Victorian historian to pronounce her "a woman whose wickedness cannot perhaps be paralleled in the history of the universe". On the other hand, there was a twinge of sympathy for a playful king, Subha, whose party trick was to change places with a servant who was his spitting image. One day, having played the trick once too often,

not the only resource to be exploited for profit, and Sri Lanka also became known as a source of precious stones, first-class elephants and spices, especially cinnamon.

However hard-earned, Dutugemunu's unification fell apart in the absence of defined rules of succession. Of Anuradhapura's early kings 15 ruled for less than a year, 22 were murdered by their successors, six were murdered by other people, four committed suicide, 13 were killed in battle, and 11 were dethroned, never to be heard of again. If any of the perpetrators had Buddhist inhibitions about using cold steel, more than 50 deadly poisons grew wild on the island. Queen Anula first poisoned her husband to gain the throne and then reached for the bottle as soon

the servant "king" who had taken his place sentenced the real king to death, and he was carted off, howling protestations, to be executed. The imposter servant reigned for four years in his turn, before himself being murdered.

Sigiriya

Murderous royal ambitions could have unexpected results and one example resulted in the creation of the eighth wonder of the world. In 478, King Dhatusena had just completed Anuradhapura's biggest reservoir yet – enclosed by a 5km (3-mile) wall of granite – when he was murdered by his son Kassapa. As was common practice in such circumstances, a second son, Mogallana, ran off to the mainland to see if he could raise an army and take the throne for himself. His negotiations took 18 years, and in the meantime Kassapa built an impregnable fortress on a 200-metre (650ft) rock that towered over the forest at a place called Sigiriya. While there was still no sign of Mogallana, he added creature comforts: a water garden, for example, and 550 frescoes of beautiful women, so beguiling that generations of visitors poured out their hearts in verse scribbled on a nearby wall. When Mogallana materialised, Kassapa went by elephant to meet his nemesis on the plain below.

The chronicles have little to say about Kassapa apart from grudging admiration for the way he died. It seems he was leading a charge on the Chola force that Mogallana had at last managed to raise when his elephant sensed they were heading for a hidden swamp and veered away. The troops behind misread this sudden evasion as a signal to retreat and broke up in confusion. Left to face the enemy alone, Kassapa raised his dagger high, drove it down his throat, re-sheathed the blade, toppled off his elephant and died. Mogallana dispatched 1,000 of his brother's courtiers and returned the capital to Anuradhapura.

The fall of Anuradhapura

Mogallana's victory betrayed the dangerous reality that the Tamil kingdoms of the Pandyans, Pallavas and the Cholas on the mainland were Anuradhapura's king-makers. Interference, however, worked both ways, and Sinhalese kings ran the risk of taking sides in disputes on the mainland. Their worst mistake was to back the Pandyans against the Cholas led by Rajaraja, a formidable king whose empire eventually stretched to Malaysia and Indonesia. Rajaraja ordered a revenge attack in 993. The Sinhalese were powerless against overwhelming forces. Mahinda V, then king of Anuradhapura, was bundled off to exile in India, the capital was sacked, and Rajaraja annexed the whole island as part of his empire. It seemed that 1,500 years of history had come to nothing.

Although this calamitous state of affairs lasted only 75 years, it did bring the curtain down on Anuradhapura, reducing to rubble a city that had once measured 25km (16

ABOVE, FROM LEFT: Abhayagiri Monastery, one of Anuradhapura's great stupas; one of the Sigiriya maidens in an unrestored state, but is she goddess or courtesan?

> As well as enjoying a safer and more strategically central location, Polonnaruwa enjoyed one other big advantage over Anuradhapura as a capital: it had fewer mosquitoes.

miles) across. Some seven centuries later, the Englishman Robert Knox walked by the scene of the Cholas' revenge on the city and wrote: "Here and there, by the side of the river, is a world of hewn stone pillars, and other heaps of hewn stones which, I suppose, formerly were buildings..."

Polonnaruwa

Anuradhapura was replaced by Polonnaruwa, an ancient military stronghold at the one point where armies could ford the Mahaweli river, and the best place to keep an eye on infiltration from the south. For all Rajaraja's might, the politics of south India were notoriously fluid. Within 50 or 60 years of the invasion, the Cholas were troubled both at home and by a nagging guerrilla campaign lead by Vijayabahu, a young relative of the exiled king, which made them cut their losses and leave in 1070. For the sake of tradition, Vijayabahu had himself crowned in the rubble of Anuradhapura but, like the departed Cholas, elected to rule from Polonnaruwa. Described by the chronicles as

The boastful Nissanka Malla ordered teams of elephants to drag a 25-tonne rock across 100km (60 miles) so that scribes could engrave an indelible record of his work.

"a brave man and distinguished by his good conduct", Vijayabahu kept the peace for over 40 years, being "extraordinarily skilled in the use of the many expedients such as kindness".

Parakramabahu the Great

The chronicle saved its unbridled adula-

tion instead for Parakramabahu I, who more than made amends for Vijayabahu's coolness towards the Buddhist clergy. Thus, a tremendous thunderstorm had no effect on a royal procession, when Parakramabahu rode with his queen in a tower erected across the backs of two elephants. Not a drop of water touched them, "a striking instance", the chronicle noted, "of the power of Buddha".

But it was another drop which made Parakramabahu famous and is still very much quoted. When announcing plans for more ambitious irrigation schemes than had ever been attempted in Anuradhapura, he declared that "not one drop of water must flow into the ocean without serving the purposes of man".

His showpiece, the Parakrama Samudra, made a mockery of the later British term "tank". At 2,100 hectares (5,600 acres), it was more like an inland sea.

Parakramabahu's huge vision extended to foreign policy, too. He may not have been the first Sinhalese king to send troops to India, but none had contemplated a naval force – commanded by a Malabar general, Adikaram – to invade Burma and, as things turned out, kill its king.

The fall of Polonnaruwa

Tangles at the imperial court after Parakramabahu's death had a familiar ring. His nephew Vijayabahu II murdered a shepherd who hesitated to hand over his beautiful daughter and was at once murdered himself by another who thought he better deserved her. His successor lasted five days. The rot stopped with the coronation of Parakramabahu's Indian brother-in-law, Nissanka Malla.

Nissanka oversaw a baroque flourishing of the arts, with sinuous lotus-stem pillars and elaborately entwined carvings. He also taxed later scholars by adding inscriptions to existing buildings so that other kings' work appeared as his own, but most agree that he commissioned one of the greatest works of sculpture in any age: the imposing Gal Vihara, four giant Buddhas carved from a single wall of granite.

If Parakramabahu's prodigality had stretched the treasury, Nissanka Malla's vanity finished it off. His death without leaving a designated heir triggered the usual chaos and once again there was an opportunist on the mainland ready to step in. The chroniclers were inconsolable: "This Magha, who was like unto a fierce drought, commanded his army of strong men to ransack the kingdom of Lanka, even as a wild fire doth a forest. Thereupon, these wicked disturbers of the peace stalked about the land hither and thither crying out boastfully, 'Lo! we are the giants of Kerala.'"

His atrocities are catalogued: the amputation of limbs; rich men tortured until they surrendered their valuables; believers beaten up at their prayers; children flogged wholesale; temples and libraries destroyed; slave labour and so on. "Alas! Alas! Even so did those Tamil giants, like the giants of Mara, destroy the kingdom and the religion of the land... and robbed all the treasures that were therein with all the pearls and precious stones."

When Magha died in 1255 there were no members of the ruling class still around to make a bid for the throne. With the city and its irrigation system left unattended, the jungle closed in. Although the Polonnaruwa era had lasted less than three centuries, compared with Anuradhapura's 13, it had matched it in magnificence. Like Anuradhapura, its memory faded until 1886 when S.M. Burrows, a British colonial officer, came across the remains of the Thuparama, one of the city's best-preserved monuments. "The entrance to and interior of this curious building was almost entirely blocked up with fallen masonry and other

Kurunegala, then on to the cities of Gampola and Dedigama, where rival kings established themselves by around 1340. The Tamils, whose numbers had grown significantly, looked after themselves in an independent kingdom centred on Jaffna. A scion of the Gampola royal family later set himself as king of an obscure town in the hills, Senkadagala, which would subsequently become known as Kandy and provide the Sinhalese with their last and one of their most glorious kingdoms. The Dedigama kings, meanwhile, were eclipsed by a new set of rulers on the coast, based at the city of Kotte, close to the modern city of Colombo.

debris," he wrote. "This has been removed at a considerable cost of labour, for most of the fallen blocks of masonry were so large that they had to be broken up with the pickaxe before removal was possible. But the labour was well expended..."

Ephemeral capitals

Driven out of Polonnaruwa, the Sinhalese nobility drifted gradually south, taking their capital with them from Yapahuwa to

ABOVE, FROM LEFT: the ruined temples at Polonnaruwa are roofless and weather-beaten but retain their religious power; a 19th-century postcard gives an historic view.

Thus fragmented from the 13th to 15th centuries, the island was prey to invaders from unexpected quarters. Cheng Ho, a Chinese admiral, carried off one of the Sinhalese kings and his prime minister to China. A Malayan king invaded for reasons which remain a mystery, and there is similar uncertainty about incursions by the king of Pegu in Burma or even a sultan of Egypt.

Then, at the beginning of the 16th century, a fleet of storm-battered ships appeared off the west coast near Kotte. The occupants wore armour, carried firearms, and appeared to eat stones and drink blood. It was the island's first sight of the Europeans who would dominate its history for the next four and a half centuries.

INDI.

Boreum
pmo

Sufuara

MARE INDI

Talacori
Galidi

Modutti

Margana
Iogana

Anubingara

Phasis fl.

Anurogrammum
regia

Nagadiba
Maagram
mum

Anarifmudi
pmo

Oxia
pmo

Soani

Galibi montes

Ganges fl.

Procuri

Soana fl.

Semni

Adifamu

TAPROBANA.

Solif por

que ante fe
Poduce Habet infulas
1378

Sincocanda

Sandocandæ

Abaratha
Tarachi

Malea mons

Bocana

Annubingara

Bocani

Barachus fl.

Sin°
rafodif

Bumafani

Elephantum

Nubartha

fl.

Pafena

Æq

Axanus

Vlifpada
Rhogadani

Nacaduna

Nanigiri
Bachi oppidum

Hodoca

Anium
prom

Dagana

Corcobara

Caladadrua

yone

Arana

Alaba

Baffa

Balaca

Canathra

rangana

COLONIALISM AND KANDY

The Portuguese came for spice, the Dutch and British planted Western institutions and gardens of tea, but through it all Kandy preserved Sinhalese culture intact.

From the 16th century onwards, waves of Portuguese, Dutch and British invaders successively came and conquered Sri Lanka, or at least its coastal lowlands; not till 1815 were they able to subdue the remote Kandyan kingdom, hidden in the hills at the centre of the island.

In 1497, the Portuguese navigator Vasco da Gama proved that sailing round Africa offered a better route to the East than Columbus's course, which ran into an unexpected continent that stood in his way. Eight years later, Dom Lourenço de Almeida, a Portuguese naval commander, was hunting for Arab spice vessels off the Indian coast when adverse winds forced his fleet of nine ships to anchor in the very river mouth where the spice-traders collected one of their most valuable commodities: cinnamon.

Their arrival did not go unnoticed. "There are now in our harbour of Colombo," a scout reported to the king of Kotte, "a race of men, exceeding white and beautiful. They wear boots and hats of iron, and they are always in motion. They eat white stones and they drink blood. They have guns which make a noise like thunder, and a ball shot from one of them, after flying some leagues, will break a castle of granite, or even of iron." The mistaken diet of white bread and red wine apart, the newcomers lived up to these terrifying first impressions.

Taking the Portuguese to Kotte

The king of Kotte saw the Portuguese as an answer to belligerent Tamil states as well as the

machinations of domestic rivals. He wished to meet de Almeida. To this day, "taking the Portuguese to Kotte" is a wry joke recalling the merry path they were led to disguise the smallness of the Kotte kingdom, and the fact that the capital was just 13km (8 miles) away from where the Portuguese boats had moored. The slog through the jungle took at least three days. As the ships fired a cannon on the hour and the roar was always audible, the weary envoys knew exactly what was going on. A Portuguese soldier remarked in his journal that in his opinion every single person born on the island was treacherous.

The king offered 110,000kg (250,000lb) of cinnamon a year, an astonishing sum, for Portuguese protection. The Portuguese were slow to realise

---

LEFT: a reproduction of the Greek geographer Ptolemy's 2nd-century map of "Taprobane". **RIGHT:** a new threat on the horizon in the shape of Portuguese warships.

just how good a bargain they were being offered. The island was strategically placed to defend their trade routes, which stretched from Brazil to Macao. By the time they reopened negotiations in 1521, however, local politics had taken a characteristically confused turn.

Wars of succession

King Vijaya VI and his elder brother were both married to the same queen, so there were doubts about the paternity of her three sons. The king was more confident about being the father of a fourth boy by a second queen and designated him as heir. The three slighted sons seized power and carved up the kingdom among themselves. In 1540 the eldest, who took over Kotte, asked Portugal to guarantee the succession of his favourite grandson. The boy was duly groomed for the throne, given a Christian education and baptised as Dom João Dharmapala, whilst his effigy was shipped off to Lisbon and crowned there with great ceremony. The Portuguese even found a way of speeding the boy's accession: his

grandfather was taking the air at an open window of the royal pavilion when a shot rang out and hit him square in the head. A Portuguese soldier said he was aiming at a pigeon.

Dom João Dharmapala's dalliances with the Portuguese and conversion to Christianity had not, however, gone down well with the local Sinhalese, and his reign was immediately challenged by his uncle, Maydunne, and later by his cousin, Rajasinha, who captured large parts of the kingdom of Kotte. Portuguese troops were despatched to remove this bellicose cousin, but when the booty in the palace proved less than expected, they resorted to "robbing houses and violating women with great insolence and high-handedness". Under local rules, a Portuguese historian noted, Sinhalese soldiers smashed up property and killed one another but left women alone. "A great disgrace to Christians that Pagans should be more moderate in this."

Realising that they could not hold Kotte indefinitely, the Portuguese installed Dom João Dharmapala in Colombo. He was a sitting target, and in due course an uncle managed to get at him with some poison. The dose wasn't fatal, but the hapless Dom João lost all his teeth and was a physical wreck for the rest of his long and unhappy life.

A cunning queen

Having been driven out of Kotte, Rajasinha turned his attentions inland, campaigning through the jungle and scooping up petty principalities until he was in control of Kandy, by now the major centre of Sinhalese power in the island's interior. Rajasinha left in his wake a flotsam of royal refugees, among them a couple of young princes who washed up on Portugal's doorstep. Unfortunately, there was only one prospective bride, Dona Caterina, another refugee who had a claim to the Kandy crown which Portugal intended to enforce. This was a virtual death warrant; with polyandrous arrangements now out of the question, one young prince was soon clutching his stomach.

Soon afterwards, the wretched Dom João Dharmapala was persuaded to give up his throne to the Portuguese, and a baptised Christian named Konappu Bandara was engaged to lead the army into Kandy against Rajasinha. The idea was that Bandara would install a suitably dutiful puppet ruler on the throne. Instead, he celebrated the army's victory by seizing the throne for himself as King Vimala Dharma Suriya I. The retreating Rajasinha stood on a bamboo splinter and contracted fatal blood poisoning. The Buddhist chroniclers shed no tears: "Verily this sinner did rule with a strong arm."

Clearly a hard man was needed to sort things out, and none came harder than General Conquistador Pedro Lopez de Souza. It was agreed that he should make a start by getting young Dona Caterina on the Kandyan throne come what may. In the event, Kandy was taken with hardly any opposition, since Vimala Dharma Suriya I had made a strategic withdrawal – something that was to prove a recurrent feature

subdue the north. "The viceroy, whose charger had been shot under him, fought his way to the vanguard on foot amid a cloud of arrows and bullets." The Tamil prince was eventually driven out of the city and the Portuguese went in for the spoils. Among the prisoners was the prince's wife, who afterwards became a Christian. The prince had slipped out of the fortress at night, leaving behind the heads of 12 chiefs who had suggested he might like to make peace with the Portuguese. He was later reinstated, but proved to be an inveterate plotter. His last successor was sent to Goa to be beheaded. After almost a century, Portugal controlled the whole island, apart from Kandy.

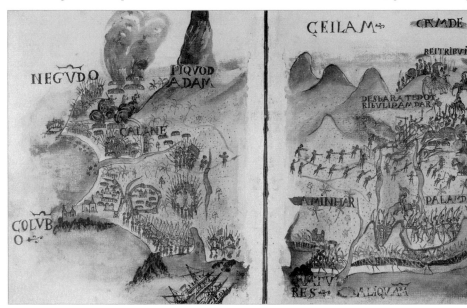

of Kandyan military tactics – and was lying in wait for De Souza on his way back to Colombo. The General Conquistador was in for a multiple humiliation: a military trouncing, the capture of Dona Caterina, and the fact that she then married Vimala Dharma Suriya I, a change of sides that shows she was a consummate political survivor.

The arrival of the Dutch

Meanwhile Jaffna remained a base for pirates who preyed on Portuguese shipping. In 1560, the viceroy accompanied 1,200 troops from Goa to

Unfortunately, in the meantime they had lost control of the seas. In 1612, two English ships beat off four Portuguese galleons and 26 frigates, while the powerful fleet of the Dutch East India Company (the Vereenigde Oost-Indische Compagnie, or VOC) had also meantime been carving out a miniature trading empire in the East Indies, centred on their capital at Batavia (present-day Jakarta). Of the two potential threats, it was the VOC that was of the most immediate concern. Founded in 1602 (in response to the creation, in 1600, of the British East India Company), the VOC had taken control of the formerly disorganised and competing efforts of rival Dutch trading companies in Asia, and had rapidly acquired

ABOVE, FROM LEFT: Dom João Dharmapala, the puppet king; a 16th-century map of a battle between the Portuguese and Sri Lankans.

enormous economic and military power. Under Dutch law, the VOC was permitted to enlist troops, build forts and sign foreign treaties – in short, to act more or less like an independent sovereign power, although its ultimate goal was always to increase profits for the shareholders back in the Netherlands.

The Dutch Admiral Joris van Spilbergen had met Vimala Dharma Suriya I in Kandy and offered help against the Portuguese. His compatriot Sebald de Weert arrived a few months later with a small fleet and went with some of his officers to see the king, inviting him to come back and inspect his ships. The king seemed

reluctant to do so, saying that he did not like to leave his queen alone. The admiral, who had been drinking, unwisely quipped that from what he had heard, it was most unlikely that Queen Dona Caterina would be alone for long. To be fair, the king's precise instructions to his men were *"bandapan me balla"* ("bind this dog"), but one of them took this to mean he should grab the admiral by the hair and split his head open with a sword. On reflection, the king decided this was no bad thing and ordered the other officers to be given the same treatment. The king sent a note, in Portuguese, to the captain of the ships, drawing his attention to the danger of drink.

Vimala Dharma Suriya died of fever in 1604. The king's half-brother Senerat was a leading contender for the throne, and Dona Caterina married him, elevating him to the throne with instructions to open negotiations with the Dutch with a view to getting rid of her former guardians, the Portuguese.

The Dutch take control

The Dutch campaign to unseat the Portuguese extended to seeking an alliance with, of all people, the Danes. An eager expedition took two years to make the voyage from Denmark only to find that it had been overtaken by fast-moving local events and that their assistance was no longer required. Faced with the long voyage home, the dejected crew stopped off on the Indian Coromandel coast for supplies, found they liked the place, and decided they might as well start a Danish colony there.

They were not needed on the island because by 1630 the Dutch forces of the VOC had the sea power necessary to blockade Goa, preventing Portuguese reinforcements from reaching the island while Rajasinha II, who had succeeded Senarat, fought his own battles. His forces inflicted a major defeat on the Portuguese commander Constantine de Sa. But the Sinhalese king was not inclined to gloat when presented with de Sa's head, despite the victory: "How often did I ask thee not to make war on men, nor destroy my lands, but to let me live in peace, the Portuguese remaining absolute lords of the best part of Ceylon."

After 20 grim years of fighting, the Dutch had closed in on the most important Portuguese possession on the island, the fort at Colombo. After a long and bloody siege, the Portuguese finally capitulated. A Portuguese survivor described the end: "At three o'clock on the afternoon of the 12th May, 1656, we came out of the city, 73 very emaciated soldiers, all that remained there, including some with broken arms and minus a leg, and all looking like dead people... We then entered the house where we met the Dutch general and major, who received us very warmly and gave us a toast..." The Dutch officers said they looked forward to meeting the rest of the brave defenders. They were told no more had survived. "At this they changed colour, a great sadness following the cheerfulness with which they had received us."

The Portuguese garrison in Jaffna managed to hold on until 1658, but this was simply a sideshow to Rajasinha's arrival to claim Colombo under his agreement with the Dutch. He found the gates shut against him. In fury, Rajasinha torched everything around the city before withdrawing to Kandy. According to the Sinhalese proverb, "we gave pepper and got ginger".

The Dutch era

It is said that in their ultimate victory over the Portuguese at the siege of Jaffna in 1658, the pragmatic Dutch used Portuguese tombstones as mortar bombs, packed the defeated men off to captivity in Batavia, kept the women, declared a special day of thanksgiving for their victory over "popery and idolatrous practices"

the Company's position is at the same time assured". The subjects taught were Latin, Greek, Hebrew, theology and the control of natural passions. If this seemed a tall order, by 1740 a schools inspector reported his astonishment at the facility with which the locals could "chatter in Latin and construe Greek".

The Dutch brand of austere Calvinism was too much even for those islanders who could comfortably worship the Buddha, a pantheon of Hindu gods and the Virgin Mary at more or less the same time. The Dutch did not really care; their main goal was building exports of cinnamon, elephants, pearls, salt and areca or

and looked forward to making money. After the Portuguese, the historian Philalethos concluded, "the Dutch did not bend before the grim Moloch of religious bigotry, nor did they worship at the shrine of superstition; but cent per cent was their faith, gold was their object, and Mammon was their god".

In fact, Dutch missionaries did try to convert the island to Calvinism, and the secular administration of the VOC helped the cause by reserving jobs in the civil service exclusively for Christians. Education was perceived as "work whereby God's glory was promoted and

ABOVE, FROM LEFT: the emphatic Dutch victory over the Portuguese; Colombo's harbour in the 18th century.

THE SILK TONGUE OF PERSUASION

The author Michael Ondaatje mentions that the Sri Lankans' power of silky persuasion was in the gift of the thalagoya, a cross between an iguana and a giant lizard which is common on the island but almost unknown anywhere else. Its prickly tongue – used to snare prey – was removed, after knocking the creature senseless, and placed between two slices of banana like a sandwich, and swallowed whole.

"I am not sure what other side effects there are," he says, "apart from possible death." There is a myth that if a child is given a thalagoya tongue to eat he will become brilliantly articulate.

Robert Knox

**It was in the reign of Rajasinha II
that life in Kandy came under the
extraordinary microscope of a
19-year-old Londoner.**

I n 1660, a 19-year-old Londoner named Robert
Knox was among a party of English sailors who
went ashore near the mouth of the Mahaweli
River and were taken prisoner by soldiers of King
Rajasinha of Kandy. To Knox's surprise, he and his

shipmates were not the king's only European
"guests": Rajasinha had imprisoned quite a number of Europeans, of which the most bad-tempered,
at least to begin with, was Louis XIV of France's
personal envoy, M. de la Narolle.

Knox kept an account of his "19 years, six
months and odd days" in captivity. He was allowed
enough freedom to move around and talk to people
– even to start a business and buy a house – and,
even though it carries the imprint of European
mores of the time, his *Historical Relation of Ceylon*
is a valuable document. Unlike the Buddhist chronicles, it is concerned with the lives of ordinary people, not just kings, and subsequently inspired parts
of Daniel Defoe's novel *Robinson Crusoe*.

Knox chose not to marry because he wanted to

avoid ties that might dissuade him from escaping
when the opportunity arose. There was no question
of simply bolting. The jungle was dense, the paths
through it were carefully watched and no one was
allowed to use them without a kind of passport.
Nevertheless, Knox seemed struck with the liberal
attitude to sex. Even married women, he noted,
had affairs with anyone they liked, if necessary
leaving their husbands at home to look after the
children. Problems only arose "should they lay with
a man of inferior quality to themselves". When
important visitors called, husbands "commonly will
send their wives or daughters to bear them company in their chamber". Both men and women
would marry four or five times before settling down,
although polyandry, in which two or more brothers
shared a wife or one man married a number of sis-
ters, was fairly unusual, if acceptable.

If the people of Kandy appeared lazy, it was
because the moment they acquired anything above
the bare necessities of life, it was snatched away by
hordes of assessment officers, customs officials,
rent collectors and tax gatherers. Justice was dis-
pensed by a court of local chiefs and officials, and
appeals to the king were risky: he might decide that
the petitioners were wasting his time, in which case
they could expect a trial by ordeal – which meant
plunging their hands into boiling oil. Only the king
could order corporal punishment, although never
for women; and capital punishment by elephant
seemed an effective deterrent, as Knox knew of
only a few examples, observing "they will run their
teeth through the body, and then tear it in pieces
and throw it limb from limb. They have a sharp iron
which they put on their teeth at such times".

Knox escapes

In the end, Knox made a run for the Dutch-controlled
north with another Englishman, abandoning with
some regret his house and estate, an old man who
looked after them and, most of all, a girl named
Lucea, who was the daughter of a fellow captive. By
1698, Knox was back in the East as a ship's captain.
In China, he ran into one of his fellow prisoners, who
had been released after Rajasinha's death. On
learning that other old friends were still in Kandy, he
wrote to let them know that life in England was hard
and that he was still a bachelor. He enclosed a picture of himself with the request that it be passed on
to Lucea: "You know that I loved the Child and since
have no cause to hate her."

LEFT: Robert Knox, from the frontispiece of his journal.

betel nuts. Cinnamon (see page 167) was particularly important, growing in abundant quantities in the wild, although the Dutch eventually
cultivated cinnamon around Colombo, partly
because harvesting in the wild was expensive
and resulted in territorial clashes with Kandy.

After initial difficulties arising from the kingdom's delay in settling in cinnamon its huge
debt to the Dutch for their help against the
Portuguese, the VOC governor Van Goens left a
word of advice for his son, who succeeded him.
"It can easily be seen what a mischievous and
horrible thing war is... All our efforts should
be directed in future to reduce our expenses by

round the country to prevent foreign nations
and enemies from coming in." Such flattery was
lapped up by the king, who seemed oblivious
to the fact that the Dutch were not just the new
invaders but one of those "foreign nations" too.

The relationship could not be sustained, however, and in 1766, the Dutch sacked Kandy and
imposed a 1.6km (1-mile) wide cordon between
the kingdom and the sea. Apart from the physical and perhaps psychological isolation, this
cordon denied Kandy access to precious salt in
coastal lagoons. The idea was that the kingdom
should buy its salt from the company, paying
in cinnamon, but it proved unenforceable. "The

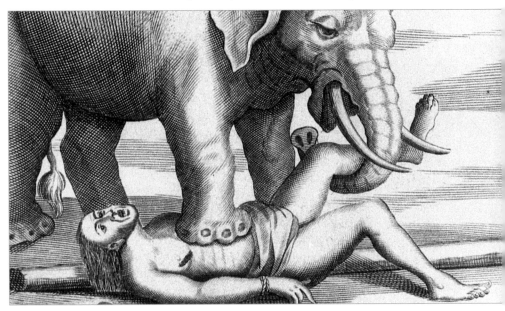

a well-regulated establishment and to increase
our profits by faithful economy."

Dealings with Kandy

As a matter of VOC policy in dealings with
the king of Kandy, the better part of valour was
obsequiousness. The Dutch took full advantage
of the king's proud spirit by flattering him with
an army of ambassadors who told him that they
were his ever loyal humble servants and subjects.
"It is out of loyalty to him," wrote a disgusted
Robert Knox when he witnessed their activities
in court, "that they build forts and keep watches

inhabitants of this Province do not purchase
salt," a Lieutenant Schneider noted, "having
sufficient opportunities to steal it from the salt
pans – as much as they want, perhaps more."

Dutch law

Governors sitting in Colombo applied the
principles of Roman–Dutch law. Certain matters were judged according to codified Tamil
and Muslim law, but the Sinhalese were a pas-
sionately litigious people who had developed a
legal system so complex that it was beyond any
outsider's comprehension. While the Dutch
gave up trying to turn local practices into
statutory law, the Sinhalese for their part took
to the Dutch system like ducks to water. The

ABOVE: execution by elephant helped Kandy keep
discipline.

country remains to this day a bottomless pit of extremely able lawyers and barristers.

By modern standards, Dutch law was ferocious but reasonably impartial, as indeed one of the Dutch governors found out. Petrus Vuyst was as close as the Dutch got to matching the Portuguese crocodile keeper Dom Jeronimo de Azavedo. Disappointed not to have been given a larger country to govern, he landed in 1726 with a hand over one eye, saying he could see quite enough that way. His half-blind administration became one of systematic sadism, and he was sent home after three years, impeached and executed.

The British move in

Meanwhile, the British East India Company had begun showing an interest in the island, mainly thanks to the magnificent natural deep-water harbour at Trincomalee. The Napoleonic Wars provided a pretext for its capture, and when France invaded Holland in 1794, the British asked the Dutch whether a protective British presence in Ceylon would give them one less thing to worry about. There was no colonial war between Britain and the Dutch. The issue was settled by British naval supremacy, although the finale was provided by the secret service with the help of a large Dutch cheese.

Having landed at Trincomalee against only light opposition, 1,200 British troops and two battalions of sepoys from the British Indian Army began the long trudge around the coast to confront the Dutch garrison at Colombo, which, for some years past, had been reinforced by crack Swiss mercenaries under a certain Comte de Meuron. The British troops were shadowed on one flank by a Kandyan army eager to join battle with their new ally against an old enemy. They had a written, albeit unsigned, agreement that for helping Britain Kandy would be awarded one of the Dutch ports, thus ending the kingdom's crippling inland isolation.

It was only in the 20th century that the truth about the decisive battle for Colombo came to light. Some months before Britain made its move, it seems, Comte de Meuron had been holidaying in Europe when he bumped into Hugh Cleghorn, a professor at St Andrew's University in Scotland who also, it transpired, did odd jobs for the British secret service. The count confided, probably over a drink, that some of his creditors were pressing. Cleghorn established that the sum of £4,000 would keep the creditors quiet.

De Meuron's brother Pierre, who had been left in charge of the Swiss mercenaries in Colombo, was surprised to receive an unsolicited gift from India in the form of a large Dutch cheese. Of course, the cheese contained a secret communication. If, some time later, the British troops and Indian sepoys approaching Colombo wondered what had happened to the Swiss mercenaries – why there was no resistance apart from some Malay mercenaries – they had no way of knowing that the Swiss no longer worked for the Dutch. The cheese had advised Pierre and his men that they were contracted to join the British army and their new posting, with immediate effect, was in Canada. With their services unrequired, the shadowing Kandyan forces never did get a signature on the promise of a port. Instead, the kingdom was allowed access to the sea – but only for the purpose of obtaining fish and salt.

Britain's prime minister, William Pitt, described the island as "the most valuable colonial possession on the globe... giving to our Indian empire a security it had not enjoyed from its first establishment". It was entrusted to the Hon. Frederick North, aged 32, a son of George III's prime minister and a classics scholar with a passionate interest in ancient Greece. He became the first British governor.

The conquest of Kandy

Shortly after North's appointment, Sri Wikrama Rajasinha was crowned king of Kandy. North paid his respects by presenting him with an elaborate stagecoach plus a team of horses. The coach had to be delivered in pieces because, apart from a thoroughfare in the capital wide enough to stage elephant fights, there were no proper roads in or to the kingdom. Nothing had changed since the mighty Rajasinha banned bridges and even the widening of paths through the jungle. Its impenetrability was the kingdom's defence against European armies.

When the young king demonstrated in no

Under Kandyan law, people who failed to pay fines had stones piled on top of them until they complied. Either that or they were made to stand with bare legs apart while a thorn bush was rubbed briskly to and fro.

for supper at the Cocoa-Nut Club overlooking the Kelani River.

Reality took on a sterner complexion when the column entered the jungle. Leeches got in everywhere, and at no time was there any protection against mosquitoes, jungle fever or the debilitat-

uncertain manner that he was not to be bought with gifts, North was inclined to depose him by force. To do so required some sort of pretext. It wasn't much, but it was enough, when an army officer at a remote outpost reported that Kandyan officials had snatched some betel nuts from Moorish traders and refused to pay for them or give them back. Bugles echoed round the army base in Colombo and a battalion of the 51st Foot marched out "with the countenances of the soldiers full of cheerfulness and joy". Some 6.4km (4 miles) out of town, a halt was called so that the officers could join friends

ABOVE, FROM LEFT: the East India Company's coat of arms; the Temple of the Tooth.

ing combination of roasting heat and torrential rain. If their rations ran out, beriberi caused limbs to swell agonisingly to elephantine proportions. The jungle was Kandy's defence in depth – draw the enemy in and let nature kill them off.

In contrast, the bulk of the Kandyan army were conscripts from the royal estates. Not more than a third of the available men were mobilised at a time, and then for a maximum of 15 days. They reported for duty with an assortment of ancient muskets or, in some cases, bow and arrows. Other equipment consisted of an umbrella-cum-sunshade made of palm leaves, a cooking pot and enough rice, cakes and coconuts to last the prescribed 15 days. On being relieved by a fresh intake, they returned to their villages.

The army also had Malabar regulars smartly turned out in turbans, red jackets and blue trousers. Malays, who had usually come over from the Dutch, served as the king's bodyguard. They were not only fearless but, as outsiders, had none of the blood-ties that would otherwise make them susceptible to plots against the crown. They trusted the kriss, a knife known affectionately as swammy, or "little god". No king of Kandy was ever killed by his Malay guard.

A hollow victory

The British troops found the capital abandoned and in ashes, the Kandyans having evaporated

into the jungle. The city had been sacked so often by the Portuguese and Dutch that Kandyans no longer built for posterity. Most of the smouldering houses were no more than mud huts. The only building that had not been put to the torch before the tactical withdrawal was the Dalada Maligawa, the Temple of the Tooth. On the other hand, British officers recognised the charred remains of North's presentation stagecoach: someone had at least gone to the trouble of assembling it. North installed Muttusamy, the forlorn but not undignified puppet he had selected to be king, in the blackened palace. While the main force returned to Colombo, a detachment was left behind to look after him. Most of them were soon ill. "God only knows what will

become of us here," one of them wrote, "for if we are ordered to evacuate the place, there is scarce a single European that could walk a mile."

The bedridden soldiers were butchered as the Kandyans regained their capital, but the grimness was relieved by the intervention of the king to save the life of the last surviving patient, a Sergeant Theon. He was invited to live in the kingdom on a royal pension. Theon accepted and over the course of the next 12 years married a local girl and had a son. Muttusamy bravely surrendered himself to save the lives of his guards and was subsequently executed. The guards were also executed, although one corporal somehow survived a blow that did not quite take off his head. He made a miraculous return to Colombo still supporting his head with his hands and survived to tell the tale.

The end of the Kandyan kingdom

In the end, the Kandyan kingdom was subdued, not by military might, but by diplomatic subterfuge. The key players were the last king of Kandy, Sri Wickrama Rajasinha, and the wily British diplomat Sir John D'Oyly. Sri Wickrama had made himself increasingly unpopular with his subjects during his reign, thanks to his insensitivity to local Buddhist traditions (Sri Wickrama himself was a Hindu Tamil born in southern India) and his increasingly megalomaniac tendencies – those who objected to his decision to create a huge lake in the centre of Kandy, for instance, found themselves impaled on stakes at its bottom.

Sensing a weakness in the kingdom's political fabric, D'Oyly plotted over a number of years with members of the Sinhalese nobility to launch a rebellion to overthrow Sri Wickrama. One such noble, Ehelepola, declared war on the king in 1814, with tacit British support. Sri Wickrama crushed the revolt with sickening thoroughness, executing all those suspected of conspiring against him, including Ehelepola's wife and children, a slaughter which revolted the Kandyans so deeply that they invited the British to take possession of the kingdom and relieve them of their unwanted monarch, who was exiled to India to live out his days at British expense. After centuries of dogged resistance, the Kandyan kingdom thus ended not with a bang, but a whimper.

It took only a couple of years, however, for the Kandyans to grow weary of their new masters. In 1817, the Kandyan Rebellion swept rapidly across the highlands and for a time threatened to drive the British back to the coast, but for the timely arrival of several regiments of Indian troops. It was the near-success of the rebellion that encouraged the British to build a railway and good roads to Kandy and beyond, allowing the swift movement of troops throughout the highlands and finally bringing the formerly remote and inaccessible kingdom within a four-hour train ride of Colombo.

The British era

Following the Kandyan Rebellion, Britain's control of the island was never seriously tested. Once the British had pushed roads through the jungle, it could no longer hide a clandestine independent state. A more accurate gauge of the new situation was that in 1821 Kandy staged its first horserace meeting. The last of the royal pretenders made his bid in 1848, which coincided with unrest triggered by a rumour that local women were to be taxed on the size of their breasts, not an unreasonable assumption given the attitude of colonial officers towards the female population. On the whole, however, Ceylon was a peaceful place until the communal rioting that led to civil war after independence.

Plantations

Profound changes came on the economic front. With new roads crisscrossing the highlands, which were ideal for growing coffee, word flew round England that fortunes were to be made. "The first ardent adventurers," wrote Sir Emerson Tennent of the inevitable rush, "pioneered the way through pathless woods, and lived for months in log huts." The new life in the jungle was full of excitement and romance. So dazzling was the prospect that expenditure was unlimited, its profusion only equalled by the ignorance and inexperience of those to whom it was entrusted.

Planters thought the reluctance of local peasants to provide labour was innate indolence; they failed to appreciate that virtually all had plots of their own that kept them fully occupied. Sinhalese kings of old had imported labourers from India to peel cinnamon, and Britain followed their example. With south India then teetering on the brink of famine, the prospects in Ceylon sounded like Eldorado. Indians swarmed across the narrow straits in catamarans and on

rafts in order to set out on the long walk to the plantations. A quarter of them never made it, dying at the roadside to await burial by the police. Moreover, the harvest was seasonal, so they went home afterwards with whatever they had managed to save and ran the gauntlet all over again the following year.

The flourishing coffee industry, however, was not to last. During the 1870s, the *hemileia vastatrix* leaf disease wiped out all the island's major plantations. The place of coffee was taken by tea, and it was soon discovered that the island's uplands offered the perfect terrain for growing this increasingly popular beverage. "The new

generation of tea planters," a contemporary wrote, "have only to step into the poor collapsed coffee planter's shoes and comfortable and accessible quarters."

The transition for the Indian labourers was more problematic. Unlike coffee, tea was picked all year round and therefore required a permanent labour force. In the space of 15 years, nearly a million men, women and children arrived. They lived in plantation compounds, as many as 10 people cooking, eating and sleeping in a compartment just a few metres across. They were landless aliens, which put an unbridgeable gulf between them and Tamils who had been established, mainly in the north, from the 3rd century BC. The British government was alarmed: "Every

ABOVE, FROM LEFT: effigy of the last Kandyan king at Dambulla; the railroad ended Kandy's isolation.

attempt must be made to secure protection for the immigrant, not only as a matter of humanity, but also as one of public interest."

The plantation economy became a ladder of opportunity not only for the Sinhalese but also for long-established Tamils and descendants of Dutch colonists, or "Burghers", who were already part of the cosmopolitan milieu. The familiar route was to use working capital made from selling drink to buy into tea or rubber plantations or the mining of graphite. The de Soysa family, genuine tycoons, prided themselves on managing their estates with no Europeans on the payroll.

Political advancement

The prickly imperial question of how much political representation should be given to the indigenous population resulted in a divergence between the authorities in London, who were inclined to be liberal, and officials on the spot, who spluttered about their subjects being "utterly deficient of the requisite elements". Effective political representation was a long time coming. The Ceylon National Congress was formed after World War I as an amalgam of all the main communities, although there was an omen of the divisions ahead when the Tamils broke away to form a separate organisation. Meanwhile, Ceylon

In general administration and education, the British colonial authorities built on the Dutch foundation. Formal recognition was given to "the religion of Boodhoo", and the Tooth Relic, which had fallen by accident into British hands, was given back. Sinhalese, Tamils and Europeans went to separate schools in Colombo, although the theory was that they would emerge with the ability to compete on equal terms and, no less importantly, with ingrained respect for "order and the present government". Right from the start, North had urged that the brightest pupils go on to universities in England and two sons of the Mudaliyar de Saram thus left for Cambridge University in 1811, leading the way for many distinguished successors.

became the first colonial dependency in Asia to be given universal suffrage without literacy, property, income or gender qualifications.

World War II

To the ordinary people of Ceylon, World War II began as a dispute on the other side of the world about things that did not concern them. This changed in early 1942, when Singapore, Rangoon and the Dutch East Indies fell to Japan and the assumption that India was the next target put Ceylon in the front line. If Calcutta were put out of commission, Britain had no other ports closer than East Africa or Australia. Ceylon's air defences against the Japanese carrier fleet that had attacked Pearl

Harbor amounted to a few Catalina flying boats and some antiquated Wildebeest bombers known to their crews, with some understatement, as "flying coffins". As more airworthy reinforcements were rushed out, followers of the turf saw their beloved Colombo racecourse turned into an aerodrome. The hot-weather exodus from Colombo to the hill stations seemed to start a little earlier that year.

On Sunday, 5 April, aircraft from Japanese carriers bombed Colombo, although not before their approach was spotted by Squadron Leader L.J. Birchall of the Canadian Royal Air Force in one of the Catalinas. He managed to get off a signal before being shot down and taken prisoner. Two merchant ships in the harbour were hit and a bomb landed on a mental hospital a little way out of town. Sirens wailed in Trincomalee four days later, and a number of British warships in nearby waters were sunk, including the carrier *Hermes*.

An invasion was not on Japan's immediate agenda, however; the main objective was to destroy Britain's Eastern fleet. Thanks to the one-sided advantage of radar, however, the fleet was able to keep out of the way in the Maldives.

By the end of the year Ceylon became the springboard for offensive operations eastward. Lord Louis Mountbatten set up his South East Asia Command headquarters in Kandy, Trincomalee was the base for the "advanced operations school" of the British Special Operations Executive, who infiltrated saboteurs and resistance organisers behind Japanese lines. As one of many new airstrips all over the island happened to be at the foot of the Sigiriya rock fortress, the saucy murals were swathed in bamboo and cotton wool, although against the vibrations of heavy engines rather than longing eyes.

Preparing for Independence

As the war drew to a close, the Tamils proposed a "50–50 Scheme" that would give half the seats in a future legislature to the Sinhalese (roughly 70 percent of the population) and reserve the other half for all minorities combined but excluding the Indian immigrant labourers, who would lose the vote they had under existing British rules. It was stated in London in July 1945 that "His Majesty's Government are in sympathy with the desire of the people of Ceylon to advance towards dominion status..."

London made no secret of its preference for the United National Party (UNP), a moderate organisation which, under the stewardship of D.S. Senanayake, cut across the island's ethnic and religious lines. Meanwhile the opposition represented specific sectional groups and an eclectic range of Bolshevik–Leninist, Trotskyist and Stalinist communists. Senanayake's party won an overwhelming victory and, in British eyes, all bode well for a seamless transition to independence.

ABOVE, FROM LEFT: a British colonial official meets the local chiefs; Tamil workers harvesting tea at the mountain station of Nuwara Eliya.

BROTHERS IN ARMS

Allied troops swarming all over the island had nothing but praise for local hospitality. "They were much made of," says E.F.C. Ludowyk in his *Story of Ceylon*, "not because they were regarded as defenders of the island, but as interesting people with whom there was much in common… For the first time Ceylonese came in contact with the European as an ordinary human being, a person like themselves in fact, stripped to the waist in tropical heat and working on the same laborious tasks they knew only too well – road-making, clearing the jungle and moving heavy loads from place to place."

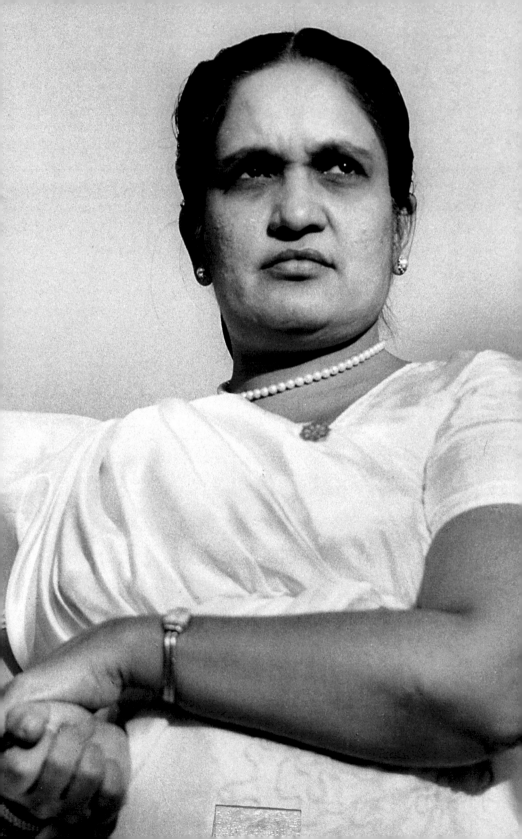

INDEPENDENCE

During six decades of Independence, Sri Lanka
has strived to build a future but found itself
beset by demons from the past.

When Ceylon embarked on Independence on 4 February 1948, it was in good shape. Wartime demand for rubber and the British military presence on the island had created jobs and opportunities for keen-eyed entrepreneurs. The military had also launched a blitz on mosquitoes, taking Ceylon to the threshold of becoming the first country in Asia to eradicate malaria.

Unfortunately, the boom was deceptive. The economy was unable to weather volatile international demand for its narrow range of natural products. Uneven wealth distribution among the rising population (which had slumped during most of the period of colonial rule) added pressure. The premier's persuasive charm, too, showed signs of fading as patience began to run out at the slow rate of change. The seeds of the conflict that was eventually to engulf the island were also being sown.

The Tamil question

Independent Sri Lanka's first prime minister, D.S. Senanayake, entered negotiations with his Indian counterpart, Pandit Jawaharlal Nehru, over an issue that would tarnish relations between the neighbours for years to come. Now pushing an overtly pro-Sinhalese agenda, he insisted that the Tamil plantation workers, even if some had been living on the island for two or more generations and had been recognised as residents by Britain, were foreign – specifically Indian – nationals. It would not have escaped his notice that they used the franchise

LEFT: Sirimavo Bandaranaike, the world's first female prime minister. RIGHT: the first prime minister of independent Ceylon, D.S. Senanayake.

given to some of them by Britain to vote for their own sectarian candidates, not his own United National Party (UNP).

Soon afterwards, S.W.R.D. Bandaranaike defected to form the Sri Lanka Freedom Party (SLFP). Ostensibly it represented a more radical, but still multiracial, departure from the UNP's neo-colonial outlook. Bandaranaike was a member of the Kandyan nobility torn between a Westernised upbringing – he had taken the well-trodden road to Oxford University – and Kandyan pride in their tradition of championing the cause of Sinhalese Buddhism. He had given an early hint of his political direction when, on returning from Oxford before the war, he shed both Western

When UNP prime minister Dudley Senanayake resigned in 1953 he was succeeded by his uncle, John Kotelawala, earning the UNP the popular nickname of "Uncle Nephew Party".

clothing and Christianity and pronounced himself "Sinhalese to the core". Before long, that just about summed up the SLFP. The audience it addressed was the rising generation who had been educated in Sinhalese, wondered why the official language was still English, and were disappointed, economically, by Independence.

There was a brief interregnum before Bandaranaike stormed into office on a platform of making Sinhalese the official language. The formal introduction of his cabinet was an echo of his gesture on returning from Oxford: they wore a length of white cloth draped from the waist and loose, long-sleeved white shirts. It was, of course, a political statement, akin to Chairman Mao's buttoned tunic, but it bemused the population at large who had never seen anything like it except on Indian politicians. Subsequent presidents stuck to the innovation, bravely ignoring sniggers.

The language campaign catapulted Band-

The Sinhalese find their tongue

D.S. Senanayake died in 1952, after falling from his horse whilst riding on Galle Face Green in Colombo. His son, Dudley Senanayake, succeeded and the pattern was set for an extraordinary demonstration of dynastic tennis: Senanayake and the UNP in one court; opposite them, a succession of Bandaranaikes in various permutations of the SLFP.

With soaring inflation and unemployment, Dudley Senanayake took the advice of economic experts and cut the subsidy on imported rice. The result was island-wide rioting that was ended only by the declaration of a full-scale state of emergency. Senanayake resigned with his tail between his legs.

aranaike into office with a huge majority, but when the appropriate bill was read in parliament, delighted Sinhalese and resentful Tamils – who communicated with one another in English – came to blows in the streets. Neither the prospect of a new official language, nor nationalisation of key industries such as transport and ports made any difference to a deepening economic crisis. Tamils demonstrated their lack of confidence by deserting en masse to their ancestral lands in the north and raising the cry for an independent Tamil state as of old. The implications were not lost on Bandaranaike, but his opening of talks with the Tamil leadership served only to whip up extremists in both camps. These included a

Buddhist monk who was so incensed by the fact that Bandaranaike was negotiating with the Tamils that he emptied a revolver into the prime minister at point-blank range, thus bringing Bandaranaike's dramatic political career to a sudden end.

The JVP rebellion

After a brief interlude, Mrs Sirimavo Bandaranaike, the assassinated premier's widow, was ushered into office on a wave of sympathy, becoming the world's first female prime minister. She began by picking on the one group that could hardly fight back: 500,000 "Indian" plantation workers were deported to India, the quid pro quo being that another 300,000 would be allowed to stay. Although winning considerable stature abroad, and not merely as a female prime minister, Mrs Bandaranaike's stumbling record at home led to an attempted coup by army officers and, soon afterwards, a heavy defeat at the polls. Dudley Senanayake returned to power and lasted five years as her successor but fared little better, abandoning an attempt to run the country according to the Buddhist lunar year. Mrs Bandaranaike was returned to power again, but if she had any new ideas, they did not work. Something had to give.

Faced with increasingly dim career and economic prospects, the country's disillusioned young people vented their collective frustrations through the Janata Vimuktu Peramuna (JVP), an extreme left-wing party. In 1971 the JVP launched an armed insurrection against Mrs Bandaranaike's government, with a frenzy of bomb attacks against government installations and an attempt to kidnap the prime minister herself. After the initial shock had passed, the Sri Lankan Army made short work of the poorly organised rebels, most of whom were young students, massacring thousands of activists.

Towards civil war

Mrs Bandaranaike redoubled her nationalisation programme, expropriating all private agriculture and the tea estates, the only two areas of the economy that were still functioning. At the same time, she pushed through constitutional amendments, turning Ceylon into the Republic

of Sri Lanka and giving herself, with dubious legality, two extra years in office. The response, orchestrated by disaffected members of the ruling coalition, was the worst wave of strikes in 20 years. Mrs Bandaranaike went to the polls – the one tradition from which no island politician has ever deviated – and received the thumbs-down from 86.7 percent of the electorate.

The new prime minister, J.R. Jayawardene, broke new ground in two respects. He was someone other than a Senanayake running the UNP and his economic theories were the antithesis of Mrs Bandaranaike's loose-cannon socialism. His model was Singapore; the flag-

ship of his economic initiative was a free-trade zone north of Colombo. Tamil and English were elevated to the status of national – less than official – languages. Jayawardene was also responsible for changing the constitution to introduce an executive presidency along French lines – something which has proved disastrous both in terms of the amount of power it concentrates in one person's hands, and for the political chaos which almost inevitably ensues if president and prime minister come from opposing parties.

The rise of the Tamil Tigers

Despite economic success and limited concessions, however, Jayawardene singularly failed

ABOVE, FROM LEFT: opening of Sri Lanka's first parliament in 1948; Indian PM Indira Gandhi meets Dudley Senanayake.

to tackle increasing Tamil disillusionment, which grew throughout the 1970s in the face of state-sponsored discrimination and the heavy-handed behaviour of Sinhalese policemen and soldiers stationed in Tamil areas. The late 1970s saw the emergence of a new generation of radical Tamils who decided that the only solution to Sinhalese discrimination was to be found in taking up arms. One of these groups was the Liberation Tigers of Tamil Eelam (LTTE), popularly known as the Tamil Tigers, led by a fanatical young man named Velupillai Prabhakaran. Throughout the late 1970s and early 1980s, the LTTE began systematically to attack Sri Lankan

turn fled from the north. The battle lines had thus been drawn between the Sri Lankan Army and the Tamil Tigers for a conflict that was to rage for more than two decades and claim perhaps as many as 100,000 lives.

The early years of civil war

Following the riots of 1983, clashes between the LTTE and the Sri Lankan Army became an established feature of Sri Lankan life, while punitive operations by the armed forces accelerated the exodus of Tamil refugees to India, the total climbing towards 100,000. Ostensibly to stem the flow, the Indian air force began drop-

government targets, as well as murdering all their Tamil political rivals.

In 1983, the LTTE ambushed an army patrol, killing 12 soldiers. The incident provoked a Sinhalese backlash against Tamil civilians which resulted in scenes of communal savagery across the country, subsequently christened "Black July". In Colombo, mobs roamed the capital, armed with electoral registers to pinpoint Tamil households. Perhaps as many as 2,000 Tamils were murdered by these mobs, with Sinhalese police doing very little to halt the killings.

The point of no return in Sinhalese–Tamil relations had been reached. Many Tamils left their homes in southern Sri Lanka and fled north, or abroad, while Sinhalese families in

ping food parcels over northern towns. Supplies by sea led to clashes between the Indian and Sri Lankan navies.

In July 1987, Indian premier Rajiv Gandhi and the Sri Lankan president Jayawardene announced that 45,000 Indian troops – the so-called Indian Peace-Keeping Force (IPKF) – would be sent to Sri Lanka to enforce a ceasefire between the SLA and LTTE. The Tigers, yet again, proved themselves to be tenacious fighters. Never more than 10,000 strong, they tied down the IPKF and forced Sri Lanka to increase its national forces to around 100,000. Although the jungle was their natural terrain, they did not shrink from mounting head-on attacks on military bases or sending Sea Tigers against naval warships.

Then, in parallel with the increasingly anarchic situation in the north, in 1987–8 the JVP launched a second rebellion in the south, assassinating political opponents and launching strikes which brought the already enfeebled country to its knees. As it had in 1971, the government responded with massacres of all known or suspected JVP members or sympathisers, killing perhaps as many as 17,000 people.

Suicide bombings

The IPKF withdrew in 1990 after losing more than 1,000 of its peacekeepers and the LTTE promptly reoccupied Jaffna, from which the IPKF had driven them at a huge cost in human life. Meanwhile, President Jayawardene had stepped down in December 1988 to make way for Ranasinghe Premadasa. Born in a shack in a run-down area of Colombo, Premadasa vowed to rejuvenate the economy and end the war. The Tigers, however, now unleashed a new weapon, the suicide bomber, using them to bring terror to the heart of Colombo and other parts of the south which had been protected by distance from the effects of the war. In 1991, former Indian prime minister Rajiv Gandhi, the man who had ordered the deployment of the IPKF, paid the ultimate price for his intervention when he was assassinated in Tamil Nadu by an LTTE suicide bomber; and in Sri Lanka President Premadasa became another high-profile victim of a suicide bomber when he was blown up in Colombo in 1993.

A change of government in 1994 brought a new face, but an old name, into the political arena. The incoming leader was Chandrika Bandaranaike Kumaratunga, daughter of S.W.R.D. Bandaranaike and his widow Sirimavo and, at 49, herself a widow, whose husband had been assassinated by the JVP in 1988. The party had now exchanged rabid Sinhalese nationalism for market economics and national reconciliation, especially with the Tamils.

The government put forward a plan that would make the Tamil communities in Jaffna and the east virtually self-governing but not quite fully independent. A huge military offensive, "Operation Leap Forward", was aimed at silencing the Tigers while aid was sent to rebuild the region's infrastructure. Tamil and Muslim parliamentary parties liked the idea of a federation of states, but the reactionary Buddhist clergy and Sinhala extremists condemned it as a sell-out. The Tigers' reaction was to send suicide bombers into the heart of Colombo. President Chandrika Kumaratunga survived an assassination attack from a Tamil suicide bomber in 1999 and went on to win a new term in office a few days later.

Uneasy ceasefire

The new millennium dawned with no apparent end in sight to the island's ethnic conflict.

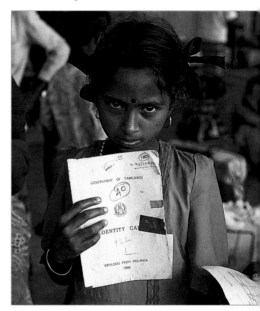

THE IPKF

The deployment of the Indian Peace-Keeping Force (IPKF) was hugely controversial with both Sinhalese and Tamils in Sri Lanka. Many nationalistic Sinhalese saw them as nothing more than an invading force, while the LTTE regarded them as a threat to their growing military power in the north. In the event, the IPKF notably failed in their mission to keep the peace: quickly becoming embroiled in clashes with the LTTE, they soon mounted a massive military operation to drive the Tigers out of Jaffna, which they did, but only after a three-week bloodbath – attacking the very people they were meant to be protecting.

ABOVE, FROM LEFT: Prime Minister Sirimavo Bandaranaike and President J.R. Jayawardene meet in 1980; a Tamil refugee.

In 2000 the LTTE recaptured the strategic Elephant Pass from the SLA, perhaps their most notable military triumph of the entire war; in 2001 LTTE suicide bombers launched a daring raid against the international airport, destroying half the island's fleet of airliners – a savage blow against the island's economy and tourist industry.

The breakthrough arrived following the election of a new UNP government led by Ranil Wickramasinghe. In December 2001, the Tigers announced a ceasefire, one which was made permanent following talks between the government and the LTTE – helped by Norwegian

The tsunami and after

The subsequent 2004 general election saw Mrs Kumaratunga's SLFP-led coalition, the People's Alliance, beat the UNP, with the populist southern politician Mahinda Rajapakse becoming prime minister. Political events, however, were suddenly overtaken by the catastrophic tsunami of 26 December (see page 58), which claimed in a matter of minutes more lives than the entire civil war had in 20 years.

Tourist areas of the coast were reconstructed with impressive speed and thoroughness, although poorer islanders were, in many cases, left more or less to fend for themselves despite

negotiators – in February 2002. A wave of euphoria swept across the island, the economy boomed, and parts of the north and east, which had been closed for decades, finally reopened to casual visitors.

The euphoria lasted not much more than a year. Although the ceasefire survived, increasing disillusionment with the peace process and Sinhalese suspicion of LTTE motives increased. In April 2003, the LTTE pulled out of talks, and by late 2003, the political tensions between President Kumaratunga and her Prime Minister, Ranil Wickramasinghe of the rival UNP, boiled over, prompting the president to declare a state of emergency and suspend parliament.

the vast amounts of foreign aid received by the government. The government's incompetent response to the crisis was expected to prove crucial during the presidential elections of November 2005. In the event their candidate, Mahinda Rajapakse, scraped home as the victor, having beaten former Prime Minister Ranil Wickramasinghe by the narrowest of margins.

The war resumes

The first half of 2006 was marked by a huge upsurge of violence which left the ceasefire in tatters. Then in July 2006, full-scale fighting between the LTTE and the Sri Lankan Army resumed after more than four years of ceasefire. As the SLA (now better funded and equipped than at any time in its history) gradually drove the Tigers out of the east, Rajapakse's determination to deal with the LTTE once and for all became apparent. By June 2007, the whole of the region was under government control for the first time in two decades.

Having dealt with the LTTE in the east, come 2008 the SLA began a major offensive in the north. A year of fierce fighting ensued, and in January 2009 the SLA finally captured the LTTE's de facto capital at Kilinochchi, followed rapidly by the important coastal town of Mullaitivu and the strategic Elephant Pass. The end finally came in May 2009, when the final patch of LTTE-held territory was overrun by the SLA, and the rebels' reclusive leader, Prabakharan, killed, finally bringing to an end over 25 years of fighting during which an estimated 80,000–100,000 people died.

Peace and beyond

Despite the outbreak of euphoria and triumphalism that enveloped much of the country following the end of the war, however, serious questions remained to be answered. Allegations of massive human-rights abuses were levelled against both the SLA and LTTE by a range of international governments and NGOs including the US, UK, EU and Amnesty International, mainly centred on the thousands of civilian casualties during the closing stages of the war, many of which were blamed on indiscriminate shelling by the SLA. The government rebuffed all such claims, setting up a committee – the Lessons Learnt and Reconciliation Committee – to investigate these claims, although this was largely seen as a cover-up.

Shortly afterwards, Mahinda Rajapakse was re-elected president for a second term, defeating his former ally, army chief General Sarath Fonseka. (Fonseka was subsequently arrested for "military offences" and is currently serving a three-year jail term.) Having seen off Fonseka, Rajapakse has further consolidated his grip on power. His brothers Basil and Gotabhaya continue to occupy senior ministerial posts with control over most military and state affairs, while numerous other members of the extended Rajapakse family now hold a range of important political and business positions. All media criticism is routinely

suppressed (sometimes with violence), while the increasingly enfeebled opposition offers little effective resistance. In addition, a new amendment to the constitution introduced in 2010 will in future allow Sri Lankan presidents to stand for office in perpetuity (previous heads of state having been limited, as in the US, to a maximum of two terms in office), raising the possibility that Mahinda Rajapakse may yet cling onto the reins of power indefinitely. For all its proud democratic traditions, Sri Lanka increasingly feels like a quasi-dictatorship, although this is a price that many of its citizens appear prepared to pay in return for peace and stability.

In the meantime, a booming tourist industry and attention-grabbing infrastructure projects including a new international airport and huge new deep-water port at Rajapakse's home town of Hambantota give the impression of a country looking confidently to the future, although the island's economy continues to suffer from deep-seated weaknesses, including huge levels of debt accumulated during the civil war. In addition, no answers are yet forthcoming as to how Rajapakse's government plans to meet the aspirations of its impoverished and exhausted Tamil citizens, while the long-term political consequences of the ever-expanding network of Rajapakse family nepotism have yet to be seen. The future, in short, is far from clear.

ABOVE, FROM LEFT: a checkpoint operated by female soldiers; PM Ranil Wickramasinghe receives gifts of thanks from loyal party members.

Tsunami

The tsunami that struck on Boxing Day in 2004 caused devastation on an immense scale, including the loss of 30,000 Sri Lankan lives.

The horror unfolds

At first, they thought that the sea was retreating. On the eastern coast, villagers peered perplexed at the vast expanse of sand before them, where the ocean should have been. Many fishermen had

It would be almost an hour after the initial deluge that the more densely populated south and west coasts were submerged. Some beach resorts, such as Bentota, were protected by mangroves and trees and suffered little. Yet as far north as Moratuwa, just south of Colombo, communities were shattered.

A town ravaged

But it was perhaps the historic town of Galle that gave the world its most graphic images of the horrors caused as a result of an earthquake that shook the ocean floor off the coast of faraway Indonesia. Plenty of places were hit harder than Galle, but it was the very fact that Galle was recognisable that made

stayed at home with their wives, tidying up after the previous day's Christmas festivities and oblivious to what the waters that had provided their livelihood were about to do. Excited children scrambled to watch the bizarre behaviour of the ocean they had grown up alongside. And then, at 8.30am on 26 December 2004, it turned on them.

The onslaught began as a low surge that pushed beyond beaches and drenched houses. What followed was a cataclysm of biblical proportions. Second and third waves of up to 15 metres (50ft) came charging ashore, instantly wiping out over 10,000 lives in the Batticaloa and Ampara Districts. Along the coast, towns and villages were violently erased. For the next 50 minutes terror reigned from the Jaffna peninsula all the way down to Hambantota.

it so shocking. It was recognisable to the cricket fans who had flocked to its distinctive international stadium. It was recognisable to the many tourists who had wandered along the ramparts of its historic fort.

Galle also had a bus station, internet cafés, hotels and a hospital. And their ravaged remains were left exposed for all to view. Those who saw Galle, even if it was only on television, saw their own home town for a fraction of a second.

Buses were strewn across the cricket pitch like die-cast toys. Bodies lay everywhere. A train that had been on its way to the town never reached its destination. And neither did more than 1,000 of its passengers – victims of the world's worst single rail disaster on a day when the very term "disaster" seemed inadequate. At its end, at least 250,000 lives had been lost across South Asia. Of those, more than 30,000 were Sri Lankans. Another 100,000 on the island were without homes. For them, the nightmare was just beginning.

The relief effort

As Galle had provided a backdrop against which to gauge the raw brutality of the ocean, it also became the focal point for the relief effort. Galle was the largest town on the island to be badly hit, and the pressure was on to get emergency medical equipment, food and water there as soon as possible.

Huge quantities of Western money poured into the country, but almost from the start relief efforts were

metres/yds of the sea were prevented from rebuilding houses on their former sites. Officially intended to protect villagers from the effects of possible future tsunamis, the move was widely seen as a cynical land-grab by a government keen to acquire coastal plots for lucrative tourist developments.

As a result, 18 months after the disaster many of those made homeless were still living in tents and surviving on handouts – even while smart new tourist developments were springing up around them. And while tourists may have been invited back to the island to help speed up its economic recovery, the tourism industry has been blamed for the lopsided and inequitable form reconstruction

fraught with controversy. The government appeared to be doing its utmost to impede rather than expedite matters, sitting on large sums of foreign aid and keeping essential goods stuck in Colombo port while bureaucrats fiddled with forms. Political controversy erupted, too, over plans to distribute some aid in the north to the LTTE. In short, the tsunami looked set to reopen wounds rather than unite split communities.

Just when it looked like things could not get any worse for those made homeless by the disaster, the government enacted its notorious "100-metre rule", whereby those who had previously lived within 100

ABOVE, FROM LEFT: satellite photo of the tsunami just after it struck the coast at Kalutara, south of Colombo, 26 December 2004; the devastation wreaked in Galle.

has taken, with five-star hotels and luxury villas prioritised above the needs of the unfortunates.

Now, over seven years on, much of coastal Sri Lanka looks better than it ever did. Scarcely any physical evidence of the disaster remains, at least along the heavily touristed west and south coasts, and many of the homeless have been rehoused, often in custom-built concrete-box villages located at "safe" distances from the coast. However, the invisible traces of the tragedy linger on. Unseen psychological scars are likely to take a generation or longer to heal; while the redistribution of land and relocation of villages have left a lasting and unwelcome social and economic legacy, separating fishing communities from the sea and their livelihood and forcing many survivors into new and unexpected poverty.

PEOPLE

Sinhalese, Tamil, Muslim, European and Veddha
– Sri Lanka's rich ethnic diversity has produced
a kaleidoscopic variety of cultures.

Sri Lanka is entangled in a mass of florid vegetation teeming with strange animals, but its human population is no less exotic. The fertile Sri Lankan soil has had to support not one population but many, and whilst this racial diversity has been the cause of much strife, it compensates with a diversity of culture and skills, as well as a grudging degree of mutual respect between the different races despite the long-raging civil war.

Interracial rivalry is fought out with games of "we got here first". The Sinhalese have an exact (albeit legendary) date for their arrival by boat from northern India, while the Tamils claim that their Dravidian ancestors got to the island even earlier, simply walking across when there was a land link to their former homeland in Southern India. Both groups continue to argue about precedence, though both are easily beaten by the fast-vanishing Veddhas, who arrived thousands of years before either

> The term Veddha comes from the Sanskrit word meaning "hunter with bow and arrow", although Veddhas prefer to call themselves the "people of the forest" or Wanniyala-Aetto.

Sinhalese or Tamils but are now, sadly, on the point of disappearing from Sri Lanka's ethnic map altogether. The Muslims in turn can trace their presence in the island back for over a

PRECEDING PAGES: tea-picking in the Hill Country plantations. **LEFT:** after-school fun, Polonnaruwa. **RIGHT:** the late chief Tissahami, a champion of Veddha rights.

millennium, though the Burghers, descended from Portuguese, Dutch and other European colonists, are relative newcomers.

THE VEDDHAS

Sri Lanka's first inhabitants were the Veddhas, who walked over from India (when sea levels were low) at least 16,000 years ago (and perhaps much earlier) when Sri Lanka was still connected to the rest of Asia. These Stone Age hunter-gatherers have more racial affinities with African Bushmen and Australian Aborigines than with any of the island's other Aryan and Dravidian settlers, though like the Aborigines of Australia, they have struggled to achieve proper recognition in recent years.

Spirit peoples

The Buddhist chronicles of the *Mahavamsa* describe the Veddhas as *yaksas* and *nagas* – spirits or ghosts. This is a tribute to how little impact they made on their environment, flitting through the thick jungle and leaving no sign of their presence. The Veddhas themselves trace their ancestry back to Prince Vijaya who is also traditionally regarded as the progenitor of the Sinhalese. The tale goes that he married a woman of the Yaksa tribe who produced a son and a daughter. These two went forth and multiplied, allegedly producing the Veddha race. Whether or not this story has any foun-

whole community to move to a new dwelling. However, perhaps as consolation for bereavement and for having to move house, a widow was permitted to marry her husband's brother.

Modern-age hunters

Centuries of settlement by Sinhalese and Tamils have gradually stripped the Veddhas of their traditional lands, forcing them to live in ever-shrinking pockets of forest. By the end of the 19th century there were no more than 5,000 Veddhas scattered around the eastern and north central provinces, while the 20th century saw the land available to them progressively

dation in fact, the Veddhas and Sinhalese have certainly lived in close proximity over many centuries – as far back as the 17th century the English writer Robert Knox was describing the Veddhas as speaking Sinhalese. Throughout that time, however, Sinhalese culture has always been dominant, and intermarriages between the two groups have led to a decline in Veddha numbers and identity.

Socially, women are equal to men and descent passes matrilineally. In the wedding ceremony the bride ties a bark rope (which she has twisted herself) around the waist of her husband to be. Traditionally, when a death occurred in a cave dwelling, it was the practice to cover the body with dried leaves and for the

squeezed as large-scale irrigation works and agriculture took away yet more of their traditional hunting grounds. A belated fight for official recognition began in the 1980s following the creation of the Maduru Oya National Park, which deprived the Veddhas of yet more of their ancestral lands. The government eventually responded by creating Veddha "sanctuaries" around the edge of the park, though this belated concession was generally regarded as being far too little, far too late.

Faced with these pressures, most Veddhas have now given up their traditional hunter-gatherer lifestyle, while many have intermarried with Sinhalese and adopted the Buddhist faith, abandoning their traditional animist beliefs. Their last remaining villages are now to be found mainly in the east of the country, in the area around Mahiyangana, east of Kandy. At present, only about 2,000 Veddhas survive, of whom perhaps as few as two hundred still maintain their traditional lifestyle; the island's oldest human culture stands on the brink of extinction, with all too many Veddhas reduced to putting on a show for curious tourists.

THE SINHALESE

Claiming descent from a lion and a headstrong princess, the Sinhalese migrated to Sri Lanka from north India around the 4th century BC, and have never looked back. Although their North Indian heritage survives in aspects of their language and culture, the Sinhalese have developed a unique cultural identity during their long centuries on the island. The adoption of Buddhism – central to Sinhalese identity – set them apart from the other peoples of the subcontinent early on in their history, while their long centuries of cohabitation alongside and intermarriage with the island's Tamils has also been of profound importance – although this is not something you will hear much discussed in the current political climate. Likewise, their prolonged contact with Muslim traders and Portuguese, Dutch and British invaders has also influenced Sinhalese society and attitudes at many, often unexpressed, levels.

Vijaya, lion prince

The legendary origins of the Sinhalese are contained in the colourful legend of Prince Vijaya and his family, as described in the island's great Buddhist chronicle, the *Mahavamsa*. The story begins in North India, with Vijaya's grandmother, a restless princess. ("Very fair was she and very amorous, and for shame the king and queen could not suffer her.") The princess leaves home and falls in with a caravan, with which she is travelling when a lion attacks. As the *Mahavamsa* relates:

When the lion had taken his prey and was leaving the spot he beheld her from afar, love for her laid hold on him, and he came towards her with waving tail and ears laid back. Seeing him without fear she caressed him, stroking his limbs. The lion, roused to

fiercest passion by her touch, took her upon his back and bore her with all speed to his cave, and there he was united with her, and from this union the princess in time bore twin children, a son and a daughter.

The son, named Sinhabahu, became the ruler of Sinhapura in North India (in present-day Gujarat), married his sister and produced no fewer than 16 sons, the eldest of whom was named Vijaya. Vijaya and his friends, however, become so troublesome and disruptive that his father was obliged to send him and 700 of his companions into exile. This disorderly crowd were put into boats and driven off to sea. They first landed on an island situated near present-

day Mumbai, but received a hostile reception and were forced to sail off again, eventually arriving on the west coast of Sri Lanka at a spot near the modern town of Puttalam.

Arriving at the island, Vijaya and his followers found that it was already inhabited by demons (Yaksas). Vijaya married one of them, named Kuveni, who bore him two children – traditionally believed to be the ancestors of the Veddhas – but then drove her away and sent to South India for brides for him and his companions. Despite marrying a Pandyan princess, Vijaya was unable to produce an heir, and so towards the end of his life sent back to his home for a younger brother to succeed him. His brother, however, was unwilling to

ABOVE, FROM LEFT: visiting the Gal Vihara rock sculptures, Polonnaruwa: legend has it that the Sinhalese are descended from a lion.

leave home and instead sent his youngest son, Panduvasudeva, who duly arrived and continued the Vijaya dynasty.

Exactly what this strange myth signifies is unclear. Vijaya himself is possibly a symbolic figure (his name means "victory"), while the story of his marriage to Kuveni probably reflects the intermingling of early Sinhalese settlers with the already established Veddhas. The arrival of Panduvasudeva probably symbolises the arrival of a second wave of settlers from Orissa or Bengal. At least this is the traditionally accepted theory: modern historians continue to argue over exactly who arrived where and when,

a bit later, in 247 BC, during the reign of King Devanampiya Tissa (c.250–210 BC), when the island was converted by the missionary Mahinda, the brother (or perhaps son) of the great Indian Buddhist emperor Asoka.

This new religion gave the Sinhalese a sense of self-identity which persists to this day. Some 93 percent of Sinhalese are Buddhists, and there are virtually no non-Sinhalese Buddhists in Sri Lanka. The connection between race and religion is thus unusually clear-cut and still of vital importance to most islanders, who feel that to be Sinhalese is to be Buddhist, and vice versa (despite the small but significant number

and what it all means, arguments that became increasingly charged with political significance over the past decades as Sinhalese and Tamils argued for historical precedence.

Buddhism and the Sinhalese

According to that mouthpiece of Buddhist orthodoxy, the *Mahavamsa*, the Buddha himself paid three visits to Sri Lanka, and then, on his deathbed, declared a blessing on Vijaya and on the island, announcing that it would be "a place where his doctrine should thereafter shine in glory" – indeed, traditionally Vijaya is meant to have landed on the island at the exact moment when the Buddha passed into nirvana. In fact, Buddhism didn't arrive in Sri Lanka until quite

of Sinhalese Christians, mainly found along the west coast around Negombo). The belief amongst more nationalistic Sinhalese and the clergy that Sri Lanka is the chosen land of Buddhism added further fuel to the fire during the civil war with the LTTE, while many right-wing Sinhalese continue vociferously to oppose the aspirations of their fellow Hindu citizens even following the conclusion of hostilities.

Sinhalese in a changing world

Historically, it was the Buddhist faith that allowed the Sinhalese to survive centuries of Indian influence and European rule with their sense of self-worth and cultural integrity largely unshaken, pointing to the island's Buddhist traditions and a long line of kings who have upheld this state of affairs (a dynasty reaching back 2,300 years and comprising an unbroken chain of 167 monarchs that ended only with the surrender of Kandy in 1815). This sense has survived despite the myriad foreign influences which have poured into the island over the centuries: intermarriages between Sinhalese and Veddhas had probably long been frequent; while a tradition of Sri Lankan kings (dating right back to Vijaya himself) of sending off to South India for Tamil queens, not to mention the huge numbers of Tamil immigrants to the island over the years, added a significant splash of South Indian blood to the Sinhalese

> *Caste divisions in Sri Lanka have always been more muted than in India, though the system continues to have a subtle but pervasive influence – despite the fact that the Buddha himself repudiated the system.*

now regard themselves as being culturally and racially purer than their low-country brothers.

The caste system

The caste system originated in India and divided people into four main categories, with brah-

mins (priests) at the top of the tree, followed in descending order by warriors, merchants and farmers, and the casteless "untouchables" at the bottom.

The Sri Lankan caste system lacks the brahmin and warrior castes of India; the leading caste is instead the numerically dominant farmers' caste, the goyigama. There are also castes for numerous different professions such as toddy-tapping, cinnamon-peeling, drumming, laundering, the making of pottery and jewellery, and fishing, to name just a few. Caste has played a major role in politics: all but one of the country's prime ministers and presidents have been goyigama, as have most cabinet ministers – indeed, resentment

gene pool. Further dashes of European blood were also added to the mix during colonial times – even the reclusive kingdom of Kandy received a share of this, because as many as 1,000 British, French, Dutch and Portuguese prisoners have been held by its kings at various times, all of whom were allowed to take local wives.

As time went on, the Sinhalese began to further subdivide into so-called low-country Sinhalese, living in coastal regions and having prolonged exposure to European values, commerce and religion; and the more conservative up-country or Kandyan Sinhalese, who even

ABOVE, FROM LEFT: young monks at Sigiriya: pre-school children enjoying a lesson.

by non-goyigamas at the lack of opportunity available to them was probably one factor in the catastrophic JVP insurrections of 1971 and 1989. All castes are welcome in Buddhist temples (though one of the island's Buddhist sects, the Siam Nikaya, only accepts goyigama monks) and caste remains an important factor in marriage, with marriage advertisements in papers still generally stating the caste of the advertiser. Some surnames have particular caste associations and it's not unknown for people to take new, caste-neutral names or to modify their existing name in order to conceal their caste.

Planetary and spirit influences

The Sinhalese take the influence of the heavens very seriously. Marriages are planned on the advice of astrologers and gurus, while auspicious hours, days and months are carefully considered before conducting any major business or social activity – astrologers are always particularly busy with the horoscopes of politicians come election time. Every Sinhalese child has a horoscope based on the time of his or her birth. The position of the stars and planets is carefully analysed by an astrologer to determine the flow of the child's early life. Thereafter, five-year horoscopes are cast to

ADVERTISING FOR A MATE

"Sinhala Goyigama (Farmer Caste) Buddhist parents seek a well educated non-working, beautiful, slim, well charactered and well mannered girl from a Kandyan or Low Country Buddhist family with a profound Goyigama cultural background, for their son who holds a senior executive position, owns a house and a new car. Mars in the seventh house. Responses must be in own handwriting, with full particulars and horoscope."

This advertisement for a bride appearing in a local newspaper highlights the importance of caste integrity in supporting family life. The reference to astrology betrays another Sinhalese preoccupation.

predict good times and bad, wealth, job and marriage prospects and their effects on family members. Most marriage adverts ask for prospective partners to send their horoscopes so that their compatibility, or otherwise, can be scrutinised.

Negative influences can be countered by devotion to the Buddha, and propitiation ceremonies can be prescribed to forestall danger or earn favours at work or elsewhere. Should sickness or ill-fortune strike, it is possible to turn to the realm of the supernatural: exorcism ceremonies (*bali;* see page 100) intended to ward off malevolent spirits are still sometimes staged in remote rural villages right up to the present day.

THE TAMILS OF SRI LANKA

The Tamils are Sri Lanka's second-largest ethnic group, although much less numerous than the Sinhalese, comprising around 18 percent of the population. However, whereas the Sinhalese are found only in Sri Lanka, the 3.5 million or so Sri Lankan Tamils represent only a small proportion of the vast Tamil population (over 70 million) found over the Palk Strait in the Indian state of Tamil Nadu – not to mention the further millions of Tamils living abroad in countries as diverse as Canada, England, Malaysia and Norway.

Exactly when the first Tamils, or their Dravidian ancestors, arrived in Sri Lanka remains a matter seizing control of the entire island for extended periods. Their most decisive and destructive incursion was in 993, when Chola armies destroyed Anuradhapura and established a new capital at Polonnaruwa. At the same time, thousands of Tamil traders, artisans and farmers also settled on the island, where they have been ever since.

The descendants of these long-established Tamil settlers, traditionally known as "Sri Lankan Tamils", now make up around 12.5 percent of the population, living mainly in the north and east of the island, although significant numbers can be found throughout the country, particularly in Colombo.

of considerable speculation; although they were on the island no later than the 2nd century BC, and possibly much earlier, before the Sinhalese, having walked across to Sri Lanka from India at a time when the island and mainland were still connected. Tamil influence on Sri Lanka became more pronounced from the 2nd century BC onwards, when the first of the numerous Tamil invaders who were to seize the island over the centuries established themselves on the throne at Anuradhapura. Tamil kings and mercenaries came and went over the following centuries,

ABOVE, FROM LEFT: procession through the streets of Kandy; tea factory portrait – Tamil tea pickers at Nuwara Eliya.

The "Plantation Tamils"

The remaining 5.5 percent of the island's Tamil population is made up of so-called "Plantation Tamils". This second wave of Tamil migrants arrived in the 19th century thanks to the British. Faced with massive labour shortages on their coffee plantations, the British recruited hundreds of thousands of Tamil labourers from India to work on the estates. Employment in the coffee plantations was seasonal, however, so Tamil workers were forced to return to India for part of the year. The collapse of the coffee industry during the 1860s and its replacement with tea planting had one crucial side effect. Unlike coffee, the tea plantations required year-round labour, so the Tamils who had previously migrated to Sri Lanka on a seasonal basis now settled permanently in the hills, where their descendants still live to this very day.

The slightly incongruous sight of Tamil tea pickers in colourful saris working in the island's tea plantations is one of Sri Lanka's most picturesque and defining images, though the reality behind the picture-postcard image is altogether grimmer. Many early Tamil settlers died on the journey from India and on the early estates, and their latter-day descendants fare little better, suffering some of the poorest living standards in the island and marginalised both by the Sinhalese government in Colombo and the much longer-established Jaffna Tamils alike. Tamil tea workers remain amongst the worst paid in the country, often living in cold and insanitary conditions and working long and exhausting hours for often just a few dollars a day.

They have also suffered continual political discrimination (one of the Sri Lankan government's first acts following Independence in 1948 was to strip the Plantation Tamils of the vote they had previously been given by the British), and even the longer-established Jaffna Tamils tend to look down their noses at them – which has at least had the benefit of allowing the plantation workers largely to keep out of the civil war.

THE NORTH–SOUTH DIVIDE

The divisions between the Sinhalese and Tamils which have racked the island during recent decades appear not to have been as entrenched during the early periods of Sri Lanka's history. Up until the 4th century AD, many Sri Lankan Tamils were actually Buddhist, while both races seem to have lived together peacefully and intermarried extensively for long periods. The ethnic and linguistic divide which now separates the mainly Tamil north from the Sinhalese south only began to establish itself during the 14th century, when the island's first significant Tamil kingdom was established in the north at Jaffnapatnam (present-day Jaffna), surviving until 1619 when it was subdued by the Portuguese. The northern part of the island – that closest to India – became predominantly Tamil and has remained so to this day, with Jaffna, the unofficial capital of Tamil Sri Lanka, regarded as the traditional home of Tamil culture in the island, rather as Kandy is seen by the Sinhalese. Even so, significant numbers of Tamils still live throughout the south in Sinhalese areas and in the hill country, though virtually all Sinhalese were driven out of the north by the Tamil Tigers (LTTE) – an inequality which the Sinhalese often refer to as proof of the LTTE's intransigence and racism. For their part, Tamils living in Sinhalese areas faced mounting difficulties as a result of the renewed war against the LTTE *(see Urban Tamils of Colombo).*

Urban Tamils of Colombo

Tamils continue to live throughout the rest of the country, perhaps most notably in Colombo, a city on which they continue to have a notable influence despite the riots of 1983 during which as many as 2,000 Tamils were killed or driven out of the city. The city's freewheeling Pettah district, always a traditionally Tamil area, is quite different from anywhere else in Sri Lanka, with its hectic commercial life and dozens of churches and tiny Hindu temples – but hardly a Buddhist temple in sight. Tamil influence is also to be seen in newer parts of the city: nowhere else in the country will you

were expelled from the city for no better reason than that they were unemployed, prompting allegations of ethnic cleansing – something the Sinhalese government had always claimed was the exclusive preserve of the LTTE. Things have improved since, although Tamils continue to suffer regular discrimination and intimidation at the hands of the security forces.

Liberation Tamil Tigers of Eelam

The island's most notorious Tamils were the members of the LTTE, the Liberation Tamil Tigers of Eelam, led by Velupillai Prabhakaran, who as a teenager, rumour has it, watched

see so many purely vegetarian South Indian restaurants, with huge crispy *dosas* inside and colourful sweets piled up in glass cases at the door.

Nonetheless, life in Colombo, in particular, is no bed of roses for both established and migrant Tamils. The situation was particularly acute during the final years of the civil war, when local Tamils were regularly stopped, searched, harassed and sometimes arbitrarily detained and imprisoned. In one particularly notorious incident (June 2007), hundreds of innocent Tamil civilians living in Colombo

an uncle being burned in oil by soldiers and announced, "I will make you sorry". The United States credited him with creating what was once the most deadly guerrilla force in the world, whose relatively small but fiercely committed band of fighters was able to keep the far larger and better equipped Sri Lankan Army on the run during two decades of civil war, until they were finally crushed (and their leader, Prabhakaran, killed) during the massive army offensive of 2008–9.

But despite their undoubted military skill and bravery in battle, and the ideological commitment of some of their recruits, the LTTE always had a dark side, which undermined the essential rightness of its original cause and

ABOVE, FROM LEFT: a Tamil woman toils in the tea plantations; a Tamil Tigress, ready to fight for independence.

justified those who branded it a "terrorist" organisation. The massacre of innocent civilians and the use of suicide bombers (whose technology the Tigers pioneered, and are thought to have exported to the Middle East); the forcible recruitment of young men and children as soldiers; the widespread extortion of money, at home and amongst Tamils overseas; the ethnic cleansing of non-Tamils from LTTE-controlled areas; the ruthless killing of all Tamils who opposed the LTTE; and the often heavy-handed treatment of the people they were meant to be fighting for (it has been estimated that more Tamil civilians have been killed by the LTTE

up to Jaffna. Both religions have co-existed side by side quite happily ever since – some Hindus even accept Jesus as one of their own gods, and depict him sitting on a fish – and both communities happily take part in each other's festivals.

Caste still plays a significant role in the lives of both Tamil Hindus and their Christian counterparts, although the system has now taken on a distinctly Sri Lankan form. Unlike in India, there are very few Brahmins (priests) in Sri Lanka, and no Kshatriyas (warriors) at all on the island.

The dominant caste is the Vellala, the equivalent to the Sinhalese goyigama, mainly living

than by the Sri Lankan armed forces) left the movement's image in tatters – whilst the apparent use of thousands of innocent Tamil civilians as a human shield during their final stand in 2009 did nothing to enhance their reputation.

Religion and caste

Most Sri Lankan Tamils are Hindus – usually followers of Siva or Skanda (for more on Sri Lankan Hinduism, see page 88). However, there are also significant numbers of Christian Tamils, mostly Roman Catholics whose ancestors were converted by the Portuguese during their fervent missionary sweep around the island's west coast, leaving a swathe of Christian Tamils from Negombo in the south

in the Jaffna peninsula. Over 50 percent of Sri Lankan Tamils belong to this caste, whose members are traditionally landowners and cultivators, although during the colonial period many took advantage of new educational possibilities and the availability of administrative jobs to move away from agriculture. Following the Vellala are the Karaiya (equivalent to the Sinhalese Karava), originally fishermen who subsequently branched out into commerce, and the Chetti merchant castes, many of whom can still be found in Colombo. At the bottom of the system come the Palla. The Plantation Tamils are mostly from the lowest castes in India, a fact which has contributed to their isolation from both the Sri Lankan Tamils and the Sinhalese.

MUSLIMS

Muslims and Islam have been present in Sri Lanka since the early days of the religion. The first Arab settlers are said to have landed in Beruwala during the 8th century (at the site of the present Kachimalai Mosque) and soon established a string of settlements up and down the coast. Their numbers were subsequently boosted by the arrival in the 18th and 19th centuries of further Muslim immigrants – the so-called "Malays", who arrived during the Dutch colonial period from Java and Malaysia, and the Indian Muslims, comprising soldiers and traders who came to the island from India during the British era.

Today's Muslim community constitutes just over 7 percent of the population, with the original Arab Muslims accounting for 95 percent of this total number.

to Arabia, although ethnic lines have become significantly blurred over the centuries.

The majority of the island's 2 million or so Muslims (roughly 8 percent of the population) continue to live close to the coast, forming the majority of the population in some towns in the east, while there are also signifi-

Muslim leaders played a prominent role in the struggle for the country's independence. S.W.R.D. Bandaranaike said "The Ceylon Moors have been in Ceylon as long as we Sinhalese. A close bond of friendship exists between the communities." Perhaps the reason they integrated with ease was intermarriage. Most Muslim settlers arrived here without womenfolk of their own, and subsequently married Sinhalese and Tamils. The vast majority (over 90 percent) of Sri Lanka's Muslims – or "Moors", as they're sometimes called – trace their roots back

ABOVE, FROM LEFT: returning refugees bear the burden of war, losing their homes and family members; Tamil fisherman mending his nets in the port at Galle.

cant Muslim communities inland at places like Kandy and Bandarawela. Muslims are still traditionally regarded as traders and businessmen, and Muslim families continue to play an important role in certain trades, especially gems and jewellery. Many poorer Muslims, however, work as farmers and fishermen, mainly on the east coast and in the area around Mannar and Puttalam on the west. Historically, Sri Lankan Muslims have tended to speak Tamil (with numerous Arabic loan-words) rather than Sinhalese, though Muslims living on the west coast are likely to speak both languages, while a few Malay Muslims still preserve their own language, Bahasa Melayu, similar to that spoken in modern Malaysia and Indonesia (although

One Burgher, Emil Daniels, when asked for his nationality by a British governor, answered "God alone knows, your excellency", thus neatly summing up the varied heritage of the Sri Lankan Burgher.

again with numerous Sinhalese and Tamil loan-words added).

Muslims in the modern world

Muslims have traditionally supported the island's two main political parties, the SLFP

1990 by the horrific killing of 120 Muslims, massacred whilst at prayer in a mosque near Batticaloa by LTTE gunmen. Thankfully, the conclusion of fighting in the east in 2007 and the expulsion of the LTTE from the area has made life a lot easier – although many of the Muslims driven out of the north remain stuck in refugee camps more than two decades after the event.

BURGHERS

One of the island's smallest but most colour-ful ethnic groups, the Burghers are white, English-speaking Sri Lankans descended

and UNP, both of which have had Muslim cabinet ministers – indeed some Muslims have been elected to represent predominantly Sinhalese constituencies. The first exclusively Muslim political party, the Sri Lanka Muslim Congress, was formed in 1981, shortly before the outbreak of the civil war. The war was particularly traumatic for the Muslim community. The 75,000 Muslims who formerly lived in Mannar and the northern province were driven out by the LTTE in 1991, while east-coast Muslims were repeatedly caught between Sinhalese and Tamil forces. The LTTE traditionally regarded the east as Tamil terri-tory despite a large Muslim population for whom it showed scant concern, epitomised in

from European settlers – mainly Dutch and Portuguese. When the British took over the island from the Dutch in 1797, a significant number of employees of the Dutch East India Company stayed on in the island. Most of them were, of course, Dutch, but those who stayed also included other nationalities, amongst them Portuguese, Germans, Danes, French, Italians and even, ironically, British. This group formed a distinctive English-speaking Christian community – although they always maintained a certain distance from the new British masters, who kept a similar distance from them, regarding them as natives who were not altogether to be trusted.

European descent

Strictly speaking, a Sri Lankan Burgher is one who can claim unbroken paternal descent back to a European employee of the original Dutch East India Company. The more conservative Burghers still regard themselves as Dutch (the term "Dutch Burghers" is often preferred to "Burghers"). Those who attend the Dutch Burgher Union's Christmas dinner in Colombo are traditionally required to stand and sing the hymn "Het Lieve Vaderland ("Dear Fatherland"), though ironically it is now sung in English because, apart from the title of the hymn, no one knows the Dutch words.

French Huguenot descent, a Dutch father and a mother of mixed Dutch, Scottish and Sinhalese descent.

Despite the fact that they were never totally accepted by the British colonial establishment, many Burghers rose to considerable prominence in the colonial administration and other middle-class professions. Small in number, they have played a disproportionately large role in the country's history, although the Sri Lankan government's declaration, following Independence, that Sinhalese was henceforth to be the sole national language, led to mass emigrations: perhaps as many as half the island's

In practice, however, the term is used to describe all Sri Lankans of European descent. Burgher numbers were significantly increased during the British period by Portuguese who came to work on the new railways and settled along the coast between Colombo and Negombo, while the constant intermingling of Muslim, Tamil and Sinhalese blood added further flavours to the ethnic cocktail. One of Sri Lanka's most famous modern Burghers, the architect Geoffrey Bawa, had a Muslim grandfather, an English grandmother of

ABOVE, FROM LEFT: two Muslim girls at Colombo's Id ul-Fitr festival marking the end of Ramadan; author Michael Ondaatje.

Burghers departed, mainly to Canada, Britain and Australia.

Cultural role

Significant numbers remain, however, mainly in Colombo, where they continue to play a disproportionate role: their names now read like a cultural Who's Who of contemporary Sri Lanka, including Geoffrey Bawa, artists George Keyt and Lionel Wendt, designers Barbara Sansoni and Ena de Silva, and novelist Carl Muller – not to mention Sri Lankan-born but Canadian-raised Michael Ondaatje, whose family memoir and travel diary, *Running in the Family* (1982), provides a warm and marvellous snapshot of Burgher society in the mid-20th century.

CONTEMPORARY SOCIETY

Modern Sri Lanka is a cat's cradle of contradictions – at once traditional and modern, conservative and cosmopolitan, fundamentally peace-loving and yet scarred by the turmoil of civil war.

In the smart restaurants of Colombo, the English-speaking business elite talk share prices over power lunches, while a hundred kilometres away peasants in loincloths wade through flooded rice paddies and the Veddhas gather wild honey in the lowland jungles. In Galle, wealthy European expats plot the opening of a luxury beachside villa, while in the north, where until recently desperate Tamil refugees risked death on an hourly basis, dodging the guns and artillery of the Sri Lankan Army and LTTE, the slow rebuilding of everyday life has begun. In short, whatever generalisation you try to make about Sri Lanka, the opposite will also be true.

Ancient and modern

Large parts of Sri Lanka remain deeply rural. Much of the population does what it has always done: working in the fields, visiting the local temple, and dining daily on rice and curry. Marriages are arranged, and propitious dates for nuptials (and other important events) determined after consultation with a professional astrologer – even the days of elections and the opening of parliament are still often fixed according to the stars.

The south, in particular, remains a stronghold of the Sri Lankan rural way of life – a bastion of traditional Sinhalese values, fuelled by the anti-Tamil rhetoric of the Buddhist clergy and providing unwavering political support for local Hambantota-boy Mahinda Rajapakse who currently holds the reins of power in the island's capital.

Meanwhile, in the chic cafés of Colombo, a very different version of modern Sri Lanka is in progress. English is the preferred language

here, an obligatory status symbol; while sharp suits and gorgeous outfits, from chic boutiques like Barefoot and Odel, are the order of the day, with the latest smartphone as an essential designer accessory. This is the other Sri Lanka – cosmopolitan, liberal and internationalist, and a world away from the rice paddies and Buddhist temples of the hinterlands.

Workers of the world

Tea and tourism still play a crucial role in the economic life of Sri Lanka, but the island increasingly relies on its cheap labour and the financial desperation of its impoverished inhabitants to make ends meet. The country's leading export industry is now garment-making, with hundreds of factories churning out clothes for major Western chains. Most of the employees are women under the age of 25, often working for a pittance in insalubrious surroundings – although conditions are gradually improving.

And then there's the country's second-largest "export", the thousands of workers who leave their families at home to labour in the Gulf and elsewhere and whose remittances provide another important prop to the massively indebted Sri Lankan economy. A lucky few manage to secure remunerative white-collar jobs; but the majority, mainly women, go abroad to work in low-paid positions as

peace and justice for all members of Sri Lankan society. The island's proud democratic traditions are also beginning to look increasingly frayed as Mahinda, his brothers Basil and Gotabhaya and other members of the extended Rajapakse clan exercise an increasingly suffocating influence on all affairs of state – the last person to contest a presidential election against Mahinda currently languishes in jail, while journalists who fail to tow the party line are routinely threatened, or worse. Alleged human-rights violations during the closing stages of the war have also yet to be satisfactorily answered, and probably now never will be, while Tamil civilians in the north and east

housemaids and nannies, frequently suffering abuse by their employers – who often seem to regard Sri Lankan expats as little better than indentured slaves – and further exploited by the agents who take a significant slice of their earnings.

Dysfunctioning democracy

President Mahinda Rajapakse and his government may have won the military battle against the LTTE in the north and east but have yet to prove that they are capable of delivering lasting

ABOVE, FROM LEFT: almost every part of the versatile coconut tree can be worked to provide shelter, food, fuel and medicine; Galle Face Beach, Colombo.

continue to disappear with alarming regularity.

The peace that Sri Lankans have dreamed of for a generation has finally arrived, but now carries an ambiguous flavour. A spate of ambitious new infrastructure projects and a booming tourist industry give the impression of a country on the mend, but serious questions remain about deep-seated flaws in the island's economy. Meanwhile, the question of Tamil autonomy and self-determination remains unresolved, while most Sri Lankans have already resigned themselves to living under a quasi-dictatorship as the necessary price to be paid for continued peace and stability. The battle, in short, may have been won, but the future of post-war Sri Lanka remains far from clear.

RELIGION

Sri Lanka is the spiritual heartland of Theravada Buddhism, and also plays host to three of the world's other major religions.

Religion plays a crucial role in Sri Lankan life, irrespective of race and creed. Central to the island's religious life is Buddhism, the faith of the vast majority of the country's Sinhalese. Hinduism is the dominant religion of Sri Lanka's Tamils, though significant numbers are Christian. The fourth of the island's faiths, Islam, is professed by Muslims living mainly along the west and, particularly, east coasts.

The presence of four such diverse religions squeezed together in such geographical proximity has resulted in a significant blurring of boundaries in places. Hindu deities are commonly found in Buddhist temples, while Hindus reciprocate by declaring the Buddha to be an avatar or incarnation of Vishnu. Catholic saints are easily accepted as further additions to the accumulated clutter of religious images, and are accorded due reverence by adherents of other faiths careful not to miss out on any spiritual merit, wherever it might be found.

Followers of all four religions visit one another's festivals and pilgrimage places. This state of cheerful cohabitation is summed up by the revered pilgrimage town of Kataragama, where a Hindu temple, Buddhist stupa and mosque sit side by side; and by the sacred mountain of Adam's Peak, whose mysterious "footprint" has been claimed in turn by Buddhists, Hindus, Muslims and Christians, all of whom assert that it was made, variously, by the Buddha, Siva, Adam and St Thomas.

PRECEDING PAGES: Colombo 2012, Sri Lankan Buddhist monks protest over the US-led move to censure Sri Lanka at the UN Human Rights Council sessions over its alleged war crimes while crushing Tamil rebels in 2009. **LEFT:** monk at the Gangaramaya Temple in Colombo. **RIGHT:** a young pilgrim brings floral offerings to Anuradhapura.

BUDDHISM

Buddhism is central to the life and beliefs of the island's Sinhalese. Almost more than a religion, it has also given the Sinhalese a sense of national identity, and fostered a view of their island as the so-called "chosen land" of Buddhism, as the island's more extreme monks like to put it – it's said that the Buddha himself pronounced a blessing on the island from his deathbed, and claimed it as a future stronghold of the faith. In addition, Sri Lanka was one of the first places converted to the religion, meaning that, since Buddhism has now virtually disappeared from India, Sri Lanka has the distinction of being one of the world's oldest Buddhist countries, as well as preserving the faith in its "pure" original form, the so-called Theravada tradition. It was also in Sri Lanka, at Aluvihara (see page 221), that the most important Theravada texts, the *Tripitaka*, were first written down, while the Tooth Relic at Kandy is perhaps the world's most venerated Buddhist relic.

The life of the Buddha

The future Buddha, Siddhartha, was the son of King Shuddhodana of Kapilavastu and his queen, Maya. He was born at Lumbini in the Himalayan foothills, in what is now Nepal. His family name was Gautama and he belonged to the Shakya clan, hence his alternative name,

kingdom. Yashodhara bore him a son. But the seeds of disenchantment had already sprouted in Siddhartha's heart. He named his son Rahula (Impediment).

Suffering and enlightenment

As prophesied, Siddhartha saw the three signs of suffering: sickness, old age and death. On the night of the full moon in the month of Vaisakha (or Vesak, as it's called in Sri Lanka), Siddhartha prepared for the Great Renunciation. He stood at the door of his bedchamber, looked at his sleeping wife and son for a few moments, and then left the palace.

Shakyamuni (Shakya Sage) or Shakyasimha (Shakya Lion). Among his other epithets are Amitabha (Infinite Light) and Tathagata (He Who Has Arrived At Perfection).

Queen Maya died a week after delivering the prince. At Siddhartha's birth, the royal astrologer prophesied that he would one day become disillusioned with worldly pleasures and become a mendicant in search of the wisdom to overcome suffering. Siddhartha grew up into a handsome youth, gentle and compassionate, skilled in all the arts. The king, remembering the astrologer's prophecy, tried to save his son from unpleasant sights. He was surrounded by luxury. The king found for him a lovely wife, Yashodhara, princess of a neighbouring

Siddhartha sat at the feet of famous masters, but none of them could explain to him the cause of sorrow. For a while he joined a group of ascetics and performed severe physical austerities. He became extremely weak in body and mind, and realised that wisdom could not be attained through self-mortification. At last, meditating under a Bo tree near Gaya, he attained Bodhi (Illumination). Prince Siddhartha had become the Buddha, the Enlightened One.

After becoming enlightened, Gautama the Buddha could have immediately released himself from the cycle of rebirths and attained nirvana, supreme liberation. But the compassionate side of his nature prevented him from tasting the fruit of liberation so long as a single living creature was in pain. His first sermon was preached in the Deer Park at Sarnath, near the holy city of Varanasi. According to legend, deer from the forest listened enraptured to the Buddha, sensing that his message was for all living beings. It contained the Four Noble Truths, which form the basis of Buddhist thought (*see box*).

As the number of his followers increased, the Bhikshusangha (Order of Monks) was formed. At first, only men were admitted. But later, urged by his foster mother Gotami, the Buddha admitted women and an Order of Nuns was formed.

After a few months the Buddha visited Kapilavastu and met his father, wife and son. He had left as a prince: he returned as a mendicant. He was hailed as a hero, a conqueror in the spiritual realm.

During the remaining 40 years of his life the Buddha travelled from village to village, preaching the message of love, compassion, tolerance and self-restraint. He led a humble life, and died in 483 BC, in his 80th year, at Kusinara, not far from the place of his birth. His last words were to his favourite disciple, Ananda: "A Buddha can only point the way. Become a lamp unto yourself. Work out your own salvation diligently."

The Buddha's teachings

The Buddha's first sermon is called the Sermon of the Middle Way and steers between two sets of extremes: on the ethical plane, the extremes of self-indulgence and asceticism; on the philosophical plane, the extremes of naive acceptance of everything as real and the total rejection of everything as unreal. While Hindu thought was preoccupied with the essential nature of Absolute Reality, the Buddha avoided metaphysical controversies. "The arising of sorrow, the termination of sorrow, that is all I teach," he once said.

The starting point of Buddhist teaching is the Four Noble Truths: that life is suffering; that suffering is the result of craving; that it is possible to put an end to craving and thus suffering; and that there is a path which leads to the end of suffering. This path is summed up in the Noble Eightfold Path, a kind of Buddhist Ten Commandments comprising a simple set of

rules to encourage one to live virtuously. These are right conduct, right motive, right resolve, right speech, right livelihood, right attention, right effort and right meditation. By following this path of restraint and self-perfection, one can conquer craving and put oneself on the path towards nirvana, the transcendental state of complete emancipation.

Shortly after the Buddha's death, his oldest disciple, Kashyapa, convened a Council at Rajagriha. The master's oral teachings were classified into three sections, known as *Tripitaka* (Three Baskets). These, along with later commentaries, became the principal scriptures of

THE FOUR NOBLE TRUTHS

The Buddha preached his first sermon in the Deer Park at Sarnath, where the ascetics from whom he had parted company a few months earlier became his first audience. The Buddha's Four Noble Truths outline the key problems underlying man's existence:

1. Life is suffering.
2. Suffering is caused by desire and attachment.
3. If you extinguish desire and attachment, suffering will cease.
4. The Middle Path leads to the end of desire and attachment (to be steered between sad and useless asceticism and ignoble hedonism).

ABOVE, FROM LEFT: the Temple of the Tooth at Kandy; flags over Kandy.

Buddhism, and it was in Sri Lanka that they were first written down on palm leaves, then loosely bound to make books (at the monastery of Aluvihara, just north of Kandy).

Buddhism in Sri Lanka

Buddhism arrived in Sri Lanka, according to tradition, in 247 BC, when the missionary Mahinda, sent to the island by the great Indian Buddhist emperor Asoka, converted the king of Anuradhapura, Devanampiya Tissa, and his followers. Buddhism quickly established itself as the state religion, giving the Sinhalese a new-found sense of self-identity.

and the growing influence of Hinduism during the Polonnaruwan period. As the state religion, Buddhism suffered following the collapse of Sinhalese power in the north, with the island's increasingly enfeebled kings no longer able to support the huge monasteries of previous eras, or to discipline errant monks. The religion further suffered with the arrival of Europeans and missionary Christianity from the 16th century onwards, while the throne of Kandy passed into Tamil hands, leading to renewed Hindu influence on Sinhalese affairs.

The lowest point arrived in 1753, when it was discovered that there were not enough monks

Buddhism and the state remained closely linked throughout the Anuradhapura period. The city's kings were seen as upholders of the faith, judged by their piety and commitment to raising great monasteries and other religious edifices – the origins of the great sequence of monasteries and stupas that still dominate the ruined city. The successful network of irrigation works constructed by the city's rulers also provided an agricultural surplus which allowed it to support a large community of monks, giving the early city the character of an enormous theocracy.

Buddhism gradually disappeared from India but continued as the pre-eminent religion in Sri Lanka, despite repeated Tamil incursions

left to ordain any new clergy. The king of Kandy sent to Thailand for qualified priests, who duly arrived and ordained a fresh set of monks, the first members of the so-called Siyam Nikaya, the Siam Order, an exclusive Buddhist sect which survives to this day.

The Theravada tradition

Sri Lankan Buddhism preserves the religion in its original and "purest" form, the Theravada tradition, or "Law of the Elders". This is also the dominant form of the religion in Southeast Asian Buddhist countries such as Burma and Thailand, who look to Sri Lanka as the traditional heartland of the religion, thanks to its geographical proximity to India and the fact that Buddhism has been established there for so long. The Theravada tradition stresses, as did the Buddha himself, that one is personally responsible for one's own spiritual welfare, and that the only route to nirvana is through constant spiritual striving – a long and difficult path that will usually require millions of lifetimes to achieve. As such, the Theravada tradition contrasts markedly with the far more populist Mahayana tradition that subsequently developed in Tibet, China and Japan, which holds that nirvana can be achieved, not through personal self-knowledge, but through devotion and prayer to the various deities, or

been co-opted into the Sri Lankan Buddhist belief system. This isn't as inconsistent as one might think: the Buddha himself accepted the existence and powers of the myriad gods of India (and according to tradition even ascended to the heavens to preach to them), but simply argued that they were subject to the same laws of karma and rebirth as all other creatures.

Vishnu (often called Upulvan) is regarded as a protector of Buddhism in Sri Lanka, and his image can often be found standing next to the main Buddha image in Buddhist shrines – he also often has freestanding shrines dedicated to

Bodhisattvas (Buddhas-to-be) of the Mahayana pantheon. Despite the fact that Mahayana Buddhism promises a much swifter and less challenging route to nirvana, it enjoyed only a brief and limited period of influence in Sri Lanka, and had more or less disappeared by the 10th century.

Buddhist pantheon in Sri Lanka

Buddhism in Sri Lanka has become deeply intermingled with Hindu beliefs over the centuries, and many of the gods of Hinduism have

ABOVE, FROM LEFT: flags drape a sacred Bo tree in Kandy; at Dambulla, home to the most impressive Buddhist cave temples in the land.

him, or even complete temples, as at the Vishnu Devale in Kandy.

Kataragama is another popular god who is believed to protect the island. Originally a local deity from the remote southern town of Kataragama, his cult subsequently spread across the island; Hindu Tamils regard him as a manifestation of the great Hindu god Skanda, a son of Siva – a characteristically Sri Lankan mingling of Buddhist and Hindu beliefs. His traditional colour is red, and he is usually shown with a peacock and holding his characteristic trident (*vel*).

Another famous local god, Saman, is believed to reside at Adam's Peak and protect pilgrims to that sacred mountain – he is often portrayed

> *There are no longer large-scale monasteries in Sri Lanka; most monks live in villages and play an active role in the community, serving as teachers, advisers, astrologers, and even doctors.*

with a white elephant and a picture of the mountain behind. The elephant-headed Hindu god Ganesh (also known locally as Ganapathi) is widely worshipped, while the cults of the ferocious female Hindu goddesses Kali and Durga have also grown in recent years.

The Sangha

Although much reduced in number since the days of the great Anuradhapuran monasteries, the community of Buddhist monks in Sri Lanka – the Sangha – still plays an important symbolic and practical role in the country; there's also a small order of Buddhist nuns. Young boys are recruited into the Sangha if they show a particular interest in religious matters, and if their horoscope is propitious. Practical considerations can also be an important factor, since boy monks are guaranteed an education and a basic level of material security which the island's poorer families would not always be able to provide for

POYA DAYS

The Buddha urged his disciples to undertake special spiritual practices on every full moon *(Poya)* day, and the practice has stood the test of time. Buddhists still venerate *Poya* days, which the more devout spend in worship. The most important is Vesak *Poya* (May), while the Esala and Poson *Poyas* are also associated with major festivals. All 12 *Poya* days are public holidays, and Sri Lankans often travel around the island on pilgrimage or to visit family, particularly if the *Poya* day falls on a Friday or Monday. Hotels and transport get very busy and no alcohol is supposed to be sold, though some tourist hotels will discreetly serve foreign guests.

them. Suitable candidates are first initiated into the Sangha as novices around the age of 10, with full ordination occurring at 20. Monks are supposed to enter the Sangha for life; there is no tradition, as in Thailand and Burma, of laymen entering monasteries for a short period before returning to normal life.

On entering the Sangha, the boy monk shaves his head, dons the characteristic orange or red robes and takes the vow to commit himself to the stringent monastic code of behaviour, whose 250 rules will henceforth govern his existence.

Chosen land

One unfortunate by-product of contemporary Sri Lankan Buddhism has been its monks' increasing involvement, since Independence, in ultra-nationalist politics. Many of the more conservative monks regard Sri Lanka as the "chosen land" of Buddhism, and their attitudes to their fellow Sri Lankan Tamils is often disturbingly reminiscent of the anti-Arab rhetoric of hardline Jewish rabbis in Israel. In 1959, Prime Minister S.W.R.D. Bandaranaike was shot dead by a Buddhist monk in revenge for making modest concessions to the Tamils. Monks have regularly taken to the streets throughout the civil war to demonstrate against peace initiatives, recalling the example of the legendary King Dutugemunu, who went to war accompanied by 50 holy men who sought

simply visit their temple whenever they wish, to pray, meditate and make offerings of fruit, food, flowers or other items, or to light oil lamps. Temples are busiest on *Poya* (full moon) days *(see box)*, which are traditionally regarded as particularly important and when more devout Buddhists will dress in white and retire to the temple for the day to muse on religious matters or recite scriptures. On special occasions, lay people may also arrange for the chanting of Buddhist scriptures by monks, a practice known as *pirith*, and the nearest Buddhist equivalent to the traditional Hindu *puja*.

to legitimise the trail of slaughter he left behind him in his conquest of the island. The Sangha now have their own political party, the Jathika Hela Urumaya (JHU), or Heritage Party. The first monk was elected to parliament in 2001, and the party is now part of Mahinda Rajapakse's ruling coalition, using their popular support to push an intransigently pro-Buddhist, anti-Tamil agenda.

Daily Buddhist ritual and belief

Unlike Islam and Christianity, Buddhism has no organised form of worship – devotees

ABOVE, FROM LEFT: the Buddha's transcendental qualities are colourfully highlighted; inside the Temple of the Tooth (Dalada Maligawa), Kandy.

HINDUISM

The complex and disparate collection of beliefs known generically as Hinduism has been long established alongside Buddhism in Sri Lanka. Buddhism was born from Hinduism, and the two religions share many assumptions about the world: that we are born over and over again; that our present deeds and accumulated karma determine the course of our future lives; and that we may one day hope to escape the endless cycle of rebirths, a longed-for deliverance which Hindus call *moksha*. In Sri Lanka, the exact boundary between the two religions has become decidedly blurred, and many gods from the Hindu pantheon occupy important positions in Sri Lankan Buddhism.

Hinduism in Sri Lanka is the exclusive preserve of the island's Tamils, who practise a form of the religion similar to that found in Tamil Nadu on the Indian mainland. Tamil Hinduism has little time for the complex metaphysical speculations which have characterised some schools of Indian thought, and tends to express itself instead in shows of ecstatic personal devotion towards the chosen deity. During Sri Lanka's great Hindu religious festivals, such as those at Kataragama and at the Nallur Kandaswamy Temple in Jaffna, devotees affirm their love of the god by performing gruesome (to Western eyes) acts of self-mortification, driving skewers through the flesh of their cheeks, limbs and back – though they assert that their god protects them from all feelings of pain. Other devotees express their devotion by walking barefoot across burning coals – perhaps a distant folk memory of the events narrated at the culmination of the Ramayana, whose heroine, Sita, is forced to walk over fire at the end to prove her purity to her husband Rama. (Firewalking has also caught on in Buddhist parts of the island and now forms an integral part of the nightly dance shows put on around Kandy for tourists.)

THE RAMAYANA

The great Hindu epic, the *Ramayana*, tells the story of the epic battle between Rama, the eldest son of King Dasharatha of Ayodhya, northern India, and Ravana, the demon king of Lanka, who abducts Rama's wife, Sita, before being finally defeated by Rama, his brother, Laksmana, and an army of monkeys led by Hanuman. Rama is revealed to be an avatar (incarnation) of Vishnu himself. Several places in Sri Lanka are popularly linked with the great poem: rival locations at Ella and Nuwara Eliya both claim to be where Ravana imprisoned the unfortunate Sita, while Adam's Bridge – the chain of islets that runs between India and Sri Lanka – is said to have been built by Hanuman to facilitate the passage of his monkey armies. A trio of rocky outcrops also stands as testament to Hanuman's mighty powers. Hanuman was sent by Rama to the Himalayas to search for a rare medicinal herb to save the life of Laksmana, wounded in battle. Arriving at the Himalayas, the absent-minded monkey-god realised that he had completely forgotten which type of herb was required, so decided to uproot an entire mountain and take the whole thing back to Sri Lanka in the hope that the required plant could be found somewhere upon it. The specific herb was found, and Laksmana recovered, to fight another day. The rocks at Hakgala, Ritigala and Unawatuna are popularly believed to be fragments fallen from this peak.

Most Sri Lankan Tamils are followers of Siva, one of the great three gods of Hinduism, or his son Skanda. Skanda (also known as Murugan) has particular local significance, having become hopelessly muddled up with the Buddhist god Kataragama, and is now worshipped under both names by both faiths, particularly at his shrine in the pilgrimage town of Kataragama. Siva's other son, the elephant-headed Ganesh, is also popular, as is the south Indian goddess Pattini, the paragon of wifely devotion. Kataragama, Ganesh and Pattini are also often found in Buddhist temples, or in independent shrines, such as the *devales* at Kandy, although these are visited mainly by Buddhists.

Temples dedicated to the other great Hindu god, Vishnu, are few and far between – ironically, you're more likely to find images of Vishnu in a Buddhist temple than a Hindu one, given that he's regarded as the protector of Buddhism in the island (while according to some schools of Hindu thought, the Buddha was actually an incarnation of Vishnu). There are, however, a number of temples associated with Vishnu's human incarnation Rama and his wife Sita, the hero and heroine of the great Indian epic the *Ramayana*, significant parts of which are set in Sri Lanka *(see box)*.

Temples

Important Siva temples can be found all around the island – at Chilaw, Colombo, Trincomalee, Jaffna and many other places. Sri Lankan temples follow the plan of their Tamil cousins, although only the Nallur Kandaswamy Temple in Jaffna rivals the great temples of the subcontinent in size. The principal gateway is usually marked with a soaring tower, or *gopuram*, usually garishly painted and covered in hundreds of tiny carvings of gods and goddesses – a symbolic representation in stone of the sacred Mt Kailash, the Himalayan home of Siva and myriad other deities. Most Sri Lankan Hindu temples have a simple interior plan, with a central shrine *(cella)* in which the temple's principal image is kept, surrounded by an ambulatory, which is usually lined with further subsidiary shrines. In Siva temples the god is symbolised by the lingam, a traditional phallic symbol, and a yoni, a symbolic representation

of the female sexual organ, placed at the base of the lingam. Skanda's principal symbols are his mount, the peacock and the vel (spear); during festivals worshippers often carry kavadis: paired pieces of semicircular wood or metal decorated with flowers and peacock feathers.

Temples are at their most vibrant during the island's myriad Hindu festivals. Most feature processions in which enormous, colourfully decorated and illuminated chariots are pulled around the streets by hugh crowds of bare-chested devotees – a more free-form alternative to the classic Buddhist *perahera* (parade). The most famous chariot procession occurs during the Vel festi-

val in Colombo (see page 96), though there are many others across the island. Outside festival times, the chariot can usually be found parked somewhere in or outside the temple.

CHRISTIANITY

Unlike Buddhism, Hinduism and Islam, Christianity is the one religion in Sri Lanka which crosses ethnic lines, at least to a small degree. There are no Buddhist Tamils or Hindu Sinhalese, but a small number of Sinhalese and a significant number of Tamils profess Christianity, as do the island's Burghers.

According to local tradition, Christianity was first brought to Sri Lanka by St Thomas, one of the original disciples, who is believed

ABOVE, FROM LEFT: breathtakingly intricate details on a Hindu temple, Matale; a humble coconut becomes a holy offering.

to have introduced the religion to India, where he was martyred (at Mylapore, in modern Chennai). According to local Christian tradition, it is his footprint, rather than the Buddha's, which is imprinted into the rock at the summit of Adam's Peak.

The real history of Christianity in Sri Lanka, however, begins with the arrival of the Portuguese in 1505. The Portuguese were ferociously zealous missionaries, and converting the local population to Roman Catholicism was one of their most cherished missions – one which, sadly, was accompanied by the widespread destruction of Buddhist and Hindu temples.

Christian churches developed an enviable network of schools – today, many of the island's best schools and colleges carry the names of Christian saints, even if nearly all their pupils are Buddhist or Hindu.

and introduced other denominations – including Baptist, Methodist and Pentecostal – to the island.

Christianity today

Perhaps not surprisingly, the proportion of Christian Sri Lankans has fallen since

The preferential treatment accorded Christians by the Portuguese encouraged the conversion of many local people, ancestors of the large number of Christians who live along the west coast from Colombo all the way to Jaffna and whose Portuguese surnames – Perera, Silva, de Soysa and so on – remain common to this day.

Following the Dutch conquest of the island, Roman Catholicism was banned and the Calvinist form of Protestantism introduced, with the establishment of the Dutch Reformed Church – although compared to the Portuguese, the Dutch were more interested in making money than in saving souls. Missionary Christianity revived somewhat under the British, who established the Anglican Church of Ceylon

Independence from over 9 percent to the current 7.5 percent; conversions to Christianity are now rare, except occasionally amongst Plantation Tamils. Ninety percent of the island's Christians are Roman Catholic, and their florid churches and wayside shrines are still a major feature of the landscape along the west coast between Negombo and Jaffna. The island's foremost Christian centre of pilgrimage is in the north, at Madhu, whose church is home to the miracle-working statue of Our Lady of Madhu, images of whom can be found in churches all over the country. The statue's power to protect devotees (against snakebite, in particular) appeals to members of all faiths – the annual Madhu festival (August) regularly attracts half a million visitors.

ISLAM

Islam has a long history in Sri Lanka. The religion arrived in the island soon after its foundation, brought by Arab traders and settlers to the coastal regions – the Kachimalai Mosque in Beruwala is said to mark the spot where the first Muslim settlers landed, sometime in the 8th century. A string of large Muslim trading settlements subsequently grew up all along the western coast from Jaffna to Galle. The Muslims had a virtual monopoly on trade on the island until the Portuguese conquered the coastal provinces and began to persecute them. This forced them to seek protection from the king by the Dutch. Further Muslims arrived from India during the British period, including soldiers and merchants from Tamil Nadu and Kerala who came to the island searching for business opportunities and never left, while other Indian Muslims to arrive during the 19th century included groups of Memon Muslims from Sind (in modern Pakistan) and Bohras and Khoja Muslims from Gujarat in India.

Muslims now make up around 10 percent of the island's population, mainly settled along the west and east coasts in places such as Galle, Aluthgama and Hambantota. Most Sri Lankan Muslims follow the Sunni sect of

of Kandy, who offered them refuge in inland towns such as Gampola, Mawanella, Welimada and Akuressa where many of their descendants still live today, the men instantly recognisable thanks to their distinctive skull caps and beards.

This long-established community of Arab-descended Muslims (formerly known as the Moors, though the term is no longer much used) were subsequently joined by further co-religionists. A wave of so-called "Malay" settlers arrived during the Dutch period from Malay and Java, most of them soldiers brought over

Islam, although there is also a small number of Shi'a Muslims (descended from the Bohra and Khoja settlers from Gujarat). Mosques are a common sight around the coast (there are around 5,000 in Sri Lanka in total), and the call to prayer is a distinctive feature of local life in many places, often competing for attention with amplified chanting from nearby Buddhist temples. All the major Islamic festivals are also observed, including Id-ul-Fitr (see page 97), Milad-un-Nabi (The Prophet's Birthday) and Id-ul-Adha (The Festival of the Sacrifice), although these remain largely private affairs within the Muslim community, and aren't celebrated with the public flamboyance of major Buddhist and Hindu events.

ABOVE, FROM LEFT: Holy Rosary Church, serving the needs of Colombo's Christian community; Muslim men taking a stroll in Galle.

SHRINES AND OFFERINGS

Effigies of demonic spirits and roadside shrines are just two indications of the vital role religious (and supernatural) beliefs play in Sri Lankans' everyday life.

Evidence of the spirit world is everywhere you look in Sri Lanka. Most obviously, it's visible in the innumerable Buddhist temples (not to mention churches, mosques and Hindu temples) that litter the landscape. It can also be seen, less flagrantly but equally pervasively, in many smaller forms. Buddhist roadside shrines sprout up everywhere, usually consisting of a few tiny Buddha statuettes and a scattering of offerings placed beneath a venerable old Bo tree, its branches decorated with colourful prayer flags. Elsewhere, shrines and alms-boxes have been set up next to busy roadsides, and passing drivers will stop and offer a few coins in the hope of a safe journey.

The Christians of the west coast and the Hindus of Jaffna have followed suit: almost every street in Negombo sports a small shrine to a Catholic saint, usually imprisoned in a glass box and festooned with garlands; while roadside shrines to Hindu deities, such as Ganesh and Shiva, can be found throughout the north.

Older and more atavistic traditions have also survived. In the south there's scarcely a house where you won't see, fastened to some part of its facade, a luridly painted wooden mask, usually depicting the pop-eyed Gurulu Raksha – a fearsome mythical bird that is believed to drive away bad spirits and protect against snakes.

ABOVE: pilgrims to Anuradhapura appropriately clad in white.

RIGHT: a colourful family of effigies is set up at the roadside to scar away evil spirits, in particular those that appear as wild elephants.

BELOW: devotees place offerings at the base of the Aukana Buddha

ABOVE: candles symbolise the dispelling of darkness or ignorance through the gift of light.

LEFT: many of the Catholic saints introduced by the Portuguese have become the object of veneration, even by non-Christians.

ALMS-GIVING

Buddhist monks and nuns are forbidden from preparing their own food, and are not supposed to eat after midday, a form of daily fasting intended to sharpen their physical and spiritual discipline. But there's no danger of going hungry, thanks to the practice of *dana* or alms-giving.

Providing food for monks is a religious duty for lay Buddhists by which they earn merit, and the possibility of achieving a more advanced rebirth on the spiritual ladder. The ancient origins of Sri Lankan alms-giving are shown by the vast "rice boats" found in the ruins of Mihintale, which were filled with donations of food. Today a monk is likely to have a regular lunch appointment with a devout family who are honoured to lay an extra place at table. Others go from door to door to beg for their morning meal.

ABOVE: food is placed as offerings in front of a Buddha statue at Gangaramaya Temple in Colombo on a *poya* or full moon day – deemed significant as many events in the Buddha's life are said to have occurred on these days.

RIGHT: the lotus flower is sacred to Buddhists: seven of them bloomed as Buddha took his first steps, and again at the moment when he reached Enlightenment.

FESTIVALS

Sri Lanka's festival calendar holds a wealth of religious pageantry, with spectacular processions, caparisoned elephants, and drummers and dancers aplenty.

Sri Lankans sometimes claim that they have more festivals than any other country, and though it's difficult to prove the veracity of this claim, there's no mistaking the number and importance of the religious celebrations and other festivals which regularly bring life on the island to a standstill. The current calendar lists 25 public holidays, including various religious festivals celebrated by the island's Buddhists, Hindus, Christians and Muslims, as well as secular holidays such as May Day and Independence Day, while smaller religious holidays and temple festivals are observed in various places around the island.

Most of the island's festivals are religious. Not surprisingly, Buddhist festivals take pride of place, from the *Poya* day holidays that are observed every full moon to the great *peraheras* (parades) held at Kandy, Colombo and elsewhere, in which hundreds of drummers, dancers, acrobats and other performers march through the streets accompanied by dozens of colourfully dressed elephants. Hindu festivals also figure largely, from Colombo's spectacular Vel festival and the great temple festivals of Jaffna and the north, to the remarkable Kataragama festival, where devotees of Skanda walk on hot coals or pierce their flesh with skewers to demonstrate their devotion to the god. Muslim and Christian festivals tend to be more private affairs, although even these can sometimes attract huge crowds. Many festivals cross religious and ethnic divides, combining elements of different faiths and attracting visitors of all religious persuasions.

Full moon (*Poya*) days are considered particularly auspicious by Sri Lanka's Buddhists; all 12 are public holidays, and the most important ones, especially Vesak, rank amongst the island's most significant festivals. The fact that *Poya* days and other Buddhist festivals follow the lunar calendar means that exact dates vary by a week or two from year to year. Muslim festivals follow a lunar calendar without the compensatory days that are inserted into the Buddhist lunar calendar, meaning that festival dates fall about 11 days earlier from year to year, gradually moving backwards through the calendar.

The word Poya derives from the Pali and Sanskrit uposatha, meaning a day of fasting, and many shops and most businesses are closed on Poya days.

New Year

The Sinhalese and Tamil New Year (13–14 April) is celebrated by Hindus and Buddhists alike. The festival was originally agricultural, marking the end of the harvest and the beginning of the southwest monsoon, and old rituals – such as lighting the hearth and eating for the first time in the new year – are still carried out at astrologically auspicious times by more traditional islanders, while horoscopes are also cast and special foods made and offered to the gods. Businesses close for the duration and many people return to their villages, put on new clothes and celebrate with games and fireworks. Nuwara

cars are decorated with streamers and garlands, shops and streets decked out with myriad paper lanterns. Tiny clay coconut-oil lamps are lit in villages, while in the cities illuminated structures called *pandals* are put up, with richly decorated panels depicting events in the Buddha's life.

Because it is considered meritorious to offer gifts of food and drink during the festival, you will find specially constructed roadside booths (*dansal*) where both are offered free of charge. The fare on offer ranges from rice and curry to Vesak sweetmeats. The devout dress in white and visit their local temples to spend the day performing religious observances, fasting and praying.

Eliya is particularly busy over New Year and the weeks before and after, with a lively programme of sporting and social events such as horse racing, golf tournaments and a mini-carnival.

Vesak

Vesak, celebrated on the day of the full moon in May, is the most hallowed of Buddhist festivals, celebrating the Buddha's birth, enlightenment and death, all of which are believed to have occurred on this one day – like Christmas, Easter and Whitsun rolled into one. Buses and

ABOVE, FROM LEFT: a monk robes a statue at a Colombo temple during the holiest Buddhist festival of Vesak; a *Poya* day dancer..

THE NEW WAVE OF FESTIVALS

Not all Sri Lankan festivals are religious. The Galle Literary Festival (late Jan/early Feb; www.galle literaryfestival.com), first held in 2007, has already established itself as a major feature on the international literary scene, attracting leading authors from around the world, along with eminent Sri Lankan scribes. The success of this has inspired a spate of other new festivals ranging from the Colombo Art Biennale (Feb; colomboartbiennale. com) through to the Electric Peacock Music Festival (Dec; www.electricpeacockfestival.com), and the Hikka Beach Fest (late July/early Aug), during which revellers take over the beach at Hikkaduwa.

> Ask a pilgrim to Kataragama what time he plans to get there and he will reply: "In God's good time." He will not presume to have any control over his plans.

Poson

Poson *Poya* (June) commemorates the introduction of Buddhism to Sri Lanka. The day is celebrated at temples all over the island, but the biggest celebrations are at Mihintale, where the Buddhist emissary Mahinda converted King Devanampiya in 247 BC, establish-

and more lavish over the 10 days of the festival, until by the final night it has swollen to include a cast of hundreds of elephants and thousands of dancers, drummers, fire-eaters, acrobats and many others – an extraordinary sight without parallel anywhere else in Sri Lanka, if not the whole of Asia.

Kataragama Festival

Held at the same time as Kandy's Esala Perahera, the Kataragama Festival is the main event of the year at the remote southern pilgrimage town of Kataragama. Whereas the main focus of the Esala Perahera is on spec-

ing Buddhism as the national religion of the Sinhalese.

Esala Perahera

The lunar month of Esala is a month for festivals and *peraheras* all around the island. Easily the finest and most famous is the Esala Perahera held at Kandy over the 10 days leading up to the Esala *Poya* day (late July or early August). The festival dates back to ancient Anuradhapura, when the Tooth Relic (see page 192) was taken through the city in procession, and the pattern continues to this day, with the relic carried at the head of an enormous procession which winds its way round and round the city by night. The *perahera* becomes gradually longer

tacle and pageant, the Kataragama Festival is more about individual acts of devotion and penance – much more Hindu in inspiration, although the town and festival attract pilgrims from all four of the island's main faiths. Devotees perform ritual acts of self-mutilation, piercing their cheeks, arms, legs or backs with skewers as an act of devotion to the god Kataragama, who is believed by Hindus to be a form of Skanda (also known as Murugan), a son of Siva.

Vel

Another Skanda-inspired event is the Hindu festival of Vel, held in Colombo (July or August) to venerate the god's trident (*vel*).

Every year, Skanda's *vel* is placed in a great gilded temple chariot and pulled by hundreds of devotees dressed in white and smeared with holy ash. The procession starts at the Sea Street temple in the Pettah district and moves on to a temple in either Bambalapitiya or Wellawatta, in the south of the city. The journey across town proceeds at a snail's pace and takes a whole day.

Other festivals honouring Skanda are held elsewhere in the island at this time, especially around Jaffna, the largest being the Nallur Festival, held at the great Nallur Kandaswamy Temple on the edge of Jaffna. This mammoth

to welcome Lakshmi, the goddess of prosperity – symbolic of the triumph of good over evil.

Id-ul-Fitr

The most important Muslim festival is the celebratory Id-ul-Fitr (due to be held on 8 August 2013; date changes annually by 11 days) marking the end of Ramadan, the month of religious observances during which devout Muslims observe a daily fast from dawn till dusk.

Duruthu Perahera

The Duruthu Perahera, held at the Raja Maha Vihara temple in Kelaniya, 8km (5 miles) outside

event lasts 26 days, featuring chariot processions around town, and attracts thousands of pilgrims during its spectacular final days, including a devoted few who subject themselves to bloody acts of self-mutilation and physical penance to express their love of Skanda.

Deepavali

Deepavali, the Hindu festival of lights, is celebrated in late October or early November. Thousands of flickering oil lamps are lit to celebrate Rama's return after his period of exile and

ABOVE, FROM LEFT: the Esala Perahera in Kandy; Sri Lankan Hindus offer prayers at a Colombo temple on the occasion of the four-day Pongal festival.

Colombo, is second only to the Kandy Perahera in spectacle. Staged annually in January, the *perahera* commemorates the first visit of the Buddha to Sri Lanka over 2,500 years ago, with a lavish procession of elephants, dancers and drummers.

Pongal

Here at least is one festival you can count on taking place on the same day every year (14 January), as Hindus celebrate in honour of the sun god. The word *ponkkol* means "boiling over" and, after worship at the kovil (temple), a huge pot of rice is ceremonially cooked in spicy sweetened milk and left to boil over. The direction of the spilling indicates good or bad luck in the coming year – and the rest makes a delicious sacramental feast.

DANCE AND MUSIC

Sri Lankan dance ranges from the flamboyant
classical traditions of Kandy to the populist
dance-dramas and exorcism ceremonies
of the south.

Music plays a relatively small role in traditional Sri Lankan culture, a reflection of the arts' generally low place in the Buddhist scheme of things. What the island lacks in the way of traditional vocal and instrumental music, however, it more than makes up for with its rich dance traditions and by its extraordinary style of drumming, one of the loudest and most exuberant in the world.

The traditional dances of Sri Lanka are generally divided into two groups: up-country, or Kandyan, encompassing the aristocratic classical dance traditions of the former Kandyan kingdom, with their lavishly costumed dancers and highly stylised choreography; and low-country, covering the much more populist traditions of the south including masked *kolam* dance-dramas (usually a satirical portrayal of village life) and exorcism ceremonies.

Kandyan drumming

The performing arts of the Kandyan kingdom started life in the temple, with drumming and dancing enacted in honour of the gods – it's thought that the kingdom's dances were first performed for a deity called Kohomba (who is still believed to be the god who inspired the *ves*, Kandy's most famous dance). Kandy's distinctive style of drumming and dancing subsequently spread from the temple into the cultural mainstream. Drummers still accompany the thrice-daily pujas at the Temple of the Tooth in Kandy and can also now be seen (and heard) in numerous other ceremonies and celebrations across the island, ranging from traditional festivals to tourist beach weddings.

Sri Lankan drummers are usually deployed in ensembles *(hewisi)* of anything between three and, in the largest festivals, 50 performers. Many ensembles display incredible levels of virtuosity, and the extraordinary sound of a group of top Kandyan drummers in full flight is one of the island's most distinctive and pulse-quickening experiences. Solo wind instruments are also occasionally employed, but most performances feature drums on their own, compensating for the total absence of melodic interest with a barrage of extraordinarily complex rhythmic effects. The style of Kandyan drumming is quite unlike the equally virtuoso, but far more metrically regular, style of North Indian classical music. Instead, Kandyan drumming is distinguished by its frequent sudden changes of tempo and highly irregular rhythmic patterns which ebb and flow in a series of percussive onslaughts – the almost telepathic coordination displayed by the members of top drum groups during performances can seem almost magical.

There are various types of traditional drum. The most important is the classic Kandyan drum, the *geta bera* (literally "boss drum"; called the *yak bera* in the low country). This is a double-headed drum, measuring exactly 67cm (26in) long, slightly bigger in the middle than at the ends. The drum is suspended from the player's waist by a piece of rope and played with both hands. Different skins are used for the two drum heads (monkey or goat on one side, for example, and

oboe-like instrument (not unlike the South Indian *nagaswaram*), whose player performs a set of simple melodic patterns above the riotous drumming. Like the dancers they usually accompany, Kandyan drummers wear a traditional costume: white turban, breastplate, broad waistband and copious sarong. Important musical points are signalled with an accompanying shake of the head, which sends the topknot of the turban flying through the air in a sympathetic flourish.

Kandyan dancing

There are various different genres of Kandyan dance, with slight differences in costume and

cow on the other) to produce contrasting tones. The shorter but larger *daule* is another double-headed drum which is hung from the player's waist and played with a stick in the right hand and the palm of the left hand. The *tammettana bera* consists of a pair of tiny kettledrums (often erroneously described as tom-toms) tied together and beaten with a pair of sticks. You're likely to see ensembles using all three types of drum during the bigger dance shows at Kandy, sometimes along with a *horanava*, a quadruple-reed

ABOVE, FROM LEFT: a dancer performs during the Daha Ata Sanniya ritual, held to exorcise disease from the body; a Kandyan dancer, in traditional, silver-laden *ves* costume.

THE VES DANCE

Most spectacular of all the Kandyan dances is the ves. Performed solely by men, this is the pinnacle of the Kandyan dancer's art, featuring limb-contorting feats of athleticism, back flips, high-kicks and pirouettes combined with carefully stylised hand and feet movements. The overall effect is of a kind of hyperactive but carefully choreographed abandon which is sometimes compared to the famous *kathakali* dance of South India. The elaborate costume is equally stunning, with the traditional dancer's costume topped by an extraordinary silver crown-like headpiece, an item which is considered sacred to the god Kohomba.

> Exorcism ceremonies, or bali (also called thovil or balithovil) can last all night, with neighbours and relatives in attendance, and involve drumming, dancing, sacrificial ritual and chanting.

choreography: the five main types are *ves*, *pantheru*, *udekki*, *naiyandi* and *vannam*. The dancers are mainly men, who wear striking, elaborately decorated costumes (each varies depending on the dance being performed) featuring beadwork chest decorations, waistband, beaded necklaces, silver chains, brass shoulder plates,

such as *assadhrusa* (in praise of the Buddha) and *uduhara* (expressing the majesty of the king).

Low-country devil dances

Sri Lankans traditionally believe that illnesses can be caused by malevolent spirits, and the south has developed a rich tradition of "devil dances" used in exorcism ceremonies (bali) to propitiate and expel such demons. The "possessed" could be a sick person, a fisherman whose nets are always empty, or a farmer with a poor harvest. The basic aim of the ceremony is to summon up the troublesome spirit, make offerings to it and then ask it to leave the afflicted person. Dancers wear

anklets and more. Dancers are sometimes required to sing and/or play musical instruments whilst dancing, as in the *pantheru* dance, during which they beat time using small, skinless tambourines, while in the *udekki* they play small hourglass-shaped drums.

The *vannams* (from the Sinhala word *varnana*, meaning descriptive praise) are somewhat different in concept and began life as songs, before developing into dances. There are 18 classical *vannams*, variously inspired by nature, history and legend, each of which describes a certain emotion or object (*rasaya*). The *vannams* include animal-inspired dances such as *mayura* (peacock), *gajaga* (elephant), *sinharaja* (lion) and *naga* (cobra), as well as more abstract themes

gruesome masks to represent particular spirits or diseases, and the principal dancer is said to become possessed by the spirit he is attempting to appease, while the person suffering from the illness might also become drawn into the dancing. It's almost impossible for a casual visitor to see one of these very private village ceremonies, though the masks (see page 124) used in them have become Sri Lanka's top tourist souvenir.

Kolam and folk dances

Masks are also a feature of the south's other unique art form, *kolam*. A type of dance-drama, *kolam* may originally have developed as an offshoot of devil dancing, though it subsequently developed a markedly more Buddhist aspect. Traditional *kolam* performances feature a sequence of dances of various genres: satirical portrayals of lecherous villagers or drunken drummers; friendly demons and wild animals; stately royal dances and Buddhist sermons.

In addition to southern *kolam* and *bali* dances, there are also various folk dances associated with local rural activities and festivals; jazzed-up versions of these have become popular as part of the dance shows performed in Kandy and elsewhere. Common folk dances include the *leekeli* (stick dance), *kulu* (harvest dance), *kalageldi* (pot dance) and *raban*, a particularly popular genre (although it's more of a circus trick than a dance), during

while dancing and drumming can occasionally be seen at other temples around town – try the Vishnu Devale in Kandy.

The easiest way to get an introductory taster is to attend one of the three "cultural shows" that are staged nightly at venues around Kandy (the YMBA; Kandyan Arts and Crafts Association and Lake Club). These are undeniably touristy, but well performed. Programmes generally comprise a pot-pourri of up-country and low-country dances featuring alternating casts of male and female dancers: you'll typically get to see *ves* and *pantheru* dances, a *vannam*, a southern masked devil dance, and a folk dance

which *rabans* (a flat drum – it looks like a thick wooden plate) are spun in the air on fingers or sticks balanced on the hands or head, or in the mouth – a real adept can keep up to eight spinning from various parts of the body simultaneously.

Where to see dancing

Kandyan dancing (which originated in the Central Highlands region) and drumming can still be seen in its original context during the great Esala Perahera festival in Kandy, and at other festivals around the island. Drummers perform thrice daily at the Temple of the Tooth,

(the drum-spinning *raban* dance is a universal favourite, as is the *kulu* harvest dance), rounded off with a spot of fire-walking. Touring dance troupes also perform regularly at the larger hotels, though obviously it's very much a matter of chance whether you happen to coincide with one. Expect a similar medley of dances to those performed in the cultural shows in Kandy.

The Bandu Wijesooriya Dance Academy (tel: 091 225 8948; www.banduwijesooriyadanceacademy.org) in Ambalagoda, opposite the Mask Museum, stages full performances of southern dances about six times a year; alternatively, you can usually watch students rehearsing in the afternoons (Mon–Fri from around 3.30pm). Ask at the Mask Museum for details (see page 174).

ABOVE, FROM LEFT: traditional drumming during the Esala Perahera, Kandy; Kandyan women dancing.

ART AND ARCHITECTURE

From the great stupas of Anuradhapura to the colonial townscapes of Galle and Colombo, Sri Lanka's art and architecture bear witness to a wealth of influences.

Sri Lanka's enormously varied art and architecture have been shaped by two key factors. The first is the nation's Buddhist heritage, which has provided a cultural benchmark for the island's artists and architects since the conversion of King Devanampiya Tissa in 247 BC right up to the present day. The second is the influence of the myriad foreign invaders who have shaped the island's history, from the Tamil soldiers, traders and craftsmen who established and embellished the great early Sinhalese capital of Polonnaruwa through to the Dutch and British colonisers, whose buildings still form a major part of the island's architectural heritage.

The artistic history of Sri Lanka closely reflects political developments in the island as a whole, and the changing influences of different cultures and ethnic groups. The key artistic phases roughly correspond to the island's major historical periods: the Anuradhapura Period (247 BC–AD 993); the Polonnaruwa Period (993–1215); the Kandyan Period (roughly 1400–1815); the Dutch and British colonial periods (roughly 1650–1948); and the modern era from Independence to the present day.

The Anuradhapura period

The art and architecture of the Anuradhapura period was almost entirely religious in inspiration. Buddhism played a key role in the political and cultural life of Anuradhapura, providing the ancient Sinhalese with a powerful sense of identity and cultural purpose. The city's kings, for their part, were expected to

LEFT: Wewurukannala Vihara near Dikwella.
RIGHT: the post office building at Nuwara Eliya.

express their devotion to the faith by organising the creation of religious monuments, devoting huge resources and enormous manpower to raise the sequence of great monasteries, stupas and other religious buildings that still dot the ancient city today. These early building works represented a collective creative effort rarely matched in human history since the construction of the Egyptian pyramids, which the great Anuradhapuran stupas rival in size.

The pre-eminent physical symbol of early Buddhism in Sri Lanka is the stupa – one of the first acts of King Devanampiya Tissa on being converted to the faith in 247 BC was to erect the Thuparama stupa in the heart of Anuradhapura. Stupas (or dagobas, as they're

There are numerous subtle variations in stupa style and design. Traditionally, six different basic shapes are recognised, from the perfectly hemispherical dagobas of Anuradhapura to the more elongated bell-shaped stupas of modern times.

usually known in Sri Lanka) traditionally enshrine relics of the Buddha or other illustrious holy persons, serving as physical symbols of the Buddhist faith and objects of religious contemplation. Their elegantly simple domed shape has attracted various symbolic

interpretations over time. The popular explanation is that the Buddha himself, when asked what form a monument to the faith should take, folded his robe into a square and placed his upturned begging bowl and walking stick on top of it. The metaphysical explanation is that the stupa is a symbol of the physical and spiritual realms, with the main dome, or *anda*, built in the shape of a hill and said to represent Mount Meru, the sacred peak at the heart of the Buddhist universe, while the spire (or *chattravli*) symbolises the cosmic pillar, which connects earth and heaven, and leads upwards towards Nirvana.

Grand stupas

The relatively modest Thuparama at Anuradhapura was soon eclipsed by three far grander stupas – the Jetavana, Abhayagiri and Ruvanvalisaya – larger than anything in the ancient world save the two biggest Egyptian pyramids. The tallest, the Jetavana, originally stood around 120 metres (390ft) tall and still tops 70 metres (230ft) and used, according to the estimate of Victorian archaeologist Emerson Tennant, more than 90 million bricks. It remains the world's largest structure made entirely of bricks and provides a potent symbol, not only of the Buddhist faith, but of the overwhelming importance that religion played in ancient Sri Lanka.

The design of stupas continued to evolve throughout the Anuradhapuran period and beyond, although no later structures, except the Rankot Vihara at Polonnaruwa, rival the great stupas of Anuradhapura in size.

MOONSTONES

One of the most distinctive forms of Sinhalese art is the moonstone, a decorative semicircular slab of polished granite at the entrance to important shrines. The moonstone serves as a kind of spiritual doorstep, concentrating the mind of worshippers walking over it into the shrine and providing an allegorical representation of the passage from the distractions of the physical world to nirvana.

The finest examples are found at Polonnaruwa and Anuradhapura. Details vary from stone to stone, but some or all of the following elements are usually present. The outermost ring shows flames (symbolising desire). Within these can be found representations of

four animals: the elephant (birth); the horse (old age); the lion (sickness); and the bull (death). Surrounding these animals are vines, or snakes, representing the attachment to life, and geese (purity). Having crossed these bands, one arrives at the far side of the stone, and a carved lotus: the achievement of Nirvana.

Designs evolved through the Polonnaruwan and Kandyan periods. The lion (royal symbol of the Sinhalese) and the bull (an important Hindu symbol) were increasingly omitted, being considered too important to step on. Later the moonstone lost most of its symbolism, and even its semicircular shape, evolving into a decorative device embellished with floral patterns.

Early Buddha images

Not all early Sinhalese art was purely monumental. At the opposite end of the spectrum from the city's vast stupas, the craftsmen of Anuradhapura also achieved remarkable levels of artistry in the execution of small-scale carvings – Buddha images, moonstones, *naga* stones, guardstones, *makara toranas* and other designs, both religious and decorative. Buddha statues can be found all around the ancient city, such as the famous Samadhi Buddha, a serene figure that symbolises many of the main features of Sinhalese Buddhist sculpture, seated in the meditation *(samadhi)* posture (a particular

is also rich in so-called "guardstones" *(dvarapalas)*, images of *nagarajas* (snake kings, shaded by cobra hoods), often carved in incredible detail, which were placed next to the entrances of temples and royal palaces to protect against evil influences. *Nagarajas* are often accompanied by dwarfs (symbolising wealth), while elephants and other more unusual animals can often be seen, such as the playfully naturalistic elephants carved onto the rocks by the Royal Pleasure Gardens or the remarkable sculpture portraits on display at the Isurumuniya temple. Another mythical animal which became an ever-present artistic motif during the Polonnaruwan and

favourite of Sri Lankan sculptors), and modelled with gently rounded, humanised features – a far cry from the more outlandish representations of the Buddha found in other parts of South and Southeast Asia.

The full artistry of Anuradhapura's sculptors, however, can be seen in the other forms of stone carving which abound throughout the city. Most intricate are the remarkable moonstones *(see box)* which were traditionally placed at the threshold of shrines and embellished with minutely detailed depictions of lions, bulls and other animals carved in low relief. The city

Kandyan eras is the *makara*, a composite monster formed from a combination of fish, lion, monkey, elephant, peacock, pig and crocodile. Two *makaras* joined to a central dragon's mouth create the ubiquitous *makara torana* (dragon arch), used to frame doorways and statues in temples all over the island.

The Polonnaruwa period

In 993, the South Indian Chola dynasty invaded Sri Lanka, razed Anuradhapura, and established a new capital at Polonnaruwa, from where they reigned for most of the following century until evicted by the Sinhalese. The Sinhalese made the city their new capital in turn, and created a sequence of buildings to rival the

ABOVE, FROM LEFT: the Ruwanweliseya stupa at Anuradhapura; a classic moonstone at Kataragama.

Buddhist Mudras

Buddha statues are traditionally highly stylised works of art which aim to represent the Buddha's transcendental qualities.

Buddha statues aim to show the Buddha's transcendental qualities, rather than attempting to depict a human personality (unlike, say, Christian representations of Jesus). There are detailed rules concerning the correct

was meditating and on the point of achieving enlightenment, the demon Mara attempted to break his concentration by shaking the earth beneath him.

Vitarka mudra (Gesture of Explanation pose) shows the Buddha teaching: with the thumb and forefinger of one hand he forms a wheel, representing the cycle of dharma. Used in both sitting and standing positions.

Parinirvana mudra shows the Buddha reclining at the moment of his death (or, more correctly, passing into nirvana). More common in Sri Lanka, however, is the very similar sleeping pose. There are five subtle iconographic differences between

creation of Buddha images, which artists are expected to adhere to strictly. Statues traditionally show the Buddha in one of various canonical poses, or mudras, either standing, seated, or reclining. Some of the most widely used in Sri Lankan art are:

Abhaya mudra (Have no Fear pose) shows the Buddha standing with his right palm raised in a gesture of reassurance.

Samadhi mudra shows the Buddha seated in meditation in the lotus position, with hands joined on his lap.

Bhumisparsha mudra (Earth Witness pose) shows the Buddha seated, touching the ground with the fingers of his left hand. The mudra commemorates the moment when, as the Buddha

the two poses – for example, in the former, the Buddha's feet are not in a straight line and the hem at the bottom of his robe is uneven.

Despite the importance ascribed to these traditional poses, not all Buddha images are sculpted in one of these positions. The famous Aukana Buddha, for instance, is in the unusual *Asisa*, or Blessing, position, with hand turned sideways on to the viewer; while the equally famous standing figure at the Gal Vihara, with arms crossed over his chest, is unique in Sri Lanka and follows no established pattern whatsoever.

ABOVE: a reclining Buddha statue at Anuradhapura. This is an example of the Parinirvana mudra, when the Buddha passed into nirvana.

abandoned Anuradhapura (although in the event Polonnaruwa endured only a fraction of the time of its illustrious predecessor). Many of the religious monuments at Polonnaruwa are a direct continuation of the artistic traditions of Anuradhapura – the Sinhalese continued to build huge stupas, such as the Rankot Vihara and Demala Maha Seya, and make beautifully carved moonstones and guardstones, but new influences and artistic styles also made their presence felt.

Politically and culturally the Polonnaruwa period was marked by prolonged and profound Indian influence – even after the expulsion of the Cholas, Tamil traders, soldiers and craftsmen played an important role in the life of the city. A new, hybridised style gradually developed, as Buddhist shrines began to borrow many of the architectural motifs traditionally associated with South Indian Hindu temples. Perhaps the most remarkable example of this composite style is the temple at Nalanda, north of Kandy – a purely Buddhist temple built in a completely Hindu design (even including a couple of faded tantric carvings). In Polonnaruwa this new hybrid style can be seen in the city's three *gediges* – the Thuparama, Tivanka Patamaghara and Lankatilaka – heavy-set rectangular stone structures with thick walls embellished with characteristically South Indian pillars and niched windows.

The Quadrangle

The eclectic array of stylistic influences at work in Polonnaruwa can best be seen in the remarkable Quadrangle. The extraordinary collection of buildings here ranges from the traditional Sinhalese shrines of the Hatadage through to the Indian-style Thuparama and the bizarre Satmahal Pasada, a unique, ziggurat-like shrine that looks more like an ancient Khmer temple from Angkor rather than anything remotely Sri Lankan. The beautiful Lotus Mandapa, with its delicately curved pillars (modelled on lotus flowers) and unusual stone "fence", is another unique architectural curiosity. Best of all, however, is the exquisite Vatadage, perhaps the most beautiful building in the island, designed to hold the famous Tooth Relic, with rich carvings on its circular outer walls and four Buddhas placed carefully within.

RIGHT: the Water Gardens at Sigiriya.

Buddha statues

Another notable development during the Polonnaruwan period was a new-found craze for building enormous Buddha statues, such as those at the Lankatilaka, a standing figure that completely fills the lofty, two-storey building in which it's housed; and the four great Buddhas of the Gal Vihara. Further massive Buddha statues from the same period can also be found across the island at Aukana, Sasseruwa, Buduruwagala and Maligawila. The new emphasis on such sculptural collosi may be a result of the Mahayana Buddhist influence, which enjoyed a brief vogue in the island

during this period. Mahayana teachings placed greater emphasis than the Theravada tradition on the Buddha's superhuman, transcendental powers – meaning that statues of the master became increasingly huge. This culminated in the 16-metre (52ft) high standing image at Buduruwagala, although even this is dwarfed by the giant modern Buddhas at Dambulla, Wehurukannala, Weherehena and elsewhere, which touch the 50-metre (165ft) mark.

Rocks and water

Not all Sinhalese architecture, however, displayed the grandeur and formality of the great monastic and palace complexes of Anuradhapura and Polonnaruwa. Many early shrines were built within caves or between rock outcrops, as at Aluvihara, Mulkirigala and, most famously, Dambulla, to name just three. As well as their obvious practical function of protecting and supporting buildings, the use of massive rocks as either a structural or decorative element lends a striking naturalistic quality to much early Sinhalese design, as at the Boulder Gardens in Sigiriya, with its scatter of huge rocks, rock-cut shrines and monastic cave dwellings.

Water also played a major role in Sinhalese design. Superbly carved bathing pools can be found all over Anuradhapura and Polonnaruwa, ranging from the vast Et Pokuna at the former to the tiny, beautifully stylised Lotus Pond just south of the Tivanka Patamaghara at the latter. Water channels, moats and ponds were also important features of forest monasteries such as Ritigala and Arankele, and also (especially) at Sigiriya, whose elegant water gardens resemble a medieval South Asian Versailles, with a symmetrical design of ponds linked with water channels and dotted with fountains.

The Kandyan period

Following the fall and subsequent abandonment of Polonnaruwa in the 13th century, the

TEMPLES

Sri Lanka's Buddhist temples vary enormously, but most contain the following elements. At the heart of the temple lies the image house (*pilimage* or *patimaghara*), home to the temple's principal Buddha images. Nearby you'll generally find a Bo tree enclosure *(bodhighara)*, a feature unique to Sri Lanka, comprising a Bo tree, its branches usually strung with prayer flags. Larger temples will often have one or more subsidiary shrines *(devales)* to other deities considered important – such as Vishnu, a protector of Buddhism on the island.

Large monastic temples will also have a *poyage* (literally Full Moon House, though sometimes translated as "chapter house") in which the temple's monks gather on full moon *(poya)* days to recite Buddhist scriptures and confess breaches of monastic discipline. Some Kandyan temples also have a *digge*, usually an open-air pavilion, in which drummers and dancers attached to the temple traditionally perform. Other types of building occasionally seen are the *vatadage*, a circular shrine comprising a miniature stupa surrounded by pillars and topped by a roof; and the *gedige*, a name used to describe the thickly walled and decorated stone shrines found at Polonnaruwa, Nalanda and a few other places. Typically, the entire temple is enclosed by a white perimeter wall, sometimes fancifully decorated with low-relief carvings of elephant heads.

A vihara (or viharaya) is a Buddhist temple; a kovil is a Hindu temple. A devale is a shrine devoted to a particular deity, either freestanding or part of a larger temple. Devales are nominally Buddhist, though often show strong Hindu influence.

Sinhalese gradually drifted south towards the hill country. This phase of Sri Lankan history was marked by a steady decline in the power of the Sinhalese kings. The island's monarchs no longer had the manpower and revenues to pour into major building projects, and even the most striking monument from this period – the great stone stairway at Yapahuwa (see page 223) – is relatively modest compared to previous undertakings.

From around the 16th century the Sinhalese finally established a secure new capital in the middle of the inaccessible hills at Kandy. At last free from Indian interference, and protected by the hills from the newly arrived Europeans on the coast, the city of Kandy developed a rich cultural tradition exemplified by its remarkable performing arts (see page 98). The kingdom's art and architecture also began to develop their own distinctive character, although the city's buildings were still relatively modest by the standards of Anuradhapura and Polonnaruwa.

Wood, rather than stone, became the principal building material, often featuring elaborately designed pillars decorated with carvings of drummers, dancers, lions, geese and other motifs (as at numerous temples in the Kandy area such as the Embekke Devale and the Padeniya Raja Mahavihara). Buildings were usually topped by slightly Chinese-looking hipped roofs, and their sides sometimes left open to create elegant pavilions – the Audience Chamber in the Royal Palace complex at Kandy is a classic example.

Murals

The Kandyan era also saw a renewed interest in the art of murals. Painting had already been long established in Sri Lanka, as proven by the world-famous Sigiriya Damsels, dating back to the 5th century BC, a marvellous picture gallery of 20-odd celestial nymphs painted halfway up the sheer rockface of Sigiriya rock. But – damsels excepted – little has survived from earlier eras. Under the patronage of the Kandyan kings, temples all over Sri Lanka were restored and embellished, with marvellous murals often added. These are typically arranged in strip panels and feature a variety of Buddhist subjects such as *peraheras* (religious parades) or scenes from the *jataka* stories (fables describing the previous lives of the Buddha), usually executed in

vivid shades of red – there are good examples at Mulkirigala and at several temples around Kandy, including a magnificent sequence at Degaldoruwa.

Easily the finest Sri Lankan murals, however, can be found at the famous rock temples of Dambulla, especially in Cave 2, a kind of Sri Lankan Sistine Chapel. Here large areas of the ceiling have been covered in a sequence of magnificent murals showing, most memorably, the Buddha's celebrated tangle with Mara (the *Defeat of Mara*, or *Mara Parajaya*) and subsequent temptation by a bevy of comely maidens (*Daughters of Mara*), among many other scenes from popular Buddhist mythology.

ABOVE, FROM LEFT: circular Relic House at Medirigiriya; the murals in the cave temple at Dambulla have been skilfully painted to follow the contours of the rock.

Colonial architecture

Fresh influence from abroad arrived in the shape of the three colonial powers which successively ruled Sri Lanka from the 16th to 20th centuries. Scarcely any physical evidence of the Portuguese period survives, but their successors, the Dutch, left a rich architectural legacy, exemplified by the wonderful Fort at Galle, a perfectly preserved colonial townscape of low-rise villas enclosed by enormous walls and bastions. The Dutch also established the prototype for the classic Sri Lankan villa, centred around one (or more) inner courtyards, and with thick walls, which kept the interior cool, large street-banks, post offices, official residences and the like, a generic and rather bland neoclassical style was usually preferred – good examples include the National Museum building in Colombo and the Queen's Hotel in Kandy, along with the many grandiose (though now sadly more-or-less derelict) edifices that line the streets of Colombo's Fort district. Their domestic architecture was perhaps more successful, and countless chintzy little British-era bungalows still dot the island, often decorated with fanciful *mal lali* (floral panel) wooden eaves that give some residences a positively fairy-tale appearance.

facing verandahs *(stoeps)* and big overhanging tiled roofs supported by columns (although this plan itself owed much to traditional Sinhalese manor houses, or *walauwes*, and the residences of Arab traders). This pattern was much copied throughout the colonial period, and later reinvigorated by modern architects such as Geoffrey Bawa. The Dutch also built a number of important churches, such as those at Galle, Matara and on Wolfendahl Street in Colombo, plus a string of large forts around the coast at places including Galle, Matara, Batticaloa, Kalpitiya and Jaffna.

British banks and bungalows

British contributions to Sri Lankan architecture were mixed. For public buildings such as

It was also during the British period that the island acquired many of the florid neo-Baroque Roman Catholic churches that line the west coast from Negombo all the way up to Jaffna. Imported architectural styles also had an unexpectedly strong influence on local temple design, and many Buddhist shrines built during the colonial era sport incongruous foreign touches – anything from classical Greek columns and pediments through to little free-standing bell towers built in imitation of European churches. Similarly, many colonial-era mosques, such as the principal mosques at Galle and Matara, resemble Baroque churches far more than traditional Islamic buildings.

Bawa

Modern Sri Lankan architecture has been dominated by the work of Geoffrey Bawa (1919–2003), one of the later 20th century's foremost Asian architects, who virtually single-handedly created a style of Sri Lankan architecture which continues to shape the work of many younger designers. Bawa's earliest buildings date from the early 1960s: a striking series of very contemporary-looking constructions, in a style loosely known as "Tropical Modernism", built in collaboration with Danish architect Ulrik Plesner.

Bawa gradually became dissatisfied with this imported idiom, however, and began using rooms to avoid the need for energy-hungry air conditioning, along with spacious verandahs and large overhanging eaves to protect against monsoonal downpours and the tropical sun. The seamless blending of modern and traditional forms, the use of local materials, and an overriding concern for the environmental context of his buildings lends them a unique style and charm, and also served as a vital example of ecologically sound design in an island whose natural beauty was – and still is – at severe risk from insensitive development.

Many of Bawa's finest works were hotels, mostly found along the west coast. This means

more traditional materials and styles. A concern with nature and the natural setting of his buildings became a guiding principle, producing structures designed to blend seamlessly with their environment – typified by the spectacular Kandalama Hotel near Dambulla, built up against a rock outcrop and almost completely buried beneath a thick layer of tropical vegetation. The forms of Dutch colonial villas and traditional Sinhalese *walauwe* (houses) were also revived by Bawa, with the use of large courtyards and open-sided interconnecting

that visitors can enjoy his work at a very immediate level, whether grand creations such as the Kandalama or Lighthouse hotels (at Dambulla and Galle), or more intimate establishments such as Club Villa and the Villa Mohotti (both at Bentota, where Bawa himself owned a house and estate, Lunuganga, which is now open to the public – see page 172). In Colombo, Bawa's former offices have now been converted into the beautiful Gallery Café, offering a perfect snapshot of his architectural magic. With a pair of linked courtyards, strategically placed urns and shaded verandahs, it offers both a serene retreat from the urban chaos outside and a compelling model of how the future of Sri Lankan architecture might proceed.

ABOVE, FROM LEFT: the Dutch East India Company's coat of arms; the Lighthouse Hotel, Galle, designed by Geoffrey Bawa.

THE ART OF SRI LANKA'S MURALISTS

Caves, rock shelters and temples provide a home for the island's remarkable collection of wall paintings, from prehistory to the present.

Sri Lanka's rich tradition of wall painting stretches far back into antiquity. Primitive drawings and daubs by the island's first inhabitants, the Veddhas, can be found in over 30 rock shelters at various locations, portraying stylised animal forms, hunting figures and symbolic motifs, and offering a tantalising glimpse into the imagination and lifestyles of the island's earliest inhabitants.

Few paintings survive from medieval Sri Lanka – most have now been reduced to fragmentary splashes of colour with the exception of the celebrated Sigiriya damsels, an extraordinary picture gallery of heavenly beauties painted halfway up the sheer rockface of Sigiriya. It was during the Kandyan period, from 1650 to 1815, however, that the art of the Sri Lankan muralists really blossomed. Temples across the island still preserve vivid paintings from this era, most portraying religious themes (scenes from the life of the Buddha and religious processions) and combining the intricate detail of an Indian miniature with vivid colour schemes and grand designs – the cave temples at Dambulla being the classic example.

Mural painting continued to flourish during the later colonial period, often borrowing details from European art – pictures of Italian cherubs, classical architecture and exotic foreign clothes. Further 20th-century temple paintings can also be found, often inspired by European artistic movements of the day.

ABOVE: mural of the Buddha's arrival at the Kelaniya Raja Maha Vihara, created during the 1930s–40s by renowned artist Soliya Mendis using paints he mixed himself from organic matter.

BELOW: at Dambulla, the gilded interior murals in the Kandyan tradition – which used heavy line work for visual impact – follow the natural rock so closely that they are often mistaken for cloth.

LEFT: Purvarama temple at Kataluva, whose murals may have taken four years to paint, has some of the finest examples from the southern tradition.

LANKA'S EARLY PORTRAITS

Art dating from the 5th century is extremely rare because organic pigments do not often survive many hundreds of years. In several temples, ancient art has been overpainted in more recent times in a style that makes the Buddhist texts easily intelligible to today's worshipper.

The ancient rock palace of Sigiriya, with its bare-breasted women, either celestial beings, queens or ladies-in-waiting, received priority restoration treatment from Unesco on account of its great age, beauty and rarity. Of the original 550 figures, fewer than two dozen remain today due to vandalism through the centuries. Thought to represent clouds and thunder, they are notable for being the only non-religious frescoes in Sri Lanka.

The Sigiriya artists used a mix of alluvial clay, paddy husks, sand, lime and vegetable fibres to paint onto three layers of plaster. For colour they used vegetable dyes, in a style similar to the Ajanta rock paintings of India. To view these legendary women at their glowing best, visit the temple in soft late-afternoon light.

BELOW: the little-known Subhodrama temple, in the suburbs of Colombo, has naive figures costumed in textiles and geometric motifs juxtaposed with cherubs.

BOVE: at the Sunandarama Temple in Ambalangoda, a Buddhist ɪonk points out a scene in a splendid mural typical of the southern ɕhool; followers of the southern tradition would depict various ɔisodes of a story, often subtly defined by shading.

FOOD AND DRINK

Tropical fruits, rare spices, unusual vegetables
and fat prawns – just a few of the ingredients
in Sri Lanka's colourful and unique cuisine.

Far more than a local variation on the classic cuisines of neighbouring India, Sri Lankan cooking has its own unique and distinctive set of dishes and flavours, inspired by the island's abundant natural produce and the huge variety of spices grown here. Rice and curry remains culinary king, but with fiercer flavours than in neighbouring India and with sauces based on coconut milk and fiery chilli sambols – somewhere between Indian and Thai cooking in style. As well as rice and curry, the island has numerous other local specialities like hoppers, string hoppers, *kiribath* and *wattalapam*, to name just a few. Sri Lanka's culinary traditions have also been enriched over the centuries by a wide range of foreign influences, from Tamil *vadais* and *dosas* and Muslim *rottys* and *pittus* through to colonial-era introductions like Dutch *lamprais* and British tea and coffee.

Where to eat

There are some outstanding restaurants in the island's top hotels where you can sample the best the island has to offer, as well as other international dishes, while at the other end of the scale some unpretentious little guesthouses dish up excellent Sri Lankan home cooking at bargain prices. Standards are variable in all price ranges, however, and outside Colombo good places to eat are often thin on the ground – although the recent opening of a string of ambitious and upmarket new restaurants in places like Galle and Bentota is going some way to boosting the island's culinary credentials,

offering top-notch Sri Lankan fine-dining, often in memorable colonial or beachside settings (see Eating Out, pages 296 – 300 for suggestions on good places to eat around the island).

For the time being, the island's principal foodie destination is unquestionably Colombo, which boasts an excellent range of restaurants offering plenty of Sri Lankan cooking along with most international cuisines, from Chinese and Thai to Italian and Swiss. It's also the best place in the island for more downmarket fare, including innumerable down-at-heel little kottu rotty cafés (often, confusingly, called hotels) and a fine selection of unpretentious South Indian pure-vegetarian restaurants, where you can eat mouthwatering heaps of *dosas*, *idlis* and *uttapam* at giveaway prices.

PRECEDING PAGES: Australian-born painter Donald Friend found his muse in Sri Lanka. **LEFT:** a curd stall in Konketiya. **RIGHT:** fishmonger at Galle market.

Rice and curry

Sri Lankan cooking has evolved around rice. The national meal is not referred to as "curry" but as "rice and curry": a mountainous plate of rice generally accompanied by assorted meat and/or vegetable curries, various pickles, (*sambols*), and a handful of tiny poppadums. More than 15 varieties of rice are grown on the island, from tiny white translucent varieties to long-grained basmati and the nutty red kakuluhaal. Locals will take balls of cooked rice and rub the highly spiced accompaniments into them, massaging the mixture gently between the fingers to blend the flavours (*see box*).

The rice and curries served in the island's better hotels, guesthouses and restaurants, however, have evolved far beyond this basic formula and often comprise a sumptuous miniature banquet, with a plateful of rice accompanied by at least five, and sometimes as many as 15, side dishes. These typically feature a culinary compendium of contrasting textures and flavours, from highly spiced meat and fish curries to gently flavoured dishes of pineapple, sweet potato or aubergine, plus servings of unusual local vegetables – anything from drumsticks (*murunga*, a bit like okra), ash plantain or *jak* fruit to other, more arcane regional foodstuffs

– as well as the classic *mallung* (shredded green vegetables cooked with grated coconut and turmeric). You'll also be given a bowl of dhal, some crispy little poppadums and at least one or two dishes of sambol.

Spicy sambols

No rice and curry is complete without a few accompanying *sambols*, the Sri Lankan version of the Indian pickle, used to add an extra dash of flavour (and heat) to the dishes on offer. The standard ingredient in Sri Lankan *sambols* is chilli, either freshly chopped or powdered. As a result, many *sambols* can be fiery hot, so approach with caution and always do a taste test on a tiny amount before ladling spoonfuls all over your meal. In the event of over-heating, a mouthful of rice cools the mouth far more quickly than water. The simplest *sambol*, *lunu miris* (salted chilli), contains chilli powder, onions, Maldive fish (a salty, intensely flavoured sun-dried tuna) and salt. Add fine white grated coconut to this and you get the classic *pol sambol*. More gentle is the sweet-and-sour *seeni sambol* (sugar *sambol*).

International influences

The Dutch, who had already cut their teeth on Indonesian cooking when they arrived in Sri Lanka, took one taste of the local cuisine and

brought to the island by generations of Tamils. Standard South Indian dishes regularly found in Sri Lanka include *dosas* (a rice pancake served in various forms, most commonly as *masala dosa*, in which the pancake is wrapped around a spicy potato curry), *uttapam* (another, thicker, type of rice pancake), and *idlis* (steamed rice cakes served with curry). A classic Tamil titbit, which has been enthusiastically embraced by all Sri Lankans, is the *vadai*, a spicy snack made from deep-fried lentils, which are sold by roving hawkers on trains and buses everywhere.

Muslim cooking has also found its way into

decided it was good enough to wrap up and take home: they came up with *lamprais* (from the Dutch *lomprijst*). A helping of rice is cooked in stock, placed in a wrapping of plantain leaf and piled high with a medley of different flavours; perhaps a sour/spicy aubergine concoction, a prawn paste, a portion of curried chicken or mutton; and a dab of *sambol*. Tied up and then gently baked, the result is a prized restaurant dish or takeaway.

Another of the island's lasting culinary influences has been South Indian food

the Sri Lankan culinary mainstream, especially *rotty* (also spelt rotti and roti, but not to be confused with the completely different North Indian roti, or chapati, which can also be found in the island's better North Indian restaurants). This doughy pancake is used to wrap up little parcels of curried vegetables – watching the cook knead the little balls of dough out into wafer-thin sheets, then folding them up again, is half the fun. Alternatively, *rotty* is chopped up into slivers – like thick, fat noodles – and stir-fried with pretty much any ingredient that takes the cook's fancy to make *kottu rotty*; if you want to know where it's being made, just listen out for the incessant metallic banging which *kottu rotty* chefs,

ABOVE, FROM LEFT: vegetarians should have no problem in Sri Lanka; it would be a sin not to indulge in Sri Lanka's abundance of tropical fruits.

usually armed with a pair of large metal cleavers, make while chopping up their ingredients. Muslim Malays also introduced *pittu* to the island. This rice flour and shredded coconut preparation, similar to coarse couscous, is steamed inside a bamboo (or aluminium) tube and either eaten as part of breakfast or, increasingly, used as a rice substitute in evening meals.

Hoppers and string hoppers

The hopper *(appa)* is another classic example of a humble food that has achieved gourmet status. The hopper has a delicate, puffy, crêpe-

like texture, much like a pancake, and is eaten as a traditional Sri Lankan breakfast or after-dark snack. Proper hoppers are made from a batter containing coconut milk and palm toddy which is left to sit for a whole night to give it time to ferment – although most cooks now use instant hopper mix. Its cousin, the egg hopper, is an ordinary hopper with an egg broken into the centre. Break off the crisp, lacy outer rim at the top of the hopper and dip it into the runny egg yolk at the bottom for a true taste of culinary heaven.

No relation to the hopper, string hoppers *(indiappa)* are tangled mounds of rice vermicelli steamed over a low fire and usually eaten at breakfast with curry and *sambol*.

Fish and seafood

There's an abundant variety of freshly caught fish and seafood around the coast, including seer, amberjack, skipjack, herring, pomfret, bonito, shark and mullet. The closer you are to the coast, the better it's likely to be. Preparation is usually simple (grilled, fried, breadcrumbed or marinaded in a mild garlic sauce). Fish curries are also ubiquitous, normally cooked in a hot, coconut milk-based *kiri hodhi* sauce. Intensely flavoured pinches of sun-dried fish and seafood, such as prawns, are widely used to add flavour to curries – "Maldive fish" (sun-dried tuna) being the most common.

The best seafood traditionally comes from the Negombo lagoon and includes crab, cuttlefish, lobster and huge, succulent tiger prawns. Locals love nothing better than to crack open a bottle of *arrack* and sit down over a plate of spicy seafood: crab, prawns or lobster either devilled or cooked in tangy chilli or garlic sauces – chilli crab is a particular favourite.

Desserts

Pure ambrosia can be had in the form of buffalo curd, a wonderfully creamy yoghurt usually served with a thick, dark brown treacle known as *kitul* (made with sap from the kitul palm). You will be offered this as dessert, but it also makes an ideal light breakfast and a perfect foil to spicy food. The Malay-inspired *wattalapam*, a rich, coconut-flavoured crème caramel made with cashew nuts and *jaggery* (a raw sugar sweetener created from *kitul* treacle), has practically turned itself into the national pudding. Another characteristic local dessert is *kiribath*, rice cooked with milk. The resultant slightly sticky rice is traditionally cut up into diamond-shaped pieces and is a popular snack on festive occasions and at weddings.

Fruit

The island's cornucopia of tropical fruits includes pineapple, passion fruit, pomegranate, papaya, avocados, mangoes, several kinds of guava, more than a dozen varieties of banana, and many more exotic offerings which you're unlikely to have seen back home. Look out for the deep purple, delicately grape-flavoured mangosteen and the unmistakable sweet-tasting *rambutan*, red and hairy on the outside, but similar to lychee on the inside. Other local specialities include

> The balance of glucose and potassium in coconut milk makes it a delicious health drink for convalescents, and in emergencies it can even be used as a drip.

sweet-tasting star apples, red cherry-like *lovi-lovi*, and the strange wood apple, covered in an indestructible woody shell and usually served with honey to soften the taste of its bitter bright-red, pulpy flesh.

Then there is the maverick *durian*, a huge green fruit whose smell, often compared to a

over the island, especially in the southwest, where most of the island's 10 million or so coconut palms can be found. Coconut juice is a safe bet if you are dubious about the local drinking water as it comes ready-sealed in the heart of the coconut, while also being an effective pick-me-up for a hangover.

Another local beverage made from the coconut palm is toddy. This is tapped from the flower of the coconut and left to ferment. New toddy is light and refreshing; fermented, it can be as alcoholic as cider. A distilled spirit made from the toddy becomes *arrack*, the nation's favourite tipple, which is widely used

blocked drain, usually puts people off sampling its delicious, nougat-flavoured flesh – although its popular reputation as an aphrodisiac assures it a loyal local following. Even bigger than the durian – in fact the world's largest fruit – is the *jak*, a massive green monster, like a bloated marrow in shape, whose fruit is either eaten raw or used cooked in curries.

Drinks

Machete-wielding hawkers sell golden bunches of young coconut (*thambili*) by the roadside all

in punches and cocktails but also drunk neat or mixed with coke, lemonade, soda water or other mixers.

Inexpensive Sri Lankan lagers (Lion and Three Coins are the two leading brands, along with locally produced Carlsberg) are available everywhere.

Despite the reputation of its tea, Sri Lanka isn't the best place to drink it. Most of the really good stuff gets exported, and tea drinkers are usually left with a beverage made from low-grade Liptons tea bags, or something similar, usually served with powdered milk, or sometimes evaporated milk. Coffee offers a good alternative – most is locally grown in small plantations and is usually perfectly palatable.

ABOVE, FROM LEFT: aubergine curry; a favourite island breakfast is a selection of stuffed *rotty* accompanied by locally grown tea.

SHOPPING

Outlandish masks, lace and batiks, carved wooden elephants and gorgeous cotton fabrics – just some of the myriad crafts that await the visitor to Sri Lanka.

Sri Lanka's rich artistic traditions rival those of pretty much anywhere in the world – as a visit to any one of its superbly sculpted and painted temples will immediately prove. The island's artisans excel in many different media, from the wood, stone and ebony used in religious carvings through to more recent forms such as lace, lacquer and batik (introduced during the Dutch colonial period); while a string of innovative modern designers have added their own novel twists to the island's traditional crafts.

Many souvenirs on sale at the major resorts are – as you'd probably expect – stereotypical in design and often slapdash in quality. If you're prepared to shop around, however, there are still excellent crafts to be found at often modest prices, making even heirloom-quality objects relatively affordable. Be aware, however, that you'll need a licence to export any genuine antiques (defined as any object more than 50 years old): consult the tourist board or the shop you're buying from for details on securing the necessary paperwork.

Where to buy crafts

The government emporium Laksala has branches in most of the island's major towns and makes a handy place to check out the full range of crafts available and get an idea of prices – although the stock at these shops generally shows Sri Lankan craftsmanship at its shoddiest and most insipid. In Colombo, there are plenty of superior craft shops, including a clutch of excellent boutiques (see Activities page 304) offering contemporary takes on traditional crafts. The other main places

to buy are Kandy, which has a veritable deluge of shops selling pretty much the complete range of Sri Lankan crafts; and Galle, traditionally famous for its gems, jewellery, lace and Dutch antiques, and now also home to a number of smart designer boutiques. All the main tourist resorts along the west coast have plenty of souvenir shops, though quality and choice vary wildly and there are considerable quantities of tat.

On the west coast, you'll be regularly approached by the hawkers who trawl up and down the beach with bags of clothes and tourist trinkets – a good opportunity to pick up a few bargains if you're prepared to barter hard. Bargaining is also the order of the day in smaller shops, and in all but the smartest

LEFT: clay wares for sale in Anuradhapura.
RIGHT: detail of a batik fabric.

boutiques a request for a "small discount" or "special price" can sometimes work if you're making a big purchase or buying several items.

Masks

The most obvious of Sri Lanka's many crafts are the gruesome masks, traditionally used in performances of ritual *kolam* dances or in exorcism ceremonies *(bali)* to propitiate malevolent deities (see page 100). Many of the masks depict wild-eyed demons, and when you see them at close range – with their fearsome gaze and tangle of hair – you will understand why locals believe in their efficacy in

frightening off bad spirits.

The most commonly seen mask depicts the bug-eyed bird monster Gurulu Raksha, believed to ward off malign influences, and many Sri Lankans hang one of these masks outside their houses for safe measure. Not all masks depict demons, however. Some show royal personages or comic characters associated with *kolam*, while others show different ethnic characters such as wild Veddha hunters, gap-toothed Tamils or red-faced English soldiers.

The masks are carved from soft kaduru wood from the *Nux vomica* tree, which is soaked to soften it before carving. Early examples grace the collections of museums around the island, but modern examples are no longer painted with

An excellent overview of the full range of Sri Lankan crafts can be found at www.craft revival.org (follow the Sri Lanka link under "Crafts").

vegetable-based dyes, using gaudy colours instead. Some masks are now artificially aged to resemble antique ones – an attractive alternative to freshly painted masks, and a lot easier on the eye.

The centre of Sri Lankan mask-making is the west coast town of Ambalangoda, which has a number of workshops open to visitors. The Ariyapala and Sons Mask Museum (see page 174) has a big workshop and shop selling reasonable-quality masks. Alternatively, Southland Masks, close by at 353 Main Road, has an excellent and wide-ranging selection of quality creations.

Woodcarvings

Woodcarvings are found everywhere in Sri Lanka – everything from the worst sort of tourist junk to heirloom-quality statuettes in a variety of hard and soft woods including ebony, sandalwood, teak, mahogany and satinwood. Elephants are the preferred subject of many carvers, and the island produces literally millions of these wooden beasts, large and small, for tourists, some of them painted with colourful polka-dot designs, others simply left bare and varnished. The best are carved from ebony, though shortages of this wood have forced artisans to find other materials. Second in popularity to elephants, Buddha carvings, traditionally hewn from sandalwood, can also be found everywhere, in all sorts of different sizes and qualities.

Attractive wooden models of carts, trucks and tuktuks are also widely available on the west coast, especially in Negombo, and make great children's toys (although they tend to fall apart quite quickly). Other popular wooden toys include jigsaw puzzles, alphabet sets, bookends and educational games.

Batiks

The art of making batiks was introduced from Indonesia by the Dutch and numerous factories and smaller workshops around the island now churn out considerable quantities of batik clothes and pictures. At whichever end of the scale, all are made through the same time-consuming process of carefully applying wax to the areas not to be dyed. After each dying, the fabric must be fixed, the old wax washed out, and then more wax reapplied for the next dyeing. In this way, the pictures gradually develop in colour washes as the batik-maker works from light to dark.

Cheap batik clothes are comfortable and colourful and available at beachside stalls and shops all down the west coast – though don't expect them to last long. More durable are the batik wall-hangings produced by many workshops. The majority show clichéd beach scenes, gambolling elephants or the nubile Sigiriya Damsels, though there is more interesting and original stuff to be found if you hunt around, either modern designs or more traditional batik – inspired by old Indonesian designs.

For Picasso-inspired batik pieces that have been exhibited in galleries in Europe, visit Dudley Silva at his home-cum-workshop, 53 Elpitiya Road, Ambalangoda. There are also excellent batiks to be had at Jezlook, at St Yehiya Road in Matara (www.jezlookbatik.com), whose owner, Jezima Mohamed, can count Queen Elizabeth II amongst her customers.

Lace

Lacemaking was introduced to Sri Lanka in the 16th century by the Portuguese. Hours of painstaking work are needed to produce just a few centimetres and, as in Europe, lacemakers are mainly women. Galle is the most famous centre of lacemaking in Sri Lanka – you may be approached by hawkers bearing samples of intricate handmade lace as you wander around the lighthouse area of the fort – while Weligama is another centre of production. A good place to shop for lace is the Shoba Display Gallery at 67a Pedlar Street in Galle (www.shobafashion.org), which showcases the work of local lacemakers. Alternatively, visit Dickwella Lace Centre, a women's cooperative established to revive this venerable island craft, or the nearby Sewa Lanka Lace Showroom, both a short drive further along the coast at the village of Dickwella.

Metalwork and lacquerware

Metalwork is also widely produced, especially around Kandy, the source of the ceremonial brass lamps which are used in temples, at weddings and on Sinhala New Year. Striking, if sadly a bit too big for the suitcase. Metalworkers also produce lavishly detailed trays and decorative items, laboriously indented to create delicate patterns, although these are generally too fussy for most Western tastes. Attractive metalwork statuettes can also sometimes be found.

Lacquer bowls, containers and other objects originate from Matale near Kandy but are now found everywhere. Many of these are just painted and coated with varnish but you can find work finished with lac. This is a resinous substance that is secreted by the lac insect when it punctures the bark of certain trees. The resin is removed, melted

ABOVE, FROM LEFT: masks and other woodcarvings, Sigiriya; lacemaker at work in Galle, a town renowned for its lace production.

down and strained through muslin and worked while it is still soft with the pigment.

Contemporary crafts

Sri Lanka has a small but vibrant selection of places offering contemporary twists on traditional crafts. Foremost amongst these is Barefoot (704 Galle Road, Colombo 3; also branches in the Dutch Fort in Fort district, Colombo and at 49 Pedlar Street, Galle; www.barefoot.lk), a lovely shop founded by designer Barbara Sansoni that has almost single-handedly created a new style of modern Sri Lankan chic. The shop's gorgeous hand-woven cotton textiles in luminous shades

of deep orange, red, green and blue are made into all sorts of things, from clothes and tablecloths to cuddly toys and stationery.

Rivalling Barefoot as a source of stylish contemporary knick-knacks, Paradise Road (213 Dharmapala Mawatha, Colombo 7; also branches at 2 Alfred House Road, Col 3, and at Paradise Road The Villa, Bentota) is another of Colombo's top names in design, with modern takes on traditional crafts. Outside Colombo, the Matale Heritage Centre, tel: 066-222 2404, in Aluvihare 15km (9 miles) north of Kandy, is the brainchild of renowned designer Ena de Silva. Created in 1984, the centre was known initially for its fine handwoven tapestries and batiks, but has also become respected for its wood, brasswork and other handicrafts.

Marine products

Various shops and itinerant hawkers around the west and south coasts offer marine products – usually polished shells and pieces of coral – for sale. Remember that buying such items directly contributes to the destruction of Sri Lanka's fragile and seriously endangered marine environment. In addition, the export of marine (and all other animal) products is illegal, and their import into most foreign countries also proscribed, so you'll be looking at a hefty fine as well if you're caught.

Gems

The gems of Sri Lanka have been famous since biblical times. It was to Ratnapura, the City of Gems, that King Solomon sent emissaries to procure the jewel which won him the heart of

GODS AND GEMS

The methods used in mining gems today remain unchanged from when the first precious stones were mined. All that is required is patience, excellent eyesight, a tolerance of damp working conditions, and a great deal of luck. It is to ensure the latter that an elaborate series of rituals has been developed.

A male astrologer is always used to investigate the horoscopes of miners – women are never used for this task. He not only calculates their chances of finding a gem but also advises on the most auspicious moment for a ritual known as the "sod-cutting ceremony". This takes a full day and starts with the offering of a venerable *puja* (act of worship) to the guardian gods. It ends

precisely 24 hours later when a priest blesses the chosen miner at the exact time that the sod is cut.

A miner, clad only in a loin cloth, then sinks into the pit, praying that the gods will bring him luck. The astrologer no doubt shares his anxiety, as do other people whose livelihoods depend on him finding a glint or sparkle in the pit.

First in line to share the spoils is the financier of the pit, along with the licensee who pays the government for the mineral rights; next comes the pump operator, followed by the gemmer, a connoisseur of the true gem. Last of all to gain from the find is the supposedly star-blessed man who toils in the mud.

Queen Sheba. In *1001 Arabian Nights*, Sinbad tipped off his master, Haroun Al Rashid, that the best gems were to be found in Serendib (as the Arabs then called Sri Lanka), while Marco Polo described the island's wealth of precious stones in loving detail, including sapphires, topaz, amethysts and a massive ruby, "the finest and biggest in the world; about a palm in length, and as thick as a man's arm".

More recently British royals have been struck by Sri Lanka's exquisite stones. A cat's eye discovered in a rice paddy and weighing 105 carats had the distinction of being admired and caressed by four British royals in turn – Edward VII, George V, Edward VIII and Elizabeth II – when they visited the island. Indeed, the largest sapphire in the British crown is the Blue Belle of Asia, found in a village near Ratnapura. The famous Panther Brooch made by Cartier in the 1930s for the Duchess of Windsor, Wallis Simpson, holds another Sri Lankan sapphire of 152.35 carats.

Sri Lanka's wealth of precious stones originates in the ancient rocks of the hill country, from where they are washed down from the mountains in the waters of fast-flowing rivers mixed up with tons of coarse water-borne gravel called illam. A variety of gems are often found together in river bed gem pits including spinels, corundums (sapphire and ruby) and star stones. Aquamarines, tourmalines, topaz, garnets, amethysts, cats' eyes and zircons are also found. But most outstanding of all are the glistening rubies and sapphires for which Sri Lanka has been one of the oldest sources in the world.

Caution is required, however, if you want to buy gems yourself. Beware a friendly Sri Lankan with a handful of glinting "gems" which turn out to be pieces of worthless cut glass. Choose a dealer or a shop belonging to the Sri Lanka Gem Traders' Association or the International Coloured Gemstone Association. The words "Tourist Board Approved" sometimes displayed in shops have no official backing. Remember, you are the buyer – don't be pressured into making a snap decision.

Jewellery

Jewellery, traditionally considered to be a Sri Lankan woman's portable wealth, is found in

The famous Star of India is in fact a Sri Lankan sapphire, the largest such stone in the world (roughly the size of a golf ball). It was presented to the American Museum of Natural History by famous banker J.P. Morgan in 1900.

towns all over the island. Gold rings, earrings and chains are bought when times are good, as a badge of success, and as a form of insurance in case fortunes change. Silver and silver-plated jewellery is also common and ranges from very simple designs to chunky Indian-style work to

delicate filigree necklaces. Kandyan artisans are renowned for their gem-setting and intricate workmanship.

In Colombo, the traditional place to shop for silver and gold is Sea Street in the Pettah, home to dozens of small shops stuffed with precious metals; alternatively, visit the modern Sri Lanka Gem & Jewellery Exchange on Level 4 of the World Trade Center in Fort district, home to almost 40 jewellers' outlets. (Here, for a modest fee, you can have the authenticity of gems tested, assuming, that is, that the jewellers are prepared to let you borrow the stone, or accompany you there.)

In Galle, try Laksana at 30 Hospital Street, which stocks a good range of modern and antique silver jewellery.

ABOVE, FROM LEFT: first stop for stylish homewares – the Barefoot shop in Colombo; a jeweller concentrates on his task at the moonstone mines, Mitiyagoda.

WILDLIFE

Sri Lanka is home to abundant wildlife ranging from elephants and whales through to leopards, crocodiles, and a huge array of colourful birds.

Sri Lanka remains a predominantly rural island, relatively undeveloped despite a burgeoning population and increasing pressure on land. Huge areas of the island are protected as national parks and reserves, a fact which partly reflects traditional Buddhist concern for all forms of life, and partly the increasingly important role of ecotourism in the nation's vital tourist industry.

The country is home to a wide range of rich and absorbing wildlife. Leading attractions include the majestic elephant herds which can be found in many of the national parks and the abundant leopards which stalk Yala, as well as a treasure trove of bird species, many of them unique to the island. In addition, the coastal waters around Sri Lanka boast a wealth of marine life including turtles, dolphins and whales. The national parks are, of course, the best places to spot wildlife, but colourful birds and unusual animals can be seen almost anywhere: brilliant blue kingfishers perched on roadside telephone cables; working elephants marching across fields; or huge land monitor lizards ambling sedately down the dusty tracks of small villages – even Colombo has a healthy population of tropical water birds that descend daily on Dehiwela Zoo for free food.

Not that the island's wildlife is without its challenges. Ongoing conflicts between villagers and roaming herds of elephants claim hundreds of animal and human lives every year, while the continuous destruction of habitat, increasing pollution and unrestrained tourist development have also cast a long shadow over

the island's natural environment – from the virtual destruction of formerly pristine coral reefs at various points around the coast to the steady disappearance of the spectacular lizards that live at Horton Plains (killed, according to different theories, either by acid rain caused by traffic pollution, or by hungry crows attracted by thoughtlessly dumped litter).

Elephants

The Sri Lankan elephant (*Elephas maximus maximus*) is a subspecies of the Asian elephant. They are smaller than their African cousins, and with less prominent ears, while only about 10 percent of males (so-called tuskers) have tusks. They usually live in family groups of around

LEFT: baby elephant on the approach to Lion Rock.
RIGHT: the white-throated kingfisher.

15, led by an elderly matriarch. Elephants need plenty of room to survive – each adult requires around 5 sq km (2 sq miles) on account of the huge amount of water they drink and vegetation they consume. Their destructive impact can be seen in Uda Walawe National Park, where the large resident population has more or less killed off most vegetation in significant swathes of the park. Herds usually migrate along so-called elephant corridors in search of food and, especially, water – some can wander for considerable distances over the island, a common cause of conflicts with humans. The most famous elephant corridor is in the north,

linking Minneriya, Kaudulla and Wasgomuwa national parks. Elsewhere, wild elephants can be seen in virtually all of the island's national parks, or in captivity most famously at the Pinnawela Elephant Orphanage.

Estimates puts the number of wild elephants in Sri Lanka at around 3,000, though this is only a small proportion of the numbers that originally inhabited the island. Numbers declined dramatically during the colonial period thanks to overzealous European hunters, and have continued to fall since Independence owing to increasing loss of habitat, while many elephants were also killed during the civil war – although numbers have begun to recover since the conclusion of hostilities. Conflicts between humans and elephants – with regular fatalities on both sides – are another tragic but common feature of island life.

Leopards

Spend much time in Sri Lanka, and it's pretty much impossible not to see at least a few elephants. The same can't be said about the island's other most famous wild inhabitant, the leopard (*Panthera pardus*). Sri Lanka has more of these animals than almost any other country. There are estimated to be around 800 in the entire island, with the majority being found in Yala National Park, whose population density (amounting to one leopard per square kilometre in parts of the park) is reckoned to be the highest in the world.

If you're lucky enough to glimpse a leopard in the wild, it's a sight not easily forgotten. These superb big cats can grow to more than 2 metres (6ft 6in) in length and live within a set territory, feeding off a diverse diet that includes anything from insects to smaller mammals, such as deer or even humans – the infamous man-eater of Punanai was finally shot in 1923 after lunching on 20 unfortunate villagers. As well as excelling in speed and strength, they are also expert climbers and can be spotted sitting perched in trees or sunning themselves on top of large rocks.

Monkeys

Monkeys are everywhere to be seen in Sri Lanka. There are three species, the most common of which is the graceful grey langur, a delicate creature with long limbs covered in silver-grey fur and a small black face. Grey langurs can be found in many places, especially along the south coast, both in national parks and towns (Kataragama has a particularly large population, as do Yala and Bundala national parks). Curious but skittish, they often sit and stare at human goings-on, but tend to scamper away nervously if approached.

Sri Lanka's other common monkey is the altogether less attractive and considerably more belligerent toque macaque, a solidly built reddish-brown monkey that looks slightly baboon-like. They also have baboon-like aggressive tendencies and can become fierce when looking for food – don't try to offer them a banana. The third native species is the much rarer purple-faced langur, similar in build to the grey langur, but with darker and thicker fur, plus a pair of neat white side whiskers. They are most often seen in the hill country, where you might also see the shaggy bear monkey, one of four subspecies of the purple-faced langur.

Other mammals

Easily topping Sri Lanka's list of cute wildlife is the engaging sloth bear, a shaggy bundle of fur that can occasionally be seen shambling around the undergrowth in various national parks – Yala is the likeliest place to spot one. Slightly less endearing but far more common are the island's deer. Commonly sighted species include the spotted deer, sambur deer and barking deer (or muntjac); these can be seen in pretty much

You might also see wild rabbits – rare in Sri Lanka, and a source of considerable excitement to locals, though for once in Sri Lanka you're unlikely to be as impressed.

have to be very lucky to see island rarities such as the fishing cat and porcupine, both of which are largely nocturnal.

Birds

Sri Lanka has a wonderfully rich array of birdlife, one which appeals to dedicated orni-

every park in the country, from the highlands of Horton Plains (where a few usually hang out around the ticket office waiting for tourist hand-outs) to Yala (where they make up a large part of the local leopards' diet). Squirrels are also a regular sight, from the delicate little palm squirrels that scamper around trees on beaches all round the coast, to rare giant squirrels that live high up in the canopy of mountain forests. Giant fruit-eating bats, or flying foxes, are widespread, wild boars are also reasonably common, and you might spot a mongoose or two – though you'll

ABOVE, FROM LEFT: Yala National Park is one of the best places to see wildlife in Sri Lanka – such as these monkeys; Water buffalo, Yala National Park.

thologists and casual visitors alike – it's quite possible to spot over 100 different species in a single day at one of the country's national parks if you go with a good guide. The island is home to 233 resident species (including 33 endemic species found nowhere else in the world), while its equatorial location close to the Indian mainland also makes it a favoured spot for seasonal migrants, attracting around 200 species from northern India, other parts of Asia, and even as far away as Denmark. The island's physical diversity and wide range of habitats also encourages avian diversity – from the village gardens and paddy fields of the coast to unspoilt rain and cloudforests further inland. Some species are restricted to particular areas, with altitude and rainfall often being the crucial factors – most of Sri Lanka's endemic species are found in the wet zone.

Both coastal and inland wetlands provide great birdwatching opportunities. Cormorants are the diving champions, whilst plovers and waders keep to the muddy banks. The painted stork ventures further in search of crabs, frogs and water snakes, and with luck you may spot a kingfisher waiting to pounce. One bird even the most amateurish ornithologist will be able to identify is the spoonbill, swishing the water from side to side like a diner searching for something in his soup.

Birds of prey are also regularly seen, particularly hawks and eagles. Most of the island's reservoirs sport populations of fishing-tank eagles or white-bellied sea eagles. Mountain cliffs are frequented by the black eagle, the mountain hawk eagle, the brahminy kite and the serpent eagle.

More difficult to spot unless you are travelling with a specialist guide are the rarer rainforest and mountain birds. The brilliant blue magpie lives in groups in the hill forests, feeding on insects. The pied ground thrush got its name because it has variegated markings on its wings and is often found foraging through leaf litter. The Malabar trogon is widespread in Sri Lanka, the male easily identifiable by his bright-red breast and black head. The raucous call of the bizarre-looking Malabar pied hornbill in the dry zone will guide you to the flocks that live in the tallest tree tops.

There are many birds that seem to be as much at home in the city as in the country. At first it seems that the ever-present crows are the only birds in town, rooting through dustbins and dodging traffic, but a dawn walk will provide a fair bird list. Viharamahadevi Park in Colombo is a good place for birdspotting, while the city's Beira Lake attracts flocks of aquatic birds, such as egrets and pelicans – although neither can rival the extraordinary troupes of birds that congregate on the lake at Dehiwala Zoo for the daily afternoon feeding sessions.

Reptiles

There are plenty of reptiles in Sri Lanka: two species of crocodile, 80 types of snake and a huge array of lizards, some of which are still being

THE GATHERING

One of Sri Lanka's – and indeed Asia's – most spectacular natural sights is the so-called Gathering of the Elephants. During the dry season, more than 300 elephants converge on the retreating waters of the Minneriya Tank in Minneriya National Park – the largest such gathering of elephants anywhere in Asia. Small family herds of elephants congregate from all across the northeastern plains, walking 80km (50 miles) or more along traditional migratory routes to drink and bathe in the precious waters, and to feed on the freshly sprouting grass which grows up from the lake bed as the waters retreat. There's a decidedly social element to the whole occasion, as animals who have not seen one another for a year renew old acquaintanceships. Matriarchs lead their herds to the water, carefully protecting their youngsters en route, while adult bull elephants wander amidst the crowds, intermittently tussling for dominance while sniffing the air with their trunks in search of receptive females. The ultimate pachyderm party, if you like.

The Gathering takes place from July to October every year (but is usually at its best during August and September). A similar, if slightly smaller, gathering of elephants occurs annually at Kaudulla National Park, just down the road from Minneriya, where up to 200 elephants are present during September and October.

classified, ranging from tiny geckos to enormous land monitors. Crocodiles are widespread in the coastal national parks and are either freshwater (mugger) or the less common saltwater. The largest can tackle animals as big as a deer, and big saltwater crocs will occasionally attack humans – although since there may now be only around 300 left in the entire island, the odds against meeting one in a bad mood are pretty high.

Far more dangerous are the island's five species of venomous snake, which claim a considerable number of human victims every year: it's worth bearing in mind that Sri Lanka has one of the world's highest rates of death from snake-

rivers or just walking along roads, while many smaller species also inhabit the island, including numerous types of gecko, chameleons and other lizards, some of them brightly coloured.

Whales

Over the past few years, Sri Lanka has begun to emerge as one of the world's leading whale-watching destinations, following pioneering work by UK marine biologist Charles Anderson which demonstrated that hundreds of cetaceans regularly migrate around the shores of southern Sri Lanka on a biannual basis, passing within a few kilometres of the coast. This means that Sri

bite (6 per 100,000 annually) before wandering through long grass with unprotected legs. All five venomous varieties are relatively common, especially in the north, and include cobras and vipers, such as the extremely dangerous Russell's viper. However non-venomous species, ranging from large rock pythons to reclusive, worm-like blind snakes, are, thankfully, in the vast majority.

Lizards are also common throughout the island. Enormous land and water monitors (the latter can grow to up to 2.5 metres/8ft in length) are frequently spotted by the side of

Lanka now ranks among the top two or three places in the world to spot blue and sperm whales, and is perhaps the best place on the planet to see these two majestic species swimming together. There have also been sightings of other marine creatures, including killer whales, Bryde's whales, and large pods of spinner dolphins.

The main centre for whale-watching is currently Mirissa (see page 307), on the south coast (with the whale-watching season running from December to January, as the whales travel in one direction, and then again throughout April, as they return, during which periods you are more or less guaranteed a sighting of at least one or two of the gargantuan creatures). In addition, whale-watching trips have recently

ABOVE, FROM LEFT: a spotted deer stag in Yala National Park; an inquisitive giant squirrel (*Ratufa macroura*); male green garden lizard (*Calotes calotes*).

been launched at Trincomalee and Kalpitiya, meaning that it's now possible to spot cetaceans somewhere around the coast for at least ten months out of every 12, a figure which might rise even higher in future as further data become available about the precise movements of these majestic mammals.

Turtles

Sri Lanka is a major stopping-off point on the Indian Ocean's turtle trails, and all of the world's five major species of marine turtle visit the island to nest on beaches, most commonly the green turtle, along with the loggerhead, the hawksbill, olive

Kosgoda, south of Bentota, where nightly turtle watches allow you to spot these remarkable creatures dragging themselves up onto the sand to lay their eggs. For every 1,000 eggs laid by a sea turtle, only one mature adult turtle is likely to survive.

Protected areas

Respect for the natural environment has long been ingrained in the national consciousness – the country's first wildlife sanctuary is said to have been created in the 3rd century BC by the island's first Buddhist king, Devanampiya Tissa, while modern reserves, such as Udawattakelle Sanctuary in Kandy and the Sinharaja rainforest,

ridley and leatherback. Sadly, loss of coastal habitats and poaching of eggs has seriously affected turtle populations in Sri Lanka – as throughout most of the world. A string of turtle hatcheries has been set up along the west coast with the professed aim of protecting local turtle populations. These places buy turtles eggs from local poachers, allow them to hatch and then return the resultant baby turtles to the sea, although serious questions have been raised about the practical effectiveness and ethical credentials of many hatcheries – some of which appear to be more concerned with squeezing cash out of passing tourists rather than with genuine wildlife conservation.

At present the only places to watch turtles on the beach are at Rekawa, near Tangalla, and at

can also trace their origins back centuries to the days when they were royal reserves. Protected areas now cover 13 percent of the country. These are classified variously as national parks, nature reserves, sanctuaries and strict nature reserves (where entry is prohibited).

National parks

Of most interest to visitors are the country's 22 national parks. The most famous of these is Yala National Park, which covers a vast swathe of countryside in the southeast of the island beyond Tissamaharama. Much of the park is closed to visitors, but the area which is open has probably the richest and most varied collection of wildlife in the country, including a substantial elephant population, elusive sloth bears, gorgeous birdlife and, most famously, a significant leopard population. Although they're not easy to spot, you've reasonable odds of seeing one if you spend some time in the park with a reputable outfit.

A little further west along the coast is another of Sri Lanka's top reserves, Bundala National Park. Comprising a system of coastal lagoons and wetlands, Bundala is a watery wonderland of aquatic birdlife, including great flocks of migratory flamingoes, as well as crocodiles and a few more elephants. Inland from Bundala, spread across the dry plains at the southern foot of the hill country, the popular Uda Walawe National Park is one of the country's best places to spot elephants – most of the park is covered in light, arid scrub, with very little forest cover.

Up in the hills themselves, the best known reserve is Horton Plains National Park. Quite unlike any other national park in the country, there's relatively little wildlife here (though the park is one of the top spots in the island for spotting montane bird species), the main attraction being the scenery. Wild, misty moorlands, studded with beautiful stands of cloudforest, roll down to the breathtaking precipice of World's End, where the cliffs marking the southern edge of the hill country fall sheer for the best part of a kilometre (0.5 miles) to the plains below.

The Cultural Triangle is home to another pair of popular parks, Minneriya and Kaudulla, close to Polonnaruwa. Both are built around two of the innumerable ancient man-made reservoirs that dot the north, and once again the principal attraction is elephants – the parks lie on an elephant corridor along which animals migrate seasonally between the two, as well as to nearby (though much less visited) Wasgomuwa National Park. August and September in Minneriya is particularly memorable, as hundreds of elephants congregate around Minneriya Tank, the largest meeting of Asian elephants in the world – popularly dubbed "The Gathering" (see page 132).

Other reserves

National parks aside, there are plenty of other protected areas dotted around the island. Just east of Uda Walawe National Park lies the most

remarkable, Sinharaja, a swathe of perfectly preserved tropical rainforest strung out along the undulating southern outliers of the hill country. This is a particularly good birdwatching location, home to a string of rare endemics, though the density of the forest cover can make sightings difficult without an expert guide.

Some other reserves are also good for birdwatchers – Kalametiya, on the southern coast near Bundala, and Hakgala, in the hills near Nuwara Eliya, are two of the island's top birding destinations. Udawattakelle sanctuary, almost in the centre of Kandy, is another good spot to head for.

CORAL REEFS

El Niño, fishing boats and the tsunami have all played havoc with Sri Lanka's coral reefs, and to really appreciate Sri Lanka's submarine environment you'll need to go diving, and well away from the shore. Along the coastline, only a few patches of live coral remain. Perhaps the most impressive stretch of reef is at the Hikkaduwa Coral Sanctuary, rich in tropical fish (and the odd turtle), although much of the coral is now dead. Elsewhere, you'll find outcrops of live coral at Unawatuna, at Polhena (near Matara) and at Pigeon Island at Nilaveli. All can be snorkelled to, although they're fairly unimpressive compared to reefs elsewhere in Asia.

ABOVE, FROM LEFT: hawksbill turtles are lucky to have several hatching sanctuaries on the island; the little egret.

INTRODUCTION

A detailed guide to the entire country,
with principal sites cross-referenced
by number to the maps.

A papal legate six centuries ago wrote that "From Ceylon to Paradise, according to native legend, is 40 miles; there may be heard the sound of the fountains of Paradise." For those unable to enter Paradise itself, its neighbour has enough diversity to make one forget about eternal salvation: mountains, jungles, ruined cities, vast man-made lakes, fertile uplands where tea estates stretch as far as the eye can see; elephants, leopards, birds, turtles, whales and darting tropical fish.

Gateway to the island for all travellers is Colombo, a fascinatingly eclectic city which offers an absorbing introduction to contemporary Sri Lanka. South of Colombo, the coast presents a long swathe of golden sand shaded by forests of palm trees. This is also where you'll find some of the island's finest wildlife reserves, including the magnificent Yala National Park, as well as whale-watching expeditions from Mirissa, the sacred town of Kataragama, and the superb Dutch-era fort at Galle, one of Sri Lanka's most memorably time-warped destinations.

Inland from Colombo lies the historic city of Kandy, the last capital of the Sinhalese kings and still a vibrant crucible of the island's traditional arts and architecture. Heading south, endless tea estates swathe the dramatic heights of the hill country around the old colonial town of Nuwara Eliya, from where there are spectacular excursions.

North of Kandy, the so-called Cultural Triangle is where you'll find the island's most absorbing archaeological remains centred on the ruins of the great cities of Anuradhapura and Polonnaruwa, the spectacular rock citadel of Sigiriya, and the exquisite cave temples of Dambulla.

The east coast preserves a string of magnificent beaches and still sees only a handful of tourists outside the lively surfing centre of Arugam Bay. Even fewer outsiders venture to the north, recently reopened to visitors after the civil war, and offering a fascinating glimpse into the vibrant culture of the Sri Lankan Tamils.

PRECEDING PAGES: passengers on the train stopped at Ella; stilt fishermen off the coast of Galle; Mihintale. **LEFT:** the steps to the Terrace Garden, Sigiriya.
ABOVE, FROM LEFT: the Great Stupa, Anuradhapura; the south coast at Galle.

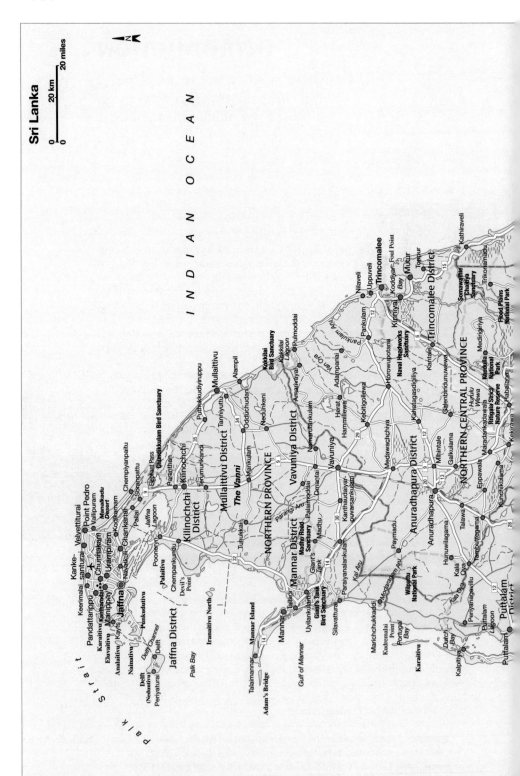

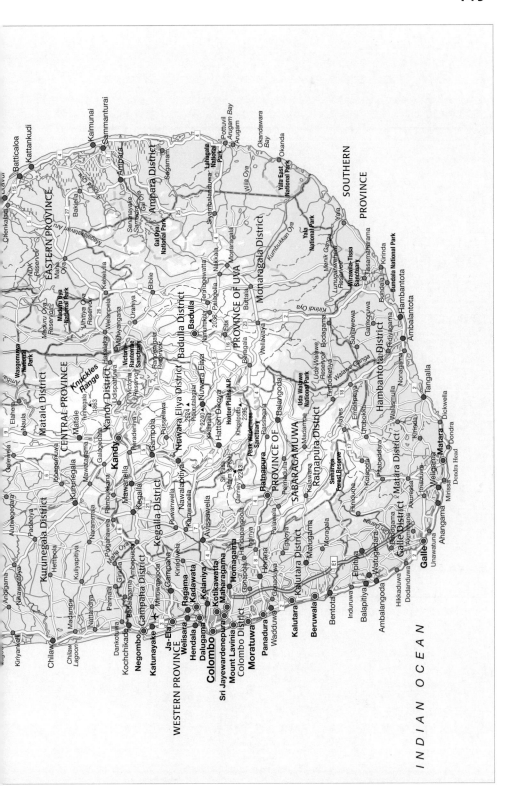

Colombo

COLOMBO

Colombo's crowded and chaotic surface hides a rewarding city whose contrasting mix of cultures and sights shows the country at its most diverse and progressive.

The city of Colombo is a relative newcomer by Sri Lankan standards. Although the area has long been settled, particularly by Muslim seafarers who established a small trading port here from the 8th century onwards, the town remained at the margins of Sri Lankan history until the arrival of Europeans in the 16th century.

In 1517 the recently arrived Portuguese built a fort here, their first foothold on the island, from where they launched their conquest of the Sri Lankan lowlands. It was this fort that subsequently formed the nucleus of the modern city. The Dutch expanded the fortifications and gave the fledgling city new suburbs and an extensive system of canals, though it was not until the arrival of the British that Colombo really began to take off, as improvements to its harbour transformed it into the island's principal port and an important staging post on the Indian Ocean's maritime routes. In 1815, Colombo was declared the capital of Ceylon. The modern city, which a population of around 3 million calls home, has grown exponentially since Independence and now spreads its tentacular suburbs along the coast for the best part of 60km (37 miles).

LEFT: Jami-ul-Alfar Mosque, the Pettah.
RIGHT: chappals at the Gangaramaya Temple.

A colonial capital

Much of this ever-expanding metropolis is now a disorienting morass of mildewed concrete and gridlocked traffic; but though initial impressions may be unwelcoming, Colombo's handful of low-key sights, its fascinating contrasts of colonial and modern, and its sheer hustle and bustle reward all those who take the time to spend a few days absorbing something of its unique character.

Colombo's relatively modern origins and colonial character – not to mention its sheer size, far bigger than any

Main attractions
THE PETTAH
GALLE FACE GREEN
SEEMA MALAKA AND
　GANGARAMAYA
VIHARAMAHADEVI PARK
NATIONAL MUSEUM
DEHIWALA ZOO
MOUNT LAVINIA
KELANIYA RAJA MAHA VIHARA

A new lighthouse, built to replace the old Lighthouse Clock Tower, stands on oceanfront Marine Drive, on the west side of Fort.

other city on the island – have given it a distinctly different atmosphere from the rest of Sri Lanka. There's relatively little visible evidence of Buddhism or traditional Sinhalese values here. Instead, the city's population comprises a cosmopolitan spread of cultures, with important Tamil and Muslim communities, as well as Burghers and a considerable number of expats. Mosques, churches and Hindu temples remain as visible as Buddhas and stupas, while conversations in the city's smarter suburbs are as likely to be in English as in Sinhala or Tamil.

And compared to the more conservative towns elsewhere in Sri Lanka, Colombo remains resolutely forward-thinking. This is a vibrant crucible of contemporary Sri Lankan life, its eyes fixed firmly on the outside world, with every latest fad and fashion hitting the streets of the capital some time before they reach the rest of the island – if, indeed, they ever do.

Old Fort, new district

BELOW: street scene from 1910.

At the centre of colonial Colombo is Fort district. The original fort was built by the Portuguese in 1517, and later expanded by the Dutch to protect their valuable trade in sapphires, elephants, cinnamon and ivory. As Colombo expanded during the 19th century under British rule, and the need for fortifications passed, the old defences were gradually dismantled and their place taken by streets of grandiose neo-classical buildings, which announced the new European overlords' mastery of their attractive new dominion.

The heart of Fort retains a time-warped British character, with huge old crumbling colonial buildings lining its small grid of streets, a couple of which – such as York and Chatham streets – still bear their original names. Much of the area's 19th-century charm vanished during the civil war, however, when repeated Tamil Tiger (LTTE) bombings drove most commercial life out to the southern suburbs and reduced parts of Fort to near dereliction. Roads around the President's House remain cordoned off for security reasons, and although long overdue renovation work has finally begun on some of the old

Main Street. Colombo.

Victorian buildings, the whole place remains somewhat forlorn, its largely deserted streets cut up by numerous security checkpoints, and with a heavy police presence throughout.

At the end of Chatham Street, the heart of Fort is marked by its most distinctive landmark, the **Lighthouse Clock Tower Ⓐ**, designed by a British governor's wife in an attempt to instil punctuality into the notoriously bad timekeepers under her husband's rule. Ten years after it was built, a light was added to the top of the structure, and the hybrid clock tower-cum-lighthouse went on to serve as the city's major shipping beacon until the 1950s, when new high-rise buildings finally blocked its view from the sea.

Immediately north of here, through the security fences and barbed wire, you might be able to catch a glimpse of the **President's House Ⓑ** (Janadhipathi Mandiraya), the official residence of the island's head of state. This beautiful mansion was built in the late 18th century by the last Dutch governor, and subsequently served as the residence of the island's British governors. These included the indefatigable Sir Edward Barnes, who unified the country with a massive road-building effort and whose statue still stands guard at the gate. All road distances from Colombo are measured from here. The surrounding streets and landmarks, including **Gordon Gardens** and the old **General Post Office**, are currently closed to visitors.

The short walk down Chatham Street and a left-turn along York Street brings you to **Cargills**, the famous old Colombo department store whose long red-brick facade provides another of Fort's famous landmarks, though the interior has now been largely stripped of its original wooden fittings and glass display cases. At the north end of York Street, Colombo Port is off limits to casual visitors, although you can admire the vast tangle of cranes, gantries and boats' funnels from the fourth-floor Harbour Room bar-restaurant at the **Grand Oriental Hotel Ⓒ**, opposite the port entrance. Before the age of planes, this famous old hotel was the inevitable first stop for all arriving

BELOW: a classic colonial villa, typified by its verandah and overhanging roofs.

TIP

A rickshaw (or tuktuk)
is the quickest and
most enjoyable way to
weave through the
traffic congestion of
Colombo, though not
particularly comfortable
for a long journey.

passengers staggering off their boats –
in 1914 Bella Woolf (sister of Leonard,
and future sister-in-law of Virginia)
wrote: "It is said that if you waited
long enough in the hall of the Grand
Oriental, you would meet everyone
worth meeting." In 1890, an unknown
Russian writer called Anton Chekhov
checked into the famous old hotel.
His latest book hadn't done too well,
hardly surprising since it was entitled
A Dreary Story, but he perked up after
a tour of the island and went home to
try his hand at playwriting.

The Dutch Hospital and southern Fort

Due south of the Lighthouse Clock
Tower lies one of Fort's oldest buildings – and newest landmarks – the
Dutch Hospital, with three long, low
wings of verandah-shaded ochre buildings arranged around a pair of courtyards. Originally built in the 17th
century, the hospital reopened following extensive renovations in 2011 and
now provides a memorable setting for
an upmarket cluster of restaurants,
cafés and shops which have brought

some much-needed life back to this
corner of the city.

Directly opposite the hospital rise
the major landmarks of southern Fort.
This part of the district is quite different in character from the time-worn
streets further north, and its cluster
of modern high-rise towers forms an
impressive skyline – at least by Sri
Lankan standards. Three of Colombo's
five-star hotels (the Hilton, Galadari
and Ceylon Continental – the last
currently closed for renovations)
can be found here, along with the
cylindrical twin towers of the **World
Trade Centre** and the soaring **Bank
of Ceylon** skyscraper. Next to the
Galadari Hotel lies the large, heavy
colonnaded facade of the former parliament building, now known as the
Presidential Secretariat, with statues
of Sri Lanka's first four post-Inde-
pendence prime ministers posing self-
importantly in front, including the
island's first premier, D.S. Senanayake,
who died after falling off his horse on
the adjacent Galle Face Green.

Pettah's shopping bazaar

East of Fort, on the north side of
Colombo Fort Railway Station,
stretches Colombo's most absorbing
area: the **Pettah**, a tumultuous bazaar
district that is still the scene of much
of the city's vibrant commercial life,
its grid of narrow streets stuffed full
of every conceivable type of merchan-
dise, from electrical goods to rare
spices. The Pettah is Colombo at its
most deafening and hyperactive, but
anarchic as it may initially seem, there
is some method in its madness if you
can stand the crowds and noise. Many
of the district's streets are given over to
specific items, with one street devoted
to selling leather goods, another to
household wares, and so on. The most
interesting area is around **4th Cross
Street**, which is given over to the sale
of teas and Ayurvedic herbs – somewhat more fragrant than the odours of
dead fish and diesel fumes that a walk
through the Pettah usually provides.

BELOW: the
Secretariat, now
overshadowed by
modern high-rise
buildings.

A home for all faiths

Concealed among the shops and teeming streetlife of the Pettah are some of the oldest and most interesting buildings in Colombo. The **Dutch Period Museum** ❶ (Tue–Sat 9am–5pm; charge), on Prince Street, occupies a well-preserved Dutch colonial residence dating back to 1780, whose original appearance has been re-created using assorted furnishings, household goods and maps – an idyllic respite from the frenzied streetlife outside. Various exhibitions lay bare Dutch life as it was on the island. Close by on Second Cross Street is the Pettah's most striking building, the **Jami-ul-Alfar Mosque** ❷, built in 1909 and striped in red and white like a stupendous raspberry layer-cake, with candy minarets and arches shaped like bitemarks.

More reminders of Dutch rule can be found at the atmospheric **Wolvendaal Kerk** ❻, on Wolfendahl Street and Vivekanada Hill at the northeastern edge of the Pettah. Begun in 1749, the church is plain on the outside, but within its 1.5-metre (5ft) thick walls, this staunch work of Doric architecture holds a finely carved wooden font, canopied pulpit, crystal lamps, an illustrated Dutch Bible and a fine collection of silver plate. Its floor is made from tombstones brought from a Dutch church in Fort.

A short distance west is **Sea Street**, one of the most colourful streets in the Pettah, with huge fluorescent Sinhala signs advertising the long string of jewellers' shops below, which specialise in silver and gold creations. Halfway up Sea Street are the **New and Old Kathiresan Kovils** ❼, the most important of the many small Hindu temples whose garish towers dot the area's streets. The temples' long, gaudy facades make a colourful splash along the roadside and are the starting point for the annual Vel Festival dedicated to the god Skanda (see page 96). During the festival, an enormous Vel chariot, intricately carved and brightly painted, is dragged around the city, visiting all the kovils on Galle Road, followed by thousands of devotees.

Continue north along Sea Street to reach the harbour-side and an important Roman Catholic church

Wolvendaal means "Dale of wolves", but since there were never any wolves on the island, the Dutch must have mistakenly identified a pack of roaming jackals.

BELOW: shopping in the Pettah.

dedicated to **St Anthony** . Every Tuesday, people hailing from various faiths flock to this church to tap into the miraculous powers that are attributed to the saint – a good example of the inter-faith worship that happens at so many of Sri Lanka's religious sites. If you still have energy for more, continue east to Colombo's most magnificent place of worship, **St Lucia's Cathedral** , finished in 1902, which took 34 years to complete and holds 6,000 worshippers on the very rare occasions when it's full. This enormous domed cathedral, with Ionic columns, is dedicated to the Virgin St Lucy of Sicily. Legend has it that she had such alluring eyes, she pulled them out to present them to an unwelcome suitor enamoured of her beauty.

Galle Face Green

Back in the city centre, on the south side of Fort, stretches an elongated expanse of scrubby grass called **Galle Face Green** , which provides the city with important breathing space and attracts locals in their hundreds towards dusk. This is when crowds of cheerful idlers come to meet friends, fly kites or sample the strange-looking snacks sold from mobile food-carts along the oceanfront esplanade (although every few years the worn-out grass means that the whole green needs to be closed for reseeding).

A handful of newish hotels lies close to the green, including the palatial **Taj Samudra**, which overlooks the east side of the green, a Holiday Inn and the three five-stars (see page 288) at the southern end of Fort. None, however, can match the colonial aura of the venerable **Galle Face Hotel** *(see box)*, built in 1864, which bounds the southern end of the green. Even if you're not staying here, this is still the best place in Colombo to watch the sun go down. It becomes an even better experience when enjoyed while sipping a mango cocktail or an arrack and soda next to the outsize chessboard on the seafront lawn.

Slave Island

East of Galle Face Green, Slave Island was named after the slaves whom the Dutch once imprisoned here by

A hotel with allure

"**H**ere, in the course of time and travel comes sooner, or later, every man born of woman, and every woman interesting or uninteresting to man. Go where you will, go East, go West, you shall hardly avoid landing some day at the Galle Face Hotel. Not even if your aim be the Antarctic Pole." So observed Yorkshire-born botanist and traveller Reginald Farrer – credited with introducing numerous new species of rock plant to British gardens – in his book *In Old Ceylon*, published in 1908. His enthusiasm was perhaps due to one of the splendid concoctions from the verandah bar, or the cosseting from the four liveried retainers allocated to each customer in those days (the hotel still has an exceptionally high staff-to-customer ratio).

night. At the time it was completely surrounded by Beira Lake, which has since been compressed to reclaim more land. The slaves were flogged and branded if they tried to abscond, while the lake was stocked with crocodiles to further discourage them from attempting to swim to freedom.

The district retains a resolutely ramshackle and local atmosphere, despite its central location and proximity to some of the city's swankiest addresses. There are numerous mosques and temples dotted around, including several mosques built for the Malay troops once garrisoned here by the British, and the huge **Sri Subramania Hindu temple** on Kew Road, whose soaring, multicoloured tower provides the district with its major landmark.

The most unusual place of worship hereabouts, however, is the **Seema Malaka Buddhist temple** ⓛ, whose small buildings sit atop three podiums perched amid the sluggish waters of Beira Lake. Designed by Sri Lanka's foremost 20th-century architect, Geoffrey Bawa, the temple offers a modernist take on traditional

Sinhalese architectural styles. The overhanging tiled roofs are held up by walls made from collected spindles and bannisters, affording ample protection from heavy rains, but no impediment to cooling breezes. Its peaceful elegance is a haven from the noisy city and a world away from the larger and more traditional **Gangaramaya Temple** ⓜ (daily 7.30am—11.30pm; charge) close by. The latter is a good example of the modern Buddhist temples you'll see all over the island, with a main shrine filled by an enormous fluorescent orange Buddha and a host of attendant deities and disciples; a peaceful courtyard with a Bo tree on a raised platform to one side (where you may also see the temple's resident elephant feasting on piles of leaves); and various subsidiary buildings containing shrines to other gods revered by Sri Lankan Buddhists. The highlight of the temple is its bizarre museum, which is home to a vast collection of antiques, kitsch and random bric-a-brac, all presented to the temple by devotees over the centuries. Feast

Looking down the coast from Galle Face.

BELOW: intersection in the Slave Island area.

One of the Hindu bronzes in the National Museum.

your eyes on shelves chock-a-block with sandalwood and ivory carvings, brass gods and even old Parker pens and eye glasses, strewn between jade and crystal monstrosities and elephant tusks. The resident guide will be disappointed if your jaw doesn't drop.

Viharamahadevi Park and around

Southeast of Slave Island lie the expansive open spaces of **Viharamahadevi Park** . Originally known as Victoria Park, and still occasionally referred to by that name, it was renamed in 1958 after a Sri Lankan, rather than a British, queen. Ebony, mahogany, lemon, fig and eucalyptus trees grow here among lotus ponds, and if you visit just before dusk you'll see the hordes of resident fruit bats waking and stretching their wings.

Overlooking the northeastern side of the park is the **Town Hall**, built in 1927: a neoclassical wedding cake topped with a glimmering white dome and with a large, shiny golden Buddha sitting impassively opposite. Just across the street from the Town

BELOW: at the Gangaramaya Temple.

Hall is the **Devatagaha Mosque** , the oldest building in this part of Colombo, dedicated to the Muslim saint, Datar, who is buried here.

The mosque sits on the busy **De Soysa Circus**, which is now one of modern Colombo's major shopping areas. The best-known place hereabouts is the chic little **Paradise Road** emporium, close by at 213 Dharmapala Mawatha, which occupies a 19th-century mansion and sells locally made collectibles, antiques and ceramics aimed at Western tastes. The smart **Odel department store**, almost opposite the mosque at 5 Alexandra Place, is the island's glitziest department store and another popular destination for tourists and label-conscious locals.

The National Museum

The southern end of Viharamahadevi Park is home to a trio of museums. The **National Museum** (daily 9am–6pm; charge), on Albert Crescent, an elegant white colonial structure of 1877, contains regalia of the last king of Kandy and other treasures. The collection provides an excellent overview

of Sri Lankan arts and crafts, beginning with a limestone Buddha from Anuradhapura, which sits meditating in the foyer as if undisturbed by the passage of 16 centuries. The surrounding rooms are filled with an excellent collection of small Hindu bronzes, many of them taken from the temples built at Polonnaruwa by the invading Tamil Cholas.

Also here is Sri Lanka's finest collection of masks – quite unlike the stereotypical junk which is flogged at most of the island's shops. The masks here cover the whole range of the island's artisanal output, including the traditional masks made for kolam performances (see page 100) and the fearsome masks representing various diseases and demons, which were worn by the principal dancer during exorcism ceremonies. At the end of the ritual, the deity represented by the mask was asked to leave and never return. No repeat prescriptions were necessary.

A few rooms further on is the highlight of the museum, the glittering crown, throne and footstool of the last Kandyan kings. These were rudely appropriated by the British and shipped back to England, where they were housed in Windsor Castle until rightfully returned in 1934.

Other museums in the vicinity include the dog-eared **Natural History Museum** (daily 9am–5pm; charge) and, next door to it, the **National Art Gallery** at 106 Ananda Kumaraswamy Mawatha (daily 9am–5pm; free), which has an interesting collection of works by 20th-century Sri Lankan artists, though nothing is labelled.

Cinnamon Gardens

Colombo's most exclusive suburb, Cinnamon Gardens – or "Colombo 7", as it's often known, after its postcode – is named for the plantations of cinnamon which formerly grew here in Dutch times. The suburb has a peaceful and slightly patrician air, with wide, straight streets shaded by the sweeping canopies of tropical trees and lined with magnificent old villas (most of which now house foreign embassies or exclusive schools). Even the suburb's street names – Guildford Crescent, Torrington Square, Horton Place, and so

SHOP

On the north side of the National Museum and National Art Gallery, Ananda Kumaraswmy Mawatha (or Green Path) is home to one of Colombo's most enjoyable impromptu artistic events every weekend, when local artists hang their canvases from the railings along the side of the road, transforming the road into a blaze of colour. All paintings are for sale, often at surprisingly modest price.

BELOW: the Town Hall, as seen from Viharamahadevi Park.

The Legend of Viharamahadevi

Sri Lankan history numbers many famous kings, but only one celebrated queen: Viharamahadevi. According to legend, Viharamahadevi was the daughter of a certain King Tissa of Kelaniya. Tissa unjustly sentenced a Buddhist monk to death (the unfortunate man was boiled alive), whereupon, it is said, the waters of the oceans rose up and threatened to drown his kingdom. The redoubtable princess offered herself as a sacrifice to atone for her father's crime, and was duly placed in a boat and cast adrift off the coast near present-day Colombo. After a long sea journey, Viharamahadevi fetched up on the shore at Kirinda, near Tissamaharama, where she was discovered by King Kavantissa. Kavantissa, smitten by her beauty, immediately married her. The royal couple produced a son, the legendary Dutugemunu, Sri Lanka's greatest historical hero.

Like other legends of ancient Sri Lanka, the story of Viharamahadevi is probably a recycled mix of a little fact and considerable fancy, woven together over the ages and complete with the obligatory Buddhist moral (monks should not be boiled in a pot). It also neatly provides the island's greatest warrior-king with a suitably illustrious mother. Perhaps most interesting, though, is the description of the waves rising to swallow King Tissa's kingdom – previously regarded as a fanciful piece of story-telling, it has acquired a new, and sinister, relevance since the 2004 tsunami.

Municipal garden sign.

BELOW: keeping cool in school uniform.
RIGHT: going to the shops is a colourful business.

on – remain resolutely English, having so far resisted the tide of Sinhalisation that has overtaken many of the capital's other colonial street names.

The area's attractions are low-key. The **Sapumal Foundation** (32/4 Barnes Place; Thur–Sat 10am–1pm; free; www. theserendibgallery.com/sapu_found) houses a rewarding collection of Sri Lankan 20th-century art in a sprawling bungalow that was once the home and studio of Harry Pieris, one of the artists of the so-called '43 Group, whose members laid the foundations of modern art in Sri Lanka. Another artist associated with the '43 Group was the famous barrister, musician and photographer, Lionel Wendt, who is commemorated by the **Lionel Wendt Theatre and Art Gallery** (http://lionelwendt.org) at 18 Guildford Crescent. The venue hosts contemporary art and craft displays and a changing programme of musical and theatrical events. Northwest from here, at 61 Dharmapala Mawatha, the Saskia Fernando Gallery (daily 10am–6pm; free; http://saskiafernandogallery.com) showcases the work of leading living Sri Lankan visual artists.

Further south, along Cambridge Place, are two of the country's most august academic institutions, **Colombo University** and **Royal College**, which share a triangle of land with the city's forgotten racecourse on Reid Avenue. To the east is Independence Avenue and the **Independence Commemoration Hall**, a fake Kandyan audience hall of monstrously oversize proportions, built shortly after Independence. Close by on Maitland Place stands the venerable Sinhalese Sports Club, popularly known as the "Lord's of Sri Lanka" and the city's venue for test match cricket since 1984.

Galle Road

South of Galle Face Green lie the principal districts of modern Colombo: brasher, newer and quite different in character from the northern part of the city. Most of the commercial activity driven out of Fort by repeated LTTE bombings has taken refuge here, while a burgeoning number of smart shops, cafés and restaurants means that what this part of Colombo lacks in historic attractions, it more than makes up for in

amenities – if you want to eat, drink and shop in the city, this is the place to be.

The smelly and deafening **Galle Road** arrows due south from Galle Face Green, bisecting the city's main southern suburbs – Kollupitiya, Bambalapitiya and Wellawatta – before reaching Dehiwala and Mount Lavinia (see page 160). The Galle Road is the main focus of the southern city, serving as its effective high street and major traffic artery. The choking fumes and fanfares of bus horns and associated vehicular cacophony can make exploring the strip a tiring experience, though traces of traditional Sri Lankan life remain among the gimcrack modern glass and concrete architecture: tumbledown little local cafés and tiny shops, and pavement hawkers selling all sorts of odds and ends, from sacks of rice to religious posters.

Kollupitiya and Bambalapitiya

The northern end of the Galle Road has a rather forbidding atmosphere, with the US and Indian embassies hidden behind large defensive walls, and the even more heavily fortified **Temple Trees** (the Sri Lankan prime minister's official residence) protected by sandbagged gun emplacements and watchtowers, from which rifle-toting soldiers regard the passers-by below. At the north end of the suburb is the glitzy **Crescat Boulevard** shopping centre.

Things become livelier 1.6km (1 mile) or so south at Bambalapitiya, the commercial heart of southern Colombo, where a mixed bag of shops and restaurants fights for street space. These range from the large and humdrum **Majestic City** shopping mall through to the beautiful **Barefoot** shop (see page 301), whose vibrantly coloured, instantly recognisable textiles have become synonymous with contemporary Sri Lankan style.

A few minutes' walk north from Barefoot at 2 Alfred House Gardens lies The Gallery Café, another landmark of contemporary Sri Lankan style. The café (and attached shop and gallery) occupy the former offices of architect Geoffrey Bawa: the café in the urn-dotted, high-walled courtyard; the shop and gallery in the elegant

Running parallel to Galle Road a block inland is R.A. de Mel Mawatha, still usually referred to by its old name of Duplication Road, which (literally) duplicates the course of Galle Road to provide extra breathing space for the district's traffic, and further street space for restaurants and shops.

LEFT: a quiet moment in the park.
BELOW: tuktuks braving the rain.

buildings which front it. Close by, at number 11, 33rd Lane (Mon–Fri 9am–5pm; charge), Bawa's former house is also open to the public. Extensively remodelled by Bawa during the four decades he lived here, the house offers a fascinating insight into his style at its most intimate, as well as showcasing the eclectic range of artworks and arte-facts collected by him over the years.

A detail from the elaborate carvings at Raja Maha Vihara.

Dehiwala Zoo

In the southern suburb of Dehiwala, the extensive **Dehiwala Zoo Q** (daily 8.30am–6pm; charge) is home to a wide range of Sri Lankan and international wildlife and birdlife. Compared to the dismal zoos found in other parts of Asia, the inmates here enjoy tolerably humane conditions, apart from some of the unfortunate big cats, which remain shut up in horribly small cages pending further promised improvements.

The zoo's representative selection of Sri Lankan wildlife makes it a good place to visit before heading off to the national parks. Look out for all three types of local monkey, sambhur and spotted deer, sloth bears and leopards, as

BELOW: sunset swim at Mount Lavinia.

well as a wide selection of birdlife – brush up on your birdspotting skills in the large walk-through aviary. There's also a fine selection of non-Sri Lankan wildlife, including lions, tigers, chee-tahs, jaguars, giraffes, tapirs, kangaroos and a few African elephants – although you probably won't want to see these performing during the infamous daily elephant dance (5.15pm).

Mount Lavinia

The south coast is fringed with patches of sand all the way down from Fort, but the first proper beach isn't reached until you arrive at the suburb of **Mount Lavinia R**, 10km (6 miles) south of Fort. It's not the greatest stretch of sand in Sri Lanka, admittedly, but it's not bad, and the swimming is generally safe (though beware of strong undertows), while the suburb's tranquil atmosphere and a good spread of accommodation options make it a pleasant retreat from the madness of Colombo and the nearby Galle Road.

The best place to stay is the land-mark **Mount Lavinia Hotel**, sitting grandly atop the small promontory

that terminates the southern end of the beach. This sprawling wedding-cake of a hotel has grown up around an old colonial villa and was the meeting place for the world's rich and famous for many years. The hotel still maintains a certain colonial elegance and period charm, as well as a pool, and a good stretch of private beach (open to non-guests for a price) if you want to get away from the masses on the public beach – which you quite possibly will at weekends, when half of Colombo seems to descend on the sands.

Kelaniya and Kotte

On the northeastern edge of Colombo, the suburb of Kelaniya is home to one of the island's most revered Buddhist temples, the **Kelaniya Raja Maha Vihara** , which is supposed to occupy the place where the Buddha paid the last of his three mythical visits to the island – a stupa marks the exact spot. The original temple was destroyed by the Indians, then rebuilt, and then demolished by the Portuguese. The current structure is an attractive colonial-era building dating from the 18th and 19th centuries, decorated with an eye-catching sequence of modern murals by Soliya Mendis, depicting the Buddha's legendary visits to the island as described in the *Mahavamsa*. The temple is also home to the lavish two-day Duruthu Perahera, held annually every January on Duruthu Poya day (see page 97).

On the western edge of the city, around 7km (4 miles) inland from Fort, the modern suburb of Sri Jayawardenepura occupies the location of the former capital of **Kotte** ❼, one of the various transient capitals established during the long period of instability following the abandonment of Polonnaruwa. The city flourished during the 15th and 16th centuries and was the first Sinhalese settlement to come into contact with the Portuguese, who greatly admired the place, before destroying it. It's now home to the Sri Lankan parliament, occupying a large and striking Kandyan-style building designed by Geoffrey Bawa, poised in the middle of an artificial lake – a fine sight, though it's not open to the public for obvious reasons.

BELOW: festivities held during the Duruthu Perahera.

WEST COAST

Lined by a string of fine beaches, along with tourist amenities of every conceivable standard and style, this is Sri Lanka's most developed stretch of coast.

Sri Lanka's west coast shows the island at its most developed, its most Westernised, and its most tourist-oriented. A string of fine beaches, backed by hundreds of hotels and guesthouses of all sizes and standards, dot the coast from Negombo in the north to Hikkaduwa in the south. Despite increasing development in other parts of the island, the large resort hotels of Negombo, Kalutara, Beruwala and Bentota continue to serve as the main engine of the island's substantial package-tourist industry, offering two-week stays to sun-starved European visitors, particularly during the northern winter.

Development along the coast has been unplanned, uncontrolled and, in some places at least, decidedly unappealing – although even budget resorts like Hikkaduwa and Negombo have recently smartened up their acts, and almost all the massive damage from the 2004 tsunami has now been repaired. And yet despite the crassness of some parts of the coastal development, there is still much to savour along the west coast, and places that still justify the words of the late Arthur C. Clarke, once Sri Lanka's most celebrated foreign resident, who described the coast thus; "And always it is the same; the slender palm trees leaning over the white sand, the warm sun sparkling on the waves as they break on the inshore reef, the outrigger fishing boats drawn up high on the beach. This alone is real; the rest is but a dream from which I shall presently awake."

Negombo

The beach at **Negombo ❶** owes much of its popularity to its convenient location just 10km (6 miles) north of the international airport, attracting many visitors for their first (or last) night's

Main attractions
BRIEF GARDEN
BENTOTA
LUNUGANGA
INDURUWA
AMBALANGODA
HIKKADUWA

PRECEDING PAGES: Negombo port.
LEFT: Tangalla coastline. **RIGHT:** celebrating National Day on Negombo Beach.

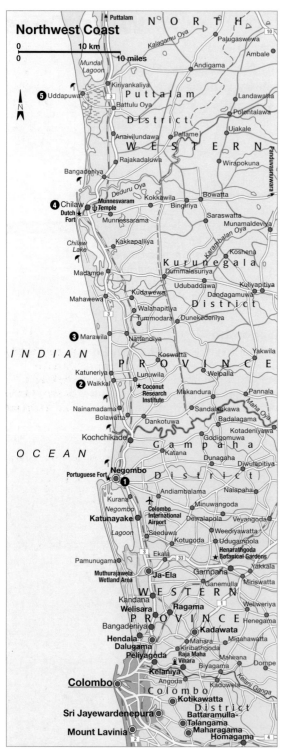

Northwest Coast

stay on the island. The beach here is wide but heavily developed and, in places, rather grubby. Although there are far nicer places to stay further south, Negombo is fine for a night, and there are myriad hotels in all price ranges to choose from. There's also a good collection of restaurants and bars, giving the resort a liveliness and a smattering of nightlife that is notably lacking in most other places along the coast.

One of the largest towns along the west coast, Negombo rose to prominence during the colonial era thanks to its abundant supplies of wild cinnamon *(see box)*. The centre of town preserves a few reminders of the Dutch period, including the slight remains of the old fort (converted by the British into a prison, and still used as such), a ramshackle old rest house, and the Dutch canal, which arrows due north from Negombo all the way to Puttalam, over 100km (62 miles) away.

In the middle of town stands the stately pink landmark of **St Mary's Church**, one of the numerous large Roman Catholic churches that dot Negombo town and the coast south to Colombo. Portuguese missionaries were particularly active in the area, converting many of the local Karava fishermen to Roman Catholicism. Their devotion to the faith of their colonial overlords can still be seen, not only in the area's many churches, but also in the dozens of colourful little wayside shrines which crop up on the main roads around town, as well as in the dramatic Passion Play, which is enacted at Duwa island, just opposite Negombo town, every Easter.

The Karavas are also famous for their fleets of distinctive *oruva* boats – a type of small outrigger canoe topped by a huge square sail. Pliny mentioned these boats in the 1st century AD, though they had probably existed for many centuries before then, and the sight of dozens of these unusual vessels sailing back to shore after a fishing trip is Negombo's most memorable sight.

Bounding the south side of the old town centre, the Negombo Lagoon is the source of some of the island's most highly prized seafood, especially its large and juicy prawns. Daily fish auctions are held early in the morning (around 7am) in the busy fish markets in the town centre and at Duwa, both of which are worth a visit at any time of the morning for the sight of crowds of locals haggling animatedly over huge piles of tuna, seer, mullet, crabs and other forms of marine bounty.

Muthurajawela

Midway between Negombo and Colombo, the beautiful wetlands of **Muthurajawela** offer a tranquil natural escape from the surrounding urban sprawl. The saltwater wetlands and lagoons here are home to abundant birdlife, as well as toque macaque monkeys, water monitors and the occasional croc. Enjoyable boat trips (daily 7am–4pm; charge) depart from the visitor centre, heading down the old Dutch Canal before reaching the southern end

of the beautiful Negombo lagoon, a breezy expanse of water running around patches of tangled mangrove swamp and with egrets, herons and kingfishers perched on the surrounding trees.

From Negombo to Chilaw

Heading north from Negombo you'll pass the villages of **Waikkal** ❷ and **Marawila** ❸. Waikkal is a major tile-producing centre, and tiles are made in the dozens of picturesque little home-spun factories, with their distinctive tall brick chimneys, which dot the countryside hereabouts, while Marawila is known for its batiks, which are offered for sale (at prices generally lower than elsewhere in the island) in a couple of large showrooms along the main highway.

The main road continues north from Mahawewa, running inland around Chilaw Lake to reach the bustling fishing town of **Chilaw** ❹. The main point of interest hereabouts is the **Munnesvaram Temple**, about 5km (3 miles) inland, one of the most important Siva temples on

> **TIP**
>
> Short trips aboard one of Negombo's *oruva* boats out to sea or into the Negombo lagoon or boat trips along the old Dutch Canal can be arranged through many places in town.

BELOW: Sri Lankan cinnamon *(Zeylanicum cinnamon)*, both in quills and ground.

Cinnamon

One of Sri Lanka's most attractive commodities, in the eyes of the Portuguese and Dutch, was the plentiful cinnamon which grew along the west coast. Cinnamon – "the bride around whom they danced" – grew wild in the jungles and was in huge demand in Europe, where it was much sought after for its distinctive flavour and for its efficacy in relieving air trapped in the bowels. The cinnamon found in the Negombo area was traditionally regarded as the sweetest and most highly prized.

Cinnamon grew wild in damp, elephant-infested jungle. Collecting it was hard, dangerous work, and the exclusive job of the Choliah caste. Tubes of cinnamon were bundled up and taken to "surgeons" who bit off pieces to assess quality, the premium being on milder varieties without an aftertaste. A ritual slice of bread was eaten between batches, not to cleanse the palate in the wine-tasting sense but to ease pain; repeated mouthfuls of cinnamon were torture on the tongue.

Cinnamon was so valuable that it was made a capital offence to damage plants, which grew up to 3 metres (10ft) in height, or to sell it on the black market. However, Arab traders were more familiar with the coastline than Dutch naval patrols, so contraband cinnamon and even elephants went out; Indian rice and textiles came the other way.

The doorway of a shop entices with shade, rather than displays of goods.

BELOW: the Tsunami memorial in Peraliya, near Hikkaduwa.

the island. The orginal temple was later destroyed by the Portuguese and the present building dates from the British colonial era. The lavishly decorated inner shrine houses the main Shiva lingam and a golden statue of his wife, Parvati, surrounded by a fine old wooden ambulatory housing shrines to various other deities and assorted chariots used in the annual temple festival (held in Aug–Sept).

North of Chilaw

At **Uddapuwa** ❺, between Mundal Lagoon and the sea, the terrain changes dramatically as you enter the dry zone. The fishing villagers here are descendants of a north Indian warrior caste who settled on this coast over 1,000 years ago. They were the first converts to Catholicism when the Portuguese arrived and mass baptisms were held, during which the converts acquired surnames like Mendis, de Silva and Fernando. Despite Christian influence, Uddapuwa is home also to a notable group of small Hindu temples located along the coast.

Just south of Puttalam, a small side road leads around the edge of the extensive Puttalam Lagoon to reach the **Kalpitiya peninsula**, a beautifully remote area hemmed in by sea and lagoon on three sides. At the tip of the peninsula, Kalpitiya town was formerly a major Dutch stronghold and still boasts the remains of an old fort, along with the colonial-era St Peter's Kirk. The area nearby has been earmarked for major new government-sponsored tourist development, although this has (mercifully) so far failed to take shape.

Tourist development on the peninsula has so far has been largely confined to the village of Alankuda, some 15km (9 miles) south of Kalpitiya town. A wonderful cluster of low-key boutique resorts (www.alankuda.com; see page 290) has sprung up on the beautiful beach here over the past few years, offering attractive but unusual lodgings close to nature in a range of characterful styles – mud-brick chalets, quirky wooden cabanas and Rajasthani-style tents. Alankuda has also developed

into a major centre for whale- and, especially, dolphin-watching. During an early-morning sea-trip here you're likely to see perhaps over a thousand of these remarkable creatures, an extraordinary sight, with pods of (mainly spinner) dolphins in every direction as far as the eye can see, skimming through the waves and occasionally leaping clean out of the water and spinning acrobatically through the air.

The A3 coast road continues to the town of **Puttalam**, another busy fishing settlement whose proximity to the north has made it a major collecting point for Muslims evicted from the north by the Tamil Tigers, some of whom have remained stranded here in refugee camps for the best part of two decades. At Puttalam the A12 turns inland to Anuradhapura, offering an alternative route to the Cultural Triangle.

En route, the road passes **Wilpattu National Park**, the largest national park in the country and formerly one of its most popular, particularly famous for its large leopard and elephant populations. Sadly the park was badly damaged – and much of its wildlife killed or dispersed – during the civil war, but it's now once again open to visitors and is gradually beginning to recover some of its former lustre.

South to Kalutara

The stretch of coastline south from Colombo is the tourist epicentre of the island, with a strip of superb beaches equipped with a sprawl of resort hotels, luxury villas and down-at-heel guesthouses. Every conceivable taste is catered for here, from the chic boutique hotels of Bentota to the budget surfers' guesthouses of Hikkaduwa.

An hour's drive south of Colombo, the large town of **Kalutara** ❻ is the first place south of the capital that still retains its own separate identity – though only just. The beach here, and at the neighbouring suburb of Wadduwa to the north, remains unspoilt, however, surprisingly so given its proximity to the capital, and is home to a cluster of large resort

The Galle Road runs between the stupa and the rest of the Gangatilaka temple. It is customary for drivers travelling further down the road to stop and drop a few coins in the strategically placed tills in the hope of ensuring a safe journey.

BELOW: Beruwala Bay.

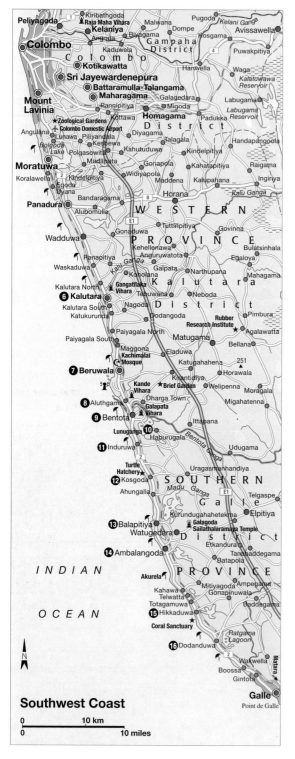

Southwest Coast

0   10 km

0   10 miles

hotels strung out along the narrow but still relatively peaceful sands.

The town itself takes its name from the Kalu Ganga, or "Black River", whose expansive mouth is crossed by a long bridge, from where there are tempting views of tranquil waters and thickets of palm trees inland. Ahead, the view is dominated by the huge white stupa of the **Gangatilaka** (donation), rising high above town. This is one of the largest stupas on the island, and also one of the few which is hollow, its cool interior decorated with 74 murals, laid out in cartoon-like strips and telling some of the Jataka stories, which deal with the Buddha's previous lives.

A few kilometres inland from Kalutara lies the intriguing old **Richmond Castle** (daily 9am–4pm; charge). This magnificent hybrid of Indian and British architecture was originally a spice plantation mansion built for a wealthy regional governor who copied the plans from an Indian Maharaja's palace, designed by a London architect.

Beruwala

About 60km (37 miles) from Colombo, **Beruwala** ❼ is the heart of Sri Lanka's package-tourist industry. The beach here is wide and beautiful, an alluring swathe of sand backed by a string of densely packed resort hotels, which cater mainly to the European package-holiday crowd. The area is also one of the island's main Ayurveda centres, and most of the hotels here offer Ayurvedic treatments in dedicated centres.

A couple of kilometres north of the resorts, the scruffy town of Beruwala is the oldest recorded Muslim settlement in Sri Lanka, and still has a large Muslim population. The town's most significant landmark, out on a rocky headland on the northern edge of town, is the white minarets of the **Kachimalai Mosque**, believed to be the oldest on the island. It is also an exquisite location from which to watch the sunset, with views over the bay and lighthouse.

Aluthgama

Immediately south of the Beruwala resort strip, the workaday little town of **Aluthgama** ❽, literally "New Town", is one of the liveliest along the west coast – a bustling place with lively fish and vegetable markets, plus a surprisingly good selection of unpretentious little shops selling masks and woodcarvings. The town also has a string of attractively low-key guesthouses backing onto the beautiful Bentota Lagoon – a good alternative to the less appealing resort hotels to the north and south.

About 1km (0.5 miles) inland from Aluthgama, the pretty little hilltop **Kande Vihara** is home to one of Sri Lanka's biggest Buddha statues, a 48-metre (157ft) colossus seated in the Bhumisparsha (Earth Witness) mudra, which was completed in 2007. The original temple dates back to 1734, and also includes an ornate Baroque 18th-century image house with some well-preserved Kandyan-era murals and a couple of resident elephants.

About 16km (10 miles) inland lies **Brief Garden** (daily 8am–5pm; charge). There was nothing remotely brief about Brief, which was a lifetime's work for its creator, the acclaimed landscape artist, sculptor and bon vivant Bevis Bawa – elder brother of Geoffrey Bawa, the celebrated architect who established his own country estate just down the road at Lunuganga. Brief got its name because Bawa's barrister father bought the land with money from a successful legal brief. Bevis Bawa cleared the surrounding rubber plantation and went on to create a verdant romantic folly of inviting alcoves, nooks and bowers. The house is even more appealing, a beautiful colonial villa stuffed full of miscellaneous artefacts and artworks – including a stunning mural of Sri Lankan life by Australian artist Donald Friend, which dominates the hall. There are also assorted mementoes of Bevis Bawa's life and times, including photographs of some of the celebrities

Beruwala suffered significant tsunami damage in 2004, and major building works continue to this day, including renovation work on the landmark Riverina hotel and the construction of the huge new Chaaya Bay resort, due to open in 2013 on the site of the former Hotel Bayroo, which was flattened by the waves.

BELOW: Bentota Beach.

A Hindu shrine.

BELOW: a hawksbill turtle, one of the kind found nesting near Kosgoda.

who visited, such as Laurence Olivier and Vivien Leigh.

Bentota

South of Beruwala, its twin resort, **Bentota ❾**, offers another superb swathe of golden sand and a further string of resort hotels, although development here has been more muted than at Beruwala, with hotels laid out at discreet intervals along the beach and a far more relaxed and hassle-free atmosphere. The southern end of the beach is home to some of the west coast's most appealing top-end accommodation options, with a number of delightful boutique hotels and villas hidden amongst the palm trees.

Bentota is also the water sports capital of the island. Backing the beach, the calm waters of the Bentota Lagoon and river offer the ideal setting for myriad activities ranging from canoeing to jet-skiing. It's also possible to arrange interesting boat rides up the river, exploring the Bentota Ganga's tangled waterways, mangrove swamps and marine life.

Between the beach and the river, Bentota village offers an interesting slice of local life – although it's impossible to explore for long before being seized by a local tout. There are a couple of interesting Buddhist temples here: the kitsch **Wanawasa Raja Maha Vihara**, and the most atmospheric **Galapata Vihara**, dating back to the 12th century, which legend claims was built by a minister of Paragramabahu the Great (1153–86), the famous ruler of Polonnaruwa. The temple is said to have been linked by a maze of subterranean tunnels to other temples in the area.

Further inland up the Bentota River lies the magical country estate of **Lunuganga ❿** (daily 9am–5pm; charge). Lunuganga was the life's work of the celebrated architect Geoffrey Bawa, who acquired the former rubber plantation and its bungalow in 1948 and spent the next half century landscaping the grounds and adding a sequence of engaging new buildings to it – a fascinating snapshot of his architectural career in miniature. The gardens ramble over two small hills,

flanked by the waters of Dedduwa Lake, with artfully contrived terraces dotted with strategically placed artworks, opening up at moments to reveal carefully planned vistas over the surrounding countryside. The original bungalow itself was systematically adapted and expanded, while Bawa added a number of new outbuildings, ranging from the diminutive "Hen House", constructed during the 1970s, to the beautiful Cinnamon Hill House of 1992.

South of Bentota, the village of **Induruwa** ⓫ is home to another fine stretch of beach, even quieter (and notably cleaner) than that at Bentota. Though it is now slowly being colonised by a further crop of hotels and guesthouses, it remains one of the nicest and most soporific destinations along the west coast.

Kosgoda and Balapitiya

Sri Lanka's oldest turtle hatchery can be found 5km (3 miles) south of Induruwa in **Kosgoda** ⓬. Like other such ventures along the west and south coasts, the hatchery works by buying eggs from local poachers (who would otherwise sell them for food), allowing them to hatch and then releasing them into the ocean. There's not much to see at the hatchery itself. The main attractions are the nightly turtle watches (donation), organised under the auspices of the Turtle Conservation Project, and during the main nesting season (Jan–May, best in Apr) there's an excellent chance of seeing at least one or two turtles hoist themselves ashore to lay their eggs on the beach.

A few kilometres further south, **Balapitiya** ⓭ is the starting point for one of the island's most interesting boatriver journeys, heading down the idyllic Madu Ganga past a host of tiny islands, only a few of which are inhabited; one is home to a garish modern Buddhist temple. Wildlife is plentiful, with water monitors, monkeys and myriad birdlife.

Ambalangoda

The town of **Ambalangoda** ⓮, 86km (54 miles) from Colombo, is most famous as the centre of the island's mask carvers, the people responsible for

During the peak nesting month of April, as many as ten turtles visit the beach nightly to lay eggs at Kosgoda; at other times of the year several nights may pass without a single visitor.

BELOW: Hikkaduwa Beach, good for the budget-conscious.

TIP

If you've had your fill of masks in Ambalangoda, excellent batik work can be seen at the workshop of Dudley Silva, who has exhibited his Picasso-inspired pieces as far afield as Europe. His workshop is at 53 Elpitiya Road (signed on the left as you walk into town from the mask museums).

the luridly painted images of demons and other figures which were originally used in performance of southern *kolam* and exorcism dances (see page 100), and which have now found new life as tourist souvenirs. Two mask museums stand opposite one another at the northern end of town. The larger and more interesting of the two is the **Ariyapala and Sons Mask Museum** (daily 8.30am–5.30pm; charge), which has fascinating displays explaining the meanings and traditions behind the masks. The shop above has a huge selection of masks and woodcarvings, and you can also watch carvers at work in the attached workshop. Directly opposite, the more modest **Ariyapala Traditional Masks** (daily 8.30am–6pm; donation) has a basement display featuring some impressively large masks, although the main focus is the shop upstairs. There are various other mask-carving workshops dotted around town where you can watch local artisans at work and explore the full range of Sri Lankan mask styles. **Southland Masks**, at 353 Main Road, a few minutes' walk south of the mask museums,

has a particularly fine selection. The town is also a major carpentry centre and well known for its reproduction colonial furniture, which you might see in workshops around town.

Opportunities to see the masks being used in the dances for which they were originally designed are sadly difficult to come by. The **Bandu Wijesuriya Dance Academy**, opposite and under the same management as the Ariyapala and Sons Mask Museum, sometimes stages performances of traditional Kandyan and Low Country dances during the tourist season (Nov–Apr). Even if nothing formal is scheduled, some of the school's 250 pupils are put through their paces from around 3pm for an hour or so, Monday to Friday, and rehearsals are open to visitors.

Some 6km (3.5 miles) inland from Ambalangoda, the obscure **Galagoda Sailathalaramaya Temple** (donation) at the village of Karandeniya is the unlikely home to Sri Lanka's largest reclining Buddha, an impressively elongated figure measuring some 35 metres (115ft) in length, and dating

BELOW: masks to lure tourists and frighten demons.

back to around the beginning of the 18th century.

Hikkaduwa

Half an hour's drive south of Ambalangoda lies the busy beach town of **Hikkaduwa** ⑮, 100km (62 miles) from Colombo, and Sri Lanka's long-est-established budget beach hangout. Uncontrolled development during the 1970s and 1980s took a heavy toll here, particularly along the northern end of the beach around Hikkaduwa town, but the sands further around Wewala south remain broad and inviting, dotted with inexpensive guesthouses and rustic palm-thatch restaurants and bars which stay busy until late at night. Hikkaduwa also offers some of the island's best surfing and diving, and offers a lively alternative to the more staid and expensive resorts at Bentota, Beruwala and Kalutara, particularly during the hedonistic Hikkaduwa Beach Festival, a three-day rave in July/ August featuring international DJs.

Hikkaduwa's principal attraction is its **Coral Sanctuary**, immediately off the beach in the middle of Hikkaduwa town. The coral gardens here suffered badly during the tsunami, but are now steadily recovering and also provide a home to a wealth of tropical fish, as well as the occasional visiting turtle. The safest way to see the marine life and few patches of surviving coral is to take a ride in one of the many glass-bottomed boats that whizz around the sanctuary. Alternatively, rent a snorkel and flippers and take to the waters yourself, though the number of boats darting around the sanctuary can make this an unnerving experience.

South of Hikkaduwa, the town of **Dodanduwa** ⑯ is home to a florid Buddhist temple, the **Kumarakanda Vihara**, whose grand flight of stairs – more reminiscent of a Portuguese Baroque church than a Buddhist temple – offers a welcome touch of distinction to the drab Galle Road. A couple of kilometres inland, the placid Ratgama Lagoon is home to rich birdlife and an island with a serene Buddhist hermitage; boat trips can be arranged through local touts, either at the lagoon or on the waterfront at Dodanduwa.

TIP

Hikkaduwa is one of the island's top surf spots, along with Arugam Bay and Midigama. The best waves are south of Hikkaduwa town at Wewala, opposite the A-Frame Surf Shop. Here is a good place for surfing information and equipment and offers surfing tours throughout the island.

BELOW: mending his nets for tomorrow's work

SOUTH COAST

Less developed than the island's west coast, the south coast offers more subtle pleasures, from the charming colonial town of Galle to Sri Lanka's finest national parks.

The south coast is one of Sri Lanka's most rewarding places to visit. This is the island in a microcosm: gorgeous beaches, colonial townscapes, stilt fishermen, superb wildlife parks and Buddhist shrines and temples aplenty – not to mention the island's most alluring selection of places to stay, from luxurious beach hotels to atmospheric colonial-era villas. Active types will find a never-ending range of things to see and do here although, despite piecemeal development around the coast, much of the region's charm lies in its somnolent and quintessentially rural atmosphere. Innumerable comatose villages nestle in the shade of toppling palm trees, and the pace of life is unashamedly indolent.

Galle

Galle ❶ is magical: the most perfectly preserved colonial town in Sri Lanka, and an atmospheric piece of time-warped island history, with streets of low-slung Dutch villas hemmed in by massive coral bastions and the breaking waves of the Indian Ocean just beyond.

Over the past few years, Galle has also become one of the island's most vibrant and cosmopolitan cities, as a sizeable influx of European expats (mainly from the UK) have moved into the old Dutch fort, buying up and restoring ageing properties and adding an unexpectedly international-ist dimension to this formerly sleepy town. The evidence of this foreign influx is apparent everywhere: in the string of bijou shops and cafés that now line the streets of the fort; in the town's new swathe of luxury villas and upmarket hotels; and in the steady string of cultural events, most notably the Galle Literary Festival (see page 95), now bringing the city to a global audience.

Main attractions
GALLE
UNAWATUNA
WELIGAMA
MIRISSA
MULGIRIGALLA
BUNDALA NATIONAL PARK
YALA NATIONAL PARK
KATARAGAMA

LEFT: stilt fishermen at sunset on the coast near Weligama. **RIGHT:** the Dutch Reformed Church, Galle.

Around the Fort

Galle divides into two parts: the bustling if nondescript new town, where you'll find the bus and train stations; and the nearby Galle Fort, enclosed by towering bastions, which is where you'll find the old Dutch town.

The contrast between the two could hardly be more striking: as you head through the imposing walls, the pace of life changes and the centuries seem to slip away. **Galle Fort** seems barely to have changed in two hundred years, with low, quiet and mercifully traffic-free streets lined with old villas, churches and other mementoes of the Dutch era. Walk first down **Church Street**, the fort's main thoroughfare. At the top of the street, the **Galle National Museum** Ⓐ (Tue–Sat 9am–5pm; charge) occupies one of the town's many fine old colonial buildings, with a beautifully whitewashed and verandahed exterior (although the displays within are disappointing). Immediately past here lies the superbly renovated **Amangalla Hotel** Ⓑ (the successor of the famous old New Oriental House),

occupying the former Dutch governor's residence of 1684.

Almost next to the Amangalla, the small **Dutch Reformed Church** Ⓒ (Groote Kerk) is the oldest Protestant place of worship in Sri Lanka – dating from 1755, although the original structure was built 100 years earlier. The rather plain interior is one of Galle's most atmospheric period pieces, its floor lined with the gravestones of former Dutch citizens and with a finely carved pulpit and organ loft and various wall tablets recording the lives (and deaths) of later British settlers. Further down the road lies the solid-looking, British-era **All Saints' Church** Ⓓ, topped with a squat spire. Just past it is the second of the fort's luxury accommodation options, the stunning **Galle Fort Hotel** Ⓔ – brilliantly converted from an old Dutch warehouse and offering all the style of the Amangalla at a considerably more modest price.

Retrace your steps for a few metres then turn right down Queen's Street, where you'll find the grandest of Galle's colonial buildings: the sprawling, ochre-walled **Great Warehouse**,

Galle

once used by the Dutch to store valuable export commodities such as cowries, cinnamon and pepper. The warehouse now provides a fine setting for Galle's new **National Maritime Museum** (daily 9am–4.30pm; charge), which fills a great deal of space with a disappointingly small number of exhibits, few of any interest.

South of here, Leyn Baan Street passes a large green and a few small law offices, still sporting their traditional hand-painted signs, before reaching the **Historical Mansion Museum** (daily 9am–6pm, closed for prayers Fri noon–2pm; optional donation). This unusual shop-cum-museum showcases a vast collection of colonial-era (and other) bric-a-brac accumulated over the past three decades by its owner, Mr Gaffar. It's also worth looking into the Olanda warehouse-shop, opposite, an old Dutch building stuffed full of colonial furniture and other bits and pieces.

South of here, Leyn Baan Street leads down to the seafront ramparts, where you'll find the florid **Meeran Jumma Mosque**, at the heart of Galle's Muslim quarter, and the town's picturesque old lighthouse. From here, you can walk all the way around the town's well-preserved old stone and coral **ramparts**, which offer breezy sea views on one side and picturesque panoramas of the red-tiled rooftops of Galle Fort on the other. It's particularly popular towards dusk, when half the town seems to come here to admire the spectacular sunsets, play impromptu games of cricket, or smooch under umbrellas.

Galle's environs

For a complete change of scenery from the colonial streetscapes of Galle, head to the **Kottawa Rainforest and Arboretum** (daily 8am–5pm; charge), some 15km (9 miles) from Galle on the road to Udugama. Although not nearly as impressive as the Sinharaja reserve (see page 215), Kottawa provides an interesting bite-sized introduction to the Sri Lankan rainforest, bisected by a 1km (0.6-mile) walking trail shaded by giant trees. There's also an impressive array of wildlife here including purple-faced langur monkeys, rare giant squirrels, and muntjac and sambur deer, not to mention plenty of endemic birds and reptiles.

There's another patch of rare rainforest at the nearby **Hiyare Rainforest Park** (daily 8am–5pm; charge), around 8km (5 miles) from Kottawa. The park is centred on the beautiful Hiyare Reservoir, while the surrounding rainforest is home to myriad birds, plus a small population of rare hog deer.

Biodiversity of a slightly different kind can be sampled at one of the island's most remarkable ecotourism projects, **Samakanda** (www.samakanda.org). This organic farm and eco-retreat was created by British environmentalist Rory Spowers, a process recorded in his entertaining book *A Year in Green Tea and Tuk-Tuks*, and offers visitors a range of excursions and

Slip back to a bygone age amidst Galle Fort's Dutch-era architecture.

BELOW: purple-faced langur monkey.

Most of Unawatuna Bay is sheltered by a line of offshore rocks, and by a small patch of live coral.

activities, from nature hikes and bikes rides to longer residential courses featuring a mix of activities including yoga, tea-picking and organic farming.

Unawatuna and around

Five km (3 miles) beyond Galle lies the bustling village of **Unawatuna ❷**, the liveliest and most popular beachside hangout in Sri Lanka. Long a favourite with visiting backpackers, the village is now in serious danger of being consumed by its own success. A seemingly ever-growing rash of concrete buildings has sprung up around the once picture-perfect bay and beach, while the hordes of tourists, late-night beach parties and booming music have all seriously eroded the village's former sleepy charm. It's still a pleasant place to spend a few days, with reasonable swimming (and a little bit of live coral) in the sheltered bay and a good selection of places to eat, drink and sleep, although visitors in search of peace, tranquillity and unspoilt nature are increasingly heading further along the coast.

Past Unawatuna, the coastal highway weaves through the straggling

settlements of Thalpe and Dalawela, increasingly popular with local expats from Galle and others wishing to escape the increasingly crowded beach at Unawatuna. The coast here is lined with a superb string of luxurious boutique villas and chic beachside restaurants and bars, although most are hidden discreetly away behind high walls, so you won't see much from the road. These include the beautiful APA Villa (www.villa-srilanka.com/apathalpe), owned by Insight Guides' founder Hans Hoefer.

Stilt fishing posts can also be seen at many places along the coast, while turtles are also occasionally sighted on the beaches here.

Koggala

Around 12km (7.5 miles) past Unawatuna, **Koggala ❸** is home to a World War II airstrip and a small, industrialised, free-trade zone abutting the large Koggala Lagoon. A rather dusty and nondescript little town it may be, but it's also the unlikely home of the superb new boutique hotel, The Fortress, and another of Sri Lanka's most stunning places to

BELOW: fishing vessel with that personal touch.

stay, Kahanda Kahanda, can be found close by. The main attraction in the town itself is the interesting **Martin Wickramasinghe Folk Art Museum** (daily 9am–5pm; charge). Set in the lovely gardens of this local author's home, the museum has an interesting selection of exhibits including traditional masks, puppets and musical instruments, as well as various displays on Martin Wickramasinghe himself.

A couple of kilometres or so inland, beyond Koggala, the beautiful little **Kataluwa Temple** is plastered with a remarkable number of murals, many of them dating back to the Kandyan era. Included are a number of unusual paintings of kaffringha dancers with a troupe of Western musicians, and a memorable portrait of a lopsided Queen Victoria, looking particularly unamused.

A few kilometres further along the coast, the scruffy town of **Ahangama** is perhaps the best place on the island to see Sri Lanka's trademark stilt fishermen in action. Just past here, the very low-key village of **Midigama** has some of the best waves in Sri Lanka, and attracts a steady stream of surfers.

Weligama

Weligama ❹, 23km (14 miles) from Unawatuna, is one of the prettiest towns on the south coast, its sleepy streets lined with chintzy old colonial-era villas decorated with ornately fretted wooden eaves and windows. The coastal road sweeps around magnificent Weligama Bay, a beautiful arc of sand stretching for several kilometres and dotted with hundreds of colourful fishing boats, either drawn up on the sands or bobbing on the waters of the bay.

The bay's main landmark is little **Taprobane Island** (known locally as Yakinige-duwa, or "She-devil's Island"), a tiny, rocky islet sprouting a dense layer of greenery. Topping the islet is a superb red-roofed colonial villa built by the French Count de Maunay in the 1930s, and subsequently occupied by American novelist Paul Bowles. You can now rent the entire villa for about $2000 a night (contact the Sun House in Galle; see page 291).

Just west of the centre of Weligama, around 1km (0.6 miles) inland, the roadside **Kustaraja** (Leper King) statue stands 3 metres (12ft) high, carved into

An idyllic south coast beach.

BELOW: Taprobane Island, Weligama.

The supply of fish on offer seems endless.

a rock face. Kustaraja is supposed to have arrived in Sri Lanka afflicted with leprosy but was cured by drinking only *thambili* (the juice of the king coconut) for three months. If you've already tried one of these ambrosial drinks, you'll know that there's no need for encouragement from mythical kings.

Mirissa

A few kilometres further east, the little village of Mirissa ❺ was formerly one of the quietest and most appealing beach hideaways along the southern coast. As at Unawatuna, the village's rapid growth and ever-increasing number of visitors seriously threaten to destroy the natural beauty and tranquillity which attracted people in the first place, although (unlike Unawatuna) development has not yet overwhelmed the natural setting, and the beach as a whole remains one of the nicest in the south, despite the crowds.

Over the past few years Mirissa has also found additional fame as the whale-watching capital of Sri Lanka (see page 307). Large numbers of cetaceans are frequently spotted relatively close to the shore, and a number of operators in the village can arrange boat trips to see them in season (Dec–Apr; best in Dec and, particularly, Apr).

Matara and Dondra

An hour's drive beyond Galle, bustling **Matara ❻**, the second-largest town on the south coast, was occupied successively by the Portuguese, Dutch and British. The old part of town, known as Matara Fort, was built by the Dutch, and still retains many of its old colonial-era villas, an impressive string of ramparts and a fine old Dutch Reformed Church dating from 1686 – like a low-key and untouristy version of Galle Fort, although tsunami damage and unrestrained development have taken their toll. There's another Dutch relic on the other side of the Nilwala Ganga River in the form of the tiny Star Fort, a quaint little hexagonal structure built in 1763 and surround by a diminutive moat in which crocodiles were formerly kept. A couple of kilometres west of the town centre, the beachside suburb of **Polhena** has an inshore reef and

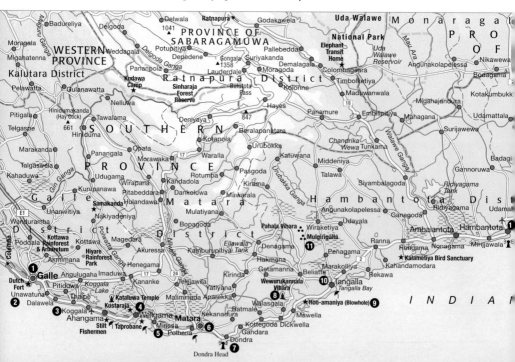

a decent slice of beach, while in the opposite direction, just east of town, the suburb of Medawatta offers good waves for surfing.

Dondra ❼, 5km (3 miles) southeast of Matara, means "the city of the gods" and is the southernmost point of Sri Lanka, marked by an octagonal lighthouse, which, at 54 metres (176ft), is the tallest on the island. From here, there's nothing but ocean until Antarctica.

Buddhas and blowholes

Follow the coastal road through **Dickwella**. About 2km (1 mile) out of town towards Beliatte is the **Wewurukannala Vihara** ❽ (daily; charge), with one of the tallest Buddhas in Sri Lanka (50 metres/164ft high), which was built in the 1960s. An eight-storey building rises up behind it, as if to emphasise the epic scale of the seated Buddha. The extensive complex contains various buildings and shrines, including numerous brightly coloured cartoon strip-style paintings of the Buddha's previous lives, and gory displays depicting the punishments

meted out in hell along with warnings of how to avoid being sent there.

Back on the coastal road just 6km (3½ miles) east of Dickwella, by the 188km (116-mile) marker, a right-hand turn leads to the spectacular **Hoo-amaniya Blowhole** ❾ (charge) at Mawella. High seas, especially during the southwest monsoon in June, force water 23 metres (75ft) vertically through a natural rock chimney and then 20 metres (65ft) up into the air. Villagers say that when the sea is really rough the jet reaches the height of three coconut trees.

Tangalla and around

The busy little town of **Tangalla** ❿ is flanked by a sequence of beautiful beaches, with picturesquely rocky coves backed by palm trees to the west, and longer and wider swathes of sand to the south (although swimmers should be wary of the steep drop-offs and strong waves at certain points along the coast). Like much of southern Sri Lanka, Tangalla is heading rapidly upmarket, and the area's formerly rather rustic selection of accommodation has recently been bolstered by a

TIP

The main temple in Dondra, the Maha Vishnu Devala, hosts one of the south's most spectacular religious festivals: a 10-day fair and *perahera* (procession) venerating the Hindu god Vishnu (as opposed to Buddha), which coincides with the Kandyan *perahera* in July/August.

BELOW: Stilt fishermen in Galle.

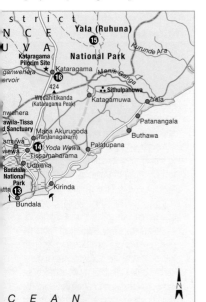

Hambantota was particularly hard hit by the 2004 tsunami. Rebuilding has been unusually swift and thorough, however, thanks in no little part to local boy, President Mahinda Rajapakse, who was accused of siphoning off large quantities of aid money to help reconstruct his home town.

string of new luxury villas, as well as the superb Amanwella resort, on one of the coast's most beautiful beaches.

Tangalla is also a good base to explore the numerous interesting sights in the surrounding countryside, including Wewurukannala Vihara and Hoo-amaniya Blowhole. Other local attractions include **Mulgirigalla** ⓫ (daily 6am–6pm; charge), 16km (10 miles) north of Tangalla. This is southern Sri Lanka's finest ancient monument, with an array of beautifully decorated ancient cave temples carved out of the flanks of an enormous rock outcrop. The temples are arranged on four separate levels and connected by around 500 steps, with wonderful views from the summit.

There are also several rewarding wildlife attractions close by. Some 10km (6 miles) east of Tangalla, the little village of **Rekawa** is famous for its nightly turtle watches, during which there's an excellent chance of seeing one of these creatures drag itself ashore to lay eggs on the beach (Jan–Apr are the best months). Keen bird-watchers will also relish a trip to the

nearby bird sanctuary at **Kalametiya**. Both Rekawa and Kalametiya also boast superb stretches of largely pristine beach, backed by meandering lagoons and dotted with a few boutique hotels popular with those fleeing the madding crowds further west.

Hambantota and Bundala

Further along the coast is the scruffy town of **Hambantota** ⓬, one of the largest on the south coast. Traditionally it's best known as the island's major centre of salt production, which is collected from the enormous evaporating saltpans that ring the town, and for its curd, made from buffalo milk, and sold from many roadside stalls – look for the strings of clay pots hanging up outside local shops.

Hambantota's fortunes have been transformed over the past few years with a string of new infrastructure projects. Most notable is the new Hambantota International Airport, which will provide Sri Lanka with only its second international hub after Bandaranaike International Airport near Colombo, offering visitors a

BELOW: a darter *(Anhinga melanogaster)* at Bundala National Park.

Kataragama Festival

Anyone who enjoys those – typically Japanese – television programmes which feature people sticking knitting needles up their noses or nailing their lips to a wall will enjoy a visit to the town's annual **Kataragama Festival**. The festival is an extravaganza of self-mutilation, during which followers of Kataragama perform a variety of gruesome acts to show their devotion to the god: ramming spikes through their tongues, walking across burning coals or, most dramatically, suspending themselves from scaffolding by means of butchers' hooks looped through their skin. It's one of South Asia's most blood-curdling spectacles, although those who put themselves through these mortifications do so willingly and in a spirit of religious ecstasy, claiming that the god protects them from any feelings of pain.

direct route into the south of the island. The vast new Hambantota Port, built by the Chinese at a cost of around US$1 billion, is also likely to provide a major economic stimulus to the area, while the new Mahinda Rajapakse International Stadium, built for the cricket World Cup in 2011, now hosts international one-day and other matches, providing the south with its first major sporting venue.

The main tourist attraction hereabouts is **Bundala National Park** ⑬, one of the country's finest, which stretches around an extensive series of wetlands and lagoons along the coast east of Hambantota. The park is particularly famous for its birdlife, especially the vast flocks of pink flamingoes, which perch prettily amongst the waters of the lagoons, while numerous crocodiles, monkeys, elephants and other wildlife can also be seen.

Tissamaharama and Yala National Park

Tissamaharama ⑭ (or "Tissa", as it's usually called) is one of the most historic towns in the south. Under the name of Mahagama it formerly served as the capital of southern Sri Lanka during the Anuradhapuran period, and still has a pair of huge stupas and a collection of ancient tanks. These include the Tissawewa and the Wirawila on the Hambantota–Wellawaya road, both of which are good places for birdwatching.

The main reason for visiting Tissamaharama, however, is as the gateway to **Yala National Park** ⑮ (see page 134), the finest reserve in the country. The park (daily 6am–6pm, closed 1 Sept–15 Oct) is best known for its leopards – the densest population of these big cats anywhere in the world – although it's also a great place to spot elephants and other mammals, as well as a wonderful array of birdlife.

Kataragama

About 29km (18 miles) north of Tissa, **Kataragama** ⑯ is one of the holiest sites

on the island, held sacred by Buddhists, Hindus and Muslims alike. Pilgrims come here all year round to worship at the shrine of the god Kataragama Deviyo (believed by Sri Lankan Tamils to be a form of Skanda, or Murugan, the 12-armed and warlike son of Siva; and by Sri Lankan Buddhists to be one of the most important protectors of the island and the Buddhist faith).

The temple complex stands on one side of the Menik River, where an extensive collection of shrines and temples lies scattered around a beautiful area of wooded parkland. Skanda's trident, or *vel*, is said to be held within Maha Devala, the most important shrine in the complex. Buddhists and Hindus worship together here (three daily services or *pujas* at 4.30am, 10.30am and 6.30pm), while Muslims attend a nearby mosque, and there's also a Buddhist dagoda dating from the 1st century BC just to the north. The temples are particularly vibrant during the evening *puja* at the Kataragama shrine, when conch shells blow, drums beat and crowds of devotees arrive laden with trays of offerings to pay homage to the god.

Hambantota has Sri Lanka's largest population of Malay Muslims – its name is said to derive from sampans, the boats that the Malays arrived in, and tota, or harbour – and you'll notice an unusually large number of mosques here, as well as the occasional decidedly Malay-looking face amidst the Sri Lankan crowds.

BELOW: Yala elephants.

KANDY AND AROUND

The historic bastion of the island's Sinhalese culture, the city of Kandy remains Sri Lanka's most vibrant centre of traditional arts, crafts and religious pageantry.

In the history of Sri Lanka, the Kingdom of Kandy retains an almost legendary place. Established deep in the impenetrable hills at the heart of the island, the kingdom resisted repeated attacks by the Portuguese and the Dutch, clinging stubbornly to its independence throughout the dark centuries during which other parts of the island fell, one after another, to the invading Europeans. Protected by its geographical position and physical remoteness, the Kandyan Kingdom remained a stable point of reference in the island's turbulent colonial history, preserving ancient religious and cultural traditions, which were subdued elsewhere by corrosive Western influences, until it, too, finally succumbed to the British in 1815.

This long history of political independence still informs many aspects of life in Kandy. The city remains a bastion of Sinhalese culture and religion, home to the island's most revered Buddhist temple, its most sacred relic and its most magnificent festival. It's also the undisputed arts and crafts capital of the island, filled with myriad temples and palaces built in the distinctive Kandyan architectural style, adorned with elaborate murals and finely carved wooden pillars, and often echoing to the

unmistakeable sound of the city's virtuoso drummers beating out rhythms in their uniquely dynamic style.

From Colombo to Kandy

The journey to Kandy is also captivating. Some 11km (7 miles) from the centre of Colombo is the Kandyan-era Buddhist temple at **Sapugaskande**, a pleasant ensemble of white-walled and red-tiled buildings sitting on top of a small but steep hill and offering superb views over the city and palm trees below. Continuing inland,

Main attractions
THE TEMPLE OF THE TOOTH, KANDY
ROYAL PALACE COMPLEX, KANDY
THE FOUR DEVALES, KANDY
PERADENIYA BOTANICAL GARDENS
PINNAWELA ELEPHANT ORPHANAGE
THE THREE TEMPLES LOOP

PRECEDING PAGES: waiting for the start of the Maha Pereha (Great Parade).
LEFT: within the Temple walls.
RIGHT: traditional Kandyan dancer.

At the end of the final hairpin bend on the road into Kandy, the road passes through a small tunnel carved out of a solid rock promontory (the new highway goes around it). A local legend speaks of the tenacity of the Kandyan Kingdom, which would not fall until an invading force pierced this solid rock encircling the city. The British fulfilled the prophecy after the Kandyan Kingdom was annexed in 1815.

just northwest of Miriswatta and 27km (17 miles) from Colombo, the **Henarathgoda Botanical Gardens** (daily; charge) contain an array of tropical plants from across the globe including Sri Lanka's first ever rubber tree, propagated from seeds taken from Brazil and smuggled down the Amazon in bales of cotton.

A few kilometres further inland on the road to Kandy is the touristy village of **Cadjugama** ❶, where young women by the wayside beckon travellers to stop and buy the delicious freshly roasted cashew nuts (*cadjunuts*) that gave the village its name. Cashews are used in many traditional Sri Lankan dishes; raw cashews, for example, can be cooked in coconut cream with spices, or "devilled" – roasted with chilli.

At **Ambepussa** junction, the road goes northwards to Kurunegala or east towards Kandy. Take the eastern route to **Nelundeniya**, where a minor road leads south to the hamlet of **Dedigama** ❷. Under the rule of Parakramabahu V (1344–59), Dedigama briefly served as one of the capitals of Sri Lanka during an anarchic period that followed

on from the collapse of Polonnaruwa. The village has a few remains from this period, including remnants of a huge stupa and an interesting little museum next to it that is filled with artefacts recovered from the stupa's relic chambers, among them a beautiful sequence of tiny gold Buddhas. Dedigama is also renowned as the birthplace of Parakramabahu I – the famous Sinhalese king who would later immortalise himself through his works at the city of Polonnaruwa.

The main road to Kandy continues through the bustling town of **Kegalle**, a jumping-off point for the famous Pinnawela Elephant Orphanage (see page 197). Beyond Kegalle the views become increasingly spectacular on the final approach to Kandy, with panoramas over the surrounding, quaintly named hills – Lion Rock, Ship Rock, Camel Hill, Tuber Rock, Balloon Rock and, especially, the dramatic, flat-topped Bible Rock. The entrance to the city is Kadugannawa Pass, at the end of a sheer ascent of 250 metres (820ft) occurring over a matter of 5km (3 miles) and complete with hairpin

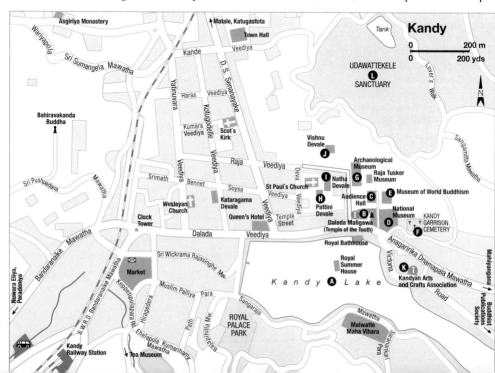

bends, from where there are breathtaking views southeast towards the ocean.

Kandy

Despite now being the island's second-largest city, **Kandy ❸** retains a surprisingly small-town feel. The centre's modest grid of low-rise streets is lined with characterful colonial-era buildings and preserves a certain old-fashioned, countrified charm, which even the often dense throngs of traffic and pedestrians can't entirely obscure.

At the west end of the centre **Kandy Lake ❹** provides the city's scenic centrepiece. This fine expanse of water is bounded by elegant white balustrades and backed by the buildings of the Temple of the Tooth and the Royal Palace complex – particularly striking when seen from the south, with the neat white buildings framed against the rich green backdrop of the Udawatakelle Sanctuary behind, and prettily reflected in the waters of the lake in front.

The Temple of the Tooth

Perched on the lakeside at the eastern end of the town centre are the serene white buildings of the **Temple of the Tooth ❸** (Dalada Maligawa; daily 5.30am–8pm; charge). This is Sri Lanka's most important Buddhist temple and home to one of Buddhism's most sacred objects, the Tooth Relic, which attracts pilgrims from all over the island and many other places in Asia besides. It also serves as an important symbol of Sinhalese identity and pride – traditionally, whoever had the relic was believed to have the right to rule the island, giving its possession a political, as well as a religious, dimension.

A Tamil Tiger bomb, detonated in front of the temple in 1998, reduced much of the facade to rubble. The damaged buildings have been lovingly restored since, though tight security now marks the approach to the shrine, giving you plenty of time to admire the temple's fine complex of white, hip-roofed buildings, set against the densely wooded backdrop of the Udawattakele Sanctuary. The striking golden roof, placed directly above the shrine in which the Tooth Relic itself is kept, was donated by President Premadasa in the late 1980s, though

Kandy town, Sri Lanka's second-largest city.

BELOW: the Shrine of the Tooth.

TIP

Look carefully at the walls of the Temple of the Tooth and you'll notice numerous images showing a hare seated inside a moon. These refer to a famous story of one of the Buddha's previous lives in which he was born a hare. A passing holy man asked the hare for food and the hare, having no food to give, threw himself into a fire, offering his own body instead.

this act of piety did the unfortunate politician little good since he was assassinated just a few years later.

Inside, the temple is surprisingly modest in size, with a single small courtyard, in the middle of which stands the richly decorated Tooth Relic shrine itself. The relic is kept upstairs in a room whose doors are only opened during the thrice-daily *pujas*, safely locked away in a golden reliquary and seen only by the most important of visitors. The three pujas are atmospheric occasions, accompanied by a deafening tattoo of traditional drumming, although the temple tends to get absolutely overrun with tourists during the mid-morning and evening ceremonies (at 9.30am and 6.30pm); the early-morning puja (at 5.30am) is a lot quieter.

Returning downstairs and continuing to the far side of the courtyard brings you into the **Alut Maligawa** (New Shrine Room), packed full of Buddhas of varying sizes and styles donated to the temple by overseas countries. Further offerings and artefacts relating to the Tooth Relic can be seen in the **Sri Dalada Museum** upstairs (no

additional charge), ranging from colonial documents to antique jewellery.

Head out from the north side of the Temple of the Tooth to reach the striking wooden **Audience Hall** , a classic Kandyan-style pavilion with ornately carved teak columns that support a hipped roof. It was here that the Kandyan chiefs signed the document handing over their kingdom to the British in 1815, hence officially ratifying the end of the last remnant of independent Sinhalese rule in the island. Continue past the Audience Hall to reach another old Kandyan building, which is now home to the **Raja Tusker Museum**, housing the stuffed remains of the massive and much-loved Raja, chief elephant in the Esala Perahera until his demise in 1988.

Royal Palace complex

The Temple of the Tooth was originally just one part of the sprawling Royal Palace complex, home to the kings of Kandy, and many of the palace's surviving buildings are dotted around the temple (including the Audience Hall and the building now housing the Raja

BELOW: in costume for the *perahera*.

Tusker Museum). Immediately behind the temple, the spacious rooms of the Queen's Palace, arranged around a central courtyard, have been converted into the **National Museum**  (Tue–Sat 9am–5pm; charge), where a wide selection of Kandyan and colonial artefacts is displayed in the rooms where courtly concubines once lounged. Although it's right next to the Temple of the Tooth, there's no direct route between it and the museum, so you'll have to go around the outside, passing the eye-catching two-storey **Royal Bathhouse** (Ulpenge) right on the lake's edge.

Continuing along the small road in front of the National Museum (around the back of the Temple of the Tooth) brings you to the fine old colonial-era neoclassical building, formerly the High Court. This now holds the bizarre new **Museum of World Buddhism** **E** (daily 8am–7pm; charge) showcasing Buddhist history, art and culture in 16 different countries across Asia, from Afghanistan to Japan. Some of the artefacts on display are undeniably impressive, although the sheer randomness of the displays (patched together from

items donated by the relevant countries) makes the whole thing look a bit like an enormous Buddhist department store, stacked high with huge quantities of glittery statues, miniature stupas and other religious bric-a-brac – not without a certain weird charm, although with zero educational value.

Just behind the National Museum, a path leads to the beautifully restored **Kandy Garrison Cemetery** **F** (Mon–Sat 8am–1pm and 2–6pm; donation), housing the gravestones of many of the city's earliest British settlers who never made it back home. Their epitaphs describe the surprising variety of ways by which the cemetery's residents met their maker, and offer a touching memento of the perils of 19th-century life in the tropics.

On the far side of the palace complex, the **Archaeological Museum** **G** (Wed–Mon 8am–5pm; donation) occupies a fine old building that was formerly part of the King's Palace, although the building itself is rather more impressive than the mishmash of exhibits inside, which include pots and fragments of carved masonry.

A fountain in the Royal Palace complex fascinates.

BELOW: the lakeside setting of the Temple and Royal Bath House.

Legend of the Tooth

Many Buddhists believe the most precious thing in the world to be the Tooth Relic of the Buddha, over which wars have been fought.

It is believed to confer kingship on whoever possesses it and is kept inside seven caskets placed inside one another, like Russian dolls. The outer casket, about 1.2 metres (5ft) in height, is of silver gilt, but all the others are of beaten gold. Perhaps not surprisingly, given its incalculable value, it is hardly ever put on public display.

This is the Tooth Relic of the Buddha, now residing in the Temple of the Tooth in Kandy. On attaining nirvana, the Buddha was cremated, but mourners managed to rescue parts of his mortal remains from the fire, including a tooth. This precious relic was kept in India for the following eight centuries, until its existence was threatened by a resurgence of militant Hinduism. It is said that the Tooth fell into Hindu hands, but attempts to destroy it with a sledgehammer succeeded only in breaking the hammer. The Hindus gave it back.

Fearing for its future, King Guhasiva of Kalinga, in present-day Orissa, hid the relic in the hair of his daughter, Hemamala, who was then spirited away to Sri Lanka. Arriving in Anuradhapura, the Tooth was installed in a specially built temple, while a lavish procession (the antecedent of today's spectacular Kandy Esala Perahera) was initiated, with the Tooth paraded through the streets of the ancient capital on the back of an elephant.

The Tooth remained in Anuradhapura for the next five centuries, until being taken to Polonnaruwa, and thence to Dambadeniya and Yapahuwa. In 1284 an invading Pandyan army captured the Tooth and took it back to India, where it stayed for four years until it was recovered by Parakramabahu III. Henceforth, a special bodyguard was assigned to watch over it.

The right to rule

Increasingly, it was believed that whoever possessed the Tooth had the right to rule Sri Lanka, transforming it into an object of enormous political, as well as spiritual, significance. Following its recovery from the Pandyans, a succession of Sinhalese kings carried it around with them as they established transient capitals in various parts of the island; first at Kurunegala, then Gampola, and then Kotte.

In the 16th century, the Portuguese captured the Tooth and shipped it to Goa where, before the assembled eyes of the Portuguese viceroy, a bishop and numerous dignitaries, it was pounded to dust, the dust burnt, and the ashes thrown into the sea. That should have put paid to the Tooth, but not so, apparently. The remnants reassembled themselves on the sea bed, enabling the Tooth to fly back to the island of its own accord. It finally arrived in Kandy in 1592, and has remained there ever since.

The British, who briefly gained possession of the Tooth after the fall of Kandy in 1815, inspected the relic and decided that the discoloured object was definitely a tooth, but that at 5cm (2 inches) in length it was more likely to have come from a crocodile than a human being. They overlooked the fact that the footprint on Adam's Peak, a strange impression on the bare rock at the summit which some believe to be the Buddha's footprint (see page 209), is 1 metre (3ft) long.

LEFT: smiling pilgrims enter the Temple of the Tooth in Kandy.

The four *devales*

The area immediately west of the Temple of the Tooth is covered by the rambling enclosures belonging to three of the city's four principal *devales*, or temples (the fourth *devale*, dedicated to Kataragama, is in the city centre on Kotugodelle Vidiya). The four gods worshipped in these four *devales* were traditionally believed to protect Kandy, and processions in their honour still form a major part of the great Esala Perahera festival *(see box)*. The temples are nominally Buddhist, but the gods worshipped in them have strong Hindu roots, a reminder of the time when the kings of Kandy were Tamils from South India.

The main entrance to the *devales* is just north of the gateway into the Temple of the Tooth. This leads directly into the **Pattini Devale ⓗ**, dominated by a majestic Bo tree growing out of a huge brick platform. The actual shrine is a small but richly decorated building off to the right, which is usually busy with supplicants begging Pattini, a popular goddess of South Indian origins considered the personification of wifely devotion and chastity for protection.

On the far side of this lies the **Natha Devale ⓘ**, a spacious enclosure dotted with shrines, small stupas and Bo trees. The main brick shrine (in front of you on the right as you enter), topped by a very Indian-looking *shikhara* (dome), is the oldest building in Kandy, dating back to the 15th century.

Turn left through here to reach the third and largest of the *devales*, the **Vishnu Devale ⓙ**, which contains an impressive collection of colourful shrines and has superb views of the Temple of the Tooth.

Whilst in the area, it's also well worth having a look inside the beautifully preserved interior of the rustic, orange-coloured **St Paul's Church**, installed by the British in 1843 right next to the city's sacred Buddhist precinct and making an incongruous sight next to the *devales*' stupas and pagoda roofs.

Around the lake

For a morning constitutional or an afternoon stroll, it's traditional

The Audience Hall, with its carved teak columns.

BELOW: the Pattini Devale.

At Pinnawela, elephant droppings are recycled in the production of some gorgeously coloured paper, here being used to make boxes.

to stretch one's legs with a circuit of **Kandy Lake**, created in 1807 by the last Sinhalese king using forced labour. The balustraded promenade around the lake offers beautiful views of the town and hills; alternatively, boat trips around the lake are run by Joy Motor Boat Service (daily 9am–6pm), departing from the western end of the lake. The island in the lake was the **Royal Summer House**, often erroneously described as the king's harem. The British, ever practical, converted it into a munitions store.

Passing the Royal Bathhouse, the promenade transforms imperceptibly from city street to parkland walk. This leads you to the **Kandyan Arts and Crafts Association Ⓚ**, which hosts colourful nightly displays of Kandyan dancing and sells a range of locally made crafts aimed squarely at visiting coach parties. Slightly further along the lakeshore is the **Buddhist Publications Society**, at 54 Sangaraja Mawatha, its shelves stocked with an overwhelming number of Buddhist tracts and treatises.

BELOW: elephants at Pinnawela.

Udawattekele and the Tea Museum

Rising directly behind the Temple of the Tooth (though only reachable via a rather convoluted walk or drive through the town's backstreets), the steep, densely forested slopes of **Udawattekele Sanctuary Ⓛ** (daily 6am–6pm; charge) offer a totally unexpected patch of untamed nature almost in the heart of the city centre. There are good paths and tracks through the woods, which are home to a wide range of montane bird species, as well as a few monkeys and – when it's been raining – an awful lot of leeches.

Around 4km (2.5 miles) south of Kandy, on the twisting road up to Hantana, the **Tea Museum** (daily 8.15am–4.30pm; charge) offers an interesting overview of Sri Lanka's most famous industry. Housed in an atmospheric old converted tea factory, the museum is home to various pieces of Victorian-era machinery rescued from defunct factories around the hill country, along with displays on the lives of some of colonial Ceylon's leading tea pioneers. These include James

Taylor (complete with a touching little array of personal effects), who established the island's first tea plantation, and the entrepreneurial Thomas Lipton, who did more than anyone to put Ceylon tea on the global map.

Peradeniya Botanical Gardens

About 6km (4 miles) from Kandy are the **Peradeniya Botanical Gardens** ❹ (daily 7.30am–5.45pm; charge), the largest and finest in Sri Lanka. Enclosed in a loop of the Mahaweli Ganga River, the lush 60-hectare (147-acre) gardens are stuffed with a baffling array of Sri Lankan, Asian and international flora, although the lack of signage can be frustrating. From the entrance the stately, much-photographed **Royal Palm Avenue** leads down to the **Great Circle** at the centre of the gardens. On your left is a handy cafeteria and the **Great Lawn**, home to a famous giant Javan fig tree, which covers an impressive 1,600 sq metres (17,222 sq ft) and is sometimes claimed to be the largest tree in the world. North of here, the gardens become wilder, with troupes of macaque monkeys foraging in the bushes and huge clusters of flying foxes dangling from the trees overhead.

Pinnawela Elephant Orphanage

Elephants young and old are given sanctuary in a natural habitat at the massively popular **Pinnawela Elephant Orphanage** ❺ (daily 8.30am–6pm; charge – extra for video cameras), just north of Kegalle and some 40km (25 miles) west of Kandy. The orphanage cares for almost 100 elephants, many of whom were either orphaned or injured in the wild – some were hurt during civil war clashes (one, the three-legged Sama, stood on a landmine), though most were injured in bloody clashes with villagers, sadly a regular occurrence in many parts of the island. Increasing numbers of elephants are also now born here, some of the tiniest, cutest pachyderms you'll ever see, hand-fed by staff out of oversized babies' milk bottles during the daily feeding sessions (9.15am, 1.15pm and 5pm). It's a good idea to time your visit

The first tea seedlings ever to be grown in Sri Lanka were nourished at the Peradeniya Botanical Gardens in 1824, half a century before it became a viable cash crop. Now there are approximately 10,000 tea trees in the gardens.

BELOW: giant fig tree at Peradeniya Botanical Gardens.

Carved detail from the temple in Embekke.

to coincide with either the morning or midday meals, after which the elephants are led over to the river to take a bath in the shallow waters of the Ma Oya – the unique spectacle of 90-odd elephants splashing around together in the river is one of Sri Lanka's most entertaining and impressive sights, and not to be missed.

A few kilometres down the road, the smaller **Millennium Elephant Foundation** ❻ (daily 8am–5pm; charge) takes a more didactic and interactive approach, with displays and exhibits on various elephant-related topics, and informative guides on hand to answer your questions. There are nine elephants here, mostly retired working animals, and visitors can help clean them, interact with them, and generally get more hands-on than is possible at Pinnawela.

Temples west of Kandy

The rolling hills around Kandy are dotted with dozens of historic Buddhist temples dating back to the 17th century and earlier, a unique repository of traditional Sinhalese religious art and architecture. Three fine temples lie close together just a 45-minute drive west of Kandy, easily combined into an attractive half-day walk known as the **Three Temples Loop**. All three date back to the 14th century – pre-dating the city of Kandy itself, having been built during the time when the northern hill country was governed from the small provincial town of **Gampola**, some 20km (12½ miles) south of Kandy.

The northernmost of the trio, 14km (8½ miles) southwest of the centre of Kandy, is the **Gadaladeniya Vihara** ❼ (daily 7.30am–6pm; charge), which was built on a hilltop some time in the 14th century. The main shrine here is a fine stone structure, lavishly carved in a distinctly South Indian style, probably by imported labourers. The temple's second shrine is an odd but engaging little cruciform structure, surmounted by a stupa-like dome, with a further mini-stupa-cum-dome topping each of its four diminutive side shrines.

A few kilometres south, the rather grand **Lankatilake Vihara** ❽ (daily 7.30am–6pm; charge) sits magnificently poised on top of a hill, reached by a long flight of precisely cut rock steps. The main shrine here is one of the largest in the area, with a fine dragon-arch entrance, a loosely fitting wooden roof and an unusual sequence of subsidiary shrines built into the exterior walls.

Another 3km (2 miles) south lies the **Kataragama Devale** ❾ (daily 7.30am–6pm; charge) at the village of **Embekke**. This small and rustic temple is notable principally for its magnificent carved wooden pillars, dating from the 14th century, decorated with myriad figures. The finest of the 500 or so figures are the dancer, a double-headed eagle, the swans and soldiers. No two carvings are alike.

East of Kandy: The Knuckles Range

There are more interesting temples immediately east of Kandy, such as the **Degaldoruwa Temple** ❿, which houses an outstanding sequence of

wall paintings in its underground shrine. Pride of place goes to the magnificently dramatic portrayal of the Buddha's Battle with Mara – a rival to the similarly fine painting on the same theme at Dambulla – along with murals depicting scenes from the jatakas (the stories of the Buddha's previous lives) and pictures of various sacred shrines around the island.

Continuing eastwards, the vista is dominated by the **Knuckles Range**, named by the militaristic British for its five peaks' alleged resemblance to the knuckles of a clenched fist – whereas the Sinhalese refer to the range by the rather more poetic name of Dumbara Kanduvetiya, or "Misty Mountains". The hills here are some of the wildest and least spoilt in Sri Lanka, with huge, though still largely unexplored, trekking and wildlife-spotting possibilities. It was this ruggedness and remoteness that led the people of Kandy, on the numerous occasions when they were threatened by invaders, to leave the city and trek out to the citadel of **Hunnasgiriya** ⓫ and camp there until the danger

had passed, taking the royal treasures, including the Tooth Relic, with them.

The switchback road around the southern edge of the Knuckles Range leads to the Mahaweli River and the **Victoria Reservoir** and its huge dam, now the source of a significant amount of the country's electricity, with views of the land once inhabited by the aboriginal tribes of Sri Lanka. This area of jungle, bounded by the river and the plains beyond, is the land of the Veddhas (see page 63), known as Bintenna.

Mahiyangana

A short drive further east is the small town of **Mahiyangana** ⓬, at the end of a hair-raising sequence of 17 hairpins down to the plains. This was one of the three places in Sri Lanka visited by the Buddha 26 centuries ago – at least according to the *Mahavamsa*, the ancient Buddhist chronicle. The aboriginal people were the immediate beneficiaries of that visit, since they converted to the practice of Buddhism after watching him levitate. A temple in Mahiyangana marks the spot where the Buddha is said to have preached.

The Knuckles Range's unique ecological significance was recognized in 2010 when it was inscribed on the list of Unesco World Heritage Sites (along with other parts of the central highlands) thanks to its remarkable wealth of endemic flora and fauna – described by Unesco as a "super biodiversity hotspot".

BELOW: Lankatilake temple.

ELEPHANTS: LANKA'S FRIENDLY GIANTS

The Sri Lankan elephant, known as Elephas maximus maximus, is more a majestic subspecies of the Asian elephant, Elephas maximus.

Despite the fact that the Sinhalese are named after the lion, it is with the elephant that they have become most closely associated over the centuries. Elephants are central to most of the island's religious festivals, and it is an elephant that is entrusted with carrying the holiest of holies, the Tooth Relic, during the great Esala Perahera festival in Kandy. Elephants were used by the ancient kings of Anuradhapura to trample down foundations for the city's massive stupas, edifices they still symbolically support – as demonstrated by the elephant-head carvings that decorate the perimeter wall of the great Ruwanveliseya stupa, and many other such structures around the island. Elephants were used by the Kandyans to execute condemned prisoners, and killing an elephant was itself a capital offence.

In more recent times elephants have been put to work pulling barges by the Dutch and helping to clear land for tea plantations by the British, and trained pachyderms are still widely used in jobs requiring serious muscle-power in many parts of the island – chances are you'll pass one lumbering along the road at some point during your visit.

ABOVE: after romping in the water at the Pinnawela Elephant Orphanage, fitful mating and a long drink, the elephants then powder themselves with dust to prevent insect bites.

BELOW: the best place for a ride on an elephant is the Millennium Elephant Foundation, near Pinnawela, but one or two tour operators in Habarana also organise rides.

LEFT: a roadside sign warns of crossing elephants, who are very shortsighted – although they can pick up vibrations through their legs and by laying their trunks on the ground.

THE MALIGAWA TUSKER

Elephants come into their own during the great religious processions, or *peraheras*, which are such a feature of island life, and nowhere more so than during the annual Esala Perahera in Kandy, one of Sri Lanka's most spectacular sights. As the festival moves towards its dramatic conclusion over successive nights, the number of elephants gradually increases. On the final couple of nights more than a hundred elephants take part in the procession, led by the so-called "Maligawa Tusker", draped from trunk to tail in a brightly coloured, embroidered cloth decorated with tiny electric light bulbs. The Maligawa Tusker is entrusted with carrying the illuminated *howdah* (elephant "saddle") which holds the gold, dagoba-shaped reliquary containing a replica of the sacred Tooth Relic.

The most famous Maligawa Tuskers are held in enormous reverence by the island's Buddhist population. The stuffed remains of the former Maligawa Tusker known as Raja, one of the island's best-loved pachyderms, are still preserved in state in a dedicated museum within the grounds of the Temple of the Tooth, while his death in 1998 prompted the government to declare a national day of mourning.

ABOVE: elephant woodcarvings, produced in droves, are a perennial favourite among tourists. The best are hewn from ebony.

LEFT: a highly decorated elephant is depicted on one of the many beautiful wall paintings in the Kataluwa Temple, near Galle.

RIGHT: the trained *mahout* (elephant driver) is so skilful at controlling an elephant – they are often together throughout the animal's life – that he can induce its hindquarters to collapse, unaided by voice.

HILL COUNTRY

Sri Lanka at its most scenic: mist-shrouded uplands dotted with old colonial settlements and the colourful figures of Tamil tea pluckers at work in the plantations.

The hill country is a world away from the rest of Sri Lanka. While the parched lowlands simmer and sweat beneath an eternal tropical summer, the uplands bask in a perpetual European spring, turning to a crisp autumnal chill at higher elevations. Tangled green mountains rise from every quarter, their lower slopes swathed in millions of verdant tea bushes. Spectacular waterfalls plunge over sheer cliffs into narrow valleys hemmed in between high mountainsides. The cloudforest above is alive with the secretive chirrupings of elusive mountain birds. As Hermann Hesse beautifully described it during a visit in 1911: "The wind had just swept clean the whole valley of Nuwara Eliya, I saw deep blue and immense, the entire high mountain system of Ceylon piled up in mighty walls, and in its midst the beautiful, ancient and holy pyramid of Adam's Peak. Beside it at an infinite depth and distance lay the flat blue sea, in between a thousand mountains, broad valleys, narrow ravines, rivers and waterfalls, in countless folds."

The British and the beginnings of tea

For most of Sri Lanka's history, this inhospitable and largely impenetrable mountain wilderness remained only sparsely settled and cultivated, and it wasn't until the arrival of the British in the 19th century that the hill country's unique commercial possibilities were recognised. The British first began to explore the highlands and clear its thick layers of forest to establish coffee plantations, but in the 1860s the virulent *Hemileia vastatrix* fungus devastated the coffee plants and ruined the fortunes of the planters who had invested in them.

It was this serendipitous turn of events that drove the unemployed

Main attractions

NUWARA ELIYA
ADAM'S PEAK
HORTON PLAINS NATIONAL PARK
LIPTON'S SEAT
ELLA
BUDURUWAGALA
SINHARAJA
UDA WALAWE NATIONAL PARK

LEFT: Devon Falls. **RIGHT:** young monks going to lessons.

planters to try a crop that would subsequently come to symbolise Sri Lanka in the eyes of the world, and which still serves as one of the mainstays of the national economy: tea. The abundant rainfall, combined with sunshine, cold nights and mists, offered the perfect climate for producing high-grown, aromatic teas – and so the world-famous industry of Ceylon tea was born.

The introduction of tea transformed the highlands from an economic backwater into a commercial hub of the colonial economy, with far-reaching consequences. The hill country's uplands were widely cleared, and blanketed in the superb swathes of glossy green tea bushes that remain to this day, while the shortage of local labour led to the immigration of thousands of Tamils to work the tea estates, forever changing the ethnic composition of the hills. The sight of brightly dressed Tamil tea pickers toiling amongst the tea bushes is one of Sri Lanka's most iconic images, though the tea pickers themselves remain among the poorest and most disadvantaged communities in the island – despite all the wealth they have helped create.

These slightly surreal cultural conjunctions lend the hill country a peculiar appeal. Old-world British colonial settlements and all their associated paraphernalia – antiquated railways, neo-Gothic churches and quaint half-timbered houses – are strangely juxtaposed with colourful little Hindu temples, sari-clad tea pickers and Tamil farm labourers in woolly hats, manhandling huge sacks of very English-looking vegetables, introduced to the highlands by Victorian gentlemen farmers such as Samuel Baker *(see box)*. Most of all, however, it's the sheer magnificence of the natural environment that draws visitors here time and time again, with its carefully manicured tea gardens and sublime vistas shadowed by the craggy grey summits of the region's highest peaks.

Kandy to Nuwara Eliya

Leaving Kandy, the road to Nuwara Eliya climbs 1,400 metres (4,700ft), hairpinning slowly upwards through a beautiful landscape of tumbling waterfalls and dramatic hills cloaked in the glistening green leaves of innumerable tea bushes. As the road ascends, the air grows cooler and the clouds crowning the peaks draw closer. A conveniently situated rest house at **Pusselawa** ⓭, halfway between the two towns, makes a good stop for lunch. About 10km (6 miles) past Pusselawa the road skirts the magnificent **Ramboda Falls** ⓮, which tumble over the cliffs in two 100-metre (328ft) high cascades. Continuing along the road, about 15km (9 miles) before Nuwara Eliya is the **Labookellie Tea Factory** (daily), where you can take a tour of the factory, walk through the beautiful estates, or just stop for a reviving cup of tea and the chance of buying freshly plucked leaves from the estate.

A longer route is via the B39 from Kandy through **Hanguranketa** ⓯, which during the 17th century served as a refuge for the Kandyan king Raja

Views are rather more limited if you manage to get stuck behind a rice wagon.

BELOW: the Tea Factory Hotel, Nuwara Eliya, has been artfully converted.

High-altitude road sign at Nuwara Eliya.

Sinha II. The **Potgul Magila Vihara** here is of some importance, as it contains an ancient collection of *ola* (palm-leaf) manuscripts bound between covers of hand-crafted silver and chased brass. The outer walls of the dagoba display murals that would normally be found locked within a temple's relic chamber.

A few kilometres south brings you to the village of **Rikillagaskada**, where route B39 meets the B40. Close to here is the **Loolecondera Estate**, the place where, in 1867, an innovative Scotsman named James Taylor established the first commercial tea plantation in Sri Lanka. You can still walk through the tea gardens of the historic estate, while the views across the valley of the Mahaweli Ganga towards Hunnasgiriya and the Knuckles Range beyond are spectacular. The **Kurundu Oya Falls**, next to the B39 beyond Rikillagaskada, drop 189 metres (630ft) above Mulhalkele

RIGHT: a British-era post box at Nuwara Eliya.

Bridge. More tea estates clad the undulating hills on the winding route towards **Ragala**.

Nuwara Eliya

The inspiring scenery that surrounds it might build up your expectations of **Nuwara Eliya** (pronounced as a single word, sounding something like "Nyureliya"), and you'll quickly see why the early British settlers fell for it. After the heat and dust of Colombo, the salubrious climate and the breathtaking landscape are a soothing balm, as Sir Edward Barnes discovered when he was governing the island in 1828 and used it as his up-country retreat. A little later the intrepid explorer Samuel Baker *(see box)* introduced English-style agriculture here, and more than 150 years later the beets, cabbages, leeks, potatoes and strawberries he brought to the region are still going strong.

Despite its impressive colonial heritage, however, recent decades have not been kind to Nuwara Eliya. Most of the centre has been taken over by rows of ugly concrete buildings,

Samuel Baker in Nuwara Eliya

Nuwara Eliya owes much of its distinctly British flavour to the British explorer Samuel Baker, famous for discovering the source of the Nile.

Baker spent some time here in the 1840s and was determined "to make it a regular settlement… a little English village round my residence". Without further ado he imported Hereford cows from home and planted strawberries, carrots and leeks, all of which thrived in the eternal spring climate.

He also had great plans to build a brewery, and sent for all he would need, plus some farmhands, artisans, a bailiff, a blacksmith with forge, farming machinery, a horse-drawn carriage and an arsenal of sporting firearms. One only wonders why he didn't ask for foxes so that he could go hunting.

The only means of transport then was through the Ramboda Pass using bullock wagons and elephant carts. Yet it all arrived safely, with the exception of the carriage.

Baker's coachman explained it to his master the best way he knew how – by letter: "Honord Zur, I'm sorry to hinform you that the carriage and osses has met with a haccident and is tumbled down a preccipice and its a mussy as I didn't go too."

while the town suffers particularly badly from traffic, whose belching fumes seem all the more noxious in the crisp mountain air. Memories of England do still cling to parts of the town: in the tranquil green spaces of **Victoria Park** (daily 7am–6.30pm; charge) and the **golf course** that thread their way through the grey town centre; in the old-fashioned half-timbered hotels and guesthouses dotted around the edge of town; and, of course, in the great piles of English vegetables which the town still churns out in huge quantities, even if they are grown by Tamil labourers in sarongs and woolly hats, rather than by English farmhands.

The best places to go if you want to get a taste of the life enjoyed by the Victorian hill planters are the town's three big colonial hotels. The most atmospheric is the splendid **Hill Club**, a hoary granite and half-timbered structure overlooking the town centre. Its interior – complete with cracked leather furnishings, stags' heads and time-worn books – is a perfect little period piece. Even if you

don't stay here it's worth visiting for dinner (note, though, that gentlemen are required to wear a tie).

The nearby **Grand Hotel**, a massive old structure that looks as if it has jumped straight out of a golf course in Surrey, grew up around a bungalow built by Sir Edward Barnes and includes a huge ballroom, a time-warped Victorian lounge and a wood-panelled bar with log fire. Tea on the lawns is heavenly. At the north end of town, the luxurious **St Andrews Hotel** overlooks the other end of the golf course, its fine early 20th-century buildings kept discreetly apart from the town centre by swathes of perfectly manicured lawns – another spot for a memorable cup of local tea.

A little way north of St Andrews stands the barred entrance to **Pidurutalagala** (or Mt Pedro, as it was rechristened by the tongue-tied British), the highest mountain in the island, though sadly you can no longer climb to its summit since it's now topped by one of the island's major air-traffic control centres. A

TIP

Despite its rather polluted urban setting, Victoria Park is one of the easiest places in Sri Lanka to see rare endemic birds, including the yellow-eared bulbul and the dull-blue flycatcher.

BELOW: the line from Nuwara Eliya to Kandy.

Hakgala Rock is said to be one of the fragments of a Himalayan peak which the monkey god Hanuman scattered across Sri Lanka, one of the many exploits described in the great Indian epic the Ramayana.

good, and less taxing alternative is the climb up **Single Tree Mountain**, south of town, reached from the Badulla Road. It's just over an hour's walk to the top, though the effort is rewarded by fine views over the town, Gregory's Lake, Hakgala and beyond. Various paths continue into the forest on the other side, leading through the beautiful tea gardens of Shantipura and on to the hilltop at Uda Radella, one of the most memorable viewpoints in the island, offering a sweeping bird's-eye panorama of the hill country as far as Adam's Peak and beyond.

Around Nuwara Eliya

For all the faded charm of Nuwara Eliya itself, the town's main attraction is as a base for exploring the magnificent surrounding countryside, notably Horton Plains National Park, Hakgala Gardens and the various tea estates, plus the scenic drives and spectacular waterfalls that dot the mountains nearby. Just a couple of kilometres from town, the extensive **Pedro Tea Estate** (daily 8.30am–6pm; charge)

offers visitors a good chance to inspect a working tea factory and see how the leaf is processed using venerable old machinery that has changed little since Victorian times.

Slightly further afield, at the village of **Kandapola**, is the striking **Tea Factory** hotel, created out of the old Hethersett tea factory, whose insides have been transformed into a stunning modern five-star establishment. The hotel is worth a visit even if you're not staying. It benefits from some of the hill country's most dramatic scenery and is surrounded by vast, immaculately manicured gardens – a rewarding destination for a morning's stroll, before lunch in the hotel.

Hakgala Gardens

South of Nuwara Eliya is another prominent peak, **Hakgala Rock**, whose sheer face rises 450 metres (1,500ft) above the surrounding countryside. At the foot of the rock lies the delightful **Hakgala Botanical Gardens** ⑰ (daily 8am–5pm; charge). Established in 1860, the gardens

BELOW: tea plantation.

started life as an experimental plantation of cinchona trees, from which the anti-malarial drug quinine is derived; but they are now best known for their roses, ferns and orchid house – and for their beautiful views. The gardens are also home to some interesting wildlife, including bear monkeys and sambur, as well as an outstanding array of montane birdlife.

About 1.6km (1 mile) back up the road towards Nuwara Eliya is the **Sita Amman Kovil**. This modest little Hindu temple is another spot that local legend associates with the events of the *Ramayana*, being said to mark the spot where Ravana kept Sita captive (although a cave near Ella makes a similar claim). Rama sent a troop of apes led by Hanuman here in search of Sita, but their appearance so enraged Ravana that he set fire to Hanuman's tail, angering the monkey god and causing him such discomfort that he tore round in a rage, setting fire to the trees of the forest. A darkened patch of soil by the temple is the result of this legendary incident.

Adam's Peak

Nuwara Eliya is also the starting point for the traditional ascent of **Adam's Peak** ⓲, reached by following the road via the town of Hatton to the small village of Dalhousie (pronounced "Del-house"; also often referred to by its Tamil name of **Nallatanniya**), on the peak's northern side. Although only the fifth-highest mountain on the island, at 2,243 metres (7,360ft), Adam's Peak is easily the most dramatic, rising in solitary splendour above the surrounding hills.

The peak has been an object of worship and pilgrimage for centuries amongst the Sinhalese, thanks to a strange impression on the bare rock at its summit that is popularly claimed to be a footprint *(Sri Pada)* made by the Buddha himself during one of his three legendary visits to the island.

Thousands of pilgrims haul themselves up thousands of steps to the mountain's summit every year to pay their devotions to the footprint. "The scene is most extraordinary," a

Giant ferns can sometimes dominate the skyline.

BELOW: a tranquil lake at Horton Plains.

Tea and Serendipity

In the 19th century, the topography of highland Sri Lanka was changed for ever by the advent of tea.

The Chinese Emperor Shen-Nung is generally credited with inventing tea 5,000 years ago, a feat he accomplished by chance when a few leaves dropped off a wild tea bush and drifted into the pot of water he was boiling. Rather than waste the contaminated water, he drank it, and so became the first person to experience the "cup that cheers".

This serendipitous event in faraway China was the first of the happy accidents that led to the establishment of tea in Sri Lanka. The second was the universal blight that destroyed the island's extensive coffee plantations during the 1860s. The afflicted coffee planters turned to tea instead, using plants brought from India, which flourished in the crisp, damp air of the central highlands. Such was the success of the new import that large tracts of the hill country were hurriedly cleared by waves of British settlers attracted by the possibilities of the island's so-called "green gold". Fortunes were rapidly made (and occasionally lost), while the environment of highland Sri Lanka was transformed within 20 years,

from dense jungle to the endless swathes of neatly manicured tea bushes that still blanket the hill country today. The old tea factories were white aerated barns, which were often constructed in England and shipped out piece by piece. These perfect relics of Victorian industrial design (as is most of the machinery within them), still stand out against the glossy green hillsides after a century or more of use.

From leaf to cup

Tea begins its journey from hillside to cup with a gentle tug between the thumb and forefinger of one of the island's thousands of Tamil tea pluckers. With baskets strapped to their backs, they work their way through the tea gardens – one of the island's most famous sights, although the tea pluckers themselves, picturesque though they appear, are among the poorest and most underprivileged of all Sri Lankans.

The freshly gathered leaves (only the topmost bud and two leaves are plucked in order to guarantee the freshness and purity of the resultant tea) are promptly carried off to be converted into tea in the nearest tea factory. The leaves are first withered in blasts of hot air to remove excess moisture, then rolled and crushed to release the remaining sap in the leaves and trigger fermentation. After a carefully calculated length of time, the leaves are fired in enormous ovens to produce bulk black tea, and sifted into different-sized particles. The entire process, from bush to finished tea, takes no more than 24 hours.

The finished teas are given elegant names based on the size of the leaf fragment, such as pekoe, orange pekoe, broken orange pekoe, broken orange pekoe fannings, and so-called dust, a low-quality tea used in tea bags. Sri Lankan teas are also ranked according to their point (and height) of origin: "high-grown" (the finest and most delicately flavoured Ceylon teas, grown at altitude in the estates around Nuwara Eliya), "mid-grown", and the fuller-flavoured but relatively coarse "low-grown" teas, produced in the foothills. Expert tea tasters will then classify the tea as "malty, pointy, bakey, thick, coppery, dull or bright" according to strength, flavour and colour, before the graded teas are finally auctioned off. Much of the best stuff ends up being exported, although an increasingly wide selection of local teas is becoming available in local shops and supermarkets. Look for unblended, single-origin teas from leading up-country estates – an authentic taste of Sri Lanka in a cup.

LEFT: weighing the tea at the factory.

European observer wrote in 1896, "men, women, old and young, some almost decrepit, some who actually die on the way, many who have to be pulled or carried up, people from India, from China, from Japan, from Burma, from Spain, from Siam, from Ceylon, from Africa, priests and laymen, princes and paupers, may be seen striving, toiling, perspiring upwards."

The arduous climb up the mountain from Dalhousie is traditionally made by night during the pilgrimage season from January to April. Arriving in time for dawn, one has the best chance, weather permitting, of seeing the extraordinary sunrise and the associated spectacle known as the "Shadow of the Peak", whereby the rising sun casts a perfectly triangular shadow of the peak's summit, which hangs miraculously suspended in mid-air for 20 minutes or so. This bizarre phenomenon has yet to be satisfactorily explained, but is commonly taken by visiting Buddhists as proof of the mountain's extraordinary supernatural qualities.

Kitulgala

North of Adam's Peak, the village of **Kitulgala** ⑲ achieved global fame thanks to its role in David Lean's classic Oscar-winning film Bridge on the River Kwai, which was shot on location here in 1957 (despite allegedly being set in Thailand). Locals will show you sights associated with the film, including the slight remains of the concrete foundations which supported the bridge itself, blown up at the climax of the film. Nowadays Kitulgala is better known as Sri Lanka's main centre for whitewater rafting thanks to its location on the Kelani Ganga, whose foaming waters provide a series of exhilarating grade 2 and 3 rapids, shooting through a dramatic landscape of sheer-sided wooded hills either side of the village. Trips can be arranged locally through a number of operators.

Horton Plains and World's End

South of Nuwara Eliya, at the southern edge of the hill country, lies **Horton Plains National Park** ⑳, a

TIP

Directly beyond Adisham lies the interesting Tangamalai Nature Reserve, a beautiful area of tropical forest that is home to a rich array of birdlife – and plenty of monkeys too.

BELOW: the view through Ella Gap.

The early morning light brings out the beauty of the Hill Country.

bleak, windswept plateau located at an altitude of around 2,000 metres (6,500ft). This is the one national park in Sri Lanka where the scenery, rather than the wildlife, is the principal attraction: a forbidding and misty landscape, often enveloped in dense cloud and rain, punctuated by rare stands of tangled cloudforest and bounded on its western and northern sides by Sri Lanka's second- and third-highest mountains, **Totapola** and Kirgalpotta.

The park offers some excellent hikes, the most popular being the 9km (5.5-mile) round trip to World's End, a stunning viewpoint at the very edge of the hill country, where the cliffs suddenly fall away beneath one's feet for the best part of a kilometre (half a mile) to the plains below. The return path takes one via **Baker's Falls**, a picturesque little cascade whose cool waters offer a perfect spot to bathe tired feet.

Haputale

BELOW: carvings at Buduruwagala.

Southeast of Nuwara Eliya, a sequence of dramatically situated towns and villages dots the southern edge of the hill country, a few of them perched right on the edge of the escarpment, offering thrilling views out across the plains below. Some of the best views are from the down-at-heel little town of **Haputale** ㉑, whose rather grubby streets contrast strangely with the swathes of beautifully tended tea plantations that surround it. East of town stretch the beautiful tea gardens belonging to the picturesque **Dambatanne tea factory** (daily 8am–6pm; charge), which is also open to visitors, and a good place to see a working tea factory in full flight. From the factory, small country lanes lead up through the tea gardens to the superb viewpoint known as **Lipton's Seat**, named in honour of the Victorian tea magnate whose name remains synonymous with tea across South Asia, and who is said to have often ridden his horse up here to enjoy the view.

A few kilometres from Haputale lies **Adisham** (Sat–Sun, *Poya* days and school holidays 9.30am–12.30pm and 1.30–4pm; charge). Now home to a Benedictine monastery, the house

was originally built as a home for the wealthy Victorian businessman Sir Thomas Villiers, who named the house after his home village in Kent and modelled some of its neo-Elizabethan features on Leeds Castle, filling it with imported carpets, porcelain, furniture and glassware. Today it is run as a Benedictine retreat, producing home-made wild guava jams and jellies and fruit cordials for sale. A couple of the time-warped original rooms are opened to the public at weekends.

Bandarawela

Half an hour's drive north of Haputale, the bustling but drab little town of **Bandarawela** ㉒ is of interest mostly for the **Bandarawela Hotel**, one of the most appealing rest stops between Nuwara Eliya and the coast. The hotel is set in a former tea planters' club, its rooms stocked with comfortable period furniture and enormous bathtubs. The beautiful hills around town are still the best area for what tea planters call "flavoury tea"; pears and strawberries also reach their prime

here as the climate is drier and milder than at Nuwara Eliya.

Just 6km (4 miles) northeast of Bandarawela, the small **Dowa Cave Temple** stands right by the road side, but is easily missed thanks to the thick woodland surrounding it. The main attraction here is a striking figure carved in low relief into the rock above the temple: either the historical Buddha or the future Buddha Maitreya, a figure also found at nearby Buduruwagala whose carvings this strongly resembles.

Ella

Half an hour's drive northeast of Bandarawela, at the southeastern cusp of the hills, the idyllic little village of **Ella** ㉓ is one of the most pleasant spots in the region, with a halcyon atmosphere approaching that of an English country hamlet – although rampant development is now beginning to slightly overwhelm its modest charms. The village's biggest attraction is the drop-dead gorgeous view through the narrow cleft in the hills – the so-called **Ella Gap** – down to the

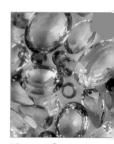

The gems of Ratnapura.

BELOW: panning for jewels.

TIP

It is bad form to ask how far it is to the top of Adam's Peak as you climb. Just exchange the greeting *Karuvanai* (peace).

hills below, one of the finest views in an island that is full of unforgettable panoramas.

There are also some good walks around the village, including the short but rewarding climb up **Little Adam's Peak** (2 hours round trip) and the longer, more challenging scramble up **Ella Rock** (4 hours round trip), the rugged summit that looms up opposite the village. Ella is also famous as one of the Sri Lankan sites most closely associated with the *Ramayana*, and particularly with the villainous Ravana, who is thought to have imprisoned Sita in the **Rawana Ella Cave**, just south of the village (though this claim is disputed by the rival Sita Amman Kovil near Hakgala – see page 208).

Around Ella

South of Ella, the road hairpins dramatically down through the hills to the **Rawana Ella Falls**, whose great cataract of water, almost 100 metres (328ft) high, tumbles down over a cliff right next to the road. Even the myriad touts and tourists who congregate here cannot detract from the spectacle. Past here, the road continues its precipitous descent to the foot of the escarpment and the dusty little town of **Wellawaya**. Five kilometres (3 miles) past Wellawaya is the evocative archaeological site of **Buduruwagala** ㉔, where seven colossal figures stand carved in low relief into a high rock face. The statues – of which the large central standing Buddha is the tallest in the island, at around 16 metres (52ft) high – are thought to date back to the 9th or 10th centuries. The trio of figures to his left is believed to represent the Mahayana Buddhist diety Avalokitesvara, along with two attendants; those on his right are thought to show the Tibetan Boddhisattva Vajrapani, the future Buddha Maitreya and Vishnu. A few kilometres beyond the statues lies the scenic Handapanagala Tank, offering fine views of the hills and a good chance of spotting wild elephants, who often come here to drink towards the end of the day.

From Wellawaya, you could loop back round to Haputale and Ella via another fine waterfall, the **Diyaluma Falls**, which drop 171 metres (560ft) in a single leap. Alternatively, from the crossroads town of Beragala it's possible to continue west towards the **Bambarakanda Falls**, the highest in the island, whose slender cascade falls a dizzying total of 241 metres (790ft). From here the road continues west to Ratnapura, hugging the beautifully wooded country at the base of the hills and passing through the small town of **Belihul Oya**, where there are several guesthouses if you want to break your journey.

Ratnapura

The lively provincial capital of **Ratnapura** ㉕ sprawls across the undulating countryside at the southern edge of the hill country, whose outlying peaks provide a picturesque backdrop to the town's workaday

BELOW: clouds can at times obscure Adam's Peak.

streets. Ratnapura (literally "city of gems") is famous for its precious stones, more of which are found in the surrounding countryside than anywhere else in the island, as they wash down from eroded rocks in the hill country and mix with gravel in the fast-flowing mountain streams and rivers. Huge quantities of stones are mined, cut and traded here, mainly along **Saviya Street** in the town centre, where crowds of locals gather daily to haggle over handfuls of uncut stones. The prospect of picking up the bargain of a lifetime may be enticing, but the fact is that amateur gem-fanciers are likely to get their fingers burnt and wallets emptied.

If you want to have a closer look at the region's mineral wonders, it's safer to admire the dazzling displays at the small but instructive **Gem Bureau Museum** (daily 9.30am–4pm; donation), a few kilometres out of town, which features an absorbing collection of coloured gems and minerals from Sri Lanka and abroad. Local touts will probably also approach you, offering visits to watch miners prospecting for gems in the impromptu mines dug out of river beds around town. If you still have time to spare, the **National Museum** (Tue–Sat 9am–5pm; charge) in the town centre has a modest selection of exhibits featuring traditional Sri Lankan crafts.

The most interesting place to visit hereabouts, however, is the sprawling **Saman Devale**, around 4km (2.5 miles) out of town. The temple was originally built by Parakramabahu in the 13th century but was demolished by the Portuguese (look for the statue by the entrance showing a Portuguese soldier killing a Sinhalese), and then built all over again in its current form – a large but harmonious complex of white Kandyan-style buildings topped by red-tiled roofs. An important *perahera* (procession) is held here annually on the Esala Poya day (late July or early Aug).

Sinharaja

Ratnapura is also the most convenient jumping-off point for a visit to the remarkable **Sinharaja Forest Reserve** (daily 7am–6pm; charge), the island's last extensive tract of undisturbed tropical rainforest. Sinharaja is quite unlike anywhere else on the island, an impenetrable expanse of intertwined trees, ferns and lianas tangled together in Amazonian exuberance and humming with the noise of cicadas and the chirrupings of birdlife. The entire reserve is an ecological treasure box, containing no fewer than 830 species of endemic flora and fauna, including numerous rare species of trees, birdlife, reptiles and insects.

For the casual visitor, it's the spectacular density of the reserve's vegetation that is likely to make the most impact. Its soaring tropical hardwoods form a dense canopy, which shuts out most sunlight and direct rainfall but locks in humidity, creating a dim, intensely humid atmosphere at ground level – akin to being in an enormous greenhouse. Many of the island's endemic bird species can be found here, along

Sri Lanka's Hindus, Muslims and Christians all came up with theories claiming the footprint on Adam's Peak to be that of, respectively, Siva, Adam and St Thomas, though none of these has ever been taken very seriously and the peak remains an essentially Buddhist place of worship.

BELOW: the "Shadow of the Peak".

Sinharaja rainforest.

with purple-faced langur monkeys and many other rare types of wildlife, ranging from squirrels to frogs and snakes, as well as myriad insect species, many of which have yet to be scientifically classified.

More than anywhere else in the island, it's worth coming to Sinharaja with an expert guide (the charge includes the services of a guide, but their command of English and knowledge of the reserve often leave much to be desired). The reserve's densely tangled flora makes little sense without expert interpretation, and it also makes it virtually impossible to spot the elusive birds, mammals and insects that live here. Palitha Ratnayake, at the Sinharaja Rest guesthouse in Deniyaya (tel: 041 227 3368), is one of the area's most experienced guides, offering day-long hikes through the forest.

Uda Walawe National Park

Lying on the plains below the hill country's southern escarpment, **Uda Walawe** has, over the past decade, developed into one of the country's most popular national parks, thanks mainly to 500 or so elephants that live in it. Elephants aside, the park is also home to the usual selection of Sri Lankan creatures, from monkeys, deer, crocodiles and (rare) leopards, to sloth bears and giant flying squirrels, plus a rich array of birdlife, including many fine birds of prey. The park's scrubby landscape is nothing much to look at, but the lack of the forest cover found in most other national parks makes wildlife spotting here comparatively easy – something you'll particularly appreciate if you've just come from exploring the impenetrable thickets and unlocatable birds of Sinharaja.

At the southern edge of the park, the **Elephant Transit Home** (usually simply called the Elephant Orphanage) serves as a temporary home for elephants orphaned in the wild. Unlike the orphanage at Pinnawela, only young elephants are kept here – at the age of five, most are released into Uda Walawe to fend for themselves. You can watch the elephants being fed here four times daily; outside feeding hours, there's not much to see.

BELOW: practical footwear for working the land.
RIGHT: afternoon refreshment.

CULTURAL TRIANGLE

Referring to the area between the former capitals of Kandy, Anuradhapura and Polonnaruwa, the Cultural Triangle contains some of the island's, if not the world's, finest ancient monuments.

The dry-zone plains north of Kandy were the heartlands of ancient Sri Lankan civilisation, and the ruins of the great cities which once flourished here are nothing less than staggering. The entire area is loosely referred to as the **Cultural Triangle**, an imaginary construct with its points at the three great Sinhalese capitals of Kandy, Polonnaruwa and Anuradhapura, which encapsulates one of the world's most extraordinary collections of Buddhist art and architecture.

Much of the region's history is contained in the remains of **Anuradhapura** (see page 231), capital of the island for well over a millennium and adorned by countless kings with a succession of extravagant buildings, including three of the largest stupas the world has ever seen. Nearby **Mihintale** (see page 240) is revered as the place where Buddhism was introduced to Sri Lanka, with a fascinating string of temples and stupas scattered across a beautiful hillside. Further south, and second only to Anuradhapura, the island's medieval capital, **Polonnaruwa** (see page 245), is a wonderful treasure trove of ancient Buddhist monuments, from royal palaces to colossal rock-cut statues. In the middle of the area lies **Sigiriya** (see page 255), where a usurper defied

engineering laws to build a royal palace in the sky on top of a giant rock – Sri Lanka's single most extraordinary sight. A good base from which to explore the area is **Habarana ❶** (see box page 225); but if you have time, spending a night or two in one of the numerous hotels around the sites gives you more of a flavour of the area.

Heading north from Kandy

A 30-minute drive north from Kandy is the celebrated monastery of **Aluvihara ❷** (no set hours; donation

Main attractions
ALUVIHARA
RIDI VIHARA
ARANKELE
YAPAHUWA
NALANDA GEDIGE
DAMBULLA CAVE TEMPLES
AUKANA AND SASSERUWA BUDDHAS
RITIGALA

PRECEDING PAGES: Golden Temple, Dambulla. **LEFT:** the Aukana Buddha. **RIGHT:** Dambulla statuary.

The Aluvihara library is one of the few places in Sri Lanka where you can still see the ancient but now dying art of writing upon ola leaf at first hand. Resident monks will demonstrate the process, first scratching out letters with a metal stylus, then rubbing ink into the leaf, causing the invisible engraved letters to magically appear.

requested). The monastery is famous as the place where the most important Theravada Buddhist doctrines, the *Tripitakaya*, were first committed to paper – or rather *ola* leaf – in the 1st century BC. The *Tripitakaya* was written in an ancient script called Pali on long leaves of the *ola* palm and then loosely bound to make books. Sadly, much of the monastery's priceless manuscripts were destroyed by the British in 1848, after a rebel leader took refuge in the complex.

The monastery occupies a series of brightly decorated cave temples carved out of a sequence of towering rock outcrops. Several are beautifully painted with frescoes; one contains a large reclining Buddha, also brightly painted; another is dedicated to the

Indian scholar Buddhagosa. The strangest of all contains a salutary depiction of the afterlife awaiting miscreants, with colourful statues of sinners being punished by demons, an unfaithful woman being chopped into pieces, and a male sex-pest having the top of his skull removed so that the demons can reach in with spoons and ladle out his brain.

Some 17km (11 miles) west of Aluvihara is **Ridigama** ❸ village, home to the very beautiful, and very ancient **Ridi Vihara** (Silver Temple; no set hours; donation requested). The temple is said to mark the spot where a precious lode of silver was discovered in the 2nd century BC. The money was used by the legendary King Dutugemunu to fund construction of the great Ruwanweliseya

stupa in Anuradhapura; in gratitude, the king also built the temple here to commemorate the find. The main temple, partly carved out of a huge rock outcrop, is decorated with old Buddha statues, while blue-and-white Dutch picture tiles add a curiously European touch. In the main temple grounds stands the little **Varakha Valandu Vihara**: an exquisite Hindu shrine that was converted to Buddhist use sometime in the 11th century.

Arankele

The forest monastery of **Arankele ❹** (daily 6am–6pm; free) is one of the Cultural Triangle's best-kept secrets, tucked away along a small side road some 24km (15 miles) north of Kurunegala. The main part of the monastery dates back to the 6th century (although a few remains from much earlier survive) and was formerly home to a group of ascetic *pamsukulika* monks who lived a reclusive life of Buddhist contemplation in caves dotted around the jungle here; their modern brethren can still be found inhabiting the small monastery at the back of the site. Like the similar forest temple of Ritigala, Arankele consists of a rather enigmatic but wonderfully atmospheric collection of ruins buried in thick jungle, including various "double platform" structures (each carefully aligned along an east–west axis and surrounded by small moats, all now dry) connected by a remarkable, arrow-straight stone pathway, formerly used for the practice of walking meditation.

Yapahuwa and Kurunegala

Following the fall of Polonnaruwa in 1236, the embattled Sinhalese kings fled south in the wake of repeated Indian attacks, establishing a series of transient capitals and royal palaces in increasingly remote and inaccessible locations, carrying the Tooth Relic (see page 191) and cuttings from the original Sri Maha Bodhi Bo tree with them. They first established themselves at Dambedeniya before arriving

at **Yapahuwa ❺** (daily 8am–6pm; charge). Here King Bhuvanekabhu I (1272–84) founded a new and short-lived capital before the Pandyans caught up with him once again and drove him further south. Little now remains of the former royal city apart from its spectacular stone staircase, one of the Cultural Triangle's greatest sights: an astonishingly well-preserved, near-vertical stairway, decorated with friezes of musicians and dancers and guarded by a pair of superb lions (one of which appears on the island's 10-rupee note). The steps lead to the top of a huge rock outcrop, though almost nothing survives of the royal palace and temple that once stood at the summit. The main reward for making the breathless climb up the sheer steps is the fine views across the plains below, and over the modest remains of the former city at the foot of the rock, protected by two semicircular ramparts and a moat.

Despite its massive fortifications, Yapahuwa served as the capital for only a dozen years. Following a brief return to Polonnaruwa, the kings

Modern-day Kurunegala, a possible base for exploring the Cultural Triangle's southwestern attractions.

BELOW: the steps of Yapahuwa fortress.

TIP

Visiting Dambulla, it's a good idea to explore the cave temples in reverse order, starting at cave 5 and working back to cave 2, which allows you to enjoy a sense of increasing size and sophistication as you move from cave to cave, and saving the best till last.

settled in **Kurunegala** ❻, where they remained for 48 years, although virtually nothing remains of the ancient city. Modern-day Kurunegala is one of the largest towns hereabouts, a bustling provincial centre centred on the breezy Kurunegala Tank and surrounded by an odd string of bare and rather lunar-looking rock outcrops. Among them, the impressive **Etagala** (Elephant Rock), topped by a large modern temple and Buddha statue, offers spectacular views of the surrounding countryside.

Nalanda Gedige

North of Aluvihara, set among lush green hills close to the majestic Mahaweli River, is the small but beautiful **Nalanda Gedige** ❼ (daily 8am–6pm; admission fee). This is one of the best examples in the country of a gedige, a type of rectangular shrine built entirely of stone and heavily influenced by the South Indian style of architecture introduced by the subcontinental settlers who flocked to the island during the Polonnaruwa period – a classic example of Sri Lankan

cross-cultural influence, comprising a Buddhist temple constructed following a classic Hindu design. True to its Indian precedents, the gedige comes complete with pillared *mandapa* (antechamber) and inner shrine encircled by an ambulatory, not to mention an extremely faded Tantric sexual carving still visible (just) on the outer wall.

Dambulla Cave Temples

More or less at the centre of the Cultural Triangle, the imposing 160-metre (52ft) **Dambulla Rock** ❽, just south of the dusty and workaday town of Dambulla, houses the most impressive and venerated Buddhist cave temples (daily 7am–7pm; admission fee) in Sri Lanka. The temples were originally created by King Valagambahu I in the 1st century BC. Valgambahu sought refuge here and stayed for 14 years after being driven out of Anuradhapura by Tamil invaders, and built the temples in gratitude after successfully reclaiming his throne. The site was repaired and further embellished by the kings of Kandy during the 17th and 18th centuries, most notably by King Kirti

BELOW: Dambulla Rock Cave Temples.

Sri Rajasinha (1747–82), who was responsible for many of the murals and statues which one sees today.

The temples, halfway up the rock itself, are reached by a steep climb up a sequence of concrete steps, offering superb views over the plains and rocky outcrops of the Cultural Triangle, including magical views of Sigiriya in the distance.

Caves

The first cave is the **Devaraja Viharaya** (Temple of the Lord of the Gods), referring to Lord Vishnu, who is popularly credited with having created the original caves. The cave is almost entirely filled by a 14-metre (46ft) sleeping Buddha carved from a single piece of rock, while his lifelong attendant and disciple, Ananda, stands solemnly at his feet. Images of Vishnu and other murals adorn the walls, many of which are faded beyond recognition due to years of incense-burning by pilgrims.

Cave 2, the **Maharaja Vihara** (Temple of Great Kings), is the largest and most spectacularly decorated of all the cave temples. The sheer size of

the cave alone is impressive: over 50 metres (165ft) long, 25 metres (82ft) wide and 7 metres (22ft) high. It's thought that the cave was created by King Valagamba, though what you see now mainly dates from the 18th century, when the cave was comprehensively restored and redecorated. The cave is home to statues of two of the island's most famous kings, hence its name: Valagamba himself (just left of the door) and Nissankamalla (hidden away behind a large reclining Buddha on the far right-hand side of the cave). Kings apart, the cave is filled to bursting with an enormous array of Buddhas, lined up around its sides.

The main Buddha statue is directly in front as you enter: a life-size image in the standing posture with his right hand in the Abhaya mudra (Have no fear) posture. Though repainted, strips of gold leaf underneath can still be seen. Flanking the Buddha are statues of Maitreya and the 1,000-armed god of compassion Avalokitesvara, an uncommon Mahayana Buddhist touch, while statues of Saman and Vishnu stand behind.

Stone Buddha in the Samadhi position of deep meditation.

LEFT: Habarana sunset.

Exploring the Cultural Triangle

There are all sorts of different itineraries through the Cultural Triangle's myriad attractions, and you'll need a week or more to really see everything the region has to offer. **Habarana**, which has several good hotels and a strategic location at the dead centre of the Triangle, is within easy striking distance of all the main attractions (although the various hotels at Dambulla, Sigiriya, Inamalawa and Giritale are only slightly less central). Public transport is sketchy, however. You really need your own vehicle to make the most of the area, especially if you plan to visit any of the more obscure sights – some of which are decidedly off the beaten track.

The one sight that must be seen is the superlative rock fortress of Sigiriya, while you should also be sure to visit the wonderful cave temples at Dambulla, given that the main road into the Triangle passes directly in front of the entrance. A visit to either Polonnaruwa or Anuradhapura (ideally, both) is also de rigueur, although it is worth making time to explore at least one or two of the Triangle's less touristed attractions. Entrance to the major sites is now decidedly pricey: $30 at Sigiriya and $25 at Polonnaruwa and Anuradhapura. The Dambulla cave temples cost $12, while most minor sites charge in the region of $5.

No less striking are the superb murals covering the walls and ceilings. The most impressive is the **Mara Parajaya** (Defeat of Mara), a set of three murals depicting the trials and temptations suffered by the Buddha on the night he attained enlightenment at Bodhgaya. In the first panel, the Buddha is shown being attacked by hordes of hairy demons, while in the second he is shown resisting the advances of a large crowd of alluring ladies. His triumph over both is shown in the third panel, in which he delivers a sermon to an assembly of richly costumed deities.

Cave 3, the **Maha Alut Viharaya** (Great New Temple), was built by one of the last great Kandyan kings, Kirti Sri Rajasinha, whose statue is positioned in front of a painting of four attendants. The cave is dominated by a meditating Buddha seated under a *makara torana* (an ornamental arch formed out of two joined makaras – a type of mythical creature made up out of pieces of fish, lion, elephants and other creatures), surrounded by 50 other Buddhas, and a colossal 9-metre (30ft) reclining Buddha, both carved out from a single piece of rock. There are further interesting murals on the ceiling. One particularly striking painting shows the future Buddha, Maitreya, preaching to groups of gods and ascetics, while to the right of the door is an unusual 19th-century painting of a garden, complete with little elephants, snakes and Buddhas.

The small Cave 4, **Pacchima Viharaya** (Western Temple), contains several finely crafted statues of sitting Buddhas lining the walls. The centrepiece is a small, cracked stupa which, legend has it, contained the jewels of Queen Somawathie, wife of King Valagamba. An attempt by thieves to steal the jewels proved it was just a myth.

Cave 5, the **Devana Alut Viharaya** (Second New Temple), was built after the four original caves, although no one knows exactly when or by whom. It is dominated by a large reclining Buddha surrounded by five smaller statues, all of brick and plaster unlike the solid-rock images found in the other caves.

At the foot of Dambulla Rock, the glitzy, modern **Golden Temple** demonstrates the considerable artistic differences between the work of the skilled

and subtle craftsmen of yesteryear and the overblown creations of today. The temple itself is large, kitsch and unquestionably ugly, although the huge, 30-metre (100ft) tall Golden Buddha that sits behind it is undeniably impressive, imbued with a certain refined simplicity and serenity perhaps not entirely out of keeping with the original cave temples on the rock above.

On the main road 100 metres/ yds south of the Golden Temple, the excellent **Dambulla Museum** (Wed–Mon 7am–5pm; charge) is devoted to the fascinating but rather neglected subject of Sri Lankan painting: beautifully executed life-size copies of important works from across the island, ranging from Veddah cave painting and Kandyan temple murals through to works by 20th-century artists like George Keyt.

Around Dambulla

Around 3km (2 miles) from the cave temples, on the road to the famous Kandalama Hotel, the **Popham Arboretum** (daily 6am–6pm; charge) comprises 14 hectares (35 acres) of beautiful dry tropical forest, crisscrossed by a series of well-maintained walking trails. The arboretum was established in 1963 by British expat Sam Popham in response to the widespread logging of Sri Lankan forests for their valuable hardwood timbers. Popham acquired a plot of deforested land, cleared away the scrub that had grown up on it and allowed nature to do the rest. Almost 50 years on, the aboretum has now sprouted more than 70 species of precious tropical trees such as ebony, rosewood and satinwood, and attracted plentiful birdlife and other wildlife – making it not only a fine example of natural reforestation in action but a beautiful place for a walk.

More rare tropical trees can be seen at the **Namal Uyana Conservation Forest** (daily 6am–6pm; charge), around 15km (9 miles) north of Dambulla. The forest is home to the biggest surviving forest of ironwood *(na)* trees in Sri Lanka, as well as a huge outcrop of rose quartz, the largest deposit of this unusual mineral in South Asia, which rises strangely out of the surrounding jungle like a miniature chain of vaguely purple-looking mountains.

Aukana and Sasseruwa Buddhas

Around 30km (18 miles) northwest of Dambulla is the stately **Aukana Buddha ❾**, the most perfectly preserved ancient statue in Sri Lanka – Aukana means "sun eating", and the statue is best seen at dawn, when the low light shines directly into its face. Standing 13 metres (43ft) high, the imposing image was carved with supreme assurance out of a single rock, in the unusual *asisa* mudra. The Buddha has his heavy right hand raised in the posture of blessing, while his other hand delicately touches his shoulder, as if holding his pleated robes in place. Although he stands erect, the body is graceful, an effect helped by the softly flowing drapery, which appears almost diaphanous. His expression is serene,

The Golden Buddha, highlight of the Golden Temple.

BELOW: the temple of the Aukana Buddha.

and from his curled hair there sprouts the flame signifying super-enlightenment. It is only when you lower your gaze to the massive feet resting on the lotus-decorated plinth, that dizziness and a crick in the neck remind you of the vastness of this statue.

Some 10km (6 miles) southwest of Aukana, the monumental Buddha at **Sasseruwa** ❿ provides a fascinating contrast with the Aukana Buddha. According to popular legend the not-quite-finished statue was the work of an apprentice sculptor who gave up after seeing the image at Aukana, and realising the failings of his own creation – although the more likely (if prosaic) explanation is that work on the statue was abandoned because of cracks in the stone. The standing image is nearly as large as the Aukana figure (12 metres/39ft), but if anything it has even greater impact, making up in vivacity what it lacks in refinement. The statue stands in a niche created by the removal of stone around it as though it had always been there, standing within the stone, waiting for the sculptor to uncover it.

Ritigala

North of Habarana, the mysterious and seldom visited remains of the forest monastery of **Ritigala** ⓫ (daily 8am–6pm; charge) lie scattered around the lower flanks of the striking Ritigala mountain. Rising 766 metres (2,513ft) above sea level, the forest monastery was discovered only in 1872 by British surveyor James Mantell. As for the mountain itself, it is popularly believed to be one of the fragments of Himalayan rock accidentally dropped by the monkey god Hanuman during the events described in the *Ramayana* (see page 88), a legendary explanation said to account for the unusual range of herbs and plants that are found on the mountain's plateau. The prosaic botanical explanation is that the mountain's relatively cool microclimate supports a much greater natural diversity than the hot plains below.

The mountain has historically attracted hermits, from the 3rd century right through until the 1970s, when JVP rebels took refuge here following their failed insurrection. Most

BELOW: working in the rice fields.

noted perhaps were the monks of the ascetic *pamsukulika* sect (meaning "red robes") who turned against the comfortable monasteries of Anuradhapura in an attempt to revive the austere lifestyle led by the Buddha following his Enlightenment. Their dedication won them many admirers including King Sena I, who built them the monastery, the remains of which can be seen today.

The ruins

Just past the entrance to the site lies the **Banda Pokuna** – a huge bathing pool lined with finely carved steps. The tank is the start of the monastery's main artery – an almost perfectly preserved stone walkway which, it is surmised, was originally built as a meditation walk for the resident monks.

Following this path takes you past a fine sequence of "double platform" structures – two raised platforms aligned east to west and connected by a small stone bridge – which are typical of ancient Sri Lanka's forest monasteries. It's thought that the larger of the two platforms would originally have served as the base of a wooden

building in which monks lived, while the smaller platform would have been used for outdoor meditation. The remains of small moats, now dry, can be seen around many of these structures, once filled with water to help cool the resident hermits.

Keep following the pavement and you'll reach the remains of a monastic hospital or bathhouse, with stone beds and stone oil baths. Past here, you come to the urinal stones. These display the sole example of iconographic carving in Ritigala, which implies their purpose was not simply for urination. Most likely, the austere monks of the *pamsukulikas* would urinate on the elaborate stones as a symbol of rebellion against the excesses of the monks at Anuradhapura.

Keep following the pavement westwards and you reach two miniature "roundabouts" on the pathway. Just before the first roundabout a path on the right leads off through enormous tree roots to a building popularly known as the fort. A fort it's clearly not, although it does offer particularly fine views over the surrounding forest.

There's been much speculation about the original function of the "roundabouts" found on the walkways of forest monasteries such as Ritigala and Arankele. One quaint theory holds that they were designed to prevent meditating monks from walking into one another. A more prosaic explanation is that they originally supported open-air pavilions, designed to provide rest and shelter in the midday heat.

BELOW: stairway to the top of Ritigala mountain.

ANURADHAPURA

A marriage of faith and engineering, this
ancient city is filled with stunning Buddhist
temples and surrounded by some of the world's
earliest examples of mass irrigation.

Anuradhapura ⑫ was the greatest monastic city of the ancient
world and the heart of Sri
Lankan civilisation for over a millennium. At its height it was home to
tens of thousands of monks at dozens of monasteries and served by a
lay population which records suggest
could have numbered nearly two million. Its flourishing Buddhist culture
and architectural achievements made
it famous across Asia and as far afield
as Europe, while even today the sheer
scale of its surviving ruins and stupas
is breathtaking.

An ancient capital

Anuradhapura was the royal capital of
113 successive kings (and four queens)
who oversaw a great flowering of the
arts, producing magnificent palaces,
intricate sculptures, ornate pleasure
gardens and a sequence of vast stupas
built to protect the most sacred relics
of Buddhism. The three main dagobas
are amongst the biggest architectural creations ever attempted in the
ancient world, surpassed in size only
by the pyramids at Giza. The gentle
sway of the Buddhist faith inspired
the kings of ancient Lanka to allow
freedom of worship and to build
the world's first hospitals for both
humans and animals alike. Perhaps the
most impressive achievement was in

irrigation, with reservoirs constructed
to preserve the monsoon rains, and a
system of sluices put in place to keep
the rice paddies productive.

The fame of the city spread;
the Greek ambassador to India,
Megasthenes, admired the limou-
sines of the ancient royalty, the state
elephants, which were an important export, along with gems and
spices. The mass of Roman coins
that have been found show that
Lanka was not short of trade and
possibly even enjoyed some early

Main attractions
SRI MAHA BODHI
RUWANWELISEYA
THUPARAMA
JETAVANARAMA
ABHAYAGIRI VIHARA
SAMADHI BUDDHA
KUTTAM POKUNA
MIRISAWETI
ISURUMUNIYA

LEFT: the Thuparama. **RIGHT:** prayer flags
swathe a Bo tree.

This stone trough at the Mahapili Refectory would have held rice to feed thousands of monks.

BELOW: a monkey slakes its thirst at a tap.

tourism. In the early 5th century, the Chinese Buddhist pilgrim Fa Hien came in search of Buddhist texts in Anuradhapura, as Buddhism was then already waning in India.

According to tradition, Anuradhapura was founded in 377 BC by the third king of the Vijaya dynasty, Pandukabhaya (reigned 380–367 BC), who established a new capital on the site of the palace of his great-uncle, a certain Anuradha – hence the city's name. In 161 BC King Dutugemunu united the island, with Anuradhapura as the capital. It was fought over and finally abandoned in 1073 when the capital was transferred to Polonnaruwa (see page 245). By that time the city had served as the capital for about 1,400 years. From then on the jungle enveloped the palaces, monasteries and stupas, which slowly began to crumble. The British explorers who first surveyed the ruins in the 19th century justifiably felt they were rediscovering a "lost" city. Subsequent archaeologists of Anuradhapura have had an invaluable aid in the form of the *Mahavamsa*, the great chronicle

which records the founding of the city's monuments in Pali verse (the sacred language of Buddhism).

A modern shrine

Restoration continues, sometimes amounting to rebuilding, since Anuradhapura is not a dead city but a living pilgrimage site. On the monthly full moon festivals *(Poya)*, more than a million Sri Lankans flock to the site.

The most crowded part is around the **Sri Maha Bodhi** Ⓐ (Sacred Bo Tree), especially during *Poson Poya* (full moon) in June, when the area is packed with worshippers. The world's most revered tree, the Sri Maha Bodhi was grown from a sapling of the original bodhi tree under which the Buddha attained Enlightenment in Bodhgaya in India. The cutting was brought here by Mahinda's sister Sanghamitta as part of the attempt to spread Buddhism in Sri Lanka.

One of the oldest trees in the world, the Sri Maha Bodhi has been tended devotedly for 23 centuries, even during the long centuries after the rest of the city was abandoned

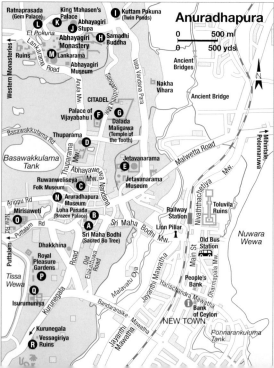

Anuradhapura

to the jungle. Cuttings from it have been planted in temples throughout the island and around the globe, creating a third generation of trees descended from the Indian original under which the Buddha attained Enlightenment. Today it is propped up on a frame of iron crutches and protected by a golden railing swathed in colourful prayer flags offered by the pilgrims.

Near the Sacred Bo Tree is the **Brazen Palace ➌** *(Loha Pasada)* – not a royal, but a monastic residence. The palace has now been reduced to an unimpressive forest of short, rough-hewn stone pillars all tilting out of the ground at varying angles. These paltry remains convey nothing of the splendours described in the *Mahavamsa*, which tell of a throne of ivory with a seat of mountain crystal set in a palace nine storeys high, and with 100 rooms to each floor. This magnificent structure was originally made entirely of wood, which unfortunately meant that it burned down more than once. The 1,600 pillars you see today are all that is left of the work begun by Dutugemunu and completed by Parakramabahu in the 12th century.

The Ruwanweliseya

The quintessential form of Buddhist architecture began as a mound of earth and developed into the stupas of India, the chedis of Thailand, and the pagodas of China and Japan. In Sri Lanka the stupa (or dagoba, as they're known) grew to unprecedented size under the patronage of Anuradhapura's fervent kings. The basic dagoba consists of a dome standing on a square base, topped with a pinnacle.

The gigantic white dome looming to the north of the Brazen Palace is the **Ruwanweliseya ➍**, also known as Maha Thupa or the Great Stupa. It was built by Dutugemunu, the hero king of the *Mahavamsa*, who was supposedly inspired by seeing a bubble floating on water. To attempt to recreate the weightless quality of a bubble on such a vast scale might seem futile, but somehow it works. You don't see the thousands of tonnes of masonry and the 100 million bricks that were

The name "Brazen Palace" refers not to the manners of the inhabitants, but to the copper roof which formerly adorned the building.

BELOW: murals within the image house at the Ruwanweliseya.

A protective gana or dwarf, an attendant of Kubera, the god of wealth.

BELOW: carved elephants guard the Great Stupa.

required to raise this dome to its full height of over 55 metres (180ft). All you see is a skin of white paint that seems to envelop a pocket of air. The dome itself represents heaven, or alternatively, you could see it as representing the head of Buddha. The conical spire is an elaborate accumulation of *chatras*, parasols that indicate kingship. They also remind one of the protuberance that appears from the Buddha's head to signify super-Enlightenment.

The stupa is raised above ground level on a huge, stone-flagged terrace. Walking clockwise around the stupa you'll pass (close to the main entrance) a subsidiary shrine containing four large limestone Buddha statues alongside a statue of the Buddha of the Future, Maitreya. Further around is another statue, very eroded, believed to be of Dutugemunu, who stands inside a glass box looking towards his masterpiece. The

terrace is bound by a high wall adorned with an army of near life-size sculpted elephants (nearly all of them modern replacements) standing ear to ear. This **elephant wall** has an imposing effect, but its function is also symbolic: the elephants seem to support the platform of the dagoba, just as in Buddhist mythology they hold up the earth.

The Thuparama and Jetavanarama dagobas

North of the Ruwanweliseya dagoba is the **Thuparama** **D**, the oldest stupa in Anuradhapura, and indeed in the island, built by King Devanampiyatissa soon after his conversion by Mahinda. It may be small, but it is very sacred to Buddhists, since it is believed to enshrine the right collarbone of the Buddha. What you see today is not ancient at all, but a reconstruction undertaken in the mid-19th century. It is not even the right shape, since the original was built in the slope-shouldered "heap of rice" form, rather than the present bell shape. The crowd of stone pillars that surround

it like windblown palms would once have supported a roof. Their capitals are decorated with carvings of *hamsas* (geese, a protective bird), with the columns arranged in four concentric circles of decreasing height.

East of the Ruwanweliseya dagoba lies the vast **Jetavanarama** monastery and stupa **E**, the largest stupa in Anuradhapura, around 122 metres (400ft) in height and 113-metre (370ft) in diameter. Elaborate shrines (*vahalkadas*) mark each of the four cardinal points, its eastern one depicting the beautiful figures of women posed so elegantly they appear to be moving, even dancing.

The stupa was the centrepiece of the great Jetavanarama monastery, founded by King Mahasena (who was also responsible for the vast Minneriya Tank). Extensive monastic remains litter the surrounding parkland, including a finely preserved bathing pool and the unusual "Buddhist railing" – like a kind of stone fence. The nearby **Jetavanarama Museum** (daily 8.30am–5.30pm; entrance with site ticket only) houses an interesting collection of precious objects recovered from the site.

Palaces and temples

North of Thuparama is the **Palace of Vijayabahu I** **F**, built for the king who liberated Sri Lanka from the Chola Empire. This was his provincial royal residence. About 100 metres/yds north are the ruins of the **Mahapali Refectory**, with an immense trough that would have been filled with donated rice. The nearby **Dalada Maligawa** **G** (Temple of the Tooth) served as the first home of the Tooth Relic after it was brought to Sri Lanka in the 4th century AD, although little of the original building has survived.

The Abhayagiri complex

On the north side of the ancient city lies the vast **Abhayagiri Monastery**, founded by King Vattagamini in 88

BC, which once housed as many as 5,000 monks and was the most powerful institution after the king. The monks here followed an eclectic and unorthodox form of Buddhism, heavily influenced by the Mahayana doctrines which had developed in places like Tibet, China and Japan. These practices enraged monks at the city's other monasteries, who followed more orthodox Theravada traditions, and were wont to look upon the clergy of Abhayagiri as blasphemous free-thinkers.

The monastery flourished under the patronage of King Mahasena (AD 276–303), sprouting palaces, bathing pools and sculpture of the highest standards. The first relic you arrive at gives only a hint of what is to come. The weathered limestone image of the **Samadhi Buddha** **H** is depicted in the serene state of *samadhi*, or deep meditation. The surrounding area is so peaceful that just walking through it has a calming effect on the weary traveller.

A little further north are the beautiful **Kuttam Pokuna** **I** (Twin Ponds),

Monks bathed in the water of the Kuttam Pokuna, which gushed out of a carved lion's head. They performed their ablutions under the protective gaze of a five-headed cobra, believed to bring good fortune.

BELOW: one of the Twin Ponds, Et Pokuna.

An example of a multi-hooded cobra or naga.

BELOW: one of the leafy roads around Anuradhapura.

which formerly served as a bathing pool for the monks of the Abhayagiri Monastery. There is no ostentation in the design, and yet the effect is impressive. They are not identical twins, however; one pond is 12 metres (40ft) longer than the other, a ratio that is carefully calculated; such perfect proportions and restraint are meant to make up for the comparative lack of ornamentation.

West from here lie the main ruins of the monastery, centred on the **Abhayagiri stupa** ◯, the third of Anuradhapura's great stupas, now standing around 70 metres (230ft) high. Unlike the Ruwanweliseya and Jetavanarama stupas, the Abhayagiri stupa is still undergoing restoration, and is currently encased in a huge mesh of scaffolding.

Sculptural jewels

West of the stupa, the threshold of **King Mahasen's Palace** ◯ is decorated with one of Anuradhapura's best moonstones (see box page 104), a wonderful semicircular doorstep adorned with finely detailed symbolic carvings.

Little survives of the palace itself, however. As with the Brazen Palace, one gets a better idea of how this place might have looked from reading the *Mahavamsa* rather than by gazing at the cracked fragments of pillars, stones and statues which lie tumbled about on the grass.

To the north are the similarly fragmented ruins of the **Ratnaprasada** ◯ (Gem Palace), the chapterhouse of the monastery. All important shrines and palaces in ancient Sri Lanka were protected by a so-called "guardstone" at the entrance, and the one here is probably the finest in Sri Lanka. The main figure is of a bejewelled *nagaraja*, or cobra king, his crown overshadowed by a seven-headed cobra. Every detail of his dress is beautifully depicted; every belt and tassel is clearly defined and miraculously well preserved. His body is caught in an exaggerated, elegant posture and the feet touch the ground lightly: he is proffering the symbols of prosperity: a *purna ghara*, or "pot of plenty", and a flowering branch. Above his head is an arch made up of four

makaras, mythological creatures made up out of the body parts of seven different animals – the body of a fish, the eye of a monkey, the ear of a pig, the foot of a lion, the trunk and tusk of an elephant, the tail of a peacock, and the mouth of a crocodile. The creatures are either consuming or regurgitating a ribbon of carvings, including two tiny humans, a pair of equally diminutive elephants and four flying dwarfs. At the foot of the *nagaraja* is an attendant dwarf, or *gana*, who seems to be chortling at the surreal scene.

South of the Abhayagiri monastery, the excellent **Abhayagiri Museum** (daily 7.30am–4.30pm; entrance with site ticket only), funded by the Chinese in honour of the 5th-century Buddhist academic Fa Hien, houses a superb array of artefacts recovered from the area, including a fine series of intricately carved guardstones displayed on the verandah outside. Southwest from here, the **Lankarama** 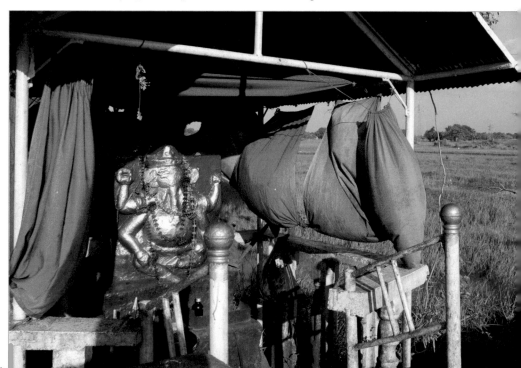, built in the 1st century BC but heavily restored since, has an unusually square stupa encircled by a crowd of pillars three deep, which would formerly have supported a roof.

Southern sites

West of the Ruwanweliseya Stupa, the **Anuradhapura Museum** (daily 8.30am–4.30pm; entrance with site ticket only) occupies a fine old British colonial building and houses a huge array of finds from Anuradhapura and nearby. The most useful for archaeologists is a reliquary found at Mihintale in the form of a model dagoba, giving vital clues as to how they originally looked. There's also an intriguing scale model of the Thuparama with its original roof intact.

Among the other curiosities is a stone urinal carved with a relief depicting the god of wealth throwing money down the hole, and a whole collection of stone toilets embellished by their makers with the representation of a rival monastery, so that by using it the monks could express their lofty contempt for their brothers. Next door is the much less interesting **Folk Museum**

The woodlands around the Abhayagiri monastery were once home to reclusive communities of pamsukulika monks, who took an extra vow to emulate the Buddha's practice of gathering rags from corpses, which they then washed and wore.

BELOW: countryside shrine.

*Relief detail at
Anuradhapura.*

(Tue–Sat 9am–5pm; charge), with exhibits depicting rural life in the north central province.

South of the museum is the imposing **Mirisaweti** stupa ❶, built by Dutugemunu – looking like a trial run for his later and even grander Ruwanweliseya stupa. Further monastic remains lie scattered about the surrounding woodland including the ruins of the refectory (on the northern side of the stupa) whose gargantuan food trough was able to hold enough food for a thousand monks.

Royal Pleasure Gardens

The area south of the Mirisaweti monastery was given over to the **Royal Pleasure Gardens** ❶. The gardens, centred on a pair of pools, were intended as a peaceful retreat from affairs of state for the rulers of Anuradhapura. The northern pool is surrounded by rocks cleverly carved with whimsical elephants, using both low relief and fully moulded carving styles, so that the animals appear to be splashing around in the cool waters, waving their trunks. Given that the pools and irrigation channels which serviced them were the result of the bulldozing efforts of these great beasts, it seems fitting that they should have their tribute.

The rock temple of Isurumuniya

South of the Royal Pleasure Gardens is the **Isurumuniya Temple** ❶ (daily 8am–6pm; charge) dating from the reign of King Devanampiyatissa in the 3rd century BC. The temple is built on and around a rocky outcrop overlooking the waters of the adjacent Tissa Wewa, and has, over the years, accumulated a roofed porch, a bell-shaped dagoba, and other architectural additions connected by stone steps and paths, which cling to the surface of the rock like barnacles on the hull of an upturned shipwreck.

A Civilisation Built on Irrigation

The great cities of ancient Sri Lanka were founded in the island's northern plains – a harsh natural environment in which long periods of uninterrupted drought are broken only by sudden downpours during the brief northeast monsoon. Capturing and harnessing the sporadic monsoon rains was key to the success of the island's largely agricultural economy, and the irrigation works constructed during the Anuradhapuran era were some of the technological marvels of the ancient world. Rains were caught in enormous "tanks" *(wewas)* and then distributed through the countryside via an elaborate system of water channels and sluices, which allowed water to be directed to wherever it was needed. The prodigious scale and sophistication of these works is unbelievable. The largest tanks are more like enormous inland seas than reservoirs, measuring 10km (6 miles) or more across, while the engineering precision of the interconnecting channels is no less impressive: the Jaya Ganga canal, for example, brought water to Anuradhapura from the vast Kalawewa tank, 90km (56 miles) distant, maintaining an exact gradient of 6 inches to the mile over its entire course. Thanks to these astonishing works, the barren plains surrounding the city were transformed into an enormous rice bowl where two crops could be grown annually, producing a surplus sufficient to support the city's vast monastic populations and fund the creation of shrines, palaces and stupas.

The temple is also home to a fascinating little museum of fine stone carvings. The museum's most famous sculpture is of the Isurumuniya Lovers, carved in the 6th century in the Indian Gupta style. Folklore identifies the young couple as Saliya, King Dutugemunu's son, and the low-caste maiden for whom he gave up the throne. According to the legend, Saliya first fell in love with the beautiful commoner while strolling through the Royal Pleasure Gardens; a less romantic interpretation is that the carving represents a Hindu god and his consort.

Further south from here, the **Vessagiriya Ruins and Caves** ® comprise a series of large rock outcrops, which once served as home to a temple complex and 500 members of the reclusive *vaisya* caste, a group of monks ordained by Mahinda, who led an austere life of renunciation in primitive caves and rock shelters scattered around the area. A few inscriptions in the extremely ancient Brahmi script can still be seen here and there, chiselled onto the faces of the stones.

Ancient waterworks

Beyond the ruins of Anuradhapura, the view everywhere is of water. Almost the entire city is surrounded by three of Sri Lanka's largest and oldest tanks. The west side of the city is girdled by two adjacent tanks. The **Basawakkulama Tank**, associated with King Pandukabhaya, was built around the 4th century BC and enlarged and improved on several occasions. South of here, the beautiful **Tissa Wewa**, constructed by King Devanampiyatissa, covers 65 hectares (160 acres) and brings water 85km (52 miles) from the Kala Wewa, feeding 70 tanks on its way. The shore of the tank is always cool and always busy with local people and visiting pilgrims, who come here to bathe and do their laundry. It's a particularly lovely place at sunset – the summit of the Isurumuniya temple provides the finest views.

On the opposite side of the city is the **Nuwara Wewa**, the largest tank in Anuradhapura, built in the 2nd century AD and now covering an area 7km (4.5 miles) across.

The Royal Pleasure Gardens were also known as the "Park of the Goldfish" on account of the goldfish which were once kept in the pools here.

BELOW: the rock temple of Isurumuniya.

MIHINTALE

Mihintale is revered as the birthplace of Buddhism in Sri Lanka, and pilgrims still flock to the town's beautiful ancient temples and dagobas.

Main attractions
KANTAKA CETIYA
AMBASTHALA DAGOBA
MAHINDA'S BED
HOSPITAL
KALUDIYA POKUNA

BELOW: the Buddha at Mihintale.

According to legend, it was at **Mihintale** ⑬ – literally "Mahinda's Hill" – that the Indian missionary Mahinda met and converted King Devanampiyatissa in 247 BC, establishing Buddhism as the island's state religion. The story goes that the king and his attendants were tracking a deer near the summit of the hill when they were met by a man dressed in monk's robes. This was Mahinda, son of the great Mauryan emperor Asoka, who had been sent by his father to bring word of the Buddha's teachings to Sri Lanka. Mahinda found a receptive audience in the king, promptly converting him and his entourage of 40,000 followers (a doubtless symbolic figure) to the new faith. Buddhism was immediately embraced with fervour by the Sinhalese people and soon became firmly established in the island – unlike in India, its birthplace, where it would subsequently fall into terminal decline.

Regardless of your beliefs, Mihintale is unforgettable: a sequence of beautiful shrines, stupas and caves strung out across wooded hills and connected by broad flights of frangipani-shaded carved steps, usually busy with crowds of devout, white-robed pilgrims.

Kantaka Cetiya

All over the world, high places are given religious significance, with the result that devotees are always climbing steps. Sometimes on their knees. Mihintale is one such place, its various shrines connected by a total of some 1,840 steps that ultimately lead to the summit – steep enough to require deep breaths and a meditative pace. They were built in the reign of Bhathika Abhaya (22 BC–AD 7), although a later paved road provides a short cut up to the first level.

At the end of the first flight, to your right, is the 2nd-century BC **Kantaka Cetiya**, one of the earliest religious monuments on the island, originally excavated in 1934. The 130-metre (425ft) base consists of three giant

steps of dressed stone, a characteristic of Sinhalese stupas symbolising the Buddhist "Triple Gem" (the Buddha, his teachings, and the Buddhist clergy, or sangha). Above them the dome has now been worn down to a heap of masonry around 12 metres (40ft) high – somewhat reduced from its original size of 30 metres (100ft). The highlights of the building are the four richly decorated shrines, or *vahalkadas*, which face the cardinal points. The eastern facade is the best preserved, with horizontal rows of carvings including fine friezes of dwarfs and elephants, while on either side the wall is finished off with a tall carved pillar holding a weathered lion aloft.

The south facade has some intricate pillars carved with symbolic animals and plants. There is also a small relief figure of a *naga*. Despite its worn appearance, you can see that it is gracefully posed – even in these archaic times the Sinhalese sculptors were very sophisticated. Facing the south side of the stupa is something even older: an inscription on a rock in large Brahmi characters, forerunner of the Pali script. It is found on a rock shelter that would

have been inhabited by Buddhist monks in the 3rd century BC. These rock shelters constituted the bare minimum in desirable residences. A channel was carved in the overhanging boulder to act as a dripstone moulding and help keep out the rain, but that was it.

The ascent

The second flight of stairs leads to another terrace surrounded by various monastic remains. To the left as you reach the top of the stairs stand the **Mihintale Tablets** – a pair of large standing stone slabs covered in medieval Sinhalese inscriptions detailing the rules and regulations that governed the monks. Behind the tablets lie the remains of the **Dana Salawa** (**Monks' Refectory**). Lying at right angles to one another among various stones that once supported the refectory's wooden buildings are two huge vats hollowed out of single blocks of rock. These would have been filled daily with rice donated to the monks by devout locals and are referred to as "rice canoes" *(bat oruva)* because of their resemblance to dug-out boats.

A guardian stone.

BELOW: a Buddhist temple.

Part of the carvings that decorate the Kantaka Cetiya.

To the summit

A third flight of steps, narrow and steep, takes you on a spiritual ascent to the highest terrace, where the diminutive **Ambasthala Dagoba,** or Mango Tree Stupa, marks where Mahinda surprised King Devanampiyatissa in mid-hunt. The stupa is supposedly built over the exact spot where Mahinda stood, and a statue of the king is placed where he stood – a respectful distance away. A large seated Buddha looks down from a rock above. Steep steps lead up to the **Rock of Convocation** *(Aradhana Gala)*, from where Mahinda preached his first sermon, while a path wends its way for five minutes through woodland to reach the enormous boulder that covers **Mahinda's Bed** *(Mihindu Guha)*. The bed itself is a smooth slab of stone, the covering rock was the roof. This is where the sage reposed, apparently oblivious to discomfort. Such spartan arrangements testify to the power of Buddhism that it could impel a prince to leave his palaces and live under a rock.

Return to the Ambasthala Dagoba, from where another flight of steps leads up to the 1st-century BC **Mahaseya Dagoba**, the largest stupa in Mihintale, which enshrines a single hair relic of the Buddha. Close by stands a second, much smaller stupa, the **Mihindu Seya**, where a small golden reliquary resembling the earliest Indian stupas surmounted by a *chattra* (umbrella) was discovered.

Further paths loop round to the **Naga Pokuna** (Pond of the Serpent), a long pool in the shadow of a large, low rock carved in low relief with a mythical five-headed cobra, or naga (serpent king). Nagas are said to be the guardians of treasure, protectors of water and makers of rain. The carving on this natural rock emphasises the nagas' association with water; it is said that the resident naga's tail reaches down to the bottom of the pool.

From just south of the Naga Pokuna, a final set of steps climbs up to the very highest point of Mihintale, crowned with the remains of a small brick dagoba, **Et Vihara** (Stupa of the Elephant), a steep ten-minute walk rewarded by panoramic views across Mihintale and out to the plains beyond.

Ancient medicine

Back down at the bottom of the site, close to the main entrance, are the ruins of a **Hospital** *(Vejja Sala)* dating back to the 3rd century AD, some 400 years before the earliest hospital in Europe. Among the remnants of walls and pillars are monolithic stone baths in which the sick would have been treated. Like the rice boats, these are hewn from a single rock, but they have a particularly gripping sculptural quality, the internal cavity being shaped to immerse a recumbent body without wasting precious herbal oils. The result is a simplified human shape that tempts you to lie down and try it for size. Excavations have unearthed many advanced medical implements.

Close by, the small site museum (currently closed for renovation) has examples of stones used for grinding medicinal herbs along with medicine jars whose blue glaze indicates that a

BELOW: schoolchildren at Mihintale.

link must have existed between Persia and the island.

Outlying remains

A five-minute drive from the main entrance brings you to the sylvan **Kaludiya Pokuna** (Pond of Black Water). This peaceful artificial lake supplied water to a monastery that stood here during the 10th or 11th centuries. A few fragmentary monastic ruins stand around the lake including a quaint little structure comprising a facade and roof built onto a natural rock overhang – half cave, half house – protected by the simplest of guardstones, lacking in any kind of sculptural decoration. The minimalist decoration is misleading, however, since these monks were definitely not roughing it like the troglodytic pioneers of Buddhism on the hillside above, but enjoyed the comforts of indoor toilets and bath houses, served by an advanced hydraulic system of artificial moats and ducts running through the buildings.

Half a kilometre (500 yards) from the pond is the **Rajagiri Kanda** (the Mountain of Kings) where a whole series of hermit caves has been cut into the hillside. Near the base of the westernmost hill is **Indikatuseya Dagoba** (the Stupa of the Needle). The base of the stupa survives, unadorned with carving, but with broad bands of dressed stone like the base of a colossal Doric column. The dome that once surmounted it has shrunk to a small mound of brick awaiting restoration. The guardstones at the foot of the steps are missing, but as you wander around the other ruins you will find a flight of steps complete with moonstone and a pair of guardstones depicting nagas in human form, although the building they embellished is reduced to a collection of stone pillars.

When you leave Mihintale you may not be converted, as King Devanampiyatissa was, but you cannot fail to be impressed by the ascetic courage that led the earliest monks to live under bare rocks, even while you admire the sophistication of the later monasteries that provided their inhabitants with ample stores of free food and an efficient plumbing system.

Indikatuseya Dagoba caused great excitement among Buddhist scholars when Sanskrit texts belonging to the Mahayana school were found here. They were transcribed into Sinhala characters and inscribed on copper plaques in the 8th or 9th century.

BELOW: Ambasthala Dagoba with the top of Mahaseya Dagoba visible behind it.

POLONNARUWA

Despite the conflicts for control that raged around it, the second of ancient Sri Lanka's two great ruined capitals preserves a wealth of superb Buddhist arts and architecture.

Second only to Anuradhapura in the ancient history of Sri Lanka, Polonnaruwa ⑭ served as the island's capital from the 11th to 13th centuries, a relatively brief but glorious epoch that witnessed a flowering of Buddhist arts and architecture – with a large dose of Indian influence. In its prime, the city stretched for many kilometres along the eastern side of the majestic Parakrama Samudra reservoir, its monasteries and sumptuous palaces and temples, both Buddhist and Hindu, protected by 6km (4 miles) of strong encircling walls. Strategically, it commanded all the crossings over the Mahaweli River, guarding the increasingly powerful southern province of Ruhuna. Its importance as a secure outpost for armies gave it the name *Kandavuru Nuvara* (Camp City). In early Sri Lankan history only Anuradhapura ranks alongside it in significance.

A contentious capital

In AD 993 the invading armies of the Tamil Cholas looted Anuradhapura and moved the island's capital to Polonnaruwa for the next 77 years. From the outset, the new city had a cosmopolitan mix of south Indian Hindu and Sinhalese Buddhist cultures. The valiant King Vijayabahu I (1055–1110) drove the Cholas out of the island in 1073, but retained Polonnaruwa as his capital. He was responsible for the resurgence of Buddhism in Sri Lanka, bringing monks down from Burma to rejuvenate the religion, which had suffered heavily under Hindu rule.

Forty years of bloody civil war followed his death, until, in 1161, Parakramabahu I captured Polonnaruwa and assumed control of the whole island. Regarded as the last great king of Sri Lanka, Parakramabahu embarked on a lavish series of building works at his

Main attractions

POLONNARUWA MUSEUM
PARAKRAMABAHU'S COUNCIL
    CHAMBER
THE QUADRANGLE
RANKOT VIHARA
LANKATILAKA
GAL VIHARA
MINNERIYA AND KAUDULLA
    NATIONAL PARKS

LEFT: the Sathmahal Pasada. **RIGHT:** looking down on the Royal Baths.

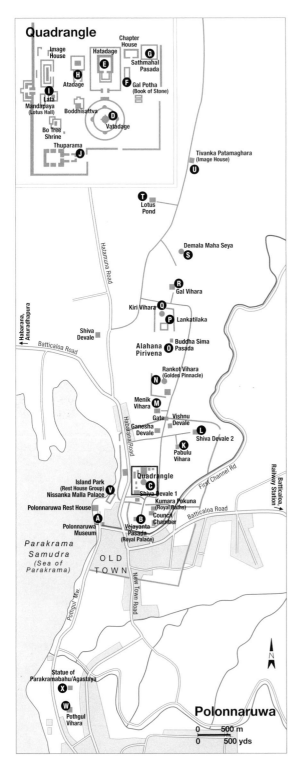

Quadrangle

- Image House
- Chapter House
- Hatadage
- **G** Sathmahal Pasada
- **E**
- **H**
- Atadage
- **F** Gal Potha (Book of Stone)
- **I**
- Lata Mandapaya (Lotus Hall)
- Boddhisattva
- **D** Vatadage
- Bo Tree Shrine
- Thuparama
- **J**

- Tivanka Patamaghara (Image House) **U**
- Lotus Pond **T**
- Demala Maha Seya **S**
- Gal Vihara **R**
- Kiri Vihara **Q**
- Lankatilaka **P**
- Shiva Devale
- Alahana Pirivena
- Buddha Sima Pasada **O**
- Rankot Vihara (Golden Pinnacle) **N**
- Menik Vihara **M**
- Gate
- Ganesha Devale
- Vishnu Devale
- Shiva Devale 2 **L**
- Pabulu Vihara **K**
- Quadrangle **C**
- Shiva Devale 1
- Kumara Pokuna (Royal Baths)
- Council Chamber
- Island Park (Rest House Group) **V**
- Nissanka Malla Palace
- Polonnaruwa Rest House
- Polonnaruwa Museum **A**
- Vejayanta Pasada (Royal Palace) **B**

- Hatamuna Road
- Batticaloa Road
- Habarana, Anuradhapura
- Habarana Road
- First Channel Rd
- Batticaloa, Railway Station
- Batticaloa Road
- New Town Road
- Pothgul Mw.
- **Parakrama Samudra** (Sea of Parakrama)
- OLD TOWN
- Statue of Parakramabahu/Agastaya **X**
- Pothgul Vihara **W**

Polonnaruwa

0 — 500 m
0 — 500 yds

N

---

new capital. King Nissanka Malla, his nephew and successor, further embellished and expanded the city, although he is best remembered for the copious inscriptions in praise of himself, which he left scattered around the city. In about 1293, Sri Lanka was once again invaded by mercenaries from South India, and Polonnaruwa was abandoned to the jungle.

The Polonnaruwa Museum

Most of the ruins of Polonnaruwa (daily 7.30am–6pm; charge) are protected within a specially fenced-off archaeological site north of the modern town. Other parts of the ancient city – most notably the Island Park (or Rest House Group) and the southern ruins – are free, and open 24 hours. Tickets to the site have to be bought from the excellent **Polonnaruwa Museum A** (daily 9am–5.30pm, and from 7.30am for the sale of tickets; entrance to the museum with site ticket only), well worth a visit for its insightful displays on life in the ancient capital, and some fine exhibits including a number of superb Chola bronzes recovered from the site.

The Inner Citadel

Entering the main archaeological site, the first thing you see are the impressive remains of the **Vejayanta Pasada B**, the royal palace of Parakramabahu, whose massive brick walls rise high above the remains of dozens of other attached rooms and outbuildings. According to the *Culavamsa* – the lesser chronicle in which the history of medieval Lanka was recorded – the palace originally rose to seven storeys, but since the upper floors were of wood, no trace of them remains. The notches in the surviving walls which once supported timber beams, pillars and floors can still be seen, while traces of the palace's original painted plaster are visible in places on the walls.

Just east of here lies Parakramabahu's **Council Chamber**, where the great king would have met advisors, administrators and petitioners. The hall consists of a raised terrace studded with columns (the roof has long since disappeared) set on top of a huge base supported by elephants carved in low relief. The entrance has two flights of steps with moonstones flanked by *makaras* – mythical creatures made out of bits of seven different animals including lion, crocodile, elephant and fish. Close by are the elegant **Kumara Pokuna**, or Royal Baths, where members of the court would have bathed.

The Quadrangle

At the heart of the city, the Dalada Maluwa (Terrace of the Tooth Relic), popularly known as the **Quadrangle ⓒ**, was the centrepiece and sacred precinct of ancient Polonnaruwa, home to the Tooth Relic and its most important cluster of religious shrines. The Quadrangle is dominated by the flamboyant **Vatadage ⓓ**, a superbly decorated circular shrine originally built by Parakramabahu and subsequently embellished by Nissanka Malla. This is perhaps the most ornate building in Sri Lanka, its outer walls

carved with friezes of lions, dwarfs and lotuses, and, at each of the four entrances, elaborate moonstones and guardstones (depicting *nagaraja* – king cobra figures with seven-hooded heads – who were believed to prevent evil from entering the premises). Steps lead up to the central shrine, presided over by four Buddhas facing the cardinal points, and a central brick dagoba in which the Tooth Relic may originally have been enshrined.

Directly opposite the Vatadage stands the far more modest **Hatadage ⓔ**, which is also believed to have housed the Tooth Relic at some point. The rather plain building has lost its original upper storey, although a pair of inscriptions dating from the reign of Nissanka Malla remain, along with a trio of Buddhas, the central statue carefully aligned with the entrance to the Vatadage opposite. Next to the Hatadage lies the enormous stone slab known as the **Gal Potha ⓕ** (Book of Stone), densely covered in glowing inscriptions praising the works of the vainglorious Nissanka Malla, who had this giant slab of rock dragged all

The ever-serene features of the Buddha.

BELOW: the ancient Vatadage.

Sathmahal Pasada means "Seven-Storey Edifice", which is all anyone knows about the building.

BELOW: a moonstone at the Vatadage.

the way from Mihintale – 100km (62 miles) distant.

Next to the Gal Potha, the eye-catching but enigmatic **Sathmahal Pasada** **G** (Seven-Storey Edifice, though only six storeys now survive) is of a simple stepped design, with niches on each floor containing the remnants of carved figures. The temple is deeply perplexing to historians. The *Culavamsa* makes no mention of it, and archaeologists are stumped as to its origin and design. One explanation is that it was designed by Khmer architects (from what is now Cambodia), and it certainly looks much more like a temple from Angkor than anything found in South Asia.

On the other side of the Hatadage are the fragmentary remains of the **Atadage** **H** (House of Eight Relics), built by Vijayabahu in the 11th century and original home of the Tooth Relic when it was first brought to the city. The neat plantation of 54 stone columns, some of them intricately carved, others embedded in brickwork, would have supported a timber upper floor in which the relic was kept. An image of

the standing Buddha almost 3 metres (10ft) high lurks among the columns.

Continuing anticlockwise around the Quadrangle, passing a lone, armless statue of what is variously claimed to be an unnamed boddhisattva or King Vijayabahu himself, brings you to the exquisite **Lata Mandapaya** **I** (Lotus Hall), built by Nissanka Malla, who is said to have sat here during Buddhist ceremonies. This tiny pavilion is notable for its extraordinary columns representative of lotus stems, with buds poised atop the delicately sinuous and seemingly Art Nouveau-inspired pillars – quite unlike anything else in Sri Lankan architecture.

Past here lies the Quadrangle's final major building, the **Thuparama** **J**, one of the precinct's oldest but best preserved structures (and the only one that has kept its original roof). The building's thick brick walls and heavily carved window niches are typical of the South Indian style of architecture that Tamil craftsmen introduced to the ancient city. The remains of no fewer than eight Buddhas stand in the crepuscular darkness inside.

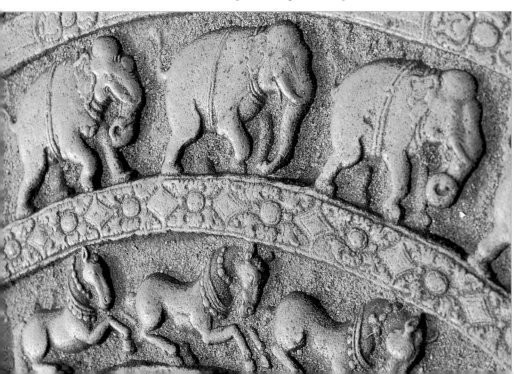

Indian influence is even more marked in the **Shiva Devale No. 1**, immediately south of the Quadrangle. This pretty little Hindu shrine dates from the Pandyan occupation of the city in the early 13th century and is just one of many small Siva temples built around the city by incoming Indian soldiers and merchants.

Beyond the city walls

Heading north, a long straight dirt road takes you through what would once have been the busy streets of the medieval city, although all but its most important buildings have now disappeared and its inhabitants have been replaced by tourists and monkeys. Turn right at the first crossroads to reach the **Pabulu Vihara Ⓚ**, a brick dagoba supposedly built by Rupavati, one of Parakramabahu's queens, and surrounded by image houses and Buddha statues – some of which may have been brought over from Anuradhapura. At the end of this road is the beautifully preserved **Shiva Devale No. 2 Ⓛ**, an attractive little domed structure which is also

the oldest building in Polonnaruwa, probably built by the south Indian Cholas in the 11th century. A number of superb bronzes found here are now on display in the Polonnaruwa Museum (see page 246).

Return to the crossroads and head north again along the main road, passing the scant remains of further Hindu temples, then on through the city's former northern gate. The area of Polonnaruwa north of here was given over to a series of large monasteries and temples. The first (on your left) is the **Menik Vihara Ⓜ**, whose small brick dagoba sits on a terrace carved with terracotta lions, while an image house with a couple of standing Buddhas lies nearby.

The north side of the Menik Vihara is dominated by Nissanka Malla's colossal (55 metre/180ft) **Rankot Vihara Ⓝ**. This huge red-brick dagoba is the only one at Polonnaruwa to rival the great stupas of Anuradhapura in size – although it is not quite as big as any of them.

Past here lie the extensive remains of the **Alahana Pirivena** monastery

Two Brahmi inscriptions found near the remains of the Alahana Pirivena monastery, above the ledge at Gopata Pabbat, are the earliest signs of human occupation at Polonnaruwa, dating back to the 2nd century BC.

BELOW: the Lankatilaka.

The Sea of Parakrama

Much like at Anuradhapura, the rulers of Polonnaruwa faced the formidable task of providing irrigation for the city's growing population. Legend has it that King Parakramabahu declared "Not even a drop of water from the rain must flow into the ocean without being made useful to man", after which he ordered the construction of the vast **Parakrama Samudra** (Sea of Parakrama). Covering an area of 2,430 hectares (6,000 acres), this monumental feat of engineering looks more like an inland sea than a man-made reservoir and had 11 channels leading off to feed a network of irrigation canals. The venerable old Rest House, right on the shoreline of the tank, is the perfect place to enjoy views of the lake over lunch or a sundowner cocktail – you can even sleep in the room where the young Queen Elizabeth II stayed in 1954.

*In order to list his
great achievements
and virtues, King
Nissanka Malla
required a slab of stone
8 metres (26ft) long.*

BELOW: the Gal
Vihara.

and royal cremation grounds, built
on the flanks of a gently shelving
wooded hillside. On the highest platform sits the **Buddha Sima Pasada**
O, the monastery's chapterhouse,
where monks would have gathered
to confess sins and reaffirm their
religious vows. Nearby, the impressive walls of the **Lankatilaka** **P**
image house soar to a height of 16
metres (55ft), enclosing a large but
headless statue of the Buddha who
stands squashed inside the high, narrow space within. A section of the
walls outside (on your left as you face
the entrance) is adorned with finely
carved reliefs of flamboyant multi-
storey houses topped with domes –
not a portrait of ancient Polonnaruwa
as is sometimes claimed, but a fanciful representation of the celestial
abodes (vimanas) of the gods. Next
door is the large dagoba known as
the **Kiri Vihara** **Q** (Milk Vihara),
named for the milk-white stucco that
once covered the entire dome (and
which has recently been restored to
something approaching its original
colour).

The Gal Vihara rock sculptures

The pinnacle of rock-carved art in
ancient Sri Lanka, the **Gal Vihara** **R**
is home to four magnificent Buddha
statues hewn out of a granite cliff-face
by unknown artists. The highlight is
the majestic 14-metre (46ft) reclining
Buddha – a figure of such enormous
but serene beauty that it inspired centuries of Sinhalese art without ever being
matched. The sculptor was working
in a medium that to some extent dic-
tated his output. Dark strata in the rock
appear as a veil of ripples washing over
the delicately carved facial features and
figure of the Buddha as he slips into nirvana, lending a beautifully fluid texture
to the mass of stone. The rock was not
always kind to the sculptor – a pale line
of it has inflicted a scar on the chin of
the Buddha – but the reverent tender-
ness with which every detail, including
the bolster-like pillow, has been carved
makes it is easy to forget how difficult
the sculptor's task must have been. Later
works in this idealised style are cold and
mechanical in comparison, but the Gal
Vihara figures manage to convey an

emotional power while sustaining the most exquisite serenity.

At the foot of the reclining Buddha is a figure standing on a lotus plinth with arms folded and eyes half-closed. This was often thought to represent Ananda, the Buddha's most faithful disciple, but it is now generally thought to depict the Buddha in the weeks following his Enlightenment. Later, in the reign of Parakramabahu, these images were joined by the two other statues: a seated Buddha meditating cross-legged against an interesting relief of buildings representing the celestial homes of the gods; and another seated Buddha set in a rock-cut niche and surrounded by attendants waving fly whisks.

Northern sites

The unfinished **Demala Maha Seya S**, conceived by Parakramabahu I, was originally planned to surpass even the giant dagobas of Anuradhapura in size – the intended height of 191 metres (625ft) would have made it the largest stone structure in the world. Unfortunately it was never completed,

despite the best efforts of the Pandyan prisoners of war who were set to work building it (*Demala* means "Tamil", hence the name). The remains of the dagoba are now almost completely covered in vegetation, making it look more like a natural hill than a man-made piece. The small dagoba on top is the work of a later and lesser king and resembles a dwarf standing on the shoulders of a giant.

Further north, on the left, is one of the few surviving relics of the Jetavana Monastery, whose 500-odd buildings, most of them still unexcavated, once covered the surrounding area. The elegant **Lotus Pond T** was built in tiers of carved eight-petalled lotus flowers, a clever and original idea that didn't really catch on, perhaps because there were too many sharp corners for comfort.

The most important building in the old Jetavana Monastery is the **Tivanka Patamaghara U** image house. Built in a markedly Indian style similar to the Thuparama in the Quadrangle, it has thick stone walls, a vaulted roof, and heavily decorated window niches

The frescoes at the Tivanka Patamaghara are in a classical style, unlike contemporary Indian paintings or later Sinhalese work, with a colour scheme confined to reddish brown, yellow ochre, green and white.

BELOW: the Lotus Pond.

The statue known as the Sage may portray King Parakramabahu I.

BELOW: the Pothgul Vihara.

studded with small statues. The name "Tivanka" derives from the image of the Buddha in the narrow interior, seen in the graceful *tivanka*, or thrice-bent, posture normally reserved for female statues. The interior is also home to the most important paintings from the Polonnaruwan period, although they're difficult to make out in the gloomy interior. The *cella* (inner room of a shrine) is decorated with scenes from the life of the Buddha, the antechamber with incidents from the *Jataka* (Buddhist tales).

The Island Park

Back in the centre of Polonnaruwa, the area immediately behind the lakeshore Rest House is known as the Island Park (or Rest House Group). It was formerly occupied by the **royal gardens and the palace of Nissanka Malla** ❶ (who was too proud to live in the palace built by his predecessor, Parakramabahu) – the surrounding water must have kept the gardens wonderfully cool throughout the year. Various remains dot the grounds, including the **Royal Baths**, whose circular and square pools were fed by underground pipes from the

tank; and a small, windowless stone **Mausoleum**, possibly marking the spot where Nissanka Malla was cremated, and which preserves some of its red, white and blue painted plaster intact.

More interesting than either, however, is Nissanka Malla's **Council Chamber**. Like Parakramabahu's similar building, the chamber comprises a large carved base topped by rows of pillars, each of which is inscribed with the title of the person who would have sat next to it during sessions of the king's council, offering a rare glimpse into the hierarchical court life of 13th-century Sri Lanka. The most important dignitaries sat closest to the king, who probably occupied a throne next to the striking lion statue which stands at the rear of the chamber.

The southern ruins

A detour south along the *bund* (embankment) to see the **Pothgul Vihara** ❶ (Southern Monastery) is worthwhile, particularly if you like puzzles. Here you will find four small dagobas surrounding a circular brick building on the central platform. The acoustics of this enigmatic building are excellent (even without the roof that once covered it), leading to suggestions that it was a kind of lecture theatre where the tenets of Buddhism were read aloud – although it might have been a library.

A little further north, the famous **Statue of Parakramabahu/Agastaya** ❶ is a huge 12th-century rock sculpture of great craftsmanship. A barefoot figure, clad only in a sarong, steps forward out of the wall of rock from which he was carved. His broad face, with its beard and walrus moustache, has a look of seriousness softened by spirituality, and he holds a sacred manuscript from which he appears to be reading aloud. The subject of the statue is a matter of debate: a Saivite *rishi* (holy man) named Agastaya is the most likely candidate, but it has also been suggested that it is a representation of the city's great hero, Parakramabahu.

Around Polonnaruwa

The area around Polonnaruwa is one of the best in which to spot Sri Lanka's legendary elephants, with **Minneriya** and **Kaudulla national parks** being the places to head for, midway between Polonnaruwa and Habarana. Both parks are centred on extensive tanks where elephants congregate in increasingly large numbers towards the end of the dry season, particularly during the famous "Gathering" at **Minneriya National Park** ⓯ (see page 132). The two parks are linked by an important "elephant corridor", designed to allow the animals to move from one park to the other as the fancy takes them – local guides should have an idea of which park has the highest elephant population at any one time. Elephants apart, both parks also host the usual range of classic Sri Lankan wildlife, and abundant birdlife.

Around 38km (24 miles) north of Polonnaruwa, via the Habarana road through Hingurakgoda, the small town of **Medirigiriya** ⓰ is home to the ruins of the **Mandalagiri Vihara** monastery, one of the Cultural Triangle's least visited attractions. At the site's centre are the remains of the superb 8th-century Vatadage, rivalling the better-known example at Polonnaruwa (although the level of craftsmanship is not quite as fine). Built atop a high terrace, the Vatadage consists of three concentric rows of pillars surrounding four seated Buddhas facing the cardinal points. Further ruins lie scattered about, including the remains of numerous shrines, a couple of small tanks and dagobas, and assorted Buddha statues in varying states of disrepair.

Southeast of Polonnaruwa the rocky mountain of **Dimbulaga** ⓱ looms over the northern side of the road to Batticaloa. The flanks of the mountain are scored with hundreds of rock caves, which have attracted reclusive monks seeking peace and solitude from the earliest Buddhist times right up to the present day. New monks are ordained in the Mahaweli River, as was the saintly monk Kassapa, who reformed and united the Buddhist order. Even now their presence in the village has a moralising influence.

A ubiquitous feature of Sinhalese buildings, moonstones symbolise the stages on the Buddhist path towards nirvana.

BELOW: the Vatadage has long since lost its conical roof.

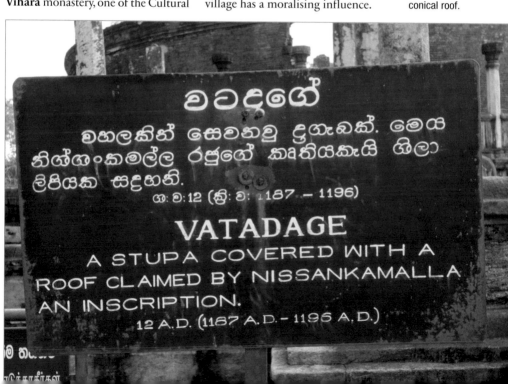

SIGIRIYA

Little can prepare you for the experience of Sigiriya, perhaps the most remarkable of all Sri Lanka's former capitals.

he towering rock outcrop of **Sigiriya** ⑱ (Lion Rock) is one of Sri Lanka's most spectacular natural landmarks: a majestic, sheer-sided outcrop of reddish gneiss rising 200 metres/yds above the surrounding plains and embellished with the extraordinary remains of one of medieval Sri Lanka's most remarkable royal palaces. The rock has long attracted settlers. A community of reclusive monks lived in the caves around the base of the rock as far back as the 3rd century BC, though it was not until the 5th century AD that Sigiriya rose to sudden and spectacular prominence in Sri Lankan affairs. The patricidal King Kassapa chose the almost inaccessible summit as the unlikely setting for his new royal palace, a courtly paradise of elegant pavilions set amid gardens and pools. The rock was transformed into an immense recumbent lion by the addition of a brick-built head and foreparts, of which only the artfully sculpted paws remain. The impact of the Lion Rock, as it is called, must have been awesome since even its remnants beggar belief. Kassapa's palace in the clouds lasted just 18 years, though its remains have drawn visitors ever since.

Kassapa's Palace

The creator of Sigiriya was one of the most interesting monarchs Sri Lanka has produced: the brave, murderous and brilliant Kassapa, who reigned between AD 477 and AD 495.

The son of King Dhatusena of Anuradhapura, Kassapa was born to a non-royal consort. On learning that Mogallana, his younger brother but of royal blood, had been proclaimed Dhatusena's heir, he seized the throne and imprisoned his father, whom he subsequently killed. Mogallana, meanwhile, fled to India, intending to raise an army and return to reclaim his throne.

Main attractions

THE WATER GARDENS
THE BOULDER GARDENS
THE SIGIRIYA DAMSELS
THE MIRROR WALL
THE SUMMIT
PIDURANGALA ROYAL CAVE TEMPLE

LEFT: the Lion Platform. **RIGHT:** making the ascent to the citadel.

The steps to the Terrace Garden.

Kassapa, in anticipation of an invasion, left the capital at Anuradhapura and established a new city at Sigiriya, with his own palace situated atop the lofty heights of the rock's summit, a defensive location surrounded by sheer rock faces on all sides. Not that military considerations appear to have been Kassapa's only concern, since he also intended his palace to emulate the legendary heavenly abode of Kubera, the god of wealth. To this end, Kassapa furnished his new abode with beautiful gardens, fabulous sculptures and an oversize picture gallery of heavenly maidens. The entire edifice, it is said, was constructed in just seven years.

The rock's natural defences were further augmented by some ingenious additional features. Broad moats and stone perimeter walls were constructed, with an outer moat built so as to flood the entire area between the two moats in the event of an enemy approach. A boulder-catapult still stands on the summit waiting to be unleashed upon an intruder. To encourage the guards to stay awake, the sentry points on the rock summit were strategically placed so that a momentary lapse of attention would send the drowsy guard plunging to his death.

The anticipated attack by Mogallana eventually materialised in AD 495, 18 years after Kassapa had seized power. Despite having created the most impregnable fortress in the country, Kassapa, in a moment of strange bravado or downright folly, descended from his lofty palace and mounted an elephant to confront Mogallana and his army on the plains below. It is said that at the height of the battle, Kassapa's elephant suddenly turned and bolted. His troops, taking this as a sign that their king was retreating, gave up the fight and fled, leaving Kassapa alone, and facing certain capture. Realising his situation, Kassapa drew his sword, and plunged it into his own throat, showing a certain honour in death which he had singularly failed to show during his life. Mogallana, triumphant, slaughtered a thousand or so of Kassapa's followers then returned the capital to Anuradhapura, handing Sigiriya back to the monks who had previously lived there for hundreds of years.

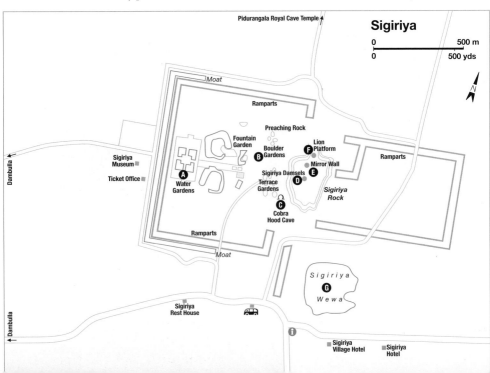

Sigiriya was not just the fortress of a paranoid tyrant, but also the palace of a ruler who wanted to assert his right to kingship with symbols, and to show through great works that he was the rightful monarch. Kassapa's reign may have been brief and murderous, his reputation murky, but his achievements have lasted for more than 15 centuries.

Sigiriya Museum and Water Gardens

Next to the entrance to the site, the impressive new Sigiriya Museum (www.sigiriyamuseum.com; daily 8.30am–5.30pm; closed first Mon of month; charge) covers the long and complex history of the site and surrounding area, showcasing a range of prehistoric finds along with other artefacts discovered at the site. There's also a bird's-eye scale model of the rock and replicas of the Sigiriya Damsel frescoes and a portion of the Mirror Wall.

Framing the main, western approach to the rock, the well-preserved **Water Gardens** Ⓐ are like a tiny piece of Versailles transported to ancient Sri Lanka, with carefully tended lawns dotted with symmetrically arranged ponds, water channels and diminutive fountains (although all of these tend to dry up during periods of low rainfall).

The first section of the gardens comprises a central island surrounded by four L-shaped pools. The island would originally have been occupied by a large pavilion, while the ponds appear to have been used as bathing pools, with polished walls, flights of steps and surrounding terraces, not unlike a modern-day swimming pool.

The second section of the gardens, the **Fountain Garden**, is home to a fanciful little array of water features including a miniature "river", marble-lined water channels and pools, plus a couple of ancient fountains with their original limestone sprinklers. These work by using the gravitational pressure generated within their feeder pipes, and still spout modest little jets of water during periods of heavy rainfall.

The Boulder Gardens and Terrace Gardens

The **Boulder Gardens** Ⓑ present a striking contrast to the classical symmetry of the Water Gardens, comprising a small swathe of picturesque forest, with winding pathways twisting between huge boulders and through quaint rock arches. Many of the boulders are scored with long lines of notches. These would originally have held supports for miniature wooden pavilions (long since vanished) which once stood on almost every boulder.

The Boulder Gardens are where the monks of Sigiriya lived before and after Kassapa's brief reign, and numerous mementoes of this ancient religious community can still be seen amongst the various rocks and cave shelters. Many of the caves would originally have been painted or plastered, and intriguing fragments of colourful abstract designs survive here and there. One of the most impressive is the picturesque **Cobra Hood Cave** Ⓒ,

TIP

If possible, try to visit Sigiriya either early or late in the day, when the heat is less intense, crowds are thinner and the low light brings out the beautiful ochre-red colours of the rock itself.

BELOW: Cobra Hood Rock.

The lovely damsels are striking for their diversity in mood and personality, face and body, clothes and make-up.

BELOW: view from the Lion Rock.

reached by a side trail running right off the main path, and topped with an unusually shaped boulder that is said to resemble a cobra – hence the name. Buddhist monks from as early as the 3rd century BC used this cave, though its painted ceiling dates from the period of Kassapa's reign.

Other nearby remains include the intriguing **Audience Hall Rock**. This was created by chopping the top off an enormous boulder. The lower half of the boulder, polished to velvety smoothness, served as the floor of the Audience Hall, on one side of which stands a 5-metre (16ft) long carved "throne" (although the hall's original pillars and roof have long since gone). Legend states that Kassapa sometimes held court here, although the building is much more likely to have had a purely religious function, with the (empty) throne representing the Buddha. A couple of similar thrones have also been carved into the surrounding rocks.

From the top of the Boulder Gardens, steps arrow directly up the rock through the **Terrace Gardens**, a series of steep terraces held up with earth-retaining walls, and the point at which the ascent of the rock begins in earnest.

The Sigiriya Damsels

At the top of the stairway up from the Terrace Gardens, an incongruous pair of Victorian-era spiral metal staircases lead up to (and down from) a sheltered recess in the rock above. This is the home of Sigiriya's single most celebrated sight, the so-called **Sigiriya Damsels ◗**. Commissioned by Kassapa in the 5th century, this exquisite mural, perhaps the largest ever attempted, is painted onto the sheer rock face and features 21 beautiful, bare-chested women, swathed in a layer of fluffy cloud from the waist down, shown scattering flower petals or offering trays of fruit.

The paintings are quite unlike anything else in Sri Lanka, whose artists have usually preferred to concentrate on the highly stylised depiction of Buddhist religious themes. The Sigiriya Damsels, by contrast, are thoroughly naturalistic and overtly sensuous – much closer to the sort of

paintings found in India at places such as the famous Ajanta Caves.

Impressive as they are, the murals you see today represent only a tiny fragment of the original picture gallery. It is thought that there were originally some 500 frescoes here, stretching for almost 150 metres (500ft) across the rock face – often claimed to be the world's largest open-air picture gallery. The exact meaning of the paintings remains tantalisingly elusive. One popular explanation is that they are portraits of celebrated beauties from Kassapa's court; another is that they are *apsaras* (celestial nymphs), in keeping with South Indian traditions. A third suggestion is that they symbolically represent clouds and lightning moving above the peak of Mount Kailasa.

The Mirror Wall

Just past the staircase up to the Damsels is another of Sigiriya's unique sights. This is the highly polished **Mirror Wall** **E**, plastered with a mixture of burnished lime, egg white, beeswax and wild honey, and covered with a dense spider's web of ancient graffiti left by visitors to the rock over the past 1,500 years. The graffiti – something akin to an enormous medieval visitors' book – include numerous short poems and other literary fragments recording early visitors' impressions of the rock, the ruins of Kassapa's palace and gardens, and, particularly, a great many tributes to the heavenly beauty of the nearby Damsels. The oldest graffiti date back to the 7th century; most are written in early Sinhalese, although there are also contributions in Sanskrit and Tamil. Taken as a whole, they offer valuable insights not only into the history of the rock, but also into the development of the Sinhalese language and literary traditions. Sadly, many of the original graffiti have now been obscured by the larger and rather less cultured scribblings of later hands.

The Lion Platform

From the Mirror Wall, the path follows a narrow and vertiginous iron walkway bolted onto the sheer rock face. Below, a huge **boulder** stands propped

Archaeological excavations have unearthed miniature terracotta figurines of the Sigiriya Damsels, which seem to have once been produced as souvenirs for visitors to the rock – making them some of the world's oldest tourist trinkets.

BELOW: centuries' worth of graffiti can be read on the Mirror Wall.

King Dhatusena

The story of King Dhatusena's murder is one of the most instructive fables in Sri Lankan history. According to legend, the rebellious Kassapa threatened his father with death if he did not reveal the whereabouts of the state treasure. Dhatusena agreed, on condition that he was allowed to bathe one final time in the waters of the great Kalawewa Tank, near Aukana, whose creation had been the major achievement of his peaceful and illustrious reign. Standing in the tank, Dhatusena gestured at the surrounding waters and announced that these, and only these, were the treasure that Kassapa so urgently sought. Kassapa, sadly, seems to have been less than impressed with his father's symbolic gesture, and soon afterwards had him walled up in a small stone cell, where he was left to die.

Just one of the myriad flights of steps and walkways.

BELOW: the summit.

up on stone crutches. The popular explanation is that in time of attack the crutches could have been knocked away, dumping the boulder onto the heads of the attackers below; a more likely explanation is that the stone supports were designed for precisely the opposite reason, to prevent the boulder tumbling unexpectedly over the edge and crushing those beneath.

From here, a final set of steep limestone steps climbs to the **Lion Platform** ❼ just beneath the summit itself, a small, flat spur projecting outwards from the rock, where enterprising locals sell welcome soft drinks, and where you can gird your loins before the final ascent. This was also home to one of ancient Sigiriya's most fanciful conceits, with the steps to the summit leading up through the mouth of a giant lion statue, though sadly only the (enormous) paws now survive – a dramatic final approach to the royal palace, and a suitable assertion of the patricidal Kassapa's royal status.

The Lion Platform is also (in)famous for its bees: look up, and you will see enormous hives dangling from the underside of the rock above – there are even a couple of wire-mesh cages provided in the event of bee swarms going on the rampage. A number of attacks by bees against humans have occurred in recent years, despite attempts to remove the hives. Some monks claim that these attacks are divine retribution for the impious behaviour of Western tourists visiting the rock. You have been warned.

The summit

From the Lion Platform, a narrow and rickety-looking colonial-era metal staircase heads up to **the summit**, cantilevered off the face of the rock and looking in places as if it is about to sail straight off into mid-air. Only those with a rock-solid head for heights will fail to feel at least a slight frisson of vertigo on this final section of the ascent. Walking up, you can spot innumerable little notches in the rock face, which would once have held wooden steps leading to the summit, and which were apparently enclosed by a high wall to block out the dizzying views – ironically, it is said that the great Kassapa, who made his home on one of the tallest rocks in the island, was afraid of heights.

After the narrowness of the steps up, the summit seems surprisingly spacious, and with peerless views in all directions. The top of the rock shelves steeply, covered in a baffling confusion of foundations and fragmentary remains which were once part of Kassapa's palace, though it's difficult to make much sense of any of them. The Royal Palace would have occupied the highest part of the summit, with the lower areas covered by the living quarters of servants and soldiers. A large tank cut from the solid rock stands between the two: water was brought to the summit using a typically ingenious hydraulic system driven by windmills. At the lowest end of the summit, a series of terraces, which were once possibly gardens, offer wonderful views over the waters of Sigiriya Wewa.

Sigiriya Wewa

On the south side of Sigiriya, the **Sigiriya Wewa** **G** tank provides a picturesque foreground to the towering rock and makes a beautiful spot for an evening stroll. As it appears today, the lake is only a fraction of its original size: it once supplied Sigiriya with all its water, from the pools and fountains of the water gardens through to the tank at the summit of the rock, to which it was connected by an intricate system of pipes and water channels. Water conservation was an important consideration in ancient Sigiriya (as, indeed, in all parts of the northern dry zone). Open channels cut into the rock were used to collect water drained from the summit, with the excess overflowing to irrigate the areas below.

Pidurangala Royal Cave Temple

For more ancient remains, and further impressive views of Sigiriya, head 2km (1.2 miles) north to **Pidurangala Royal Cave Temple**, poised atop another large rock outcrop directly opposite Sigiriya's Lion Platform.

The temple dates from the arrival of Kassapa, when the monks who had formerly been living in the caves around the base of Sigiriya Rock were evicted to make way for the new palace and gardens, although the megalomaniac king did provide some compensation by building them a new temple.

The entrance to the complex is marked by the modern white Pidurangala Sigiri Rajamaha Viharaya, right next to the roadside (a further clutch of atmospheric old monastic remains, including the ruins of a large dagoba, lie a little further down the road). From here, it's a steep 15-minute climb up to the Royal Cave Temple itself, where a large brick Buddha reclines beneath a rock overhang, flanked by figures of Vishnu and Saman. Another steep five-minute scramble along a very indistinct path leads to the summit of the rock (take care not to lose your footing on the tiny path, or break a leg on the boulders), where your efforts are rewarded by spectacular views of the north face of Sigiriya, with ant-like files of tourists and pilgrims climbing the final staircase to the top.

By building the lion sculpture, Kassapa was certainly trying to intimidate his enemies, but at the same time he was also claiming his kingship over the "lion race" – the Sinhalese.

BELOW: the rock in profile.

AYURVEDA

Sri Lanka's ancient medicines are more popular than ever, whether in treating disease or maintaining health and fitness.

Legend has it that Ayurveda, the science of life (*ayur* = knowledge, science; *veda* = life, longevity), was a gift of the Hindu God Brahma to humankind as a token of his compassion. Based on an holistic approach to health, Ayurveda has for millennia used Sri Lanka's prolific herb and plant life to cure and revitalise. Its origins can be traced back more than 5,000 years to the Vedas of India – and it has had a profound influence on Chinese and Tibetan medicine, and even Western surgery. At its core is the idea that our general wellbeing is closely related to our choice of lifestyle, and illness is caused by an imbalance of food, stress and toxins. Ayurvedic philosophy postulates that all bodies are composed of various combinations of the five basic elements – Air, Fire, Water, Earth and Ether – and that all people are subject to three *doshas*, or "life forces" – *Vatta* (air and ether), *Pitta* (fire and water) and *Kapha* (water and earth) – with illness resulting from an imbalance in the *doshas*. The aim of Ayurvedic treatments is to re-establish the three *doshas* in their correct balance, focusing on detoxification, rejuvenation, mental hygiene and spiritual healing. Oil massages, herbal remedies, and prescribed diets are the most common therapies in use.

ABOVE: Ayurvedic preparations, the basis for pills, tonics, massage packs, heat-packs and other applications, can consist of as many as 12 different ingredients. The drawers are inscribed in Sinhala.

BELOW: Ayurvedic massage incorporating heated herbal mud, here at the Siddhalepa Ayurveda Resort, often involves two therapists.

ABOVE: Shirodhara, where a patient has oil poured onto their forehead, can relieve stress and treat conditions such as hearing impairment.

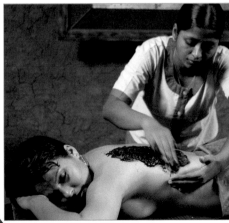

LEFT: a soothing *marma* scrub will unblock the energy channels.

CHOOSING WHERE TO HAVE TREATMENT

Because Ayurveda is such an integral part of the island's culture, it is ubiquitous – be it in the form of Ayurvedic clinics and pharmacies, locals offering oil massages on the beach or hotels and centres specialising in Ayurveda. Today, many hotels have at least a small area devoted to Ayurveda, if not an entire treatment centre. When deciding where and how to experience this ancient method of healing, you first need to determine your goals. For those simply looking for wellness, rejuvenation, or a dose of pampering, a good choice would be a hotel with a reputable treatment centre. However, you should be aware that many hotels have jumped on the bandwagon, among them a few who do not live up to standards. For those seeking a cure for a medical problem or illness, a recognised centre or retreat hotel solely devoted to Ayurveda is your best option. In general, a course of treatment lasting from two to three weeks is recommended to find relief from most maladies (see Ayurveda Resorts, page 302, and the Travel Tips section of this book for a guide to some of the best hotels and centres offering treatments).

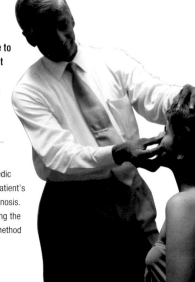

ABOVE: the ultimate relaxation, a flower bath is a wonderful way to end a day's treatment programme. The freshly picked flowers release their full aroma in the warm waters.

RIGHT: an Ayurvedic doctor checks a patient's health by iris-diagnosis. Intensively checking the pulse is another method used.

EAST COAST

Slowly emerging from civil war and tsunami, the east coast offers plenty of attractions, from superb beaches to Buddhist remains, and with hardly a tourist in sight.

S ri Lanka's east coast is unquestionably beautiful, but has often seemed cursed. The entire region suffered terrible devastation throughout the civil war years, thanks to its volatile mixture of Sinhalese, Muslim and Tamil populations, with clashes between the Sri Lankan Army (SLA) and Tamil Tigers – and widespread massacres of innocent civilians caught up in the middle of the fighting – not to mention the devastating effects of the 2004 tsunami. Lasting peace finally returned in 2007, when the SLA succeeded in driving the Tigers out and taking control of the entire area for the first time in two decades. Reconstruction since has been slow but steady, and the region is now finally looking to the future with renewed confidence. Its major towns – Trincomalee and Batticaloa – are once again bustling with life and commercial activity while ongoing development promises to finally start unlocking the massive tourism potential of the superb coast – albeit at the inevitable cost of changing its formerly remote and magically unspoilt character for ever.

Trincomalee

The ancient settlement of **Trincomalee** ❶, now the third-largest city in Sri Lanka, is best known for its famous

harbour, one of the world's largest and finest deep-water anchorages. The harbour served as the island's major port as far back as the Polonnaruwan era (when it was known as Gokana) and subsequently attracted the attentions of the Danes, Dutch, Portuguese, French and British – not to mention the Japanese Imperial Air Force, who bombed it in 1942.

The centrepiece of Trincomalee (or Trinco, as it's usually called) is **Fort Frederick**. Originally built by the Portuguese in 1623, the fort passed

Main attractions
TRINCOMALEE
UPPUVELI
NILAVELI
ARUGAM BAY
LAHUGALA NATIONAL PARK
MALIGAWILA

PRECEDING PAGES: people bathing at Pigeon Island National Park, near Trincomalee.
LEFT: Koneswaram temple, Trincomalee.
RIGHT: a Unesco mine poster.

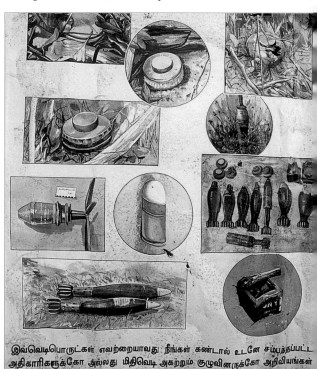

இவ்வெடிபொருட்கள் எவற்றையாவது நீங்கள் கண்டால் உடனே சம்பந்தப்பட்ட அதிகாரிகளுக்கோ அல்லது மிதிவெடி அகற்றும் குழுவினருக்கோ அறிவியுங்கள்

Trincomalee provided safe harbour for Jane Austen's "problem" brother, Sir Charles, who is buried in St Stephen's cemetery alongside a certain P.B. Molesworth, the first manager of Ceylon Rail, who dabbled in astronomy and discovered the red spot on Jupiter.

successively into Dutch and French hands, before finally being acquired by the British, who had long coveted it. It's now used as an army barracks, though casual visitors are still allowed to stroll through it en route to Swami Rock. The fort is encircled by a ring of doughty stone walls and entered through a fine old gateway, emblazoned with the British coat of arms and the motto "Mon Dieu et Mon Droit". Inside, the walls enclose a beautiful area of sylvan parkland patrolled by resident deer (and a few cows) and studded with various colonial-era buildings, including the large residence known as **Wellington House**

where the future duke of that name, then going under the more humble name of Arthur Wellesley, spent some time in 1799. According to legend, the future Iron Duke was recovering here from a bout of malaria and found his billet so comfortable that he missed the boat which was to have taken him home – and which later sank in the Gulf of Aden with the loss of all hands. In fact, the fated ship departed not from Trinco but from Bombay, and the fortunate Wellesley missed sailing on it after being struck down with a bout of the dreaded Malabar Itch.

A steep road leads up from the fort to the summit of **Swami Rock**, the commanding clifftop that dominates the coast hereabouts, topped by the modern Koneswaram temple, one of the holiest Siva shrines on the island (the original temple was toppled over the edge and into the sea by the Portuguese in the 17th century). The rock here is also popularly known as Lover's Leap, on account of a Dutch official's daughter, Francina Van Reede, who threw herself off the rock after watching her unfaithful husband

East Coast

0   20 km
0   20 miles

The Knox Tree

Ferries sail four times a day from Trinco across the bay to the Muslim town of **Mutur**, offering a pleasantly breezy dose of sea air en route. Ask around in Mutur and you may find the site of the **Knox Tree**. A stone inscription beneath the tree once read, rather erroneously: "This is White Man's tree, under which Robert Knox, captain of the ship *Ann*, was captured AD 1660. Knox was held captive by the Kandyan king for 19 years. This stone was placed here in 1893." The Robert Knox referred to was Robert Knox Senior, indeed captain of the *Ann* but actually father to the young seaman who later related his tale of imprisonment by Rajasinha II in his *Historical Relation of Ceylon*. It is thought that this book became the inspiration behind Daniel Defoe's castaway novel, *Robinson Crusoe*. For more on his story, see page 42.

desert her by sea. Her suicide attempt was unsuccessful, however, and she went on to marry for a second time eight years after her near-fatal fall.

Extending to the west and south of the fort, modern Trincomalee is an occasionally ramshackle but often characterful place. Eye-catching Hindu temples mark the centre, serving its predominantly Tamil population, while colourful streets open out to reveal views of the three bays which enclose the centre, dotted with fishing boats and larger vessels which come to dock in the waters of the Inner Harbour. Late afternoon is particularly memorable, when locals congregate along the small stretch of beach on Dutch Bay to watch the sun go down, and the bells ring out from the nearby Kali and Pillaiyar Temples.

Nilaveli and Uppuveli

Some 5km (3 miles) and 10km (6 miles) north of Trinco respectively, the beachside villages of **Uppuveli ❷** and **Nilaveli ❸** continued to attract a smattering of foreign tourists throughout the civil war years, and are still the only places you're likely to see a foreign tourist north of Arugam Bay – although development hereabouts remains extremely low-key even now. There's a rudimentary scattering of budget guesthouses at Uppuveli, plus a couple of smarter hotels (the Chaaya Blu at Uppuveli and the Nilaveli Beach Hotel at Nilaveli, both of which somehow kept going over the years despite civil war and tsunami).

Most visitors come to lounge around on the seemingly endless swathe of soft white sand which lines the coast, although increasing numbers are likely to be drawn by the newly established whale-watching tours, currently running from roughly March to September (and most easily arranged through the Chaaya Blu hotel). There's also good snorkelling around **Pigeon Island National Park**, just off the coast at Nilaveli, which boasts a fine array of live coral and plenty of tropical fish.

On the northern edge of Uppuveli village, the pristinely kept if rather sombre

Commonwealth War Cemetery holds the graves of 362 Allied servicemen of a dozen or more nationalities who died at Trinco during World War II, including soldiers and sailors killed in the Japanese air raid on Trinco in 1942.

The Hot Springs at **Kanniyai**, 8km (5 miles) inland from Uppuveli along the Anuradhapura road, are known for their therapeutic qualities. The coolest spring is 29°C (84°F) and the hottest not more than 46°C (115°F). The Tamils believe they were created by Vishnu and named after the mother of Ravanna, the demon king, to enable Vishnu to perform an ablutionary rite on his mother. Devout Hindus come here to perform religious rites after a loved one has died.

Batticaloa and the southeast

South of Trinco, the east coast's only other major settlement is the war-torn but now increasingly vibrant town of **Batticaloa ❹** (or "Batti", as it is usually called), hemmed in between the Indian Ocean and the placid waters of the meandering Batticaloa Lagoon. Batti is famous in Sri Lankan folklore

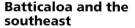

Fish drying on the beach.

BELOW: Swami Rock.

Arugam Bay's amazing waves are a magnet to surfers.

BELOW: a temple near Trincomalee.

as the home of the mysterious "singing fish". Tradition states that these are at their most vocal on nights of the full moon between April and September (and are best heard, it's alleged, by getting into a boat, sticking an oar into the water, and placing the other end by one's ear). The exact cause of the singing remains unclear, however: shoals of catfish on the bed of the lagoon, or the sound of tides rushing through empty mollusc shells or fretted rocks, are two popular explanations, although no one seems to be entirely sure.

Batticaloa also boasts an interesting colonial past. The town's fort was originally built by the Portuguese in 1628 but shortly afterwards it was captured by the Dutch – their first foothold on the island which they would soon take possession of. The fort stands next to the lagoon, its solid coral walls protected by a moat on two sides and plunging directly into the water on the other; inside, a fine old two-storey Dutch-era building flanks one side of the interior courtyard, with a small and incongruous Hindu temple in the middle. South of here stretches old Batticaloa, with

attractive streets of colonial-era houses dotted with enormous churches and the venerable old St Michael's College.

North of Batti, the bay at **Passekudah** ❺ is currently in the throes of major tourist development, with the concrete skeletons of twelve or so resort hotels currently under construction strung out around the beach, promising to bring a touch of West Coast razzamatazz to this formerly remote destination when work in finished in around 2013. The nearby village of Kalkudah remains relatively undeveloped, home to a clutch of inexpensive guesthouses and the magnificent sweep of the deserted Kalkudah Beach – still totally unspoilt and undeveloped, although probably not for long.

Arugam Bay

At the southern end of the east coast lies the little village of **Arugam Bay** ❻, far and away the east coast's most popular tourist destination, and home to an eclectic local population of Tamils, Sinhalese, Muslims and expat Europeans – a good place to hole up for a few days while enjoying the wonderful feeling of being a long way away from anywhere else. The village was first put on the tourist map by visiting surfers, who came here to ride what are reckoned to be some of the best waves in the whole of Asia – though the place now attracts plenty of non-surfers as well thanks to its very laid-back and slightly off-the-wall charm. There are no big hotel developments here (something the tightly knit local community have fought hard to resist), and if you're prepared to forego five-star comforts there are some quirky and unusual lodgings to be had in many of the village's guesthouses – rustic wooden cabanas, rickety tree houses and other homespun structures.

The beach itself is pleasant, if unexceptional, although there are plenty of activities to keep you busy. The village's world-class surf takes pride of place, with a range of breaks catering to all abilities. Various guesthouses around the village also offer interesting tours

of the nearby Pottuvil Lagoon and motor-boat expeditions out to sea in search of dolphins.

South from Arugam Bay

South of Arugam Bay, a rough dirt road threads its way down the coast, passing through a beautiful landscape of lagoon, beach and jungle to reach the atmospheric forest hermitage at **Kudimbigala**. Hundreds of Buddhist monks once lived in caves here, hidden away in dense forest between huge boulders and rock outcrops. Paths lead through the trees, passing small shrines and miniature cave temples en route, while rock-cut steps lead steeply up to the summit of the towering Belumgala rock, offering magnificent views over the wild swathes of jungle running down to the coast.

Further south, some 30km (18 miles) from Arugam Bay, the village of **Okanda** ❼ is home to one of the largest Hindu temples on the coast, said to mark the spot where the god Kataragama landed on the island. The village is also where you'll find the entrance to the little-visited **Yala East National Park** – a very peaceful alternative to its much better-known neighbour. It reputedly served as a hide-out for LTTE fighters during the civil war and has only recently officially reopened to visitors. The park's star attraction is the mangrove-fringed Kumana Wewa tank, home to an exceptionally rich array of aquatic birdlife.

Inland from Arugam Bay

Around 15km (9 miles) down the main road heading inland from Arugam Bay, the small **Lahugala National Park** consists of the Lahugala Tank and the scenic tropical dry forest that surrounds it. It's not technically open to the public at present, though the main road to Arugam Bay runs right through the middle of it, offering various viewing points from where elephants can often be seen.

Just east of the park lie the magical ruins of the **Magul Maha Vihara**, a lovely complex of weathered old brick

and stone shrines and stupas nestling in jungle.

It's another couple of hours down the road to the sleepy little provincial town of Monaragala. This is the jumping-off point for a visit to the tiny village of **Maligawila**, 17km (10 miles) distant, home to a pair of huge images that lie buried amidst unspoilt jungle. One shows the Buddha in the Abhaya ("Have no Fear") mudra; the other is thought to depict a Mahayana Bodhisattva.

Further inland, the remains of the vast Yudaganawa dagoba sit just west of the town of Buttala. The dagoba is thought to mark the site of the battle between the legendary King Dutugemunu and his brother Saddhatissa; the brothers were subsequently reconciled, and the dagoba erected to commemorate the peace. Only the base of the structure now survives, impressively huge – bigger even than the great Ruwanweliseya dagoba in Anuradhapura. A contrastingly diminutive shrine stands in front of the dagoba, dating from the Kandyan era and covered inside with a richly painted array of murals.

The east coast receives a drenching from the northeast monsoons between October and January, but otherwise it is drier than the west.

BELOW: Nilaveli beach.

JAFFNA AND THE NORTH

Bruised and bloodied, but far from bowed, the remote northern city of Jaffna remains a vibrant centre of Sri Lankan Tamil culture.

The far north of Sri Lanka is almost a different country, historically, culturally and – if the Tamil Tigers (LTTE) had had their way – literally. Separated from the rest of the country by language, religion and the wide-open spaces of the Vanni, the Tamil north looks as much to India as it does to the island's Sinhalese south, and retains a flavour and way of life which is very much its own.

It was not always so. During the early centuries of Sri Lanka's history, Tamils and Sinhalese lived shoulder to shoulder, as they still do in Colombo and many other parts of the island. With the fall of Anuradhapura and Polonnaruwa and the abandonment of the northern plains, a divide opened between the two communities. The Sinhalese drifted south, while the Tamils established a new kingdom – Jaffnapatnam, the origins of modern Jaffna – in the far north of the island.

The civil war wreaked widespread devastation across the entire north of the island, as the LTTE and Sri Lankan Army battled for control of the region. Jaffna itself changed hands on several occasions, each time accompanied by massive destruction and loss of life, although having been under continuous government control since 1995 it at least avoided the terrible

carnage associated with the closing stages of the war in 2008–09. Much of the rest of the north remained under the control of the LTTE, with their administration based in the town of Kilinochchi – which was virtually wiped from the map during the bitter final months of fighting.

Inevitably, the massive task of reconstructing and rehabilitating the north since the end of the war has been slow, and often accompanied by controversy. Three years on from the end of fighting, however, there

Main attractions
OUR LADY OF MADHU
JAFFNA TOWN AND FORT
NALLUR KANDASWAMY TEMPLE
JAFFNA PENINSULA
KAYTS
NAINATIVU
DELFT

PRECEDING PAGES: ruins of war, Jaffna.
LEFT: poster for a school, Jaffna.
RIGHT: roadside beverages.

The most obvious visible reminders of the war, during which the import of new cars was forbidden, are the superb old Morris Minors and Austin Cambridges, kept going by their owners throughout the fighting and which can still occasionally be seen plying the streets like sedate old dowagers.

are cautious signs of progress. Jaffna remains as vibrant as ever, while travel to the city up and down the A9 highway (the principal road in the north) is now unrestricted, with massive road improvements promising to cut the travel time between Kandy and Jaffna to as little as six hours. Further south, Kilinochchi is now rising from its former ashes, while Tamils driven from their homes in the Vanni are now being allowed to return, albeit with painful slowness, as the difficult process of demilitarisation, de-mining and resettlement continues.

The road to Jaffna

Past Anuradhapura, the A9 arrows due north to Jaffna via Vavuniya and Kilinochchi, linking the major towns of the north and providing the only reliable means of access to the region, short of flying. Not surprisingly, the highway was bitterly fought over for much of the civil war, during which it became known as the Highway of Death. The former narrow and potholed road is now

being comprehensively widened and reconstructed, providing (depending on your point of view) either a massively overdue boost to the neglected northern infrastructure and its long-suffering residents or a means for Sri Lankan troops to reach the area swiftly in the – hopefully unlikely – event of future trouble.

The dividing line between Sinhalese south and Tamil north is marked by the lively town of **Vavuniya**, close to the front line for much of the war. From here a side road heads west to **Mannar Island** and the village of **Talaimannar**, almost within spitting distance of India, to which it was connected by ferry until 1983. En route, the road passes the turn-off to **Madhu**, home to Sri Lanka's most revered Christian church, which in more peaceful times attracted huge numbers of pilgrims, thanks to the miracle-working statue of Our Lady of Madhu, famous for its supposed ability to protect devotees from snakebite – a very real danger in rural Sri Lanka, which has one of the world's highest rates of deaths from venomous vipers.

BELOW: Military vehicles on the streets of Vavuniya

Beyond here, the A9 rolls across endless kilometres of arid scrubland. This entire part of the island – known as the Vanni – was always sparsely populated, and 20 years of fighting succeeded in almost totally emptying the region of even the few people who formerly lived here. A few are now slowly returning, although the whole area remains almost eerily deserted, with nothing but the very occasional house and endless swathes of dense jungle lining either side of the road, whose tangled depths provided a string of secure hiding places for the LTTE leadership during the war years and allowed Prabakharan to evade capture for over three decades.

The only sizeable settlement en route is the town of **Kilinochchi**, where the Tamil Tigers had their headquarters throughout the civil war era before finally being ousted by the Sri Lankan Army in early 2009 following a two-month siege during which the town was virtually obliterated. Rebuilding continues apace, with modern offices and shops springing up incongruously amidst the ruins of the old town. A huge collapsed water tower, blown up by the Tigers during their final stand, has been left where it fell, offering a powerful monument to the destructiveness of war. Nearby stands a striking war memorial showing a huge cube of stone (symbolising the LTTE) pierced by a shell (the Sri Lankan Army) with a lotus blooming out of the cracks at the top.

Another featureless stretch of road leads to **Elephant Pass**. Guarding the entrance to the Jaffna peninsula, Elephant Pass was one of the north's most strategically important locations during the civil war and the scene of major battles in 1991, 2000 and 2009. Another oversized war memorial now stands above the police checkpoint, showing hands lifting a map of Sri Lanka with a lotus blossoming from its summit, accompanied by fatuously self-congratulatory governmental inscriptions in praise of the Rajapakse

regime. Slightly further up the road, a burnt-out LTTE armoured bulldozer stands next to the highway as a further, and somewhat more realistic, token of war. This was used by the Tigers during their attack here in 1991 and destroyed by a young soldier named Gamini Kularatne, the first recipient of the Parama Weera Vibhushanaya, Sri Lanka's highest military honour, who in a moment of suicidal courage leapt aboard and flung two grenades inside, causing the vehicle to explode.

Jaffna

The capital of the north, Jaffna remains a vibrant centre of Sri Lankan Tamil culture, its spirits undimmed despite the massive destruction it suffered during the earlier years of the civil war and its long isolation from the rest of the island. The town was repeatedly fought over between 1989 and 1995, suffering widespread destruction in the process, but has been under Sri Lankan Army control since 1995 and so avoided the destruction visited on other parts of the north during the later stages of the war

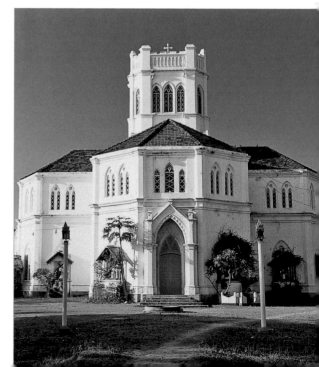

BELOW: a Jaffna church.

*The fermented flesh of
the papaya can be
used in ointment to
treat minor wounds.*

BELOW: in the Nallur
Kandaswamy
Temple.

– occasional traces of war damage can still be seen, but are increasingly few and far between.

Jaffna remains strikingly different to everywhere else in Sri Lanka, offering an absorbing blend of old-fashioned colonial charm alongside the hustle and bustle of contemporary Tamil life. The town as a whole is as reminiscent of India as of the Sinhalese south, its streets dotted with a sequence of large Hindu temples topped by soaring *gopurams*, and filled with crowds of cyclists and the distinctive blare of Tamil music issuing from cafés and shops. The almost complete absence of Sinhala writing on shopfronts and signs adds a further sense of novelty and strangeness for those who have spent time in other parts of the island.

The Dutch Fort

Immediately south of the town centre lies Jaffna's vast **Dutch Fort**, the largest Dutch bastion in Asia, built in their favoured star shape and completed in 1792. However, less than 10 years after being completed the whole thing was handed over to the British without a shot being fired. The fort finally saw serious military action during the civil war: in 1990, marooned members of the Sri Lankan Army were forced to hole up inside it for three months, surviving intense bombardment by LTTE forces, until finally being rescued. Sadly, the pounding it took during this siege finished off the old Dutch buildings inside, including the historic Great Church (*Groote Kerk*). The entire fort is now undergoing extensive renovations although in the meantime it's possible to walk into the fort and explore the largely empty courtyard within, littered with rubble, and to walk round sections of the old bastions, with fine views over the surrounding streets.

East of the town centre stretch beautiful shaded streets of colonial villas and a sequence of enormous churches – a large proportion of Jaffna Tamils are Christian. The largest is the massive **St Mary's Cathedral**. North of here on Main Street are the **Rosarian Convent** and **St Martin's Seminary**, two more attractive colonial relics.

Nallur Kandaswamy Temple

Jaffna's most impressive sight, however, is the majestic **Nallur Kandaswamy Temple**, a few kilometres from the centre on the northern edge of town. Dedicated to Murugan, this sprawling religious complex, bounded by the high, red-striped walls that traditionally indicate the presence of a Siva temple (Murugan, also known as Skanda, is Siva's son), is the finest Hindu temple in Sri Lanka, and the only one to rival the great temples of Tamil Nadu in India. The original building was destroyed – along with hundreds of others around the island – by the Portuguese; the current edifice was begun in the early 19th century. A measure of the temple's popularity and importance is the fact that there are no fewer than six daily *pujas* (men entering the temple must remove their shirts).

The temple is also the venue for one of the island's greatest religious celebrations, the Nallur Festival, which runs for almost an entire month every summer, culminating on the *Poya* day in August. During the latter nights of the festival, enormous illuminated chariots bearing images of various deities are pulled nightly by vast crowds around the city streets. As at the spectacular Kataragama festival at the opposite end of the island (see page 184), devotees also demonstrate their devotion to Murugan with spectacular acts of self-mutilation, driving hooks and skewers through their cheeks, backs and other parts of their bodies.

The Jaffna peninsula

Sitting atop the northernmost point of the island, the fertile Jaffna peninsula has long been intensively settled and cultivated, and was famous in former times for the richness of its gardens and the sweetness of its mangoes.

A string of low-key sights lies due north of Jaffna. At **Kantharodai**, 10km (6 miles) north of the city, a cluster of miniature stupas, none higher than a few metres, sit together in a small clearing. The site is quite

Following the end of the war the Sri Lankan government destroyed several sites and memorials associated with the LTTE including (most notably) Prabakharan's old family house in Velvettiturai and the LTTE cemetery at Kopai, in which hundreds of fallen Tigers were formerly buried.

BELOW: the Hindu Kovil festival in Jaffna

Palm trees line the whole coast.

BELOW: tsunami victims' graves, among the sand dunes of the Jaffna peninsula.

unlike anything else in Sri Lanka and is thought to date back perhaps 2,000 years, though its original purpose remains unclear – it's been surmised that the stupas were either built to enshrine the remains of Buddhist monks, or erected in fulfilment of answered prayers.

Two of the many grand Hindu temples that grace the peninsula – the **Naguleswaram** and **Maviddapuram** – lie close to one another north of Kantharodai, near the northern edge of the peninsula. Both temples were severely damaged in the civil war but are now being painstakingly reconstructed, with piles of statues and collapsed pillars waiting to be reassembled. Just past here, on the peninsula's northern shore, are the popular hot springs at **Keerimalai**, said to have miraculous therapeutic powers.

Further small-scale attractions cluster around the busy town of **Point Pedro**, at the far northeastern tip of the Jaffna peninsula. Here the **Point Pedro Lighthouse** marks the northernmost point in Sri Lanka, some 430km (270 miles) north of Dondra

Lighthouse at the opposite, southernmost point of the island. A few kilometres west of Point Pedro, the small town of **Velvettiturai** ("VVT") is famous as the birthplace of LTTE leader Prabakharan, whose family once owned the impressive Amman Temple, dedicated to Siva, which is the most notable landmark hereabouts. Just south of here lies the strange little **Manalkadu Desert**, a stretch of impressive coastal sand dunes that have now buried the small **St Anthony's Church**. About 2km (1 mile) north of St Anthony's, the village of **Vallipuram** is home to another of the peninsula's impressive Hindu temples.

The islands

West of Jaffna, a series of islands fans out into the shallow waters of **Palk Strait**, providing a convenient series of stepping stones for sailors travelling between Sri Lanka and India. The largest of the islands, **Kayts** (pronounced "Kites"), lies directly opposite Jaffna and is separated from the mainland only by a

narrow and shallow inlet, crossed by the narrowest of causeways. At the far end of the island from Jaffna, the modest little settlement of Kayts town is home to the beautiful shell of **St James Church**, which lost its roof and most of its interior during the war, and the more durable Dutch-era **Urundi Fort**, whose small coral-stone walls are slowly being eaten away by encroaching vegetation. Opposite here, in the middle of the waters dividing Kayts from the neighbouring island of Karaitivu, floats another well-preserved Dutch fort, **Hammenhiel** – literally "Heel of Ham", referring to the old Dutch belief that the shape of Sri Lanka resembled a leg of ham.

On the far side of Hammenhiel, **Karaitivu** island (connected to Kayts by irregular ferries, and to the mainland north of Jaffna by a causeway) is notable mainly for **Casuarina Beach**, on the island's north side, the peninsula's most popular beach, with fine golden sand and safe swimming, though no real facilities. South of Kayts, the longest of the area's various causeways crosses 5km (3 miles) of shallow water to reach the island of **Punkudutivu** – the journey there is the major attraction, with a trip along the slender causeway giving one the strange sense of driving across water.

From Punkudutivu, ferries cross to the small island of **Nainativu**, home to two important religious shrines. These include the inevitable Hindu temple – the florid **Naga Pooshani Ambal Kovil** – and, a rarity in the north, the modest **Nagadipa Vihara Buddhist temple**, which marks the spot where the Buddha is believed to have appeared during the second of his three legendary visits to the island.

It's an hour's ferry ride from Punkudutivu to **Delft**, the last of the Jaffna islands accessible without your own boat. Flat and starkly beautiful, the island feels a long way from anywhere, with its low coral-stone walls, herds of wild ponies and (just south of the ferry dock) a curious baobab tree, thought to have been brought to the island from central Africa by Portuguese sailors.

BELOW: Sri Lankan Roman Catholics gather during the pilgrimage at Saint Anthony's Church.

![Insight Guide] **TRAVEL TIPS**

SRI LANKA

TRANSPORT

GETTING THERE AND GETTING AROUND

GETTING THERE

By Air

Sri Lanka's only international airport is Bandaranaike International Airport (www.airport.lk), at Katunayake, 34km (21 miles) north of Colombo, near Negombo. A second international airport is currently under construction just outside the southern town of Hambantota, scheduled to open in late 2012.

The national carrier, SriLankan Airlines (flight code UL), has direct flights between Colombo and many destinations in Europe (including London, Paris, Frankfurt, Zürich and Milan); the Middle East (Abu Dhabi, Bahrain, Doha, Dubai, Muscat, Kuwait, Riyadh, Damman); India (Mumbai, Delhi, Chennai, Thiruvananthapuram, Kochi, Bangalore, Kozikode and Tiruchirappali); Pakistan (Karachi); southeast and east Asia (Bangkok, Hong Kong, Singapore, Kuala Lumpur, Shanghai, Beijing, Tokyo); and the Maldives (Male).

Other international carriers serving Colombo include Air Arabia, Air India, Cathay Pacific, Emirates, Etihad, Gulf Air, Jet Airways, Kingfisher, Kuwait, Malaysian Airlines, Mihin Lanka, Oman Air, Qatar, Royal Jordanian, Saudi Arabian, Spicejet, Singapore and Thai. The airport is also served by regular charter flights from Europe during the northern hemisphere winter.

Airline Offices

Offices of the major airlines flying to/ from Colombo are listed below. To dial from overseas, start with 94 11.
Cathay Pacific
Tel: 011 233 4145

www.cathaypacific.com
Emirates
Tel: 011 470 4070
www.emirates.com
Gulf Air
Tel: 011 235 9888
www.gulfair.com
Air India
Tel: 011 232 6844
www.airindia.in
Kuwait Airlines
Tel: 011 244 5531
www.kuwaitairways.com
Malaysian
Tel: 011 234 2291
www.malaysiaairlines.com.my
Oman Air
Tel: 011 446 2222
www.omanair.com
Qatar
www.qatarairways.com
Qantas
Tel: 011 476 7767
www.qantas.com
Royal Jordanian
Tel: 011 230 1626
www.rj.com
Saudi Arabian
Tel: 011 259 3914
www.saudiairlines.com
Singapore
Tel: 011 249 9699
www.singaporeair.com
SriLankan Airlines
www.srilankan.aero
Main Ticket Office:
Tel: 019 733 5500
Passenger enquiries:
Tel: 019 733 1627
Contact centre (24hr):
Tel: 1979 (from inside Sri Lanka), 00 94 777 771979 (from outside Sri Lanka)
Email: customer@srilankan.aero
Thai
Tel: 011 230 7100
www.thaiair.com

By Sea

In June 2011 ferry services were resumed, briefly, and for the first time since 1983, between Sri Lanka and India, travelling from Colombo to Tuticorin, in the southern Indian state of Tamil Nadu – and despite considerable opposition from local politicians in Tamil Nadu. Sailings were made twice-weekly aboard the Indian-chartered Scotia Prince, carrying up to 1,000 passengers and taking around 14 hours to make the journey. Unfortunately, after just six months the Scotia Prince was impounded by the Colombo High Court after a claim against the ferry's Indian owners for unpaid bills, and services currently show no sign of re-starting – meaning that it could be another 30 years before the next boat sails. Check online or with your nearest tourist office (see page 317) for latest news.

GETTING AROUND

Despite its relatively modest size, getting around Sri Lanka can be a surprisingly time-consuming affair – many first-time visitors are amazed when the apparently inconsequential journey from the airport into Colombo takes an hour or more. This is mainly a result of Sri Lanka's undeveloped and over-burdened road system. There are few dual carriageways in the island, and most highways are choked with a random assortment of slow-moving lorries and tuktuks, weaving bicycles, wandering dogs and other hazards, making road travel a slow and not particularly restful experience.

A major, ongoing programme across the island of road widening and highway upgrades is gradually improving the situation, while the recent opening of the country's first proper motorway, the E1 Southern Expressway from Colombo to Galle, has already revolutionised travel down the west coast, reducing travel time between the two cities from over three hours to just one. An extension of the highway from Colombo to the international airport is expected to open in 2013, while further extensions to Matara and Hambantota are also planned, as is a second expressway from Colombo to Kandy.

By Bus

Buses reach pretty much every town or village of any significance anywhere on the island, though services are often slow, crowded and uncomfortable. There are various types of bus operated either by the government-run SLTB (Sri Lanka Transport Board) or one of the island's myriad private operators. SLTB buses are usually painted red; private buses tend to be white (sometimes with lurid decorations). Local and non-express buses (both SLTB and private) are incredibly cheap but stop absolutely everywhere and can get horribly packed, private services in particular, as the conductor attempts to ram as many passengers as possible into any available space.

There are also various privately run "semi-express" and "express" services, which tend to make fewer stops (although they can also get packed). The fastest vehicles, usually called "inter-city express" or something similar, are usually in smaller vehicles (like large minibuses) with air conditioning, tinted windows and padded seats. These make only limited stops and don't accept standing

From the Airport

If your holiday is part of a package, transfer from the airport should be included and the local representative will be on hand to meet you. Colombo's major hotels have desks at the airport where hotel transport can be booked. If you arrive independently, there are plenty of taxis available. Fares are around Rs2,500 to Colombo (1 hour) and Rs1,500 to Negombo (20 minutes). Bus services from the airport are slow and uncomfortable, and best avoided after a long-haul flight.

passengers – at least in theory – and so are usually a lot quicker although not necessarily much more comfortable, especially for tall foreigners, since seats are small and legroom minimal.

Car Rental and Driving

Sri Lanka's anarchic traffic and idiosyncratic road rules make driving a challenge for foreigners. If you don't absolutely have to drive, the best option is to hire a driver – which is often no more expensive than hiring a car on its own. If you're determined to drive, you'll need an international driving licence plus an additional permit to drive in Sri Lanka, costing Rs1,500 and valid for up to 12 months. These can only be obtained from the Automobile Association of Ceylon (tel: 011 242 1528; www.aa ceylon.lk), 3rd floor, 40 Sir Macan Markar Mawatha, just off Galle Face Green in Colombo (a couple of buildings past the Ramada hotel).

In terms of road use, might is usually right: buses and trucks come first, followed by vans, cars and three-wheelers and finally the humble cyclist. Expect the unexpected, and be prepared for both your driving skills and patience to be tested to the utmost limits. Away from the traffic-infested capital, driving is much easier, but a good road map and phrase book are invaluable. Don't expect there to be many road signs leading you to your destination and don't rely too much on verbal directions – Sri Lankans are so accommodating that many are only too happy to "help", even if they don't know the way.

Car Rental Firms

Avis (c/o Walkers Tours)
Tel: 011 492 2141
www.avis.co.uk/CarHire/Asia/Sri-Lanka/Colombo

Casons Rent-A-Car
Tel: 011 440 5070
www.casonscar.com
Malkey Rent-A-Car
Tel: 011 236 5365
www.malkey.lk
Quickshaws
Tel: 011 258 3133
www.quickshaws.com

Chauffeur-driven Cars

These are by far the most comfortable way of getting around. There are several reputable agencies in Colombo, which offer both air-conditioned and non-air conditioned vehicles. Long-distance chauffeur-driven services are available from some hire-car companies, and are often not much more expensive than self-drive – although you'll probably also have to pay a modest amount for the driver's food and lodgings, and he will also expect a tip at the end.

For reliable chauffeurs/guides contact:
Destination Sri Lanka
Tel: 0777 840 001
www.dsltours.com
Jetwing Travels
Tel: 011 471 4830
www.jetwingtravels.com
Malkey Rent-A-Car
Tel: 011 236 5365
www.malkey.lk
Quickshaws
Tel: 011 258 3133
www.quickshaws.com
Walkers Tours
Tel: 011 230 6715
www.walkerstours.com

By Train

Sri Lanka's antiquated railway system offers a charming – if slow – way of getting around the island, especially on the scenic hill-

BELOW: a typical Sri Lankan bus – colourfully painted and carelessly driven.

country line. Fares are extremely cheap, though carriages can often get ridiculously overcrowded, and delays are the norm rather than the exception. There are three main lines starting from Colombo: the Coast Line runs north to Negombo and Puttalam and south to Galle and Matara (there are plans to extend this line to Kataragama); the Main Line goes east, via Kandy, to Nuwara Eliya and Badulla; and the Northern Line goes via Anuradhapura to Omantai, just north of Vavuniya. A side branch of the Northern Line goes to Trincomalee, while another goes to Polonnaruwa and Batticaloa. For more information visit www.railway.gov.lk.

Most trains have only 2nd and 3rd class; there's not much difference between the two, though your chances of getting a seat in the fractionally more expensive 2nd class are better. A few hill-country express trains carry a special "observation car" with big windows and (most importantly) places that can be reserved in advance, so you're guaranteed a seat. This makes for a wonderful journey through the hill country, although observation-car seats on the popular Colombo–Kandy run sell out quickly. In addition to the traditional observation car, a couple of new companies have also recently started running special tourist carriages on the main hill-country express trains, including Expo Rail (tel: 011 522 5050; www.exporail.lk) and Rajadhani Express (tel: 011 268 1446; www.blueline.lk) – relatively pricey compared to normal train tickets, but very comfortable.

By Rickshaw

Motorised rickshaws (also known as tuktuks, trishaws, three-wheelers or just "taxis") can be found everywhere in Sri Lanka and offer the most convenient way of making short journeys. They can also sometimes be useful for longer journeys in places which lack public transport. These noisy little vehicles (usually Indian-made Bajajs) can travel at surprising speed through busy traffic, and offer a fun – if sometimes slightly nerve-wracking – way of getting around. Rickshaws aren't generally metered except in Colombo, where increasing numbers of metered vehicles can be found, currently charging Rs50/km. Assuming you're going in an unmetered rickshaw, you'll need to agree the fare before setting off, and be prepared to bargain. Rickshaw drivers vary enormously in how much they'll try to overcharge you by: many are fairly honest, though a few are complete rogues. You'll usually pay a bit more in big cities like Colombo and Kandy, and less in more rural areas; the more touristy the area you're in, the more you're likely to need to barter to get a reasonable fare. It's also a good idea to have the correct change for your journey, since rickshaw drivers often claim not to have any change, in the hope that you'll let them keep the difference.

Note that a proportion of hotels and guesthouses (and also some shops, spice gardens and restaurants) pay rickshaw drivers commission for bringing them business, meaning that certain drivers may attempt to steer you away from a place that doesn't pay commission to another place that does. Ignore any driver who tells you that your chosen hotel is full, has shut down, is derelict or teeming with rats – they may conceivably be telling the truth, but it's always a good idea to check for yourself. Remember too that if a hotel pays commission to a rickshaw driver, they'll most likely try to charge you a higher rate to compensate.

BELOW: tiny tuktuks quickly navigate city streets.

By Taxi

There are numerous metered taxi services in Colombo, but the taxis don't wait on the street so you'll have to ring for one. They're generally comfortable and reliable, and can be not much more expensive than a rickshaw. Away from the capital "taxis" are usually minivans; in most towns they congregate near bus stations waiting for custom.

By Motorcycle

Motorcycles offer a quick and enjoyable way of seeing the country, if you don't mind the element of danger posed by local traffic conditions. Crash helmets must be worn at all times. Motorbikes and scooters of various sizes can be hired from outlets around the coast, including Negombo, Hikkaduwa and Unawatuna. Smaller scooters generally go for around $10 per day; larger machines from $20 and up.

By Air

SriLankan Airlines operates a comprehensive Air Taxi service from Colombo to many places around the country. All these flights use Twin Otter water planes (carrying up to 15 passengers), which are able to land on convenient lakes rather than runways (which are few and far between). Scheduled flights currently run between Colombo and Trincomalee, Ampara, Arugam Bay, Tissamaharama, Hambantota, Dickwella, Koggala, Bentota, Kandy, Nuwara Eliya and Dambulla (with more destinations in the north and east planned). There are also 30-minute scenic flights from Colombo, Kandy and Dambulla. See www.srilankan.com/airtaxi for details.

Helicopter Service is available from Deccan Air (The Landmark, 385 Galle Road, Colombo; tel: 0777 703 703; www.deccanhelicopters.com). This is a charter service, hence the cost is quite high. Expect to pay US$2,000 per charter to the south coast, US$2,500 to the Cultural Triangle for up to four passengers.

ACCOMMODATION

HOTELS, YOUTH HOSTELS, BED AND BREAKFAST

Where to Stay

There's a huge range of accommodation in Sri Lanka, from basic family guesthouses offering a handful of simple fan rooms through to five-star palaces and dozens of alluring boutique hideaways, often in magical beachside or rural locations.

In the main tourist areas, budget travellers will find plenty of inexpensive guesthouses, most of them family-run. The best places offer comfortable lodgings, good home cooking and the chance to rub shoulders with the owners, grab some insights into local life and enjoy the kind of spontaneous hospitality which you won't find in more upmarket places. Rooms in most guesthouses come with attached bathroom, fan and (except in part of the hill country) mosquito nets; some also offer air-conditioned rooms and hot water.

Mid-range hotels are relatively thinner on the ground, although again all the main tourist centres boast a decent selection of places halfway between the island's simple guesthouses and the fancier hotels. These include traditional government Rest Houses, many of which have now been attractively upgraded, but which often preserve something of their former colonial ambience.

Large-scale four- and five-star hotels can be found throughout the country. Many are clustered along the west and south coasts, and there are also a few upmarket city hotels, plus hill-country and Cultural Triangle resorts. These generally offer stylish rooms and a good array of facilities including pool, restaurants and bars, and often an Ayurveda centre or spa.

A beguiling alternative to the mainstream five-stars is offered by the island's burgeoning number of boutique hotels, usually with fewer than 20 rooms and often in marvellous natural settings – remote stretches of beach, idyllic tea plantations and the like. These offer visitors the chance to sample contemporary Sri Lankan style at its most memorable, with superb design, an intimate atmosphere and top-notch cuisine – equal to anything available anywhere in Asia, although at predictably expensive rates. Many boutique hotels occupy suave contemporary buildings, usually following the tropical-modernist template established by Geoffrey Bawa, although some can be found in restored colonial-era coastal and hill-country villas, offering an atmospheric taste of colonial Ceylon complete with all its period trappings.

An alternative (sometimes cheaper) to the island's boutique hotels is provided by the numerous private villas (a kind of Sri Lankan equivalent of the French *gîte*) which have sprung up in recent years. Many of these are found along the south coast around Galle, Unawatuna and Tangalla, and there's a further selection in the hill country, many of them in restored colonial-era tea planters' bungalow. Properties are too numerous to list here. For a good idea of what's available see www.villasinsrilanka.com, www.boutiquesrilanka.com or www.reddottours.com.

Hotel Chains

Surprisingly few of the major international hotel chains are represented in Sri Lanka. Colombo boasts a Hilton, Taj and Ramada – and that's pretty much it. The island's main hotel chains are all locally owned, although quality and service are generally of international standards, as indeed are prices. The big three are **Jetwing Hotels** (tel: 94 11 234 5700; www.jetwinghotels.com), **Aitken Spence** (tel: 94 11 2 308 308; www.aitkenspence.com), who operate a number of hotels under the "Heritance" brand, and **John Keells** (tel: 94 11 230 6600; www.johnkeellshotels.com), who operate hotels under the "Chaaya" and "Cinnamon" brands. Other leading local operators include **Amaya Resorts** (www.amayaresorts.com), **Tangerine** (www.tangerinehotels.com) and **Serendib** (www.serendibleisure.com).

Making a Reservation

Despite the continual opening of new hotels and guesthouses, Sri Lanka still struggles to accommodate the increasingly large number of visitors flocking to the island, and in popular tourist destinations from November to March, rooms can be in very short supply indeed (although from April to October things are much quieter). If travelling during peak season it's well worth booking ahead – and if you particularly want to stay in a particular hotel or guesthouse, try to book at least a month ahead. Many places now have online reservation systems, while smaller hotels and guesthouses usually (but not always) accept reservations by phone or email even if you haven't paid a deposit – although they may not hold a room for you later than 4–5pm. If you do arrive somewhere without a reservation, it generally pays to avoid the suggestions of touts and tuktuk drivers, who will either be trying to flog substandard accommodation or take you to a place where they get commission – which will then be added to your bill.

Recommended agencies for hotel bookings are: **Boutique Sri Lanka** (tel: 94 11 269 9213, www.boutiquesrilanka.com), **Red Dot Tours** (tel: 94 11 789 5810, www.reddottours.com) and **Sri Lanka In Style** (tel: 94 11 239 6666, www.srilankainstyle.com). Major Colombo hotels also have representatives in the arrivals section of the airport.

Rates

Sri Lanka is no longer the bargain it once was, and nowadays it's difficult to find any sort of accommodation for under $20 a night – while more upmarket hotels can easily top $200. Cheaper places quote prices in rupees, although more expensive places usually give rates in dollars (while along the west coast you might also occasionally see room rates quoted in euros).

Room rates vary tremendously throughout the year depending on the season and your bargaining skills. The rates indicated in the listings below are for peak season, from November through to March, although prices may drop as much as 50 percent from April to September/October.

Wherever you're going, it pays to be aware of taxes. The government curries levies around 17 percent in a range of taxes on hotel rooms, while many places also add a 10 percent service charge. Cheaper places usually quote a "net" rate inclusive of all taxes, although more upmarket places may not. Check in advance to see what is and isn't included in the quoted prices – an extra 27 percent added to your bill at the end of your stay in an exclusive boutique hotel may come as an unexpected, and not entirely pleasant, surprise.

COLOMBO

Casa Colombo
231 Galle Road, Colombo 4
Tel: 011 452 0130
www.casacolombo.com
Colombo's funkiest place to stay, occupying a patrician old colonial mansion which has been given a hip makeover with lots of quirky modern touches – watch out for the pink pool and glass sun beds. Each of the 12 individually designed suites comes equipped with all mod cons and latest high-tech gadgets, such as iPod docking stations. **$$$$**

Cinnamon Grand
77 Galle Rd, Colombo 3
Tel: 011 243 7437
www.cinnamonhotels.com
Colombo's grandest hotel, with plenty of five-star glitz and style, although rates are surprisingly affordable. In-house facilities include the city's best selection of restaurants and the lovely Angsana Spa, while rooms are attractively furnished, and come with great views over downtown Colombo. **$$$$**

Galle Face Hotel
Galle Face Green, Colombo 3
Tel: 011 254 1010
www.gallefacehotel.com
Famous old colonial landmark in a peerless position on the oceanfront at the southern end of Galle Face Green. The hotel has bags of atmosphere, although rooms in the old wing are a bit musty and old-fashioned; those in the more modern Regency Wing combine stylish modern comforts with colonial grace. There's also a fine spa, and the hotel's seafacing terrace is the best spot for a romantic cocktail or evening meal. **$$$$**

Havelock Place Bungalow
6 Havelock Place, Colombo 5
Tel: 011 258 5191
www.havelockbungalow.com
Peaceful, low-key hideaway tucked away in the southern city in a pair of stylishly converted colonial bungalows which combine period character and modern comforts. **$$$$**

Lake Lodge
Alvis Terrace, Colombo 3
Tel: 011 232 6443
www.taruhotels.com
Long-running Slave Island guesthouse which has recently been given a cool contemporary makeover by leading Sri Lankan designer Taru. Scores highly for it stylish rooms and central but peaceful location – and rates are surprisingly inexpensive. **$$$**

Ramada
30 Sir Mohamed Macan Markar Mawatha, Colombo 3
Tel: 011 242 2001
www.ramadacolombo.com
In an excellent location just off Galle Face Green, this pleasantly self-effacing hotel (formerly the Holiday Inn) makes an appealing, cheaper alternative to the nearby five-stars, with comfortable and good-value rooms. There's a fine North Indian restaurant on site, and all the facilities of the Galle Face Hotel and Cinnamon Grand are just a couple of minutes' walk away. **$$$**

Hotel Renuka & Renuka City Hotel
328 Galle Road, Colombo 3
Tel: 011 257 3598
www.renukahotel.com
Functional and comfortable business-oriented hotel on the Galle Road, conveniently central for the southern suburbs, although road noise can be intrusive – get a room at the back, if possible. There's also a small swimming pool, while the Palmyrah restaurant is known for its excellent Sri Lankan cuisine, including Jaffna-style specialities. **$$**

Taj Samudra
Galle Face Green, Colombo 3
Tel: 011 244 6622
www.tajhotels.com
One of the top hotels in Colombo, with an excellent location right on Galle Face Green, sweeping public areas and a selection of excellent restaurants (including the Navratna, perhaps the best North Indian restaurant in the country). More expensive rooms have superb views across Galle Face Green and the ocean; facilities include a health club and squash and tennis courts. **$$$$**

BELOW: Presidential Suite at the Taj Samudra.

Tintagel
65 Rosmead Place, Colombo 7
Tel: 011 460 2121
www.paradiseroadhotels.com
Luxurious boutique hotel
occupying the atmospheric
colonial mansion which was
formerly the family home of
the Bandaranaike family,
who have provided Sri
Lanka with three prime ministers since Independence.
Accommodation is in one of
ten gorgeous suites, while
facilities include a picture-
perfect little infinity pool and

a very chichi in-house restaurant and bar. **$$$$$**

Mount Lavinia

Ivory Inn
21 De Saram Road
Tel: 011 271 5006
Email: ivoryinn@hotmail.com
One of Mount Lavinia's
best budget guesthouses,
in a pleasant modern red-
brick building on a quiet
side road. Accommodation
in attractively furnished
rooms with private balcony.
$$

Mount Lavinia Hotel
100 Hotel Road
Tel: 011 271 1711
www.mountlaviniahotel.com
One of Sri Lanka's most
famous old hotels, this
sprawling white landmark
grew up around a 19th-cen-
tury governor's love nest.
Modern extensions have all
but swallowed up the origi-
nal mansion, but the hotel
retains enough colonial
touches to set it apart from
the run-of-the-mill west-
coast resorts. The superb

stretch of private beach and
seafront restaurant are also
major bonuses. **$$$$**
Rivi Ras Hotel
50 De Saram Road
Tel: 011 271 7786
www.rivirashotel.com
Attractive, laid-back estab-
lishment occupying a
sequence of detached red-
brick buildings set amidst
spacious gardens. Rooms
(with or without air condi-
tioning) are large and styl-
ishly furnished in
quasi-colonial style. **$$$**

THE WEST COAST

Ahungalla

Heritance Ahungalla
Galle Road
Tel: 091 555 5000
www.heritancehotels.com
Nestled amid a sea of palm
trees, this luxurious Geoffrey
Bawa-designed five-star is
large but cleverly laid-out to
preserve a sense of inti-
macy, with interlinked buildings backing a huge infinity
pool which seems to blend
magically with the sea. **$$$$**

Aluthgama

Anushka River Inn
97 River Avenue
Tel: 034 227 5377
www.anushka-river-inn.com
Pleasant, modern guest-
house built right out over
the waters of the beautiful
Bentota Lagoon. Rooms (all
with air conditioning) are
simple but comfortable, and
the food is excellent. **$$**
Hemadan
25 River Avenue
Tel: 034 227 5320,
www.hemadan.dk
The most characterful
accommodation in
Aluthgama, this appealing
little guesthouse has simple
but comfortable rooms in a
pleasant white building with
an attractive little garden
running down to the Bentota
Lagoon – a beautiful spot.
There is a free boat service
over to the quiet stretch of
beach. Excellent value. **$$**

Ambalangoda

Sumudu Guest House
418 Main Street

Tel: 091 225 8832
Set in a beautiful colonial
villa just behind the two
mask museums, this lovely
little guesthouse is a great
place to escape the west-
coast tourist hordes, with
cheap, comfortable rooms
(one with air conditioning), a
welcoming family atmos-
phere and excellent home
cooking. **$**

Balapitiya

The River House
70 Uthamanyana Mawathe
Tel: 011 576 9500
www.theriverhouse-balapitiya.
com
Delectable hideaway by Sri
Lanka's star designer, Taru.
The house occupies a won-
derful, wildlife-rich location
beside the Madhu River in
Balapitiya, with accommo-
dation in five large suites in
a superb contemporary/
colonial-style villa. **$$$$$**

Bentota

**Avani Bentota Resort &
Spa**
Tel: 034 494 7878
www.serendibleisure.com
Serene resort (formerly
known as the Serendib
Hotel) set in a low, elegant
white building on a pleasantly wide stretch of
Bentota beach. The whole
place has recently been
given a stylish upgrade, with
beautifully refurbished
rooms and a fancy spa,
although the atmosphere
remains pleasantly laid-
back compared to the

busier resorts further up the
coast. **$$$$$**
Club Villa
138/15 Galle Road
Tel: 034 227 5312
www.club-villa.com
One of Sri Lanka's most
attractive boutique hotels,
set in a cluster of gorgeous
Geoffrey Bawa-designed
colonial-style buildings
behind a garden running
down to the beach. The
place manages to combine
style and luxury with a
pleasantly informal atmosphere – a perfect place to
kill a few days lolling around
in the sun and filling up on
the hotel's excellent cooking. **$$$$**
Paradise Road The Villa
Galle Rd
Tel: 034 227 5311
www.paradiseroadhotels.com
Alluring bolt-hole, occupying
the superb Mohotti
Walauwe, a fine old colo-
nial-era mansion which was
restyled by Geoffrey Bawa in
the 1970s and has now
been given another makeo-
ver by Paradise Road style-
guru Shanth Fernando. The
whole place is a model of
stylish intimacy, with chic
but comfortable rooms, a
gorgeous pool and lovely
gardens running down to
the sea. **$$$$**
Saman Villas
Aturuwella
Tel: 034 227 5435
www.samanvilla.com
Ultra-luxurious boutique
hotel superbly situated on
the headland dividing

Bentota and Induruwa
beaches, with wonderful
views in either direction and
a superb infinity pool built at
the edge of the bluff, which
seems to hover in mid-air.
Rooms, within individual
chalets, lack the style of
other places nearby but
come equipped with every
conceivable mod con.
There's also a fabulous spa,
exquisitely designed in
quasi-Japanese style. **$$$$$**
Shangri-Lanka Villa
23 De Alwis Road, Horanduwa
Tel: 034 227 1181
www.shangrilankavilla.com
Tucked away in a lovely garden with pool, this tiny "boutique guesthouse" has just
three rooms, offering a
peaceful hideaway and
great value in a very wel-
coming atmosphere. **$$**
Susantha Hotel
National Holiday Resort
Tel: 034 227 5324
Reliable budget option, just
behind the railway station
and a very short walk from
the beach, with pleasant,
simple rooms (some with air
conditioning) around a
shady central courtyard. **$$**
Vivanta by Taj
National Holiday Resort

PRICE CATEGORIES

Price categories are for a
double room, no breakfast:

$ = under $30
$$ = $30–60
$$$ = $60–120
$$$$ = $120–200
$$$$$ = more than $200

Tel: 034 555 5555
www.vivantabytaj.com
Huge hotel (formerly the Taj Exotica) set in self-conscious isolation on a headland just south of the railway station. It's luxurious and stylish if a bit over-the-top for the setting, though the location is quiet and the beach beautiful. **$$$$$**

Beruwala

Barberyn Reef Ayurveda Resort
Tel: 034 227 6036
www.barberynresorts.com
One of the island's oldest Ayurveda hotels, set at the quieter northern end of Beruwala beach, and offers a range of treatment options and stress-soothing settings amidst lush oceanfront gardens and pleasantly low-key surroundings. Rates are very reasonable compared with fancier Ayurveda centres elsewhere along the west coast. **$$$$**

Hikkaduwa

Aditya
Rathgama
Tel: 091 226 7708
www.aditya-resort.com
Tucked away on a wide stretch of beach just south of Hikkaduwa, this luxurious and elegant boutique hotel offers 12 individually designed rooms and suites, each with its own plunge pool. Service is impeccable, and the food absolutely mouth-watering. **$$$$$**
Asian Jewel
Baddegama Road

Tel: 091 493 1388
www.asian-jewel.com
A real gem of a boutique hotel, set on the shores of panoramic Bird Lake just a few minutes inland from Hikkaduwa. Rooms are decorated in colonial style and set amidst beautiful gardens, and the food is top notch. **$$$$**
Kalla Bongo Lake Resort
22/8K Field View,
Baddegama Road
Tel: 091 438 3234
www.kallabongo.com
Overlooking the tranquil Bird Lake, this upmarket Dutch-owned 15-room hotel offers bright and airy lodgings with minimalist modern design and private balconies overlooking the lagoon – all at surprisingly affordable rates. **$$$**
Neela's Guest House
634 Galle Road
Tel: 091 438 3166
www.neelasguesthouse.com
One of the longest established and most popular cheapies in Hikkaduwa, Neela's offers comfortable, newly renovated rooms at bargain prices, plus good home cooking and a friendly family atmosphere. **$**
Suite Lanka
Galle Road, Thiranagama
Tel: 091 227 7136
www.suite-lanka.com
Quaint boutique hotel at the quiet southern end of Hikkaduwa, next to a broad and peaceful swathe of beach. The six spacious rooms come with either a garden terrace or balcony,

and are all neatly kitted with colonial-style furniture and four-poster beds. **$$$$**

Induruwa

Temple Tree Resort & Spa
660 Galle Road
Tel: 034 227 0700
www.templetreeresortandspa.com
Very chic designer hotel, set in a tranquil oceanfront garden filled with temple trees (frangipani). Accommodation is in huge, airy rooms with very classy tropical-minimalist decor, and facilities include a nice pool with built-in jacuzzi plus a good spa. **$$$$$**

Kalpitiya

Bar Reef Resort (formerly the Alankuda Beach Resort)
Alankuda Beach
Tel: 0777 352 200
www.barreefresort.com
The centrepiece of a marvellous little cluster of low-key, eco-oriented boutique resorts which has sprung up on Alankuda Beach over the past few years. The whole place is rather like a rustic, but very stylish, Sinhalese village, with accommodation in a handful of mud-brick cabanas and a couple of larger villas, all gorgeously designed. A stunning infinity pool runs down to the unspoilt beach, surrounded by a trio of traditional ambalama-style pavilions, while dolphin-watching trips and world-class kite-surfing are also right on the doorstep. The sister establishment, Palagama, next door, is very similar and equally beautiful (complete with funky thatched wooden cabanas), while Dolphin Beach, a short walk further down the sands, offers further accommodation in a string of beautifully appointed Rajasthani-style tents. See www.alankuda.com for full details. **$$$$**

Kalutara

Avani Kalutara Resort & Spa
Kalutara South
Tel: 034 494 0077

www.serendibleisure.com
Stylish resort hotel superbly situated on the headland dividing the Kalutara Lagoon and the ocean, with fine views over the town to one side, and with the beach directly on the other. Rooms are elegantly furnished in minimalist style, and there's an attractive spa attached. **$$$$**
Royal Palms Beach Hotel
Kalutara North
Tel: 034 222 8113
www.tangerinehotels.com
One of Kalutara's more upmarket options, with imposing modern accommodation blocks adorned with plant-filled balconies and an enormous pool which meanders halfway around the hotel. Facilities include a gym, tennis court and the Ayurveda centre at the adjacent Tangerine Beach Hotel. It's all very pleasant and comfortable, though rather lacking in style, given the hefty room rates. **$$$$$**

Negombo

Icebear Hotel
103 Lewis Place
Tel: 031 223 3862
www.icebearhotel.com
Sociable and good-value little Swiss-owned guesthouse. Rooms are attractively furnished in mock-colonial style and there's plenty of space for idle lounging in the lovely beachfront garden. **$$**
Jetwing Ayurveda Pavilions
Tel: 031 227 6719
www.jetwinghotels.com
Beautifully intimate little boutique Ayurveda hotel, with a range of courses and treatments and an army of therapists on hand to purge your system and balance your *doshas* (although you can also stay here without taking any treatments if you like). Accommodation is in beautiful self-contained bungalows with private garden, each discreetly hidden behind high ochre walls. **$$$$$**
Jetwing Beach
Tel: 031 227 3500
www.jetwinghotels.com

BELOW: waiting for trade at Negombo harbour.

Negombo's only five-star hotel, on a pleasant strip of beach at the northern end of the resort area, with superbly designed rooms, elegantly furnished with lots of dark wood, crisp white sheets and beautiful glass-walled bathrooms. There's also excellent food and a big pool. **$$$$$**
Ranweli Holiday Village
Waikkal
Tel: 031 227 7359

www.ranweli.com
Charmingly rustic, eco-friendly resort in a wonderfully unspoilt rural setting between the beach and the old Dutch canal, about 10km (6 miles) north of Negombo. Activities include birdwatching with the resident naturalist, boat trips on the canal and cycle tours. **$$$**
Silver Sands
229 Lewis Place

Tel: 031 222 2880
www.silversands.go2lk.com
Excellent, long-established budget hotel near the southern end of Negombo beach. The atmosphere is friendly and relaxing, with a good little restaurant, pleasant garden and simple, cheap rooms. **$**

Wadduwa

The Blue Water
Thalpitiya, Wadduwa

Tel: 038 223 5067
www.bluewatersrilanka.com
Large and serenely minimalist Geoffrey Bawa-designed five-star on a quiet stretch of beach in suburban Wadduwa – the location feels surprisingly sylvan, despite the proximity to Colombo. There's also a gorgeous modern spa, and the swimming pool, picturesquely dotted with coconut palms, is a stunner. **$$$$**

THE SOUTH COAST

Ahangama

South Point Villa
133 KM Post, Kathaluwa
Tel: 077 303 9404
www.southpointvilla.com
A spacious three-bedroom villa in a 560-sq-metre (6,000-sq-ft) garden, South Point Villa offers luxurious privacy along the golden beach of Kathaluwa. The exceptionally huge rooms are elegantly designed with a blend of modern and colonial furniture. Nearby, the sister property, South Point Abbey, offers similar comfort and style. **$$$$$**

Galle

Amangalla
10 Church Street, Galle Fort
Tel: 091 222 3388
www.amanresorts.com
Occupying the sensitively restored premises of Galle's famous old New Oriental Hotel, this establishment remains wonderfully faithful to the period character of its colonial predecessor, combining old-world colonial chic with the last word in contemporary luxury – a compelling combination, though at a considerable price. **$$$$$**
Beach Haven
65 Lighthouse Street
Tel: 091 223 4663
www.beachhaven-galle.com
This perennially popular guesthouse seems to have been going for ever and continues to pull in visitors thanks to its cheap and comfortable rooms, tasty home cooking and its unique friendly and sociable

family atmosphere. **$**
Closenberg Hotel
Galle Harbour
Tel: 091 222 4313
www.closenburghotel.com
Time-warped old hotel in a palatial white villa of 1858, with antique-furnished rooms and a beach-view extension. Public areas are full of period charm, while meals are served next to the exotic Fernery gazebo. **$$$$**
The Fort Printers
39 Pedlar Street, Galle Fort
Tel: 091 224 7977
www.thefortprinters.com
Characterful boutique hotel in the very heart of old Galle, occupying the barn-like building which formerly housed the town's printing shop. The hotel's five suites are little museum-pieces of Dutch colonial architecture, with creaking wooden floors and high beamed ceilings, the rather austere effect relieved by a generous dash of colourful fabrics and artworks. **$$$$**
Galle Fort Hotel
28 Church Street
Tel: 091 223 2870
www.galleforthotel.com
Stunning hotel set in a magnificently converted old Dutch warehouse – like the nearby Amangalla, it manages to combine colonial charm and contemporary luxury, though at a far more affordable price. It also dishes up some of Sri Lanka's best foreign cuisine, with a predominantly Southeast Asian slant – a pleasant change if you have

had one too many rice and curries. **$$$$$**
Jetwing Lighthouse
Dadalla
Tel: 091 222 3744
www.jetwinghotels.com
Set on a breezy stretch of seafront a couple of kilometres outside Galle, this Geoffrey Bawa-designed hotel is one of the great Sri Lankan architect's defining creations, with a simple, serene exterior, gorgeously designed rooms and splashes of local colour (such as the remarkable quirky wrought-iron staircase depicting the Portuguese arrival in Sri Lanka). Excellent food and heaps of facilities too. **$$$$$**
The Sun House
18 Upper Dickson Road
Tel: 091 438 0275
www.thesunhouse.com
This long-established boutique guesthouse is still one of the nicest places to stay in Sri Lanka, set in a beautiful old 19th-century planter's villa on a hill high above Galle, with oodles of period charm and memorable cooking. The adjacent Dutch House offers a slightly more upmarket variation on the same theme, with four huge suites in another historic colonial mansion. **$$$$$**

Koggala

The Fortress
Tel: 091 438 9400
www.thefortress.lk
One of the south's most luxurious and expensive hotels, this striking five-star resort is designed

to resemble a supersized version of one of Galle's old colonial-era Dutch villas, magnificently framed between superbly landscaped grounds, a vast infinity pool and the sea. The opulent rooms boast all mod cons, while facilities include a top-notch spa and several excellent restaurants. **$$$$$**
Kahanda Kanda
Angulugaha (near Koggala)
Tel: 091 228 6717
www.kahandakanda.com
Set in a 4-hectare (10-acre) tea estate, perched high above the magnificent Koggala Lake, this is one of the most memorable villa-style boutique hotels in the island. The luxurious, ethnic-style interior design has scooped numerous awards and the superb Thai and Sri Lankan food is worth the trip in its own right. **$$$$$**

Mirissa

Mandara Resort
Tel: 041 225 3993
www.mandararesort.com
Nestled along the estuary of Pollathu Modara River, this chic, rather minimalist modern hotel comes with 20 individually designed suites with all mod cons in a lovely

PRICE CATEGORIES

Price categories are for a double room, no breakfast:

$ = under $30
$$ = $30–60
$$$ = $60–120
$$$$ = $120–200
$$$$$ = more than $200

peaceful position at the quiet eastern end of Weligama Bay. **$$$$$**

Palace Mirissa
Tel: 041 225 1303
www.palacemirissa.com
The most upmarket option close to Mirissa beach, on a high bluff overlooking the sea with sweeping views. Accommodation is in spacious and comfortable bungalows set amidst a lush tropical garden, colourfully decorated with hand-painted ceilings. **$$$**

Villa Sea View
Mirissa
Tel: 07760 46653
Low-key and good-value guesthouse a short, sharp walk up from the beach, with fine views over the sands below. Rooms are spacious and clean, and there's good home-cooked Sri Lankan food. **$**

Tangalle

The Colony
355 Mahawella Road
Tel: 047 224 2770
www.thecolonysrilanka.com
Beautifully restored 1910s British bungalow, furnished with antiques and with excellent food. **$$$$**

Mangrove Beach Cabanas
Tel : 0777 906 018
www.beachcabana.lk
Laid-back guesthouse occupying enviably quiet beach location, with spacious wooden cabanas nestled amidst lush gardens. Free canoes are available to explore the adjacent lagoon, and there are also turtle watches some nights. The equally attractive Mangrove Chalets, a sister establishment slightly further down the beach, follows a similar theme. **$$**

Talalla

Talalla Retreat
Talalla South, Gandara
Tel: 041 225 9171
www.talallaretreat.com
Founded and operated by yoga teachers Laurie Rose and Louisa Sear, this secluded boutique hotel is predominantly themed as a retreat focusing on yoga and surfing – an unusual but appealing combination.

Accommodation is in bright and breezy rooms in two-storey villas scattered around beautifully landscaped gardens, and there's also a fine pool, plus spa and beauty treatment centre. **$$$$**

Thalpe

Apa Villa
78 M.S. Matara Road
Tel: 091 228 3320
www.villa-srilanka.com
Stylish villa with seven spacious suites facing a stunning infinity pool and the ocean. Apa's sister property Illuketia, set amidst 4 hectares (10 acres) of botanical wonderland, is a perfect hideaway for nature-lovers. Food at both properties, featuring organic veg from Illuketia, is also top notch. **$$$$$**

The Frangipani Tree
812 Matara Road
Tel: 091 228 3711
www.thefrangipanitree.com
One of the ever-growing string of svelte boutique hotels lining the coast around Thalpe, this elegant beach sanctuary offers 10 exquisitely decorated suites in four separate villas bisected by a beautiful pool running down to the sea. **$$$$$**

Unawatuna

Secret Garden
Yaddhehimulla Road
Tel: 091 224 1857
www.secretgardenunawatuna.com
Tucked away in its own lush walled garden, central and close to the beach but also very peaceful, and offering a quiet retreat from the bustling village outside. Rooms are set either in the attractive main colonial villa or in the garden bungalow outside, and there's also a pretty little dome for yoga and meditation. **$$**

Thaproban
Tel: 091 438 1722
www.thambapannileisure.com
Poking up from the centre of Unawatuna like an eccentric orange lighthouse, this unusual-looking hotel has bright and cheery rooms right above the beach, and one of

the village's best restaurants. **$$$**

Thambapanni Retreat
Tel: 091 223 4588
www.thambapannileisure.com
Set a few minutes' walk from the beach, up against the lush, jungle-covered flanks of Rumassala (the huge rocky outcrop behind Unawatuna village), this place has more the atmosphere of a rainforest eco-lodge than a beach hotel. Rooms are comfortable, with neo-colonial furnishings and all mod cons, with a small pool. **$$$$**

Kandy

Amaya Hills
Heerassagala
Tel: 081 447 4022
www.amayaresorts.com
Large pink hotel perched way up in the hills a few kilometres outside Kandy. The setting is gorgeous and the comfortable rooms are cheerfully furnished with colourful Kandyan-style touches. There's also a swimming pool (though it can get chilly up here), and an attractive spa. **$$$$**

Earl's Regency
Tennekumbura
Tel: 081 242 2122
www.aitkenspencehotels.com/earls
This large and swanky five-star hotel about 4km (2.5 miles) outside Kandy has a beautiful scenic setting by the Mahaweli Ganga, although the whole place sometimes seems a bit over the top and out of proportion with its rural setting. Rooms are plush and the service is tip-top, while facilities include a swimming pool, gym, health and Ayurveda centre. **$$$$$**

Helga's Folly
Off Mahamaya Mawatha
Tel: 081 447 4314
www.helgasfolly.com
Marvellously maverick hotel, set in a glorious position high above Kandy. The interior is like a kind of eccentric museum, filled with huge quantities of bric-a-brac ranging from animal heads and colonial photos to Indonesian puppets and huge candles covered in

clumps of solidified wax. All rooms are individually decorated with colourful murals. The lack of facilities (apart from a very shallow swimming pool) and absence of package tourists are all part of the charm. **$$$$–$$$$$**

Hunas Falls by Amaya
Elkaduwa, 27km (16.5 miles) north of Kandy
Tel: 081 494 0320
www.amayaresorts.com
Located in a sublime position 27km (17 miles) north of Kandy up in the rugged hills of the Knuckles range, this eco-oriented retreat is one of the nicest of the many hotels around Kandy, with comfortable modern facilities, a stunning setting and plenty of walks and wildlife in the surrounding countryside. **$$$$**

The Kandy House
Amunugama Walauwa, Gunnepana
Tel: 081 492 1394
www.thekandyhouse.com
One of the island's most magical boutique hotels, occupying a wonderfully atmospheric old traditional manor house tucked away in peaceful countryside 5km (3 miles) from Kandy. Rooms are beautifully furnished in traditional style, and there's good food and a picture-perfect little infinity swimming pool in the lovely landscaped gardens. **$$$$$**

Sharon Inn
59 Saranankara Road
Tel: 081 220 1400
www.hotelsharoninn.com
Neat, modern and very professionally run guesthouse with comfortable rooms, excellent food and superb views over the lake and town from its hillside setting. **$$**

Hotel Suisse
30 Sangaraja Mawatha
Tel: 081 222 2637
www.hotelsuissekandy.com
Long-established lakeside hotel (Mountbatten had his wartime headquarters here) with spacious and very comfortable rooms and a quietly understated old-fashioned colonial charm, complete with cosy bar and a fine billiards room. Excellent value. **$$$**

THE HILL COUNTRY

Bandarawela

The Bandarawela Hotel
14 Welimada Road
Tel: 057 222 2501
www.aitkenspencehotels.com/bandarawela
Atmospheric colonial-style hotel set in a 19th-century planters' club house. The rambling old wooden building is full of character, and rooms have bags of old-world ambience – all at a very reasonable price. **$$$**

Ella

Ambiente
Off Bandarawela Road, Ella Village
Tel: 057 222 8867
www.ambiente.lk
Spectacularly set on a hill high above the village, with sweeping views of Ella Gap and Little Ravana Falls. Rooms are modern and simple, though on the small side, and the food is good. **$$**

Mountain Heavens Hotel
Tel: 057 492 5757
www.mountainheavensella.com
One of the highest guest-houses in Ella, more than 900 metres (3,000ft) above sea level and offering spectacular views over Ella Gap. Rooms are bright, comfortable and clean. **$$**

The Planter's Bungalow
Wellawaya Road
Tel: 057 492 5902
www.plantersbungalow.com
Set in a gorgeous rural location 10km (6 miles) south of Ella, Planter's Bungalow offers a winning combination of contemporary comfort with a dash of colonial style. Accommodation is in three stylish rooms in the main building – a superbly restored 19th-century tea planter's bungalow – plus one cottage in the garden

outside, and there's also authentic hill country-style Sri Lankan food, including enormous breakfasts. Room rates are remarkably low given the quality. **$$$**

Waterfalls Homestay
Kithalella
Tel: 057 567 6933
www.waterfalls-guesthouse-ella.com
As the name suggests, this place is more like a homestay than a conventional guest house, tucked away just outside Ella village in an idyllic location facing Little Rawana Ella Falls. The atmosphere is very peaceful and intimate, with just three rooms (including one triple/family room), comfortably and colourfully furnished, and communal meals served in the kitchen-cum-dining room or on the lovely terrace outside. **$$**

Haputale

Kelbourne Mountain View Cottages
Tel: 011 257 3382
www.kelburnemountainview.com
Beguiling little retreat, set in a wonderful location on a lush escarpment among tea plantations, with plunging view over the hills below. Accommodation is in three pretty colonial-style cottages, all comfortably furnished and with attentive personalised service. **$$$$**

Kandapola

Heritance Tea Factory
Tel: 052 222 9600
www.aitkenspencehotels.com/teafactory
One of Sri Lanka's most ingenious hotels, occupying a converted tea factory – the exterior has been perfectly preserved but the interior

ABOVE: the Amaya Hills, perched in the hills.

magically transformed into a sleek, modern five-star hotel, combining futuristic architectural lines with lots of old tea-making memorabilia. The amazing setting is another major draw, high up in one of the most spectacular parts of the Nuwara Eliya region and surrounded by many kilometres of tea plantations. **$$$$$**

Rafter's Retreat
Tel: 036 228 7598
www.raftersretreat.com
Basic but characterful little eco-resort, with ten cabanas, made entirely from natural materials, buried in dense forest alongside the Kelani River. No frills, but a great place for hiking and white-water rafting. **$$**

Nuwara Eliya

Glendower
Grand Hotel Road
Tel: 052 222 2501
Email: hotelglendower@sltnet.lk
Small and extremely cosy little hotel set in a distinctive old colonial property with fake half-timbering in a leafy setting by the golf course. Rooms are neat and clean, and there's a welcoming bar, an excellent Chinese restaurant and a roaring log fire in the lounge. **$$$$**

Grand Hotel
Grand Hotel Road
Tel: 052 222 2881

www.tangerinehotels.com
This huge old colonial hotel is one of Nuwara Eliya's major landmarks. The imposing exterior and time-warped public areas are a superb reminder of Victorian times, although the rooms themselves disappointingly ordinary, and expensive at current rates. **$$$$$**

Hill Club
Off Grand Hotel Road
Tel: 052 222 2653
www.hillclubsrilanka.net
Set in a venerable old building close to the town centre, this famous hotel offers a real taste of colonial Ceylon. The nostalgic interior features a musty billiards room, two cosy bars and an atmospheric restaurant, plus assorted stuffed stags' heads and cracked leather furniture. Accommodation is in neat, slightly chintzy rooms with creaking wood floors. **$$$$**

Jetwing St Andrews
10 St Andrew's Drive
Tel: 052 222 3031
www.jetwinghotels.com
Nuwara Eliya's smartest hotel, occupying a beautiful colonial country club surrounded by graceful lawns running down to the golf course. The oak-panelled bar and restaurant are pure Edwardian period pieces, while rooms are cosy and comfortable. **$$$$**

THE CULTURAL TRIANGLE

Anamaduwa

The Mud House
Anamaduwa
Tel: 07730 16191
www.themudhouse.lk
This seductive dry zone

jungle retreat is situated in one of the country's undiscovered beauty spots, surrounded by abundant wildlife. Despite being made entirely out of

mud and other natural materials, rooms are very comfortable, and good, organic Sri Lankan food is also available. **$$$$**

TRANSPORT

ACCOMMODATION

EATING OUT

ACTIVITIES

A – Z

LANGUAGE

Anuradhapura

Milano Tourist Rest
J.R. Jaya Mawatha
Tel: 025 222 2364
www.milanotouristrest.com
One of the best budget hotels in the Cultural Triangle, offering a wide range of attractively furnished and competitively priced modern rooms, with or without air conditioning, plus a good attached restaurant. **$**

Palm Garden Village Hotel
Puttalam Road, Pandulagama
Tel: 025 222 3961
www.palmgardenvillage.com
Anuradhapura's smartest option, 2 kilometres (1.25 miles) from the ruins, with elegantly furnished colonial-style rooms and the largest swimming pool in the Cultural Triangle. **$$$$**

Tissawewa Grand Old Town
Tel: 025 222 2299
www.quickshaws.com
The most memorable place to stay in Anuradhapura, this marvellously atmospheric old colonial rest house has lots of period charm and an unbeatable location right at the heart of the old ruined city – the only place to stay in Anuradhapura actually inside the Sacred Precinct (though this also means that no alcohol is served). **$$$$**

Dambulla

Amaya Lake
Kap Ela, Kandalama
Tel: 066 446 8100
www.amayaresorts.com
Set in a beautiful location close to the shores of Kandalama Lake, with comfortable accommodation in individual air-conditioned chalets or eco-friendly mud huts. **$$$$**

Heritance Kandalama Hotel
Tel: 066 228 4100
www.aitkenspencetravels.com
One of Sri Lanka's most original hotels, this Bawa-designed establishment offers the ultimate marriage of architecture and nature, clinging to the side of a rocky outcrop and almost completely buried by layers of tropical vegetation. Stunning views of Sigiriya and Kandalama Lake, plush modern rooms, and one of the island's most spectacular swimming pools all add to the allure. **$$$$$**

Giritale

The Deer Park Hotel
Tel: 027 224 6272
Tranquil eco-resort discretely buried away amidst tropical jungle close to the Minneriya National Park. Accommodation is in stylish individual chalets dotted around beautiful wooded grounds, and there's also a nice pool and Ayurveda centre. **$$$$**

Habarana

Chaaya Village
Tel: 066 227 0047
www.chaayahotels.com
Resort-style hotel spread across extensive grounds running down to the beautiful Habarana Lake. Accommodation is in pleasant individual chalets, and there's also the excellent Asmara Indonesian spa in which to unwind. **$$$$**

The Lodge
Tel: 066 227 0012
www.cinnamonhotels.com
Located in the crossroads town of Habarana, and

ABOVE: keeping it eco-friendly at the Vil Uyana.

conveniently placed for day trips to all the Cultural Triangle's major sites (if you bring your own car), this is one of the nicest places to stay in the Cultural Triangle, with plush accommodation in individual villas scattered around extensive and beautiful tree-shaded grounds. **$$$$$**

Sigiriya

Elephant Corridor Hotel
Kibissa
Tel: 066 228 6950
www.elephantcorridor.com
Very exclusive boutique hotel sprawling across 80 hectares (200 acres) of unfenced natural scrubland with superb views of nearby Sigiriya. The 21 luxurious suites come with private plunge pools and every imaginable mod con and there's also an alluring spa, although the whole place comes with a very hefty price tag. **$$$$$**

Jetwing Vil Uyana
Tel: 066 228 6000
www.jetwinghotels.com
The Cultural Triangle's most memorable place to stay – and a remarkable experiment in eco-friendly tourist development. Vil Uyana is a marvellous oasis, wonderfully tranquil and rich in birdlife and other natural attractions. Accommodation is in individual chalets modelled on traditional Sinhalese village architecture but luxuriously appointed inside with all mod cons, while the main building, with restaurant, bar, spa and library, is contemporary Sri Lankan design at its most stunning. **$$$$$**

Hotel Sigiriya
Tel: 066 223 1940
www.serendibleisure.com.
Long-running resort-style hotel, occupying an attractive scatter of traditional red-tiled buildings dotted around sprawling, shady grounds. Rooms are stylishly furnished, while amenities and activities include an Ayurveda centre and swimming pool with fine views of the rock, plus rewarding nature walks with the resident naturalist. Excellent value. **$$$**

THE EAST

Trincomalee

Welcombe Hotel
66 Lower Road,
Orr's Hill
Tel: 026 222 2378
www.welcombehotel.com
Trinco's top hotel is in a superb setting on a bluff above Trincomalee harbour. The quirky modern building, topped with recycled railway sleepers, is attractive, and rooms spacious and comfortable. There's also a decent restaurant, bar and big pool. **$$$**

Arugam Bay

Aloha Cabanas
Tel: 063 224 8379
www.aloha-arugambay.com
Long-established favourite with the surfing crowd, the Aloha has a beautiful garden with cabanas, a tree house and scattered hammocks in which to while away a few hours when not riding the waves. **$$**

Arugambay Surf Resort
Tel: 063 224 8189
www.arugambay.lk
One of Arugam Bay's longest-running and best-value guesthouses (known until

recently as the Arugambay Hillton until forced to change its name by the American hotel chain). Bright rooms decorated in cheerful colours overlook a small beachfront garden, and there's also a good restaurant and a wide range of local tours and activities. **$$**

Hideaway
Tel: 063 224 8259
www.hideawayarugambay.com
The nicest place to stay in Arugam Bay (even if it's not actually on the beach), with stylish rooms either in the attractive main building or in the handful of modern cabanas and air-conditioned rooms in the lush gardens outside. **$$$**

Siam View Beach Hotel
Tel: 063 222 8195
www.arugam.com
Attached to the landmark Siam View Restaurant (the best in the village), complete with red British telephone box. Rooms are modern and spacious, and come with air conditioning, free Wi-fi, satellite TV and fridge. **$$$**

Stardust Beach Hotel
Tel: 065 224 8191
www.arugambay.com
Arugam Bay's most upmarket option, right on the beach and with bright and very comfortable modern rooms (plus a few quirky wooden cabanas), a good restaurant and open-air yoga pavilion. **$$**

Batticaloa

Riviera Resort
New Dutch Bar Road, Kallady
Tel: 065 222 2164
www.riviera-online.com
Well-run hotel, popular with visiting NGO staff, with simple but clean and comfortable rooms and chalets (with and without air conditioning) set amidst attractive grounds alongside the Batticaloa Lagoon. **$-$$$**

Nilaveli

Nilaveli Beach Hotel
Tel: 026 223 2295
www.tangerinehotels.com
Large but extremely peaceful resort hotel on a huge swathe of beach, comprehensively modernised following major tsunami damage. Rooms are excellent value (and the slightly more expensive deluxe rooms are soothingly stylish) and there's a fine pool and attractive seafront restaurant. **$$$**

Uppuveli

Chaaya Blue
Sampaltive Post
Tel: 026 222 1611
www.chaayahotels.com
This sprawling five-star resort hotel (formerly known as the Hotel Club Oceanic) is the major landmark along the coast north of Trincomalee. Recently refurbished, it now offers stylish rooms, a good spread of facilities and a fine stretch of unspoilt beach, although rates are steep. Also has a dive school and is a good place to arrange whale-watching trips even if you're not staying here. **$$$$$**

Regish French Garden
Nilaveli Road
Tel: 026 220 0397
Long-running guesthouse (known for many years as the Pragash French Garden) offering basic, inexpensive accommodation in a superb beachside location. **$**

THE NORTH

Jaffna

Expo Pavilion
40 Kandy Rd
Tel: 021 222 3790
www.expopavilion.com
The most stylish place to stay in Jaffna, in an attractive colonial-style villa with sleekly furnished modern rooms and an attractive little restaurant, although rather pricey for what you get. **$$$**

Lux Etoiles
34 Chetty Street Lane
Tel: 021 222 3966
www.luxetoiles.com
Professionally run hotel in a quiet side road near the Nallur Kandaswamy Temple. Rooms are well equipped with a/c, hot water and satelite TV, and there's the added bonus of Jaffna's biggest swimming pool. **$$$**

Morgan's Guest House
215 Temple Rd
Tel: 021 222 3666
Long-running guesthouse, popular with NGO workers, set in an attractive old colonial villa close to the landmark Nallur Temple. The comfortable rooms all come with air conditioning and hot water, and the owner has his own vehicle for tours of the city and surrounding area. **$$**

Tilko Jaffna City Hotel
70/6 KKS Rd
Tel: 021 222 5969
www.tilkojaffna.com
The biggest hotel in town, spread over two large buildings around a swathe of lawn set back from the road. Accommodation is in spacious and rather plush rooms, and facilities are the best in town, with restaurant, bar, gym and a simple spa (but no pool). **$$$**

PLANTATIONS AND TEA BREAKS

A stay on a plantation makes for an unusual insight into Sri Lanka's agricultural heritage. It is best, though not vital, to book well ahead as they are popular. Contact the following:

Horathapola Estate
Kandanagedara, inland from Negombo, west coast
Tel: 071 533 8230
www.horathapola.com
Comfortable boutique hotel occupying an old British plantation owner's villa, set in glorious gardens and with an inviting swimming pool. Wonderful meals using local produce are rustled up by the friendly staff. **$$$$$**

Kirchhayn Bungalow
Attampitiya Rd, Bandarawela
Tel: 057 492 0556
www.kirchhaynbungalow.com
Characterful old tea plantation bungalow owned by the last remaining British planting family in Sri Lanka. The interior has been sensitively and luxuriously restored, and there are beautiful walks through the surrounding tea gardens. **$$$$**

The Lavendar House
Helboda Estate, Katukitula, Pussellawa
Tel: 052 225 9928
www.thelavenderhouseceylon.com
Luxurious hill country escape occupying a painstakingly restored former tea-planter's bungalow set in 3 hectares (7 acres) of beautifully tended gardens, tucked away between lush tea plantations. **$$$$$**

Tea Trails
Tel: 011 230 3888
www.teatrails.com
Four beautiful tea estate bungalows (the Norwood, Castlereagh, Summerville and Tientsin) in the idyllic Bogawantalawa Valley area south of Nuwara Eliya. **$$$$$**

PRICE CATEGORIES

Price categories are for a double room, no breakfast:

$ = under $30
$$ = $30–60
$$$ = $60–120
$$$$ = $120–200
$$$$$ = more than $200

EATING OUT

RECOMMENDED RESTAURANTS, CAFES AND BARS

WHAT TO EAT

Sri Lankan cuisine has its own distinctive and delicious blend of flavours based on local ingredients, complemented over the centuries with Indian, Chinese, Malay, Arab and European influences. If you want to learn more about what goes into the making of the island's cuisine – or fancy trying to re-create it at home – pick up a copy of *Exotic Tastes of Sri Lanka* by Suharshini Seneviratne or *Sri Lankan Flavours: A Journey Through the Island's Food and Culture* by Channa Dassanayaka, both of which are stuffed with tempting recipes.

Rice and Curry

Many Sri Lankans will eat rice and curry three times a day. It can be made with meat, fish or vegetables and flavoured with a heady blend of spices including chillies, cinnamon, lemon grass, curry leaves, coriander, cumin, saffron, tamarind and coconut. Have a go at eating rice and curry with your fingers – watch the locals to pick up some tips.

Snacks

While in Sri Lanka, don't forget to try the sweetmeats and indigenous snack food, most famous of which are stringhoppers (*appas*) and egghoppers (*idi appas*). "Short eats" are savoury bite-sized pastries or rolls, which can be quick, easy and fun – try them with a dash of *sambol* (a red hot combination of grated coconut, chilli and spice) if you really want to set your mouth on fire. Short eats such as rolls (fried pancakes with a beef, fish, chicken or vegetable filling), cutlets,

ABOVE: curries can be served for every meal of the day.

patties, pastries and more are widely available in all local eateries.

Delicious Desserts

If you still have room for dessert after your rice and curry, go for a cup of curd topped with treacle, or try *wattalapam* – a rich pudding made with *jaggery* (a kind of fudge made from *kitul* treacle).

Festive Dishes

Sri Lanka does not have its equivalent of the Christmas turkey or similar festive dish enjoyed during an extended dinner. However, on the Sinhala/Tamil New Year, other auspicious days or as an offering to monks, *kiribhat* ("milk rice", using coconut milk) is prepared. Cut into diamond-shaped pieces, *kiribhat* is served with a fiery mixture of onions and spices, or bananas and *jaggery* for breakfast.

Drinking

Imported beverages (wines, spirits and beers) are relatively pricey, although there's a decent range of less expensive local beers – or try an authentic Sri Lankan cocktail made with arrack. Among the non-alcoholic beverages, a fresh *thambili* (coconut milk) is certainly the healthiest and least expensive. *Thambili* is sold along the roadside and on the beach. Another local speciality is ginger beer, a wonderfully refreshing soft drink with a very unusual taste.

WHERE TO EAT

Outside Colombo, there are relatively few good independent restaurants; you'll probably eat in your hotel or guesthouse, virtually all of which offer food of some sort, ranging from bland international-style buffets to excellent traditional home cooking. Many of the island's best restaurants are located in top-end hotels, some of which offer excellent cooking in luxurious surroundings. At the other end of the spectrum you'll sometimes find excellent home cooking at relatively modest little guesthouses – a great chance to enjoy proper Sri Lankan home cooking at bargain prices.

Sri Lankans themselves mainly eat in the unpretentious little cafés (often called "hotels") which you'll find on the main street of every town in the country. These usually serve up a basic range of food, usually a simple rice and curry plus short eats; some also do kottu rotty in the evenings – listen for the distinctive sound of cleavers hitting grill pans as the food is enthusiastically chopped – while others may do hoppers. Street food isn't nearly as big a deal here as in India, although you'll sometimes see roving hawkers selling vadais or other snacks from wheeled food carts or walking up and down the aisles of buses selling spicy peanuts or similar to the passengers on board.

COLOMBO

Alhambra
Ramada, 30 Sir Mohamed Macan Markar Mawatha, Colombo 3
Tel: 011 242 2001
One of the capital's longest-established North Indian restaurants, with a dependable range of standards – birianis, tandooris and the like – plus a few vegetarian and South Indian dishes served in a cosy setting. **$$**

Barefoot Gallery and Café
706 Galle Road, Colombo 3
Tel: 011 258 9305
Recover from the almost inevitable shopping spree at Barefoot in the soothing courtyard café at the back, where you'll find the best fruit juices in town plus a tempting selection of tasty light meals, snacks, salads and cakes. **$$**

Chesa Swiss
3 Deal Place A, Colombo 3
Tel: 011 257 3433
One of the best restaurants in Colombo, set in a charming colonial villa and offering a sumptuously prepared range of Swiss food, Australian steaks, seafood and vegetarian dishes. Dinner only. Closed Sun lunchtime. **$$$$**

Chutneys
Cinnamon Grand Hotel, Galle Rd, Colombo 3
Tel: 011 249 7372.
Chic South Indian restaurant with a very original twist, serving up little-known regional dishes and street food from India's four southernmost states – Kerala, Tamil Nadu, Andhra Pradesh and Karnataka. There's a particularly good vegetarian selection, plus meat and seafood mains, all bursting with chilli, tamarind and coconut flavours, served up on traditional metal plates and accompanied by authentically fiery chutneys. Excellent value. Open evenings only. **$$$**

Crescat Boulevard
89 Galle Road, Colombo 3
The lively food court in the basement of this smart shopping mall is crammed full of stalls selling everything from pizza and ice cream to Sri Lankan and Mongolian specialities. A fun place for lunch. **$$**

Cricket Club
34 Queen's Road, Colombo 3
Tel: 011 250 1384
Eternally popular cricket-themed bar-café-restaurant in an old colonial villa. Watch videos of famous matches and ogle the memorabilia plastered all over the walls whilst tucking into one of the café's well-prepared international standards – burgers, sandwiches, pasta dishes and the like. **$$$**

Curry Leaf
Hilton, Sir Chittampalam A. Gardiner Mw, Colombo 1
Tel: 011 249 1000
Rustic restaurant in the gardens of the Hilton hotel, built to resemble a kind of traditional jungle village. The design is a bit cheesy, but the nightly buffet offers an excellent introduction to the full range of Sri Lankan cuisine – rice and curry, string hoppers, hoppers, kottu rotty, wattalapan, plus fresh seafood. **$$$$**

Emperor's Wok
Colombo Hilton, 2 Sir Chittampalam A. Gardiner Mawatha, Colombo 2
Tel: 011 254 4644
Grand dining, Chinese style, with glittery decor and an excellent choice of authentic Sichuan cuisine, Peking duck, special barbecue pork dishes and dim sum. **$$$$**

Gallery Café (Paradise Road)
2 Alfred House Road, Colombo 3
Tel: 011 255 3075
Colombo's smartest café, and definitely one of the places to be seen, with a good range of international cuisine and what are claimed to be the capital's best desserts. Or just come for a drink and the chance to watch Colombo's smart set at play. **$$$$**

Green Cabin
453 Galle Road, Colombo 3
Tel: 011 228 8811
Excellent little Sri Lankan café, patronised mainly by locals but an ideal place for tourists to test drive the local cuisine. Good range of rice and curry, *lamprais* and hoppers. Bargain prices. **$**

Greenlands Hotel
3/A Shrubbery Gardens, Colombo 4
Tel: 011 258 1986
The most famous South Indian café in town, this unpretentious local institution churns out a fabulous range of *dosas*, *idlis*, *vadais* and curries, all at giveaway prices. **$**

The Lagoon
Cinnamon Grand Hotel, 77 Galle Rd, Colombo 3.
Tel: 011 249 7371
Colombo's smartest seafood venue, in a bright, modern restaurant next to the Cinnamon Grand's attractive gardens. Choose your fish or seafood from the magnificent display of the latest catch, after which it will be delivered to the chef and prepared in a style of your choosing – anything from Sri Lankan and Indian to European, Thai or Chinese. **$$$$**

Long Feng
Cinnamon Lakeside Hotel,

BELOW: fresh seafood is always a delicious option.

PRICE CATEGORIES

Price categories are per person for a two course meal:

$ = under 750 Rupees
$$ = 750–1,500 Rupees
$$$ = 1,500–2,000 Rupees
$$$$ = over 2,500 Rupees

115 Sir Chittampalam A. Gardiner Mawatha, Colombo 2
Tel: 011 249 1053
One of the city's top Chinese restaurants, this classy establishment specialises in authentic Sichuan cooking, with a few more mainstream Cantonese dishes too. **$$$**

Mango Tree
82 Dharmapala Mawatha, Colombo 3
Tel: 011 762 0620
Very popular upmarket North Indian restaurant with chic decor and reliably good, authentic Indian cuisine. Reservations advisable. **$$$**

Navaratna
Taj Samudra, 25 Galle Face Centre Road, Colombo 3
Tel: 011 244 6622
Arguably Sri Lanka's best Indian restaurant, specialising in unusual regional specialities from around the subcontinent. **$$$$**

Nihonbashi
11 Galle Face Terrace, Colombo 3
Highly rated Japanese food. There are further outlets at Odel and at Hilton Colombo Residence. **$$$$**

Royal Thai
Cinnamon Lakeside Hotel, 115 Sir Chittampalam A. Gardiner Mawatha, Colombo 2
Tel: 011 249 1000
Beautiful little Thai restaurant buried away in the Cinnamon Lakeside Hotel. The exquisite decor is matched by an excellent selection of fiery-flavoured Thai dishes, including standards like green and red curries, pad thai, and more unusual regional specialities. **$$$**

Tao
Cinnamon Grand Hotel, 7 Galle Rd,
Colombo 3
Tel: 011 249 7369
Set in the gardens of the Cinnamon Grand, whose trees twinkle magically with fairy lights after dark, Tao dishes up fine fusion cuisine blending Sri Lankan traditions with Asian and European influences. Mains range from seafood and meat standards to more innovative creations, like the combination plate of red curry chicken, grilled lamb chops and spiced tiger prawns. Open evenings only. **$$$$**

THE WEST AND SOUTH COASTS

Aluthgama

Singharaja Bakery & Restaurant
120 Galle Road
Spacious café serving tasty Sri Lankan snacks and European-style cakes on the ground floor, and a good rice and curry buffet upstairs. **$**

Tropical Anushka River Inn
97 Riverside Road
Tel: 034 227 5377
Excellent rice and curry plus seafood at this unpretentious little guesthouse tucked away at the back of Aluthgama. There are superb lagoon views from the restaurant, which is cantilevered out over the water. **$$**

Bentota

Club Villa
138/15 Galle Road, at the southern end of Bentota.
Tel: 034 227 5312
Even if you're not staying here, it's worth visiting this excellent little hotel for a chance to soak up the atmosphere and savour the well-prepared and very modestly priced international cuisine in the beautiful garden restaurant. **$$$**

Lunuganga
Dedduwa Lake
Tel: 091 428 7056
The bumpy 5km (3-mile) ride off the main road in Bentota to reach Lunuganga is well worth the effort to experience the island's most magical garden retreat, the spiritual home and country estate of renowned architect, Geoffrey Bawa. Cuisine focuses on the sort of Sri Lankan home cooking that Bawa himself enjoyed, using fresh, seasonal ingredients. Reservations are obligatory. See www.lunuganga.com for full details. **$$$$**

Malli's
Opposite The Surf Hotel
Tel: 0778 514 894
Hidden upstairs above a line of shops by the railway tracks, this unexpectedly upmarket little restaurant specialises in sophisticated Sri Lankan and Asian-style seafood and other creations (including good rice and curry) with a hint of fusion inventiveness – think pan-fried mahi-mahi with rösti and saffron sauce, for example. **$$$$**

Negombo

Alta Italia
36 Porutota Road
Tel: 031 227 9206
Pleasant, informal restaurant offering workmanlike Italian cuisine at low prices: dishes include gnocchi, polenta, lasagne, risotto and lots of pasta options, plus Italian desserts. **$$**

Bijou
44 Porutota Road
Tel: 031 531 9577
Arguably Negombo's best independent restaurant, this Swiss-owned establishment has a cosy pine interior and an excellently prepared selection of Swiss–Italian dishes (fondues, pasta and so on), plus excellent seafood. **$$$**

King Coconut
11 Porutota Road
Tel: 031 227 8043
Lively beachside restaurant known for its relaxed atmosphere and big selection of fresh seafood plus rice and curry at affordable prices. **$$**

Lords
80B Porutota Road
Tel: 0777 234 721
Attractive modern café-cum-restaurant serving up tasty and beautifully presented cuisine from around the world, although Asian flavours predominate – anything from Thai curries and chicken tikka masala through to mushroom, cashew and raisin curry. **$$$**

Tuskers
83 Ethukala Road
Tel: 031 222 6999
Smart new restaurant in an attractive open-sided pavilion just off the main tourist drag (but carefully screened from it). The menu focuses on a small but excellently prepared range of mainly European-style meat and fish dishes (and pasta) along with a few Sri Lankan- and Chinese-style mains. **$$$**

Hikkaduwa

Asian Jewel
Baddegama Road
Tel: 091 493 1388
Eclectic but excellently prepared range of Western or Asian cuisine – anything from the house speciality, shepherd's pie, through to Thai chicken curry. **$$$**

Refresh
Galle Road, Wewala
One of the West Coast's longest-running restaurants, with a romantic dining room running down to the sea and an enormous menu offering all sorts of Sri Lankan and international dishes. It remains popular, although food can be hit and miss. **$$$**

Spaghetti & Co.
644 Galle Road
Soothing Italian-owned garden restaurant offering up some of Sri Lanka's best pizza and pasta at very reasonable prices. **$$**

THE SOUTH

Galle

Amangalla
10 Church Street,
Galle Fort
Tel: 091 223 3388
This gracious old colonial-style dining room at the superb Amangalla Hotel is one of the most memorable places to eat in the south. Delicious light meals and soups are rustled up for lunch, while dinner features a mix of superb Sri Lankan and international cuisine. Alternatively (and less expensively), come for a superior high tea on the hotel's open verandah. **$$$$**

Galle Fort Hotel
28 Church Street, Galle Fort
Tel: 091 223 2870
The superb Galle Fort Hotel's memorable courtyard provides a suitably stylish home for Sri Lanka's best fusion cuisine, full of the bright, strong flavours of Southeast Asia. There's also a snack menu available at lunchtime featuring delectable light meals, plus homemade cakes in the afternoon, accompanied by fine coffee. **$$$$**

Pedlar's Inn Café
92 Pedlar Street
Small informal café with delicious snacks, juices, coffee and tea served on a verandah. Brilliant spot for a break while watching the life of Galle Fort pass by. **$**

Serendipity Arts Café
Leyn Baan Street
Popular and funky little café serving up all sorts of breakfasts, plus sandwiches, wraps, cakes and a short selection of international mains with a mostly Asian twist. Unlicensed. **$$**

Unawatuna

Thaproban Beach House
Yaddhehimulla Road
Tel: 091 438 1722
Unawatuna's smartest and liveliest restaurant offers consistently good cooking including fresh seafood, above-average pizzas, rice and curry and a smattering of international dishes. Service comes with a big smile and prices are very reasonable. **$$–$$$**

Thalpe

Apa Villa Illuketia
Thalpe, near Galle
Tel: 091 228 3320
One of the few private villas to open its doors to non-resident dinner guests. The three-course rice and curry dinner prepared with organically grown vegetables and red rice from their own grounds has a reputation that extends beyond Galle, and the lemon grass soup is to die for. Reservations are a must. **$$$**

Why House
Mihiripenna, Thalpe,
Galle
Tel: 091 222 7599
Hidden away behind large gates just 10 minutes from Galle (look for the big "WB" next to the gate), the Why House offers superb fusion cuisine in a pristine setting and immaculate surroundings. Reservations recommended. **$$$$**

Wijaya Beach Restaurant
Dalawela, Galle
Tel: 091 228 3610
This cool beachfront restaurant is a particular favourite with the Galle expat set and usually gets packed out from lunchtime onwards. Food includes excellent wood-fired pizzas, plus daily specials, wraps and homemade puddings, and there's a good drinks list including cocktails, wine and Sol beer. **$$$**

KANDY AND THE HILL COUNTRY

Kandy

Devon Restaurant
Dalada Vidiya
This functional modern restaurant is always busy with locals and tourists alike thanks to its cheap, tasty and unpretentious food, including birianis, *lamprais*, noodles, devilled dishes, and lots more, plus tasty hoppers at breakfast. **$**

Flower Song
Kotugodelle Vidiya
Tel: 081 222 3628
One of the island's best Chinese restaurants outside of Colombo, dishing up a big selection of tasty Cantonese-style mains. **$$**

The Pub
Dalada Vidiya
Tel: 081 232 4868
Catering mostly to tourists, The Pub makes a nice change from rice and curry if you fancy some spaghetti carbonara or pork chops. The balcony is a good place to have a beer and watch the hustle and bustle of Dalada Vidiya below. **$$$**

Sharon Inn
59 Saranankara Road
Tel: 081 222 2416.
The nightly rice and curry buffet (daily at 7.30pm) at the Sharon Inn guesthouse is one of the best in the island, featuring a fine spread of 15 or so dishes with the emphasis on unusual local vegetables which you'll not have tasted before. Non-guests should reserve in advance by 4pm latest. **$$$**

The White House
Dalada Vidiya
Long-established restaurant, recently given a thorough upgrade and makeover. Downstairs there's now a chic modern bakery with assorted cakes and short eats, plus rice and curry lunch-time buffets. Upstairs, a rather sedate dining room features a mix of Sri Lankan, Indian and Chinese mains along with pasta, seafood and steaks. Unlicensed. **$$$**

Nuwara Eliya

The Hill Club
Off Grand Hotel Drive
Tel: 052 222 2653
The famous dinners here offer a real taste of the colonial life of yesteryear. The food itself is average, but the time-warped atmosphere, with dinner served promptly at 8pm by white-gloved waiters in the chintzy dining room, is strangely romantic, although decidedly formal – men are only admitted if clad in the obligatory jacket and tie (available on loan free at the club if you don't have your own). **$$$$**

King Prawn
Glendower Hotel, 5 Grand Hotel Road
Good and relatively authentic Chinese food at the cosy restaurant of the Glendower Hotel, with plenty of spice to keep the hill country chills at bay. **$$**

Old Course Restaurant
St Andrew's Hotel
10 St Andrew's Drive,
Nuwara Eliya
Tel: 052 222 2445
Old fashioned wood-panelled restaurant with a cosy atmosphere and plenty of hearty Anglo-European meat dishes (plus a few fish and vegetarian options), plus a huge range of wines in the walk-in cellar. **$$$**

Ella

Dream Café
Main Street
Easily the best – and best-looking – of Ella's

PRICE CATEGORIES

Price categories are per person for a two course meal:

$ = under 750 Rupees
$$ = 750–1,500 Rupees
$$$ = 1,500–2,000 Rupees
$$$$ = over 2,500 Rupees

innumerable backpacker cafés, arranged around an attractive courtyard area, plus indoor seating too. Standards of cooking are high, and cover plenty of culinary bases, ranging from rice and curry through to pasta, burgers, wraps and salads, and the best pizza in the hill country. Also does good breakfasts, both Western and Sri Lankan. **$$$**

Ravana Heights
Wellawaya Road
Tel: 057 222 8888
Good Thai food served in this friendly little guest-house. Non-guests should book for dinner by 4pm. **$$**

THE EAST

Trincomalee

Green Park Beach Hotel
312 Dyke Street
Tel: 026 222 2369
Well-run hotel restaurant offering a vast selection of menus of North Indian food including all the usual meat, fish and vegetable classics in huge portions. Meals are served either in the sedate dining room or, come the evening, on the attractive first-floor water-front terrace. Unlicensed. **$$**

Welcombe Hotel
66 Lower Road,
Orr's Hill
Tel: 026 222 2373
The smartest restaurant in Trinco (although still rela-tively inexpensive), serving up a mix of the usual Sri Lankan standards plus a few European mains. Sit either on the beautiful outdoor terrace high above the Inner Harbour or the dining room inside. **$$**

Uppuveli
Palm Beach Resort,
Uppuveli Beach
Tel: 026 222 1250
Authentic Mediterranean cuisine at this friendly Italian-run beachfront guesthouse restaurant. **$$**

Arugam Bay

Gecko
Neat little place serving up good, healthy café fare including sandwiches (with home-made bread), home-made ice cream and cakes, all-day breakfasts, burgers, salads and pasta dishes, plus rice and curry and Sri Lankan breakfasts (most mains Rs.700–900), washed down with tasty sugar-free juices and Fairtrade coffee. You can also refill used water bottles here, saving money and plastic. Daily 6.30am until late in season, reduced opening hours at other times. **$$**

Siam View Hotel
Tel: 063 224 8195
Long-running and deserv-edly popular restaurant, set in a distinctive wooden pavilion-style building with a red British telephone box standing sentry outside. Food is mainly Thai (although they also sometimes do some non-Thai dishes in high sea-son), with a range of deli-cious and authentic classics, excellently pre-pared. The German owner also does a superb range of home-brewed beers from his basement microbrewery. **$$$**

Stardust Beach Hotel
Tel: 063 224 8191
One of Arugam Bay's more upmarket places to eat, set in an attractive pavilion restaurant next to the beach. Food comprises a varied and well-prepared selection of snacks, breakfasts and mains ranging from rice and curry through to pasta and goulash. **$$$**

THE NORTH

Jaffna

Bastian Hotel
Kandy Road
Tel: 026 222 2605
Sociable restaurant on a breezy upstairs terrace (ignore the noisy drinking den below), popular with NGOs and other Western visitors. Food is usually just a few simple rice and noo-dle dishes, although there's always a good supply of freshly chilled beer. **$**

Cosy
15 Sirambiyadi Lane
Reliable place offering a vast selection of North Indian meat and vegetable dishes (plus assorted Chinese offerings) including speciality tandoori meat dishes and breads (eve-nings only), prepared in the restaurant's own tandoor oven. Unlicensed. **$$**

Malayan Café
36–38 Grand Bazaar
A memorable slice of old Jaffna, with bargain South Indian-style thalis served up on glossy banana leaves in an atmospheric old wood-panelled dining room, heavy with the smell of incense. **$**

Rio's Ice Cream
Behind the Nallur Kandaswamy Temple
One of the best of Jaffna's numerous ice-cream par-lours serving up big helpings of colourful ice cream in unusual flavours. **$**

BELOW: the freshest of ingredients make all the difference.

PRICE CATEGORIES

Price categories are per person for a two course meal:

$ = under 750 Rupees
$$ = 750–1,500 Rupees
$$$ = 1,500–2,000 Rupees
$$$$ = over 2,500 Rupees

ACTIVITIES

FESTIVALS, THE ARTS, NIGHTLIFE, SHOPPING AND SPECTATOR SPORTS

There's a huge range of contrasting activities to keep you busy during a visit to Sri Lanka – a reflection of the island's enormous physical and cultural diversity. The island is particularly rich in natural attractions, as befits a place which is reckoned to be the most biodiverse area for its size anywhere in the world. A well-developed system of national parks boasts wildlife aplenty, along with superb birdwatching, while the coastal waters have recently established themselves as one of the globe's finest whale-watching destinations. There are also plenty of adventure activities and sports to get stuck into: heart-pounding whitewater rafting trips, magical balloon rides, some of Asia's best surf, extensive diving possibilities and numerous water sports – not to mention the island's consuming passion: cricket. Arts, shopping and nightlife still tend to be concentrated mainly in Colombo, which has an interesting selection of shops and a reasonably healthy roster of cultural events, while Galle is increasingly become a centre of culture and crafts, with a regular calendar of events centred on the globally successful Galle Literary Festival.

Major forthcoming events are listed on the tourist board's website at www.srilanka.travel. For Colombo listings, see www.whatsupcolombo.lk.

THE ARTS

Barefoot
706 Galle Road, Colombo 3
Tel: 011 250 5559
www.barefootgallery.com
Changing but always interesting exhibitions of art, sculpture and

photography in the beautiful courtyard area at the rear of this wonderful shop, which is something of an art gallery in its own right.
British Council
49 Alfred House Garden, Colombo 3
Tel: 011 452 1521
www.britishcouncil.org/srilanka
Organises a wide variety of dance and theatre performances as well as other artistic and cultural events both in Colombo and Kandy.
English Cinemas
Mainstream Hollywood and other English-language films are shown at the modern Majestic Cinema (tel: 011 258 1759), on Level 4 of the Majestic City shopping mall on Galle Road in Colombo 3. English-language blockbusters are also sometimes shown at Liberty Cinema (tel: 011 232 5265), at 35 Dharmapala Mawatha in Colombo 3, while the British Council occasionally screens arthouse movies.
Gallery Café

2 Alfred House Gardens, Colombo 3
Tel: 011 258 2162
www.paradiseroad.lk
The superb former offices of architect Geoffrey Bawa host occasional exhibitions by local artists and photographers.
Lional Wendt Theatre
18 Guildford Crescent, Colombo 7
Tel: 011 269 5794
Colombo's main performing arts venue also hosts occasional displays of photography and painting by local and international artists.
National Art Gallery
101 Ananda Coomaraswami Mawatha, Colombo 7
Tel: 011 269 3965
Open 8am–5pm daily except *Poyas*. Extensive selection of 20th-century Sri Lankan art and an array of portraits depicting Sri Lanka's Independence heroes and heads of state.
Sapumal Foundation
32/4 Barnes Place, Colombo 7

BELOW: statues and paintings at Anuradhapura.

ABOVE: an assortment of herbs used in Ayurvedic massage.

Tel: 011 269 5731
www.theserendibgallery.com/
sapu_found
Absorbing selection of Sri Lankan
visual arts from the 1920s to the
present, particularly focusing on work

by the artists of the 43 Groups.
Saskia Fernando Gallery
61 Dharmapala Mawatha, Colombo 7
Tel: 011 742 9010
www.saskiafernandogallery.com
State-of-the-art modern gallery

hosting shows by leading
contemporary Sri Lankan artists, or
international artists associated with
the island.
Serendib Gallery
36 1/1 Rosemead Place, Colombo 7

Ayurveda Resorts

A number of hotels and resorts cater
specifically to those coming to Sri
Lanka for Ayurvedic treatments, most
of them located along the west coast,
especially around Beruwala and
Bentota. Some of these are geared
up for long-stay visitors seeking
the alleviation of genuine medical
problems; others concentrate
more on "soft" Ayurveda, with the
emphasis on feel-good beauty and
de-stressing treatments. In addition
to the specialist clinics and resorts
listed below, many hotels and
guesthouses around the island have
in-house Ayurveda clinics.
Ayurveda Walauwa
Bentota
Tel: 034 227 5372
www.sribudhasa.com
Sedate and rather old-fashioned
Ayurveda resort occupying a fine old
colonial villa *(walauwe)* just behind
Bentota Beach. Moderate prices,
with the emphasis on serious long-
stay treatment programmes.
Barberyn Beach Ayurveda Resort
Weligama
Tel: 041 225 2994
www.barberyn.com
Offshoot of famous Beruwala
Barberyn Reef Resort *(see below)*,
with an unpretentious setting and a
mainly long-stay clientele.
Barberyn Reef Ayurveda Resort
Beruwala

Tel: 034 227 6036
www.barberyn.com
One of the oldest Ayurveda resorts
on the island, with a pleasantly low-
key atmosphere and a dedicated
clientele who come here for long-
stay treatments at very moderate
prices.
Lanka Princess
Beruwala
Tel: 034 227 6711
www.lankaprincess.com
Big, glitzy and expensive Ayurveda-
themed holiday resort with the
emphasis firmly on "soft" cosmetic
treatments.
Lotus Villa
Ahungalla
Tel: 091 226 4082
www.ayulotus.com
This beachside hotel was
established two decades ago by
its Austrian owner, and its targeted
Ayurvedic treatments are renowned
among those seeking alleviation
for serious health problems. A
minimum stay of two weeks is
recommended.
Paradise Island
Bentota
Tel: 034 227 5354
www.sribudhasa.com
Sister hotel to Ayurveda Walauwa,
with a low-key beachside
atmosphere and a mainly long-stay
clientele.

Shunyata Villa
660A Galle Road
Tel: 034 227 1944
www.shunyata-villa.net
Small and extremely tranquil
Ayurveda hotel on the quiet beach of
Induruwa.
**Siddhalepa Ayurveda Health
Resort**
Wadduwa
Tel: 038 229 6967
www.ayurvedaresort.com
Serious Ayurveda resort offering
medically oriented treatments
and run by Siddhalepa, who also
manufacture most of the island's
Ayurvedic medicines, including the
famous Siddhalepa Balm.
Suwa Madhu
Near Bandarawela
Tel: 057 222 2504
Small centre offering the standard
range of cosmetic Ayurveda
treatments at bargain prices. One
of the very few places that accepts
walk-in guests for individual
massages and treatments.
Wedamedura Ayurveda Centre
7 Mahamaya Mawatha, Kandy
Tel: 081 447 9484
www.ayurvedawedamedura.com
Basic Ayurveda centre offering A full
range of cosmetic treatments, plus
some longer-term programmes, all at
very reasonable prices.
Ayurvedic wrap.

Casinos

An alternative nightlife venue in Colombo is the city's five casinos, most of which stay open 24 hours. All offer roulette, blackjack and baccarat. Drinks and snacks are available free of charge to players, and some casinos may have buffet dinners and live music. Membership is in name only; anyone can sign in and play. All close on *Poya* days.

Bally's Club
14 Dharmapala Mawatha, Colombo 3
Tel: 011 233 2211
www.ballyscolombo.com

Bellagio
430 R.A. de Mel Mawatha, Colombo 3
Tel: 0755 88 66 88
www.bellagiocolombo.com

MGM Grand Casino
772 Galle Road, Colombo 4
Tel: 011 250 2268

Ritz Club
4 Galle Face Terrace, Colombo 3
Tel: 011 234 1496

Star Dust Club
9, 15th Lane, Galle Road, Colombo 3
Tel: 011 257 3493
www.stardustcasino.lk

Tel: 011 567 4578
Wide selection of Sri Lankan art, artefacts and books, from antiquity to the present day.

NIGHTLIFE

If you want raucous after-dark nightlife, Sri Lanka isn't the place to come. Only in Colombo will you find any kind of nightlife, and even this is incredibly modest for a city of around 3 million people.

Outside the capital, the island's only serious after-hours activity is at the tourist beaches of Negombo, Hikkaduwa and Unawatuna, all of which remain lively most nights until late as well as hosting occasional beach and full-moon parties.

In Colombo

Clancy's Irish Pub & Restaurant
29 Maitland Crescent, Colombo 7
Tel: 011 537 8017
There's nothing very Irish about this place, but it remains one of Colombo's most unpretentious and perennially popular drinking holes,

with regular live music and DJs, lots of pool tables and reasonable pub food.

Cricket Club Café
34 Queen's Road, Colombo 3
Tel: 011 250 1384
The cosy little Bradman's Bar at this popular café gets packed out most evenings with a mixed crowd of locals and expats.

H2O
447 Union Place, Colombo 2
Tel: 011 537 4444
The city's biggest and most state-of-the-art club, hosting Sri Lankan and international DJs and attracting a young Colombo crowd, who come to do their thing on the glass dance floor.

Kama
32B 1/1 Sir Mohamed Macan Markar Mawatha, Colombo 3
Tel: 011 233 9118
Sleek modern bar-restaurant with moody decor and Sri Lanka's first multicoloured laser lighting system. Attracts one of Colombo's posiest crowds, but don't expect much to be happening any time before 10pm.

The Library
Cinnamon Lakeside Hotel, 115 Sir Chittampalam A. Gardiner Mawatha, Colombo 2
Tel: 011 249 1000
This rather staid nightclub (it really is a library by day) attracts young professionals with its restrained music and atmosphere, although it can liven up a bit towards midnight. Entrance is technically limited to members and hotel guests, but tourists can usually blag their way in.

Rhythm and Blues Bar
Daily Villa Avenue, R.A. de Mel Mawatha (Duplication Road), Colombo 4
Tel: 011 536 3859
Long-established live music venue with acts most nights of the week.

Skky Bar
42 Sir Mohamed Macan Markar Mawatha, Colombo 3
Tel: 0775 523 316
Recently launched open-air rooftop bar on top of the AA Building just off Galle Face Green, Skky occupies one of Colombo's desirable nightlife spots (formerly occupied by the popular Tantra) with moody lighting, sultry music, a cool local crowd and a big list of cocktails and shots.

SHOPPING

What to Buy

Sri Lanka has a good range of shopping opportunities. Not

surprisingly, the biggest selection (and the funkiest outlets) are in Colombo, while Kandy is a stronghold of traditional Sinhalese arts and crafts and Galle offers a bit more choice.

Traditional artefacts and local souvenirs are perhaps the most obvious buys. Most eye-catching are the colourful kolam masks, carved from wood and usually showing pop-eyed, demonic-looking creatures. The main centre of production is in Ambalangoda, although they're sold in shops across the southern half of the island. Other carvings in sandalwood, ebony and other precious hardwoods are also common, ranging from traditional Buddha figures to stilt fishermen and endless elephants in every conceivable style. Leatherwork, lacquerware and metalwork all flourish in Sri Lanka as well and are widely available.

Tea is another popular buy. The best (and cheapest) selection can usually be found in local supermarkets such as Cargills, which usually carries a good and varied stock of local teas including rare unblended, single-estate teas. **The tea producer Mlesna** also runs a chain of specialist tea shops, selling fancy tea sets and gift-wrapped souvenir boxes. There are branches at the Colombo Hilton, Majestic City, and Colombo Hilton Residence, in Kandy City Centre in Kandy and at the airport. Spices are another good buy; again, the best place to buy is a local supermarket rather than one of the island's much touted spice gardens, where you'll pay at least five times as much for exactly the same thing.

Clothes can be another good buy. The island is a major garment-producing centre for Western

BELOW: Ayurvedic rub .

companies and seconds and overs for leading global brands can often be found at a fraction of their Western prices in shops like House of Fashions and Cotton Collection (although usually with their labels cut out). Locally designed fashions sold in shops like Odel, Barefoot and Cotton Collection are also a good and inexpensive buy. Designer "fakes" can also often be found in local markets – fine, so long as you're aware that the fantastically inexpensive CK jeans, Armani shirts and Tommy Hilfiger clothing you're buying aren't entirely kosher.

Gems are also good value in Sri Lanka, although you've a strong chance of being ripped off if you don't go to a reputable dealer. Read page 126, before purchasing any jewellery or gems.

Note that the export of "antiques" (defined as anything over 50 years old) and animal or marine products is illegal unless you can obtain the correct export licence; contact the tourist board for details.

Clothes

Arena
338 T.B. Jaya Mawatha, Colombo 10
Tel: 011 555 5338
Sri Lanka's high society shops in this leading store for designer clothing, accessories, shoes and bags. Arena also features a small eatery – the Fashion Café.
Barefoot
704 Galle Road, Colombo 3
Tel: 011 258 9305
www.barefootceylon.com
Exclusive range of stylishly simple

BELOW: the trendy Paradise Road Studio.

garments in vivid handwoven cottons and linens created by Sri Lankan artist and designer Barbara Sansoni, plus a wide selection of other gifts and an excellent bookshop. There's also a first-rate courtyard café and an interesting gallery in the courtyard at the rear. There's a second (smaller) Colombo branch in the Dutch Hospital in Fort, and another outlet at 41 Pedlar Street in Galle.
Cotton Collection
143 Dharmapala Mawatha, Colombo 7
www.cottoncollection.lk
Good range of funky and inexpensive clothes in bright colours, either part of Cotton Collection's own fashion label or heavily discounted surplus stock made locally for international brands. The sister Leather Collection store has a good range of bags, belts and other accessories. There are other branches in Colombo at 40 Flower Rd, Colombo 7; in Majestic City (see page 305); and in the Hilton Hotel, Colombo 1.
House of Fashions
R.A. de Mal Mawatha (Duplication Road), Colombo 4
This huge and enormously popular three-floor emporium acts as a clearing house for the Sri Lankan garment trade, selling off vast quantities of clothes intended for foreign labels at giveaway prices, although it can be a struggle finding anything that fits larger foreigners.
Odel
5 Alexandra Place, off De Soysa Circus (Lipton Circus), Colombo 7
Tel: 011 268 2712
www.odel.lk
Colombo's top department store, with an excellent selection of bargain designer clothing, as well as books, tea and knick-knacks. The store has now expanded across the island with numerous other branches. Other convenient stores can be found in Colombo at 38 Dickman's Road, Colombo 5; at **Majestic City** (see page 305); at Crescat Boulevard, Colombo 3; at 5 Hotel Road, Colombo 10; at the international airport; and on Level 3, Kandy City Centre, Kandy.

Gifts

Barefoot
704 Galle Road, Colombo 3
Tel: 011 258 9305
www.barefootceylon.com
In addition to its beautiful clothes (see above) this top Colombo shop uses its vibrant signature cottons to create a wonderful range of unusual cuddly toys, fabric-covered stationery and

Gems and Jewellery

Note that to export gems received as gifts, permits from the Controller of Exchange, Central Bank Colombo and the Controller of Imports and Exports, National Mutual Building, Chatham Street, Colombo 1, are required.
Colombo Jewellery Stores
1 Alfred House Gardens, Colombo 3
Tel: 011 259 7584
www.cjs.lk
Hemachandra Brothers
229 Galle Road, Colombo 3
Tel: 011 232 5147
Laksana
30 Hospital Street,
Galle
Tel: 091 381 8000
Sifani
Galle Face Hotel, Galle Face Green, Colombo 3
Tel: 011 239 5044
www.sifani.com
Also branches at the Galadari Hotel, Colombo 1, and 845 Peradeniya Road, Kandy
Zam Gems
81 Galle Road, Colombo 4
Tel: 011 258 9090
www.zamgems.com
Also branches at the Cinnamon Grand hotel, Colombo 3; 548 Peradeniya Road, Kandy; and other locations.

other collectables. Further branches in the Dutch Hospital, Colombo 1, and on Pedlar Street in Galle.
Laksala Handicraft Emporium
60 York Street, Colombo 1
Tel: 011 232 9247
The flagship store of the islandwide, government-run chain of handicraft shops. Spread over two floors, the place is stuffed with virtually every kind of Sri Lankan artefact imaginable, and offers a good overview of what's available around the island. Prices are low, although designs are stereotypical and quality is poor.
Paradise Road
213 Dharmapala Mawatha, Colombo 7
Tel: 011 268 6043
www.paradiseroad.lk
One of Colombo's most fashionable shopping haunts, this attractive little emporium has an appealing range of fancy household items, decorative knick-knacks and stylish souvenirs. There's a sister shop, The Gallery Shop, stocking similar stuff near The Gallery Café at 2 Alfred House Road, Colombo 3.

LUV SL
Dutch Hospital, Bank of Ceylon
Mawatha, Colombo 1
Tel: 011 244 8873
An offshoot of the Odel chain (see
above), selling a range of colourful
and unusual souvenirs, knick-knacks
and accessories. There's another
branch in the Queen's Hotel Building,
Dalada Vidiya, Kandy,

Books

Barefoot Bookshop
704 Galle Road, Colombo 3
Tel: 011 258 9305
www.barefoot.lk
The best bookshop in Colombo, with
a fascinating selection of titles –
everything from mainstream Western
blockbusters through to beautiful
coffee-table books, plus a huge range
of titles on Sri Lankan topics. There's
a second (smaller) Colombo branch
in the Dutch Hospital in Fort, and
another outlet at 41 Pedlar Street in
Galle.

Vijitha Yapa Bookshop
Unity Plaza, 376 Galle Road,
Colombo 3
Tel: 011 259 6960
www.vijithayapa.com
Sri Lanka's leading bookshop chain,
stocking a reasonable selection
of English-language novels and
non-fiction, plus a wide range of
Sri Lanka-related titles. There are
other branches in Colombo at
Crescat Boulevard (see below) and
32 Thurston Road, plus branches in
Negombo, Galle and Kandy.

Furniture

Olanda Furniture
30 Leyn Baan Street, Galle Fort
Tel: 0773 687 644
www.olandafurniture.com
Reproduction period furniture,
architectural artefacts and lamps. Will
ship overseas.

Sujeewa Arts & Reproductions
460 Galle Road, Ambalangoda
Tel: 091 225 7403
Wide range of antique artefacts and
colonial-style furniture. Custom-made
reproductions can be shipped to your
door.

Shopping Malls

Crescat Boulevard
Galle Road, Colombo 3
The city's smartest shopping mall,
with a series of swish outlets
including a Vijitha Yapa bookshop,
Mlesna tea shop, a Keells
supermarket, and an excellent

ABOVE: Unawatuna beach.

basement food court.

Majestic City
Galle Road
Bambalapitiya, Colombo 3
Large and (for Sri Lanka at least) glitzy
mall with lots of clothes and shoe
shops, a Cargills supermarket and the
city's best cinema.

SPORTS

For many Sri Lankans, there's only
one sport worth playing, watching
or talking about, and that's cricket.
The obsession with the exploits of
the national cricket team unites all
ages and classes (amongst men,
at least), with the leading players
inspiring an almost religious devotion
amongst their followers. Rugby is also
popular (particularly around Kandy),
while football, tennis and athletics
also attract a modest following.
Many sports clubs and associations
accept foreign visitors as temporary
members, while most major hotels
have swimming pools and tennis
courts.

Fishing

The Ceylon Anglers Club
Chatiya Road, Colombo 1
Tel: 011 239 5006
Accepts temporary members and can
provide much information on fishing
throughout the country.

The Ceylon Sea Anglers Club
China Bay, TrincomaleeTel: 011 257
3764
www.ceylonseaanglers.com

Deep-sea fishing, plus
accommodation.

Mirissa Water Sports
Mirissa Harbour
Tel: 077 359 7731
www.mirissawatersports.com
Sea trips for tuna, sailfish and other
large game fish.

Sunshine Water Sports
River Avenue, Aluthgama
Tel: 0777 941857
Four- to five-hour game-fishing trips
off the west coast with this leading
water sports operator.

Golf

Sri Lanka has several beautiful
championship-standard courses
at Colombo, Nuwara Eliya and
Kandy, and green fees are relatively
inexpensive by the standards of most
other countries.

Nuwara Eliya Golf Club
Tel: 052 222 2835
Email: negolf@sltnet.lk

The Royal Colombo Golf Club
Model Farm Road, Colombo 8
Tel: 011 269 5431
www.rcgcsl.com

Victoria Golf Club
Rajawella, Kandy
Tel: 081 237 6376
www.golfsrilanka.com

Hot-Air Ballooning

Hot-air ballooning offers a unique way
to see Sri Lanka. Typical tours take
place in the early morning, gliding over
the hill country, Cultural Triangle or
one of the national parks and lasting
for about one hour. The main balloon

Cricket

Cricket is a national obsession in Sri Lanka, and the national team's exploits are followed religiously by every man and boy in the country.

Test matches are usually played at the Sinhalese Sports Club in Colombo 7, at the Asigiriya Stadium in Kandy and at the cricket club in Galle. One-day and twenty20 matches are played at the Premadasa Stadium in Colombo, the Asigiriya Stadium in Kandy, the cricket stadium in Dambulla and the new stadium in Hambantota. Tickets are available from the individual venues.

If you want to play cricket in Sri Lanka, **Red Dot Tours** (www.reddottours.com) arrange specialist cricketing holidays for foreign clubs and teams, offering you the chance to play at some of the country's most famous venues against quality local opposition, with expert coaching included.

centre is in the Cultural Triangle with take-off near the Kandalama Hotel outside Dambulla. Flights are available in other areas of the island on a request basis, especially for larger groups. Flights generally only run from November to April, when winds are most favourable. Check www.srilankaballooning.com or www.airmagic.lk for further information.

Mountain Biking

Mountain biking is becoming increasingly popular on the island. Several tour operators have specialised in this niche market: they have bikes for rent and organise tours mostly with accompanying guides.
Adventure Sports Lanka
366/3 Rendapola Horagahakanda Lane, Talangama, Koswatta
Tel: 011 279 1584
www.actionlanka.com
Eco-Team
14 1st Lane, Gothami Road, Colombo 8
Tel: 011 583 0833
www.srilankaecotourism.com
RideLanka
7A N.J.V. Cooray Mawatha, Rajagiriya
www.ridelanka.com

Rowing, Yachting and Boat Trips

Ceylon Motor Yacht Club
Indebedda Road, Bolgoda Lake, Moratuwa

Tel: 011 421 2394
www.cmyc.lk
Colombo Rowing Club
51 Sir Chittampalam A Gardiner Mawatha, Colombo 2
Tel: 011 243 3758
Mirissa Water Sports
Mirissa Harbour
Tel: 077 359 7731
www.mirissawatersports.com
Coastal cruises, plus whale- and dolphin-watching and sea-kayaking.

Scuba Diving

There are a number of reputable and long-established diving operators around the coast, all offering PADI courses and individual dives for all standards. A three-day Open-Water PADI course will cost around US$350; individual dives tend to go for around US$35. An excellent source of information is www.divesrilanka.com. The following are the island's most reputable operators.
Blue Deep Dive Centre
Coral Reef Hotel, Hikkaduwa
Tel: 091 491 5975
www.bluedeepdiving.com
International Diving School
Coral Sands Hotel, 330 Galle Road, Hikkaduwa
Tel: 072 223 1683
www.internationaldivingschool.com
LSR Dive School
Chaaya Blue Hotel, Uppuveli (plus a second branch in Bentota, near the Bentota Beach Hotel)
www.lsr-srilanka.com
Poseidon Diving Station
Galle Road, Hikkaduwa
Tel: 091 227 7294
www.divingsrilanka.com
Unawatuna Diving Centre
Matara Road, Unawatuna
Tel: 091 224 4693
www.srilankadiving.com
Ypsylon Dive School
Beruwala
Tel: 034 227 6132
www.ypsylon-sri-lanka.de

Surfing

The island's top surfing spot is the east-coast village of Arugam Bay, while there are also good waves at Hikkaduwa, Midigama and Medawatta (just outside Matara) and other places around the coast. Surfing is best at Arugam Bay from around May to October, and on the southwest coast from November to April. There are well-equipped surf shops at Arugam Bay and Hikkaduwa, which rent boards, do board repairs and arrange surf safaris to various

ABOVE: batting practice.

spots around the coast. Numerous guesthouses in all the places above also rent boards.

Swimming

Most larger hotels have a swimming pool, which can generally be used by non-guests for a fee. Clubs offer membership and use of club facilities including tennis courts, squash courts and the bar.
Colombo Swimming Club
Storm Lodge, Galle Road, Colpetty
Tel: 011 242 1645
www.colomboswimmingclub.org
Temporary membership available.
Kinross Swimming Club
10 Station Avenue, Colombo 6
Tel: 011 258 6461
Sea bathing, lifesaving, skin diving.
Otter Aquatic Club
380/1 Bauddhaloka Mw., Colombo 7
Tel: 011 269 2308

Tennis

Many of the country's larger top-end hotels have a couple of tennis courts, although outside the big hotels it can prove difficult to find courts and players.
Sri Lanka Tennis Association
45 Marcus Fernando Mawatha, Colombo 7
Tel: 011 533 7161
www.srilankatennis.org

Water Sports and Whitewater Rafting

The main water-sports venue in Sri Lanka is Bentota, where a plethora of water-sports outfits offer everything from banana boating to jet-skiing and windsurfing. The best whitewater rafting is at Kitulgala on the Kelani River, in the hill country. Kite-surfing is also becoming increasingly popular – the breezy sea and lagoon at Kalpitiya is generally reckoned by aficionados to be the best spot.

Adventure Sports Lanka
Tel: 011 279 1584
www.actionlanka.com
Bar Reef Resort
Alankuda Beach, Kalpitiya
Tel: 077 106 0020
www.barreefresort.com/www.
alankuda.com
Ceylon Adventure
Belilena Junction, Kitulgala
Tel: 0773 603 723
www.ceylonadventure.com
Rafters Retreat
Kitulgala
Tel: 036 228 7598
www.raftersretreat.com
Sunset Araliya Water Sports
Galle Road, Kaluwamodara, Aluthgama
Tel: 034 227 2468
www.sunsetaraliyahotel.com
Sunshine Water Sports
River Avenue, Aluthgama
Tel: 0777 941857

Whale- and Dolphin-Watching

Over the past few years, Sri Lanka has emerged as one of the world's leading whale-watching destinations, and perhaps the best place on the planet to see blue whales. The main centre is Mirissa, where the season for whale-watching runs from December through to April. It's also now possible to arrange trips from Uppuveli, near Trincomalee, with the best months from around March/April to August/September, meaning that whale-watching is now possible somewhere around the Sri Lankan coast for almost the entire year. Trips were pioneered by Mirissa Water Sports (tel: 077 359 7731, www.mirissawatersports.com), although there are now at least five different operators in Mirissa offering trips. Whale-watching at Uppuveli is still in its infancy. The best place to arrange trips is currently through the Chaaya Blue Hotel, while trips can also be organised with the local Sri Lankan Navy station.

Dolphin-watching is also becoming increasingly popular – dolphins (mainly spinner) are often seen during whale-watching trips. The best place to see them is at Alankuda, on the Kalpitiya peninsula, where early-morning boat trips may reveal literally thousands of dolphins streaming through the waves in huge pods – one of Sri Lanka's most remarkable natural sights.

Yoga and Meditation

Yoga and meditation aren't nearly as well established in Sri Lanka as in neighbouring India, but are gradually becoming more popular. Increasing numbers of hotels and guesthouses are now offering yoga classes. The hills around Kandy are where you'll find most of the island's meditation centres.

Nilambe Meditation Centre
Near Galaha, around 22km (13 miles) from Kandy
Tel: 0777 804 555 or 0777 811 653
Email: upulnilambe@yahoo.com
Located in a beautifully tranquil spot in the hills, this long-running meditation centre is particularly popular with foreign visitors. All levels are welcome, whether you're a novice or an experienced meditator, and there's no minimum length of stay, although you should contact the centre at least two weeks before you plan to arrive. The cost is just Rs800 per day, including basic vegetarian food and lodging. Bring a torch, umbrella, alarm clock and warm clothing. To reach the centre, take the Deltota bus from Kandy's Goods Shed bus station and ask the conductor to put you off at Nilambe Office Junction, from where it's a 45-minute walk or short tuktuk ride.

Ulpotha.com
Embogana
Tel: 0208 123 3603 (UK)
www.ulpotha.com
Nestled between hills, paddy fields and a lake filled with water lilies, Ulpotha is a blend of eco-lodge and yoga retreat, with two-week courses led by leading international teachers. The seven adobe houses are scattered among trees, open to the elements and of an exquisite simplicity. Additional huts, hammocks, tree houses and a secluded *ambalama* (resting place) encourage complete relaxation – Ulpotha's laid-back atmosphere is a definite plus. There is no fridge and no electricity, so food is made fresh daily with ingredients organically grown in the village. Only open for about half the year. **$$$$$**

ECO-TOURISM

Ecotourism now plays an increasingly important role in Sri Lanka's tourist industry thanks to the island's remarkable wealth of animal, bird and plant life, whose massive visitor potential is gradually being realised. Both government and tourism authorities are increasingly focusing on Sri Lanka's stated aim of serving as an "earth lung" and, ultimately, becoming a carbon-neutral destination.

At the heart of Sri Lanka's ecotourism lies its extensive system of national parks, sanctuaries and reserves, occupying a remarkably high proportion of Sri Lanka's total land area. Some of these areas are completely out of bounds to casual visitors, although many are well set up for tourists, ranging from the dense rainforest of Sinharaja and the

BELOW: buffalo at Yala National Park.

cloudforests of Horton Plains through to the wildlife-rich savannahs of Yala National Park and the flamingo-filled lagoons of Bundala – not to mention various protected marine and coastal areas including the coral gardens at Hikkaduwa and Nilaveli and the turtle nesting beaches at Rekawa and Kosgoda.

Wildlife spotting is obviously the prime attraction – Sri Lanka is one of the best places in the world to see elephants, leopards and whales – while the island is also a major birdwatching destination – a number of tour operators run specialist birding and other wildlife tours. Environmentally friendly adventure tourism is also gradually taking off – hiking, cycling, whitewater rafting, ballooning and so on.

The island also boasts an excellent selection of eco-lodges and eco-inspired hotels, ranging from spectacular five-stars like Vil Uyuni through to rustic retreats with mud walls, thatched roofs and not much between you and the elements but a mosquito net – although often surprisingly comfortable and stylish even so.

Eco-Team
Tel: 011 583 0833
www.srilankaecotourism.com
A small group of nature enthusiasts who offer trekking tours, mountain biking, rainforest explorations, wildlife safaris and even volunteer programmes for the conservation of wildlife and turtles.

Jetwing Eco Holidays
Tel: 011 238 1201
www.jetwingeco.com
The pioneers of Sri Lankan wildlife- and ecotourism, and still easily the best outfit when it comes to exploring the island's natural wonders, with tours led by expert, near-fanatic wildlife aficionados.

Sri Lankan Expeditions
Tel: 0773 595411
www.srilankanexpeditions.com
Specialising in wildlife-, adventure-, expedition- and eco-holidays. Fauna and flora study tours can also be arranged.

Expeditor
Saranankara Road, Kandy
Tel: 081 490 1628
www.srilankatrekkingexpeditor.com
Experienced local guide Sumane Bandara Illangantilake and his team run superb hikes into the wild Knuckles mountains, plus visits to Veddah villages, national park trips and numerous other tours.

Kulu Safaris
Tel: 037 493 1662

www.kulusafaris.com
Luxurious overnight safaris in sturdy South African canvas tents which come with queen-sized beds, hot showers, toilets and everything else one needs after a hard day of leopard-chasing. Currently runs trips to Yala, Wilpattu and Uda Walawe national parks.

Eco-Stays

Aranya
Piliyandala, Kataragama
Tel: 011 261 5645
www.aranyayala.net
Small eco-resort, developed by former Sri Lanka cricket star Hashan Tillakaratne and located just outside Yala National Park, meaning that you're almost bound to spot wildlife during your stay. Accommodation is in four simple cottages plus a tree house, and there's also an attractive pool. **$$$**

Boulder Garden
Koswatta, Kalawana, near Sinharaja
Tel: 045 225 5812
www.bouldergarden.com
Boutique eco-hotel ingeniously built in, under and around a huge cluster of jungle-covered boulders (hence the name) – the open-air restaurant, sitting beneath a huge rock overhang, is particularly impressive. The large, stone-walled, timber-beamed rooms have a similarly rustic appearance, although with all contemporary mod cons conveniently to hand. **$$$$$**

Kumbuk River
Buttala
Tel: 011 452 7781
www.kumbukriver.com
An exclusive eco-hideout in the shape of a giant, 12-metre (40ft) high elephant, honoured by the prestigious World Travel Awards as one of the world's leading eco-lodges. Half-burnt trees were used in the structure, along with renewable materials and resources found in the area. The luxurious elephant villa is actually within the belly of the elephant; the separate Kumbuk chalet features a tree-shower and an eco-toilet in the courtyard. **$$$**

Rainforest Edge
Waddagala, near Sinharaja Rainforest
Tel: 045 225 5912
www.rainforestedge.com
Offering panoramic views of the surrounding vegetation, tea plantations and Sinharaja rainforest, Rainforest Edge has seven rustic, creatively designed rooms with beds seemingly made out of tree trunks. The retreat's centrepiece is an attractive, natural-water

pool encircled by water lilies and Indonesian pots. Energy is supplied by a combination of solar panels and kerosene lamps; fruit and veg are all grown organically within the grounds. **$$$$$**

Samakanda
Nakiyadeniya, near Galle
Tel: 0777 424 770
www.samakanda.org
Run by writer and environmentalist Rory Spowers, Samakanda is an organic farm-cum-learning centre for sustainable agriculture, with residential courses offered by visiting experts. Accommodation is in a trio of rustic bungalows and the kitchen is filled with organic vegetables, herbs, fruit and tea – while a rustic pizza-oven provides a change from rice and curry. **$$$–$$$$**

VISITING NATIONAL PARKS

Admission to Sri Lanka's national parks ranges from US$10 to $15 per person. You'll also pay a "service charge" of around $8 per group for the obligatory tracker who will accompany you, plus a couple of other small additional costs and VAT on everything at 15 percent, working out at (very roughly) around $30 for one person, $50 for two people and so on. You'll also have to pay for jeep transport around the park, which can be arranged either at the park itself or (more conveniently) through a local hotel or travel agent. Jeeps with driver usually go for around $40 for half a day. Getting out of your vehicle inside the park is strictly prohibited except at specially designated points. For the best views of wildlife you should aim to be in the park at around 6.30am or after 3.30pm.

It's also possible to stay at lodges or camp in most of the island's national parks, although the ridiculous charges levied by the Wildlife Department on foreign tourists make this an expensive business at the more popular parks – probably over $100 per person per night. Places also tend to get reserved by Sri Lankans (who pay only a fraction of what Western visitors pay) so book well in advance. Reservations can be made through the Department of Wildlife Conservation, 811A Jayanthipura Road, Battaramula, tel: 011 288 8585, www.dwc.gov. lk, although it's far easier to arrange this through a local travel agent, who will also provide all the necessary camping and other equipment.

A – Z

A HANDY SUMMARY OF PRACTICAL INFORMATION, ARRANGED ALPHABETICALLY

A

Admission Charges

Admission charges vary wildly. The top cultural sites, such as Sigiriya ($30), Polonnaruwa and Anuradhapura (both $25), attract hefty charges, as do the island's national parks. Most museums and less significant cultural attractions charge around $5 admission. Entrance to most temples is usually free, although a few places levy a $1–2 charge; alternatively you might be asked for a donation.

B

Begging

Begging is far less common in Sri Lanka than in neighbouring India, and except in Colombo and Kandy you'll often go days without seeing anyone soliciting for money. Beggars can sometimes be seen on the street, particularly in larger cities, but more usually congregate around temples and churches, or sometimes at the entrance to tourist attractions. Most such beggars are clearly elderly, infirm or disabled and deserving of whatever help is given to them. More pernicious are opportunistic requests by passing children (and occasionally even adults) for "one pen", "one sweet" or, increasingly, just "money".

Budgeting for Your Trip

Local beer: Rs200–300
Imported beer: Rs300–400

Site Charges

The cost of permits for individual sites are:
Anuradhapura US$25
Polonnaruwa US$25
Sigiriya US$30
Medirigiya US$5
Nalanda US$5
Ritigala US$5

Glass of house wine: Rs600
Main course meal: Rs400 budget; Rs700 moderate; Rs1,500 at an expensive restaurant
Hotel cost: Rs2,500 budget; Rs5,000 moderate; Rs20,000 luxury accommodation
Three-wheeler: Rs40–60/km
Bus journey: Rs2/km

C

Children

Sri Lankans adore children and usually make a great fuss over them. Children are well catered for in restaurants, and most hotels and guesthouses have family rooms. Baby food and nappies are available in major supermarkets but are very expensive. Good baby bottles are hard to find, so bring these with you. Cotton children's clothing is easily available, inexpensive and cool to wear.

Climate

The island has an unusual blend of climatic features. It is possible to travel from tropical heat to cool, misty weather, then to the dry zone, all in

CLIMATE CHART

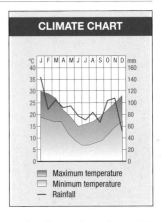

Maximum temperature
Minimum temperature
— Rainfall

one day. There are two main monsoon seasons, one in the northeast, the other in the southwest. When the northeastern monsoon blows, the southwestern side experiences peak weather and vice versa, so the weather is always good somewhere on the island.

The southwest monsoon, or Yala, brings rain from the Indian Ocean from May to September, commencing with a month of heavy rain, followed by short showers. At this time the coastal tides are dangerous and swimming is inadvisable – even the fishermen avoid it. Maha, the northeastern monsoon, blows in from the Bay of Bengal from around November to March.

An inter-monsoon period in October and November can bring thunderstorms to any part of the country. However, most days are sunny and humid, so short bursts of heavy rain are a pleasure, bringing welcome coolness and freshness. These intense, short-lived showers fill up myriad small lakes and perfume the air with the smell of damp soil and bruised frangipani blossoms.

The low-lying southern coastal regions experience the warmest temperatures. Colombo averages 27°C (81°F). The sea remains at 27°C all year round. In the central highlands, temperatures become noticeably cooler and the nights can be decidedly chilly. At 305 metres (1,000ft) Kandy averages 20°C (68°F), and Nuwara Eliya, at 1,890 metres (6,200ft), 16°C (61°F). An umbrella is never out of place in Sri Lanka. You may need it to keep the rain off, or for protection from the sun.

What to Bring

Very little, as most items you might need, such as mosquito coils to burn at night, torch, standard medicines, condoms, and so on, can be purchased locally. Sun protection is vital so bring tanning lotion and sunscreen that suits you. Bring along your favourite toiletries, as Western brands are expensive in Sri Lanka, if you can even find them.

Nappies are expensive but training pants can be a good alternative, as fewer layers of clothing make it quick and easy to clean your children. Pushchairs are not so useful, due to the condition of many roads and pavements, so a strong hands-free carrier is a good idea. Small plastic containers are handy for packing meals and a spray atomiser of mineral water helps to cool children quickly and efficiently. A fabric mesh food cover also doubles as a portable, mini-mosquito net for babies.

What to Wear

Cottons and light natural fabrics such as linen are ideal in the lowland heat. Outside tourist areas, skimpy skirts and brief shorts are not considered respectable, and will attract stares and (for women) perhaps even a certain amount of hassle. For women, loose cotton skirts or trousers and tops, and a long dress or skirt and long-sleeved blouse for visiting temples are ideal. Men will feel comfortable in cotton trousers or shorts and a T-shirt. Take a sunhat and a good pair of sunglasses, and sandals, slippers or open shoes that are easy to slip on and off. If you intend to spend some time in the hills, take a couple of light sweaters or sweatshirts. If you are planning to do any hiking, bring along a sturdy pair of walking shoes or trainers.

If you are travelling with children, bring loose cotton clothing for them and long-sleeved cotton tops to protect against mosquito bites. A sunhat, with straps that tie below the chin, is also useful. Avoid bringing too many white garments unless you don't mind washing them by hand.

Crime and Safety

Despite the end of the civil war, the political situation in Sri Lanka remains potentially volatile, and it's always worth checking the current situation before travelling to the north.

The following websites publish up-to-date travel advisories: www.smartraveller.gov.au www.fco.gov.uk www.travel.state.gov/travel

Apart from that, Sri Lanka is a reassuringly safe country. Levels of petty crime are far lower than in many other Asian countries, and violent attacks against tourists are relatively infrequent. Nevertheless, it pays to exercise caution and obey common-sense rules. Never flash valuables or leave them lying around; do not let your credit card out of your sight when making payments; avoid dark and deserted beaches at night; and do not accept lifts from strangers.

The most obvious safety hazard in Sri Lanka is traffic: the island has an abysmal record of road-related accidents and you should always stay alert when there's traffic around – vehicles often behave in unexpected and potentially dangerous ways. If you're cycling, take extra care.

Swimming is another potential hazard. Dozens of locals and the occasional tourist are drowned every year. If swimming off an unfrequented beach, always check local advice and make sure someone knows you're in the water. And never swim under the influence of alcohol.

Drugs are a problem in some coastal areas. Do not get tangled up in buying/selling/using them or get involved with those who do: it is illegal and dangerous.

(See also Touts and Con Artists.*)*

Customs Regulations

If you are bringing in over US$10,000, it should be declared at customs on arrival. Valuable equipment, gems and jewellery should also be declared. Duty-free allowances permit up to 1.5 litres of spirits, 2 bottles of wine, perfume in a quantity for personal use. Note that you are not allowed to bring cartons of duty free cigarettes into Sri Lanka; you're unlikely to be stopped at customs, but if you are a fine of Rs6,000 applies. Personal equipment such as radios, sports equipment, laptop computers, photographic equipment and so on is allowed. The import of non-prescription drugs, firearms or pornography of any form is an offence. On leaving the country, customs officers may check your luggage for items being taken out of the country without a permit. If gems are purchased in Sri Lanka, keep the receipts. Note that drugs are illegal in Sri Lanka and offenders will be prosecuted – in the worst cases potentially with the death penalty.

On Departure

Departure tax is included in the cost of your airline ticket. Up to 3kg (6½lb) of tea can be exported free; each additional kilo costs Rs5. For gifts of gems, permits are issued by the Controller of Exchange, Central Bank, Colombo. The export of "antiques" (defined as anything over 50 years old) is prohibited without a special licence, as is the export of native fauna and flora. Ask at the tourist office in Colombo (see page 317) for details. Unused Sri Lankan currency should be reconverted into foreign currency upon departure as you are not permitted to leave Sri Lanka with currency in excess of Rs250.

D

Disabled Travellers

Sri Lanka is not well equipped for those with physical disabilities. Only a few of the five-star hotels have access and facilities for people in wheelchairs – public transport has none, so a car and driver is essential. Wheelchairs, as well as a passenger Meet and Greet Service, are available at the international airport on prior request through the airlines.

E

Economy

The top foreign-exchange earners are tourism; the manufacture of garments exported to the West; and inward remittances from Sri Lankans working overseas, mostly in the Middle East.

The service sector is the largest component of GDP at around 60 percent. Industry accounts for a third of GDP with manufacturing of food, beverages and tobacco being the largest subsector in terms of value addition, followed by textiles, apparel and leather. Agriculture has lost its relative importance to the Sri Lankan economy in recent decades. It employs a third of the working population, but accounts for only about 12 percent of GDP. The main export crop is tea. Sri Lanka is one of the world's largest tea exporters, most of which is sold to the Middle East and Russia. Other important crops are rubber, coconuts and spices (mainly cinnamon). Gems, particularly Sri Lankan sapphires, are another major industry.

Economic growth fell to just 3.5 percent in 2009 as a result of the civil war, but shot up to 7 percent in 2010 and 8 percent in 2011 following the end of fighting.

Electricity

Sri Lanka uses 230–240 volts, 50 cycles, alternating current. Much of the island's electricity is generated hydroelectrically, so expect regular power cuts during periods of low rainfall, and at any time in remote villages. Most sockets are three-pronged with round pins, although you may also find UK-style three-pronged square-pin sockets, particularly in more upmarket hotels. Adaptors are cheap and readily available from all hardware shops. If you are travelling with a laptop computer, it's wise to bring a stabiliser, as power often fluctuates, even in the cities, plus a laptop plug and adaptor.

Embassies and Consulates

Australia
Australian High Commission
21 Gregory's Road, Colombo 7
Tel: 011 246 3200
www.srilanka.embassy.gov.au
Canada
High Commission of Canada
33A, 5th Lane, Colombo 3
Tel: 011 522 6232
www.canadainternational.gc.ca/
sri_lanka/
New Zealand
The New Zealand High Commission,

Emergency Numbers

Police/fire: 119
Ambulance/fire: 110 (Colombo)
Tourist Police: Anuradhapura
071 841 6007; Colombo 011
242 1451; Galle/Hikkaduwa
091 227 5554; Kandy 071 839
0664; Negombo 031 227 5555;
Polonnaruwa 027 222 3099

ABOVE: a warm welcome from the smallest villager.

New Delhi, India, is accredited to Sri Lanka.
www.nzembassy.com
South Africa
South African High Commission
114 Rosmead Place, Colombo 7
Tel: 011 246 3000
UK
British High Commission
389 Bauddhaloka Mawatha,
Colombo 7
Tel: 011 539 0639
www.ukinsrilanka.fco.gov.uk/en
USA
Embassy of The United States
210 Galle Road, Colombo 3
Tel: 011 249 8500
http://srilanka.usembassy.gov

Sri Lankan Embassies Abroad
Australia
Sri Lanka High Commission
61 Hampton Circuit, Yarralumla,
ACT 2600 Canberra
Tel: 02 6198 3756
www.slhcaust.org
Canada
Sri Lanka High Commission
333 Laurier Avenue, Ottawa,
Ontario, K1P 1C1
Tel: 613 233 8449
www.srilankahcottawa.org
South Africa
410 Alexander Street, Brooklyn,
Pretoria 0181
Tel: 012 460 7679
www.srilanka.co.za
UK
Sri Lankan High Commission
13 Hyde Park Gardens
London W2
Tel: 020 7262 1841
www.srilankahighcommission.co.uk

USA
2148 Wyoming Avenue NW,
Washington DC 20008
Tel: 202-483-4025
www.slembassyusa.org

Etiquette

Like most foreign countries, Sri Lanka offers countless opportunities to blunder. With a portion of goodwill and by watching local conduct, embarrassment can be avoided.

Few Sri Lankans use cutlery, most picking up food with their hands. However, food should be handled with the right hand only, as the left is considered unclean. When handing objects to another person, either the right hand or both hands should be used.

Away from the beach, wearing torn T-shirts, skimpy skirts, transparent clothing or displaying bare shoulders is considered highly improper, especially in temples, religious sites or in the presence of monks. When entering holy areas, it is customary to remove your shoes and walk barefoot within the designated area. (This also applies to people's homes.) Women should wear long skirts or loose trousers and a modest blouse, or a loose cotton dress. Men should wear long trousers. Even ancient ruined temples in archaeological sites are still considered sacred, and should be treated as such.

Public displays of physical affection should be avoided.

When invited to a home, it is customary to bring fruit, tea or biscuits or some other small gift.

TRANSPORT

ACCOMMODATION

EATING OUT

ACTIVITIES

A – Z

LANGUAGE

Small presents from one's home country are very much appreciated.

Courtesy is an inherent part of Sri Lankan culture, and one which you should reciprocate. The loss of temper and raising of voices will cause offence, and is very unlikely to further your cause, whatever it is. Many Sri Lankans habitually ask personal questions of all foreigners they meet: you will regularly be asked your country, possibly followed by your age, marital status and number of children. Although such questioning by strangers might be considered intrusive in Western societies, in Sri Lanka these are ordinary questions and simply reflect the emphasis locals place on family life. You may also find yourself being stared at every now and then – not something that's considered rude in the same way as it is in the West.

Body Language

The famous head "waggle" of the Indian subcontinent manages to confuse almost every foreign visitor. As throughout south Asia, shaking the head from side to side indicates a negative, while a nod indicates a positive response. However, the "waggle", a cross between a nod and a shake with the chin pointed outwards, usually indicates a simple "yes" or "okay".

If you encounter a Buddhist monk or a Hindu swami and would like to greet him in the traditional way, hold your hands together as if in prayer and raise them to your forehead. Do not shake hands. If you wish to offer a gift to a monk, do so with both hands to show that it is given freely. (Gifts of money should be placed directly in the temple box.) When sitting with a Buddhist monk, try to sit at a lower level to him and avoid pointing your toes towards him, as this is seen as a lack of respect.

G

Gay and Lesbian Travellers

Homosexuality is technically illegal in Sri Lanka, and although no one has been convicted since the 1950s, the entire subject is little understood by the majority of Sri Lankans, so discretion is advised. For information on the very secretive local scene, visit www.equal-ground.org. Reviews of gay-friendly accommodation and other tourist facilities can be found at www.utopia-asia.com/tipssri.htm.

Government

The Democratic Socialist Republic of Sri Lanka has been a democracy since Independence in 1948. The head of state is the president (currently Mahinda Rajapakse), elected by popular vote for a six-year term. There is also a 225-seat parliament, elected by a modified form of proportional representation. Members of parliament are elected for six-year terms. Parliament is led by a prime minister from the largest party, though the dual nature of the system has caused problems when president and prime minister are from different parties. Presidential and parliamentary elections are held separately. The main two parties are the populist, nationalist Sri Lanka Freedom Party (SLFP), the leading player in the People's Alliance coalition (PA), and the United National Party (UNP). As of early 2012, the SLFP/PA held both parliament and the presidency. Sri Lanka is also rare in having a party formed by Buddhist monks, the JHU.

H

Health and Medical Care

Officials do not require certificates of immunisation unless you have passed through an infected area within 14 days prior to your arrival. It is recommended that travellers have standard vaccinations. Apart from these, cholera immunisation is suggested. Malaria, dengue fever and chikungunya are quite common. Anti-malaria tablets prescribed by your doctor should be started about a week before you plan to arrive and continued for at least two weeks after you depart, depending on the type you have been prescribed. The use of mosquito repellent (best brought from home) is highly recommended. Citronella oil, readily available in Sri Lanka, is an effective natural alternative. During evening hours, long sleeves offer additional protection.

Health Insurance

The Sri Lankan health service does not cover the medical expenses of visitors to Sri Lanka. It is therefore advisable to take out a separate insurance policy for the duration of your journey.

Sun and Heat

Sunburn and even sunstroke are a genuine risk in lowland Sri Lanka, whether you're lying on the beach or exploring ancient monuments. The heat is intense, especially in the afternoon when the sun is best avoided altogether. Use a maximum-protection sun block or tanning lotion that has a high protection factor. If you go out in the midday sun, take a large hat or a parasol (Sri Lankans often use umbrellas). If you start feeling the effects of excessive sun such as nausea, dizziness and headaches, find somewhere shady to rest, drink something cool, eat some salt and bathe your face in cool water.

It is vital to drink plenty of fluids to avoid dehydration. Don't drink tap water at all, unless you know for a fact that it has been boiled. Many restaurants claim that their table water is boiled or safe, but stick to bottled water, bottled or canned fruit juices, and carbonated drinks to avoid any risk. Be aware, too, that fresh fruit juices may be made with tap water, as are most ice cubes, although ice made with purified and filtered water is sold by the bag for home use.

BELOW: always remove footwear when entering temples.

Mineral water is available at most restaurants and in all supermarkets. Stock up with small bottles to carry with you when you are out during the day. The safest and most nutritious drink available is king coconut water – *thambili* – drunk straight from the shell. It is safe, a great thirst quencher, widely available and has remarkable rehydrating properties.

Stomach Upsets

Diarrhoea can wreck a holiday, but can be avoided with a little care. Wash fruit with bottled water and peel; avoid raw vegetables and salads unless you know they have been washed in boiled water. If you are prone to "Delhi belly" carry some form of medication such as Lomatil or Pepto-Bismal with you.

Medical Services

Most hotels have a doctor on call, and most embassies can provide a referral list. There are general hospitals in Colombo (tel: 011 269 1111), Kandy (tel: 081 233 3337), Negombo (tel: 031 222 2261) and Galle (tel: 091 222 2261). Foreigners are required to pay for certain services. Although many doctors have British qualifications, state hospitals have poor facilities and crowded wards. Private hospitals are well staffed, and are generally competently run and comfortable. In Colombo, these include the Apollo Hospital, 578 Elvitigala Mawatha, Colombo 5 (tel: 011 543 0000); the Nawaloka, 23 Sri Sugathodaya Mawatha, Colombo 2 (tel: 011 254 4444, www.nawaloka.com); Oasis Hospital, 18A M E D Dabare Mawatha, Narahenpita, Colombo 5 (tel: 011 550 6000, www.oasishospital.lk).

Galle is served by the Ruhunu Hospital, Karapitiya Road (tel: 091 223 4061).

Pharmacies

Most Western medicines are available, and so are many Indian substitutes – check where your product is made. The pharmacy at the Asiri Hospital, 181 Kirula Road, Colombo 5, is open till quite late, and the Osusala Pharmacy on Union Place in Colombo 2 (tel: 011 269 4716) is open 24 hours.

Internet

Internet cafés are widely found even in the smallest towns, often incorporated in "communication centres", while increasing numbers of hotels, guesthouses and cafés are now offering Wi-fi (usually free to guests and customers).

You'll find that charges in internet cafés vary from Rs1–4 per minute. Nearly all hotels and guesthouses have at least one computer for you to get online.

Maps

The Nelles Sri Lanka map (1:450,000) has useful town maps of Colombo, Kandy, Galle and Anuradhapura.

Detailed 1:50,000 maps of the entire country are available from the Survey Department at Kirula Road, Colombo 5; tel: 011 236 8106 (take your passport).

Insight Fleximap Sri Lanka (1:560,000) combines clear cartography with informative text and photos illustrating the country's top sights. The easy-to-fold laminated finish makes it ideal in any weather.

Maps can be purchased in the UK from Stanfords, 12–14 Long Acre, Covent Garden, London WC2E 9LP, tel: 020 7836 1321; www.stanfords.co.uk. They also have branches in Bristol and Manchester.

Media

Sri Lanka has three daily English-language newspapers, and two Sunday papers; they are mainly available from stalls and pavement sellers, though can be difficult to find in place.

The *Daily News* (www.dailynews.lk) and the *Sunday Observer* (www.sundayobserver.lk) are both state-controlled and thus serve as mouthpieces for whichever government is in powe.r

Private newspapers include *The Island* (www.island.lk), which has a pronounced pro-Sinhalese bias, the more moderate *Daily Mirror* (www.dailymirror.lk) and its sister publication the *Sunday Times* (www.sundaytimes.lk).

Most hotels and reputable bookshops carry international magazines such as *Newsweek*, *Time*, *The Far Eastern Economic Review* and *The Economist*. Foreign newspapers usually take a while to reach Sri Lanka; it's much easier to read them online.

ABOVE: Kataragama temple detail.

There's also a surprisingly good range of English-language radio available, churning out a diet of mainstream pop music and cheesy chat. The best is TNL Radio (101.7 FM; www.tnlrocks.com); others worth a listen are Yes FM (89.5 FM; www.yesfmonline.com) and Sun FM (99.9 FM; www.sunfm.lk).

Sri Lankan television is unlikely to take up much of your time; the seven channels currently available broadcast mainly in Sinhala, and what little English-language programming there is tends to be fairly dire. Most upmarket hotels have in-room satellite TVs where you can watch Sky News, BBC, CNN and the various Star channels.

Money

Currency

Sri Lanka's national currency is the Sri Lankan rupee. Coins come in denominations of one, two, five and 10 rupees. Notes meanwhile are available in denominations of 10, 20, 50, 100, 500, 1,000, 2,000 and 5,000 rupees.

As elsewhere in South Asia, the term "lakh" denotes a sum of 100,000 (written 1,00,000).

Credit Cards and ATMs

Most upmarket hotels, restaurants and shops accept credit cards. Visa and MasterCard are widely accepted; American Express and Diners Club less so.

Note that some establishments may try to add a surcharge if you choose to pay by card. Be careful of credit card copying and take precautionary measures by not allowing your card out of your sight.

ABOVE: a 1,000 rupee note.

There are now hundreds of ATMs across the island that accept foreign Visa and/or MasterCards; every town of any consequence will have at least one such machine, while in larger cities there's often one every few blocks, offering an easy way to access local funds.

Exchanging Money

All banks change traveller's cheques; privately owned banks like Hatton and Sampath may be fractionally quicker than the government-controlled People's Bank and Bank of Ceylon, although nowhere is the process likely to take longer than about 15 minutes. Stick to a well-known brand (Thomas Cook and American Express are the most widely recognised in Sri Lanka) and have them denominated in pounds sterling, US dollars or euros. Money can also be withdrawn on credit cards in banks, though it's much easier and faster just to use an ATM *(see above)*. Banks are open Monday to Friday from 9/9.30am to 5/5.30pm; some branches open on Saturday mornings too. It's also straightforward to exchange notes of major currencies, though traveller's cheques attract a better exchange rate than cash. There's not usually much (if any) difference between the exchange rates offered by different banks. Many larger hotels will also change traveller's cheques and foreign currency, though at lower rates than in the banks.

Tipping

Some hotels and restaurants automatically add a 10 percent service charge to the bill; if a service charge isn't included, you might want to tip an extra 10 percent. Chauffeurs and guides will also expect to be tipped somewhere in the region of US$10 per day, depending on their skills and helpfulness. Guides who show you around temples will expect a small tip (Rs100–200 should suffice, although remember not to give money directly to monks, but to place it in a donation box).

O

Opening Hours

Most government offices and other formal businesses observe a standard five-day working week, opening Monday to Friday from around 8.30 or 9.30am and closing around 4.30 or 5.30pm. Banks open Monday to Friday from 9 or 9.30am until 5 or 5.30pm; some branches also open on Saturday mornings. Major post offices generally open from Monday to Saturday, and usually keep longer hours (typically around 7am–8pm). All shops and banks close on public holidays. Most shops close on Sunday, either all day or in the afternoon, and public offices and the majority of shops are closed on *Poya* days.

Major supermarkets in Colombo, such as branches of Keells and Cargills, stay open until 8pm and all day on Sunday. In small towns, the shopping hours seem to depend on the shop owner, with many open till late and on Sunday.

P

Postal Services

These are cheap but not particularly reliable – it's best to send urgent or valuable items by EMS express post. When sending airmail letters with stamps, it is best to make sure that they are franked in front of you, to prevent them being steamed off and re-used. All overseas packages should be stamped with a green customs label stating the contents and value. Post office working hours are 7am–5/6pm weekdays and 9am–6pm Saturday. Mail is delivered every day except Sunday and public holidays. The simplest way to mail anything is through your hotel, or do it yourself through a postal agency. There are also reliable international and domestic courier services, including the following.

DHL
148 Vauxhall Street, Colombo 2
Tel: 011 230 4304
www.dhl.com.lk

FedEx
93 1/1 Chatham Street, Colombo 1
Tel: 011 254 4357
www.fedex.com/lk/dropoff/

Public Holidays and Festivals

Sri Lanka has 25 public holidays, plus numerous other local festivals which are likely to bring places to a halt. Travelling during *Poya* (full moon) days, especially on "long weekends" (when the *Poya* day falls on a Friday or Monday), can be time-consuming, as buses and trains fill up with locals on the move. Technically, alcohol cannot be bought

Photography

Colour print film is widely available, although always check the sell-by date, and avoid buying film that might have been sitting in bright sunlight. Slide film and black-and-white film are available only from specialist photographic shops. Bring your own. Memory cards are also widely available. There are quite a few specialist camera shops in Colombo if you need to have a camera repaired (try Millers in Majestic City, Galle Road, Colombo 3); many places in tourist areas also offer one-hour or overnight printing services.

on *Poya* days, but many tourist-oriented establishments will serve guests discreetly.

The dates of most festivals follow the lunar calendar and vary from year to year *(see box)*. Forthcoming dates can be checked at www.srilanka tourism.org/event_calender.php.

Sri Lanka celebrates the Sinhala/Tamil New Year around 14 April. During this holiday, the entire island comes to a virtual standstill for at least one week following New Year's Day.

Public Toilets

Most Sri Lankan toilets are Western-style; traditional Asian squat toilets are fairly rare. Public toilets are virtually nonexistent: in an emergency, head for the nearest decent hotel. Toilets in better hotels and restaurants are usually kept reasonably clean and stocked with paper, though you might want to carry your own supply.

R

Religious Services

There are four major religions in Sri Lanka: Buddhism (espoused by roughly 70 percent of the population), Hinduism (15 percent), Christianity (7 percent) and Islam (7 percent). Almost all Sinhalese are Buddhist (there is a small number of Christian Sinhalese). The majority of Tamils are Hindu, though there are also significant numbers of Tamil Christians.

Places of Christian, Hindu and Muslim worship in Colombo are as follows:

Holidays

Public, bank and Full Moon *(Poya)* Day holidays change every year as they are based on lunar cycles. The constant national holidays are:
14–15 January Tamil Thai Pongal
4 February National Day
13–14 April Sinhalese/Tamil New Year
1 May May Day (Labour Day)
25 December Christmas Day
The Muslim holidays of Id-Ul-Fitr (Ramadan Festival Day), Id-Ul-Allah (Hajji Festival Day) and Milad-Un-Nabi (Holy Prophet's Birthday) are also national holidays celebrated on different days each year, according to the cycles of the Muslim calendar.

Other holidays occur in the following months, although there are changes every year, according to the moon and government decree:
January
Durutu Poya
February
Navan Poya
March
Mahasivarathri
Medin Poya
March/April
Good Friday
April
Bak Poya
May
Vesak Poya and day after
June
Poson Poya
July
Esala Poya
August
Nikini Poya
September
Binara Poya
October
Vap Poya
October/November
Deepavali
November
Il Poya
December
Unduvap Poya

Christian
Anglican
Cathedral of Christ the Living Saviour
368/3 Bauddhaloka Mawatha, Colombo 7
Tel: 269 6383
St Peter's Church
26 Church Street, Colombo 1
Tel: 242 2510
Bambalapitiya Dutch Reformed Church
724 Galle Road, Colombo 4
Tel: 232 3765
St Andrew's Church

73 Galle Road, Colombo 3
Tel: 222 3765

Baptist
Cinnamon Gardens Baptist Church
120 Dharmapala Mawatha, Colombo 7
Tel: 269 2414

Methodist
Methodist Church
6 Station Road, Colombo 3
Tel: 232 3033

Roman Catholic
St Philip Neri's Church
157 Olcott Mawatha, Colombo 11

BELOW: Buddhas at Gangaramaya temple.

ABOVE: Swami Rock Temple, Trincomalee.

Tel: 242 1367
St Lawrence's Church
Galle Road, Colombo 6
Tel: 258 1549
St Mary's Church
Lauries Road,
Colombo 4
Tel: 258 8745

Hindu
New Kathiresan Temple
Galle Road, Bambalapitya, Colombo 4
Sri Muthuvinayagam Swami Kovil
221 Sea Street, Colombo 11
Sri Samankodu Kadirvekanda Swami Kovil
Main Street, Colombo 11

Muslim
Bambalapitiya Mosque
Buller's Road, Colombo 4
Jami-ul-Alfar Mosque
2nd Cross Street, Colombo 11
Kollupitiya Mosque
Colombo 3

S

Sex Tourism

Unfortunately Sri Lanka has been a popular hunting ground for paedophiles. Sexual abuse of children under the age of 18 carries a mandatory sentence of 7–20 years' imprisonment with heavy fines and compensation to victims. Both male and female prostitution is illegal. If you have good reason to believe that a foreigner is committing child abuse and you know their name and nationality, contact the police or their embassy. Useful websites include: www.childwise.net and www.tourismconcern.org.

T

Telephones

Most major hotels have international direct-dialling facilities, but their rates for both local and international calls are high. It's significantly cheaper to use one of the numerous small "communication centres" (also offering fax and photocopying facilities) which can be found throughout all the island's towns. The international dialing code for Sri Lanka is 00 94.

Mobile Phones
Mobile phones offer great convenience when on the move, although roaming charges can be steep – if, in fact, your phone even works in Sri Lanka. Check with your operator before leaving, and note that most North American cellphones won't work here (apart from tri-band phones). A cheap alternative, if your phone's not locked to a particular telecom provider, is to buy a local SIM card; these cost just a few dollars from any local phone shop and give you a Sri Lankan phone number and access to significantly cheaper calls (you may be asked to produce your passport when buying the SIM). You'll have to buy scratch-card style recharge cards to top up your account as you go.

If your phone is locked or doesn't work in Sri Lanka, you can pick up a basic mobile phone plus SIM for as little as $20–25. There are plenty of mobile phone shops in even the smallest towns selling SIM cards, recharge cards, phones and other kit. The main mobile companies are Dialog (www.dialog.lk), Eitsalat (www.etisalat.lk) and Mobitel (www.mobitel.

Useful Phone Numbers

Police: 011 243 3333
Fire: 011 242 2222
Railway Tourist Information Centre: 011 243 5838
Central Bus Station: 011 232 9604/5
Colombo General Hospital: 011 269 1111
Flight information: 732 377/677
Sri Lanka Tourism hotline: 1912
Directory enquiries: 161 (local), 134 (international)
Customs: 011 242 1141

lk; the mobile arm of the national Sri Lanka Telecom).

Time Zone

Sri Lanka's clocks follow Indian Standard Time (IST). This means that Sri Lanka is at Coordinated Universal Time UTC (GMT) +5.5 – in other words 5.5 hours ahead of GMT in winter, and 4.5 hours in summer. Sri Lanka is 4.5 hours behind Australia in winter and 5.5 hours in summer; or 10.5 hours ahead of New York in winter, and 9.5 in summer.

Tour Operators

There are hundreds of tour agencies and guides around the country, of wildly varying standards; the best guides are officially accredited by the Sri Lanka Tourist Board. The following are the best established operators, and often have a degree of local expertise and knowledge which easily surpasses that offered by foreign tour operators.
Aitken Spence Travels
305 Vauxhall Street, Colombo 2
Tel: 011 230 8308
www.aitkenspencetravels.com
The travel wing of the leading hotel group offers general island tours, plus wildlife and nature tours.
Colombus Tours
221/2 Dharmapala Mawatha, Colombo 7
Tel: 011 269 7779
www.columbustourssrilanka.com
Week-long tours with the emphasis on ecotourism, camping and trekking.
Jetwing Travels
Jetwing House, 46/26 Navam Mawatha, Colombo 2
Tel: 011 462 7739
www.jetwingtravels.com.
Comprehensive selection of island-wide tours run by the travel wing of Sri Lanka's leading hotel group.
Walkers Tours
130 Glennie Street, Colombo 2

Tel: 011 230 6303
www.walkerstours.com
Long-established tour operators
with general island-wide tours
plus more unusual packages,
including mountain biking, trekking,
birdwatching, rafting, golf, water
sports and diving.

Tourist Information

Sri Lanka's Tourist Information
Centres are not quite as efficient
as in other countries; there are few
TICs in the island itself. More details
are available from the Sri Lanka
Tourist Board (www.srilanka.travel).
Major UK and Australian cities have
representatives of the Sri Lanka
Tourist Board:
London Tourist Office
Devonshire Square, London
EC2M 4WD
Tel: 0845 880 6333
Colombo
Sri Lanka Tourism Head Office,
80 Galle Road, Colombo 3
Tel: 011 243 7055
Travel Information Centre
Bandaranaike International Airport,
Arrivals Hall
Tel: 011 225 2411
Open 24 hours.
Kandy
Kandy City Centre, Dalada Vidiya
Tel: 081 222 2661
Daily 8.30am–4.15pm.

Websites

Official website of the Sri Lanka
Tourist Board: www.srilanka.travel.
Official website of the Government
of Sri Lanka with links to major
government departments: www.priu.
gov.lk
Government website which includes
details of the ceasefire and rebuilding
programme of the north and east:
www.peaceinsrilanka.org.

Touts and Con Artists

Touts frequent all main towns and
anywhere there are tourists. Most
simply want you to take a ride in their
rickshaw, or stay in a guesthouse or
visit a shop where they will receive
commission, and they can be got rid of
with a polite but firm refusal. It's worth
knowing that touts often spread lies
about guesthouses by claiming to work
there/be the owner/be the owner's
brother – so if someone tells you
somewhere is full, closed for repairs or
infested with cockroaches, it's always
a good idea to check for yourself.
    More of a menace to visitors
are the island's legion of extremely

plausible con artists (most commonly
found hanging around Galle Face
Green and Fort in Colombo; around
the lake in Kandy; in the fort and along
the beaches in Galle), who have a wide
repertoire of tricks to part you from
your money. These include soliciting
collections for fake charities; taking
you for a rickshaw ride to visit some
"festival" or other attraction, then
charging you an absurdly inflated fare;
various scams involving free/cheap
tea or gems; taking you for a drink,
then leaving you with a massively
inflated bill (whose proceeds they'll
split with the barman); or requests
for you to buy expensive tins of milk
powder for their starving family.

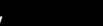

Visas and Passports

Nationals from all countries apart
from the Maldives and Singapore now
require a visa, or "ETA" (Electronic
Travel Authorisation) to visit Sri Lanka.
These can either be obtained online
before you arrive at www.eta.gov.lk or
on arrival at the airport. The fee for a
tourist visa is currently $20 if bought
in advance online ($10 for citizens of
SAARC countries), or $25 if bought on
arrival. The visa is valid for 30 days
and for two entries. Passports must
be valid for six months after arrival.
You can also buy a 30-day business
visa online (also $20).
    Visa extensions are given at the
**Department of Emigration and
Immigration** (41 Ananda Rajakaruna
Mawatha, Punchi Borella, Colombo 10;
tel: 011 532 9300; www.immigration.
gov.lk). The charge is based on what
your own country charges a visiting
Sri Lankan (see the website for a
complete list of fees). Conditions for
extensions are an onward ticket and
proof of sufficient funds to support

oneself while in the country, calculated
at US$15 a day (a credit card should
suffice). Proof of money spent in the
country may be required, so keep all
traveller's cheque receipts and ATM
receipts. Extensions normally take an
hour or two to process.

Weights and Measures

Sri Lanka uses the metric system.
Most major roads are marked in
kilometres.

Women Travellers

Sri Lankan society is conservative, and
the way you dress contributes greatly
to people's opinions of you, and also
to the way they behave towards you.
Dress conservatively (at least away
from established tourist beaches) and
you're much less likely to get hassled.
    Female travellers in tourist
spots, especially on beaches, may
attract unwanted attention. On the
west coast, around the vicinity of
Unawatuna, beach bums solicit
female European holidaymakers
looking for a local gigolo, so you may
be propositioned along these lines.
Pests can be repelled effectively if
you just walk away, avoiding contact
of any sort and saying nothing. On
the whole, eye contact is seen as a
"come-on", so avoid looking at men
who are strangers.
    You may find yourself the victim of
opportunistic groping on a crowded
bus or train. Deal with this by drawing
attention to the perpetrator and
his actions. Be wary of men who sit
beside you when there are plenty
of seats elsewhere. Your refusal
or reluctance to move away will be
interpreted as an invitation to take
matters further.

BELOW: west-coast relaxation at Bentota.

TRANSPORT

ACCOMMODATION

EATING OUT

ACTIVITIES

A – Z

LANGUAGE

Language

Understanding the Language

Introduction

The fact that so many Sri Lankans speak good English means that very few foreigners – including many people who live on the island – make the effort to learn any Sinhala or Tamil. Sri Lankans are therefore very unused to hearing foreigners attempting to speak their native languages and so usually respond to most attempts to do so with a mixture of incomprehension and hilarity. It's worth persevering, however, and once your listeners have got over the initial shock, they will usually respond enthusiastically to your attempts to mangle and mispronounce their rather tongue-twisting language. Many Sinhalese nouns are a simple adaptation of English words with an added *-eka*. A bus is *buseka*, a torch is *torcheka*. When in doubt or put on the spot, simply try this rule – it actually goes a long way. EuroTalk's Learn Sinhala CD-Rom (www. eurotalk.com) gives a good, detailed introduction to the language.

Sinhala

Greetings and Phrases

Yes Ow
No Naa
Hello/good day Ayubowan
Thank you Istuti
Thank you very much Bohoma istuti
How are you? Kohomadhe?
Fine Varadak neh
Please Karunakerara
What is your name? Nama mokadhdha?
My name is.... Mage nama....
OK/very good Hari hondai
Delicious Hari rasai
I don't understand Mata terinneh neh
Very expensive Hari ganan

No sugar please Seeni netuwa
Please stop here Metana nawaththanna
Where are you going? Koheda yanna?
Where is the hotel? Hootale kohedha?
Where is the station? Stesemeta eka ko?
What is this? Mekeh mokadeh?
May I telephone? Mata call ekak ganda poluwandeh?
How much (is this)? (Meeka) kiyadha?
Do you speak English? Ingirisi dannevada?
I don't speak Sinhala Singhala danna naa

Questions

What? Mokadhdha?
When? Kawadadha?
Where? Kohedha?
Who? Kaudha?
Why? Ayi?

Days of the Week

Monday Sanduda
Tuesday Angahauwada
Wednesday Badada
Thursday Brahaspathinda
Friday Sikurada
Saturday Senesurada
Sunday Irida

Place Names

Many Sinhalese place names are long but quite logical as they are nearly always a compound, so remember a few rules and you will pronounce them like a native.

island duwa
village gama
river ganga
street mawatha
road para
city nuwara

stream oya
town pura
port tota, tara
temple vihara
lake weva
bank bank eka
breakfast udee tee
clean pirisidu
coffee kopi
dinner paa kaama
dirty kilutu
food kaama
hotel hotela
lunch dawal kaama
small punchi
pharmacy bet sappuwa
restaurant apana sala
room kaamare
soap saban
tea tey
this/that meke/oya
water watura

Numbers

1 eka
2 deka
3 tuna
4 hatara
5 paha
6 haya
7 hata
8 ata
9 namaya
10 daaha
11 ekolaha
12 dolaha
13 daha tuna
20 vissa
30 tiha
40 hataliha
50 panaha
60 heta
70 heddawa
80 assuwa
90 annuwa
100 seeiye
1,000 daha

Tamil

Basics

Hello Vanakkam
Goodbye Poyvituvarukiren
(*Reply* Poyvituvarungal)
Yes Amam
No Illai
Perhaps Oruvelai
Thank you Nandri
How are you? Celakkiyama?
What is your name? Ungal peyar yenna?
My name is (John/Jane) Yen peyar (John/Jane)
Where is the (hotel)? (Hotel) yenge?
What is this/that? Idu/Adu yenna?
What is the price? Yenna vilai?
That is very expensive Anda vilai mikavum adikum
I want (coffee) (Kapi) Vendum
I like (dosa) (Dosai) Pudikkum
Is it possible? Mudiyuma?
I don't understand Puriyadu
Enough Podum
Toilet Tailet
Bed Kattil
Room Arai
Bedroom Patukkai arai
Train Rayil
Sari Pudavai
Dhoti Vesti
Towel Tundu
Sandals Ceruppu
Money Punam
Temple Kovil

Verbs

Come! (imperative) Varungal
Go (imperative) Pongal
Stop (imperative) Nillungal
Sleep Tungu
Eat Sappidu
Drink Kudi
Buy Vangu
Pay (money) Punam kodu (literally "give money")

Questions and "and"

How? Yeppadi?
What? Yenna?
Who? Yar?
Why? Yen?
Where? Yenge?
When? Yeppodu?
How much? Yettanai/Yevvalavu?
Questions in Tamil are usually formed by adding a long "a" to the last word of a sentence (usually the verb), e.g. "Ningal venduma?" "What do you want?".

"And" is formed by adding "um" to the end of the nouns (with an extra "y" if the noun ends in a vowel), e.g. "Kapiyum, dosaiyum", "Coffee and dosa".

ABOVE: translated temple sign

See Par
Wash (clothes) Tuvai
Wash (yourself) Kazhavu

Days of the week

Monday Tingal
Tuesday Cevvay
Wednesday Putam
Thursday Viyazhan
Friday Velli
Saturday Ceni
Sunday Nayiri
Today Inraikku
Week Varam
Month Matam
Year Varutam

Numbers

1 onru
2 irandu
3 munru
4 nanku
5 aindu
6 aru
7 yezhu
8 yettu
9 onpadu
10 pattu
11 patinonru
12 pannirandu
20 irupadu
30 muppadu
40 rarpadu
50 aimpadu
60 arupadu
70 alupadu
80 yenpadu
90 tonnuru
100 nuru
100,000 latcam
10,000,000 kodi

Health

I am sick (vomiting) Utampu cariyillai irukkiradu
I have a pain Vali irukkiradu
I have diarrhoea irrukkiradu
Doctor Taktar
Help! Utavi cey!
The English word "motions" is a common expression for diarrhoea.

Food (Sappadu)

Water Tunnir
Rice Sadum
Fruit Puzham
Vegetables Kaykuri
Milk Pal
Coconut Tengay
Mango Mampazham
Banana Valaippazham
Coffee Kapi
Tea Ti
Steamed rice cakes Idli
Pancake made from fermented dough Dosai
Thin, spicy soup, usually with a tamarind base Vadai Rasam
Dry vegetable curry Poriyal
Chicken curry Kolikarri
Lamb curry Attukkari
Sweet festival dish Payasam
Mils "Meals", similar to a North Indian thali (a selection of different small dishes), traditionally served on a banana leaf

TRANSPORT

ACCOMMODATION

EATING OUT

ACTIVITIES

A – Z

LANGUAGE

FURTHER READING

Fiction

Colpetty People Ashok Ferrey. Entertaining vignettes, full of comedy and social insights, by one of Sri Lanka's leading short story writers.

Funny Boy Shyam Selvadurai. Touching novel chronicling the life of a young Tamil boy growing up in Colombo in the years leading up to the civil war. Selvadurai's second novel, the more ambitious *Cinnamon Garden*, pursues a similar theme, exploring the twin stories of a gay man and a young girl imprisoned in the conservative society of 1930s Colombo.

The Hamilton Case Michelle de Kretser. Cleverly plotted and beautifully written whodunnit set in the British colonial era.

The Jam Fruit Tree trilogy Carl Muller. This popular trilogy of novels (*The Jam Fruit Tree, Yakada Yaka* and *Once Upon A Tender Time*) describes the comic misadventures of the slow-witted Von Bloss family, lower-class railway Burghers living in Colombo and Kandy.

Reef Romesh Gunesekera. Shortlisted for the Booker Prize, this strangely captivating novel describes the relationship between Sri Lankan marine biologist Mister Salgado and his young house-boy cook Triton, giving a distinctive flavour of the island's cooking and history.

Running in the Family Michael Ondaatje. This superbly written memoir describes the wonderfully maverick lives, loves and extended bouts of drunkeness of Ondaajte's Sri Lankan Burgher relatives, beautifully capturing the eccentric flavour of a vanished era. Ondaatje's other Sri Lankan book, the novel *Anil's Ghost*, is altogether darker, offering a lightly fictionalised account of the island during the civil war and JVP insurrection.

The Village in the Jungle Leonard Woolf. Superbly depressing tale of life in the backwaters of southern Sri Lanka – a place Woolf knew intimately from his work as a colonial administrator in Hambantota.

When Memory Dies A. Sivanandan. Epic historical novel describing the life of a Sri Lankan family from Independence to the outbreak of civil war.

History and travel

Colombo Carl Muller. Readable, lightly fictionalised look into the history and dark underbelly of the nation's capital city – and perhaps explaining why Muller himself chose to live in Kandy. Muller's *Children of the Lion* takes a similar look at the history of Sri Lanka.

An Historical Relation of Ceylon Robert Knox. Classic account of 17th-century Kandy seen through the eyes of captive English sailor Robert Knox.

A History of Sri Lanka K.M. de Silva. The best history of Sri Lanka, presenting an intelligent overview of the island's political and cultural history.

The Man-Eater of Punani Christopher Ondaatje. Michael's brother Christopher chips in with further Ondaatje family reminiscences, loosely woven around a travelogue describing a hunt for leopards in the war-torn east.

Send Us Your Thoughts

We do our best to ensure the information in our books is as accurate and up-to-date as possible. The books are updated on a regular basis using local contacts, who painstakingly add, amend and correct as required. However, some details (such as telephone numbers and opening times) are liable to change, and we are ultimately reliant on our readers to put us in the picture.

We welcome your feedback, especially your experience of using the book "on the road". Maybe we recommended a hotel that you liked (or another that you didn't), or you came across a great bar or new attraction we missed.

We will acknowledge all contributions, and we'll offer an Insight Guide to the best letters received. Please write to us at:

Insight Guides
PO Box 7910
London SE1 1WE
Or email us at:
insight@apaguide.co.uk

Only Man Is Vile William McGowan. Superbly insightful and disquieting account of war-torn Sri Lanka in the late 1980s during its twin struggles against the Tamil Tigers and JVP.

Reaping the Whirlwind K.M. de Silva. Classic account of the political background and ethnic conflict underpinning the island's long-running civil war.

Sri Lanka: Voices from a War Zone Nirupama Subramanian. Eloquent description of the later war years through the eyes of those caught up in the conflict, from Jaffna refugees to the relatives of those killed by suicide bombers in Colombo.

Tea Time with Terrorists: A Motorcycle Journey into the Heart of Sri Lanka's Civil War Mark Stephen Meadows. Insightful account of a journey through the war zones of northern Sri Lanka and the various characters encountered en route.

A Year in Green Tea and Tuk-tuks Rory Spowers. Entertaining and thought-provoking account of British environmentalist Rory Spowers' attempts to create a sustainable eco-farm in the hills above Galle.

Art and Architecture

The Architecture of an Island Barbara Sansoni, Ronald Lewcock and Laki Senanayake. Beautiful line drawings and descriptions of 95 classic Sri Lankan structures, from chicken coops to colonial cathedrals.

Geoffrey Bawa: The Complete Works David Robson. Sumptuous volume covering the work of Sri Lanka's foremost modern architect, with insightful text and superb photography.

Specialist Guides

The Cultural Triangle of Sri Lanka. Attractively illustrated overview of the main Cultural Triangle sites, with accompanying essays contributed by a team of local experts.

A Field Guide to the Birds of Sri Lanka John Harrison and Tim Worfolk. The definitive field handbook to the island's immense ornithological riches.

ART AND PHOTO CREDITS

Abu Ala Russel /Majority World/ Still Pictures 160B
akg-images 31, 39, 44, 48, 263TR
Alamy 154, 262/263T, 263BR, 263BL, 276, 280B
Amaya Resorts 293
Anzenberger/eyevine 59
Associated Newspapers of Ceylon, courtesy of Asiaweek magazine 54
AWL Images 140/141
Axiom 95
Bill Wassman 34, 181B, 225T, 234T, 236T, 241T, 242T, 248T
Biosphoto/Gunther Michel /Still Pictures 184
From Capt. O.C. O'Brien, Views in Ceylon, 1864 26, 35, 45
Corbis 4T, 6M, 92BR, 93TR, 112BR, 112/113T, 113BL, 155B, 176, 192, 197, 243
David Henley/Apa Publications 22, 29, 33, 65, 83, 84, 89, 101, 105, 106, 110, 116, 118, 119, 121, 130, 134, 148, 151, 160T, 169, 172B, 173, 174, 175, 182, 191B, 198T, 199, 209T, 209B, 213B, 216T, 238T, 239, 252B, 278T, 280T, 301B
DigitalGlobe /Rex Features 58
Dominic Sansoni 112BL, 113BR, 172T, 201BL, 213T
Dreamstime 279
Edmund Bealby-Wright 46, 256
Eric Roberts 201TR
Fotolia 8B, 9BL, 107, 185, 262ML
Getty Images 50, 52, 57, 74, 78/79, 94, 97, 98, 136/137, 161, 200BR, 281
Hans Höfer 28
Henry Sofeico/from the Bevis Bawa Collection 114/115
Howard J. Davies 55

ImageBroker/FLPA 153
Images of Sri Lanka 229
The Image Works/TopFoto 49
iStockphoto 27T, 108, 129, 133R, 155T, 164, 167, 183, 201BR, 244, 270T, 296T
Jerry Redfern/onasia.com 23R, 238B
Jetwing Hotels 11B, 294, 303
J.G Anderson 252T
Jochen Tack/Still Pictures 152, 262BR
John Powell/fotoLibra 2/3, 67, 159R
From the K.V.J. de Silva Collection 36, 38, 41
From the Leo Haks Collection 150
Lesley Player 109, 205T
Louise Renkema 63
Marcus Wilson Smith/Apa Publications 18, 66, 82, 102, 104, 120, 126, 131, 132, 149, 177, 181T, 191T, 195B, 202, 206B, 207, 208, 211, 212B, 215, 223B, 224, 230, 235, 240, 242B, 247B, 248B, 260B, 261, 266, 267, 269B, 270B, 271, 274, 275, 277, 278B, 285, 286, 287, 290, 296C, 297, 302, 304, 305, 306, 307, 311, 313, 316
Panos Pictures 56, 68, 71, 72, 100, 168T
From Philip Baldeus, A True and Exact Description of Ceylon 1703 40
Photoshot 179B, 186/187, 264/265
Pictures Colour Library 77, 99, 245, 249, 251
Piers Cavendish/Impact 93BL
From the P.R Anthonis Collection 24/25, 47
Robert Harding Picture Library

11T, 241B
From Robert Knox, An Historical Relation of Ceylon, 1681 42, 43
Roland Ammon 269T
From the Senanayake Family Collection 51, 53
Sipa Press /Rex Features 75
Sri Lanka Tourism/fotoseker 201ML
SuperStock 7MR
Sylvaine Poitau/Apa Publications 1, 3, 4B, 5, 6BR, 6BL, 7TR, 7ML, 7BL, 7TL, 7MR, 7BR, 8T, 9MR, 10T, 10B, 12/13, 14/15, 16/17, 19T, 19B, 20, 21, 23L, 27B, 32, 60/61, 62, 64, 69, 70, 73, 76, 80, 81, 85, 86, 87, 88, 90, 91, 92ML, 92/93T, 92BL, 93BR, 103, 111, 113TR, 117, 122, 123, 124, 125, 127, 128, 133L, 135, 138/139, 142, 143B, 143T, 156T, 156B, 157, 158TL, 158BL, 158BR, 159L, 162/163, 165, 168B, 171, 179T, 180, 188, 189, 193T, 193B, 194, 195T, 196B, 196T, 198B, 200/201T, 200BL, 203, 205B, 206T, 210, 212T, 214, 216B, 217, 218/219, 220, 221, 223T, 225B, 226, 227T, 227B, 228, 231, 232T, 232B, 233, 234B, 236B, 237, 247T, 250B, 250T, 253, 254, 255, 257, 258T, 258B, 259, 260T, 262BL, 282, 284, 300, 301T, 309, 312, 314, 315, 317, 318, 319
Taj Hotels Resorts and Palaces 288
Yan Minglei/Imaginechina 9TR, 96

INDEX

Main attractions are in bold type

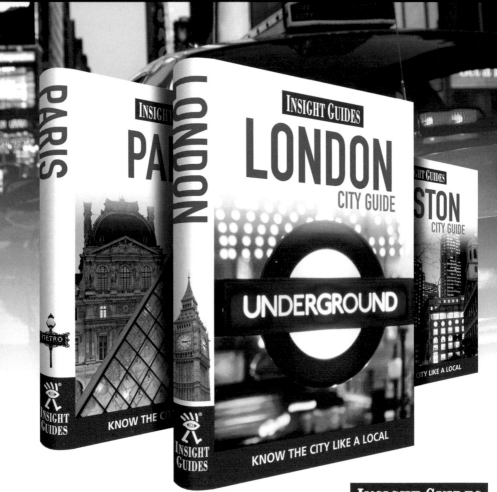